North Korea

D0169109

North Korea

The Politics of Regime Survival

Young Whan Kihl and Hong Nack Kim, editors

An East Gate Book

M.E.Sharpe
Armonk, New York
London, England

An East Gate Book

Library of Congress Cataloging-in-Publication Data

North Korea : the politics of regime survival / edited by Young Whan Kihl and Hong Nack Kim.
    p. cm.
  Includes bibliographical references and index.
  ISBN 0-7656-1638-6 (cloth : alk. paper)
  1. Korea (North)—Politics and government. 2. Political science—Korea (North)—History.
3. Korea (North)—Military policy. 4. Korea (North)—Foreign relations. 5. Korea (North)—
Economic policy. 6. Self-reliance. I. Kihl, Young W., 1932. II. Kim, Hong Nack.

JQ1729.5.A58N65 2005
320.95193—dc22   2005008401

Contents

Part III. Future Prospects

Tables and Figures

Tables

Figures

Preface

Following the death of his father (Kim Il Sung) in July 1994, Kim Jong Il became the new "Great Leader" and has ruled the communist country for more than a decade. For Kim and his people, the decade has been characterized by tough years of survival, a period of what the North has called "Konanui Haenggun" (Arduous March). Stalinist North Korea has suffered greatly from natural and man-made disasters, with mass starvation due to food shortage and economic failures, and from undue diplomatic tensions over the nuclear standoff with the United States and neighboring countries including South Korea.

Defying predictions of an early demise of the Stalinist Kim regime, the DPRK (Democratic People's Republic of Korea) has muddled through economic hardship internally and diplomatic pressures externally. The Kim regime has used the fear of U.S. attack on North Korea—real or imagined—to keep its people vigilant, while using the ideology of *juche* (self reliance) that Kim and his father jointly cultivated to sustain the popular unity and cohesion at home. In addition, reversing the "party–military" relationship, Kim Jong Il has relied heavily on the military as the main instrument of his dictatorship.

The present book on *North Korea: The Politics of Regime Survival* is designed to examine the factors, both domestic and foreign, that have contributed to the survival of the Kim regime. It is also intended to provide views and explanations regarding the key motives and policy objectives of the Kim regime. Specifically, this book examines domestic politics and the economic context of the Kim Jong Il regime survival, its strategy for regime maintenance, as well as its external links with the outside world, through analysis of North Korea's foreign relations with each of the neighboring countries of China, Russia, Japan, South Korea, and the United States. It explores "how and why" North Korea has erected a wall of seclusion, in the name of juche ideology, and assesses the potential for this artificial barrier to endure in today's world. The book is organized into three main parts: (1) domestic politics and political economy, (2) the politics of foreign relations, and (3) future prospects. It features essays by internationally renowned authors in the fields of political economy, foreign policy, security studies, and area studies on Korea.

The essays in Part I will address the context of the DPRK's domestic politics, political economy, and policymaking. These essays offer a broad and systemic perspective on the DPRK's domestic politics, economic stagnation and crisis, and reform efforts. In addition, attempts are made to analyze the linkage between Pyongyang's rigid and inflexible domestic policy to the ongoing North Korean nuclear standoff, as Pyongyang is obsessed with the survival of the Kim regime and cannot afford to take any adverse effects of alternative responses. The essays in Part II include a series of commissioned papers on North Korean foreign relations with each of the major powers including the United States, Japan, China, Russia, and South Korea. Two chapters in Part III examine, respectively, the multilateral approaches to defusing North Korea's nuclear standoff, as manifested by North Korea's participation in the Six-Party Beijing talks, and an analysis of the challenging questions of why North Korea has not collapsed despite all the odds.

North Korea's ambitious nuclear weapons program and its diplomatic standoff with the United States and other surrounding countries in the region have made it a primary focus of international media attention. Ironically, this high stakes nuclear policy dispute reflects the determination of North Korea to address both its security and the economic crisis threatening the regime's survival. A type of nuclear brinkmanship and blackmail, for instance, is intended to assure regime survival, as Pyongyang has been able to secure foreign economic and humanitarian aid by playing diplomatic hardballs while generating much needed funding through international trade in missiles and also through engaging in illegal trafficking in drugs and counterfeit currency.

The DPRK, founded in 1948, has become a modern-day "Hermit Kingdom," isolated from the rest of the world. In this age of globalization and complex interdependence, however, no country can remain secluded for long. The DPRK is certainly no exception. In July 2002, North Korea opened the door a crack by adopting limited measures of economic reform and "marketization."

Change is taking place among the major powers and their interactions with North and South Korea on the security and trade fronts. The timeliness of this volume is apparent as daily news reports highlight not only the nuclear and missile policies of the DPRK but also the context including the complex regional dynamics and the ongoing march toward globalization. Some major developments that contribute to changing regional context and dynamics include North Korea's interest in establishing special economic and trade zones and launching economic reform measures; Russian interest in trans-Siberian railway links; China's potential use of the Tumen River delta development project as the basis for developing China's Northeast region; and South Korea's grand design for turning the Korean peninsula into Northeast Asia's hub, and its ongoing effort to develop the Kaesong industrial site across the western corridor of the demilitarized zone. It remains to be seen how these developments and change will affect the future of North Korea's Kim Jong Il regime and the peace and security of the Korean Peninsula. If Pyongyang makes a prudent policy choice, it can create a "win-win" situation that can benefit both North Korea and its neighbors. On the other hand, a wrong policy choice on the part of the Kim Jong Il regime could bring about nuclear nightmares to the Korean Peninsula.

The editors wish to express their heartfelt thanks to each of the contributing authors to this collective volume. Without their strong commitment to sustain the high scholarly standards, and willingness to accept the tight schedules and deadlines, this book would not have seen the light of day in a timely fashion. All chapters are original and were written for this book project except chapter 13, which is a modified version from an earlier article appearing in *Policy Review* (no. 127, October/November, 2004:23–48). We wish to take this opportunity to express our thanks to both colleagues and office staffs in their respective university departments for their unquestioning support. We would also like to express our gratitude to the dedicated and professional guidance of the M.E. Sharpe editors, including Patty Loo and Angela Piliouras.

June 2005

Young Whan Kihl, Ames, Iowa
Hong Nack Kim, Morgantown, West Virginia

North Korea

1

Staying Power of the Socialist "Hermit Kingdom"

Young Whan Kihl

Since the death of its founding leader Kim Il Sung on July 8, 1994, the Democratic People's Republic of Korea (DPRK or North Korea) has been a failing state trapped in a cycle of economic poverty and political repression. Whereas economic stagnation and food shortages brought about overall poverty to the nation, the DPRK under Kim Jong Il (who inherited power from his deceased father) has relied on coercion as an instrument of political rule, thereby turning North Korea into a land of authoritarian repression. These characteristics of North Korea as a failing state, led by a repressive regime, are bound to be manifest in its style of domestic politics and foreign relations, including its overall dealings with South Korea.[1]

Most of the former socialist-bloc countries, since 1989, have either collapsed or changed their policies, like China and Vietnam, by incorporating market-oriented incentives and economic principles. Only Cuba and North Korea have resisted this pressure to change and remain doggedly determined to pursue the socialist economic principles of central planning. Since July 2002, however, the Kim Jong Il regime of North Korea has also introduced certain measures of economic reform in an attempt to overcome the mounting and stagnant economic problems at home.

The DPRK seems to have little option but to open its "hermit kingdom" somewhat by increasing interaction with the outside world. Since 1995 North Korea has looked outward for humanitarian assistance in order to overcome chronic starvation at home. The DPRK has received food assistance from the United Nations World Food Program (WFP), for instance, to make up for the grain shortfalls arising from crop failures, which are both natural and man-made disasters. About one-third of its 23 million people are said to rely continuously on outside food aid, which has become at risk of dwindling due to donor nation's growing sense of fatigue.[2]

The Political Economy of Reform

In addressing the subject of political economy of reform in North Korea, the socialist "hermit kingdom" seems to have resisted the change primarily for domestic political

3

reasons but had to acquiesce to delayed reform for pragmatic reasons. It is not surprising, therefore, that the Kim regime decided to pursue the path rather belatedly that was traversed by other socialist countries in Asia, like China and Vietnam. North Korea took limited measures of reform with hesitancy.

Will Economic Reform Succeed or Fail?

In July 2002 North Korea introduced limited measures for an economic reform of marketization.[3] This ongoing reform, according to Marcus Noland (2004), has had the following four major components: (1) microeconomic policy changes to increase the importance of material incentives; (2) macroeconomic policy measures decentralizing decisionmaking; (3) the establishment of special economic zones; and (4) an aid-seeking strategy from abroad.[4] These initiatives on economic reform followed an earlier policy move in 1998 to promote administrative decentralization.[5]

In an attempt to increase the role of material incentives, the DPRK has raised wage levels. Monthly payments to laborers on production lines were raised, for instance, from 110 North Korean won to 2,000 won on average. It also increased all commodity prices, with the price of rice set as the yardstick: rice purchased by the state from farmers rose from 80 jon to 40 won per kilogram, and the price of rice sold by the state to consumers jumped from 8 jon to 44 won per kilogram. (One won equals 100 jon.[6]) The purpose of these increases was to augment the volume of food entering the public distribution system. As a result, food prices to consumers dramatically increased, and within six months, the retail price of grain rose 40,000 to 60,000 percent.[7]

There has been a noticeable upsurge in small-scale retail activity, at least in the capital city of Pyongyang. But the agricultural reform in North Korea, as compared to that in either China or Vietnam, is less likely to be Pareto-improving (i.e., causing no one to be worse off) because of the relatively smaller proportion of the farm population in terms of the total population. The DPRK economy is more industrialized and urbanized today than was either China or Vietnam at the time of their agricultural reforms, and North Korea's farm sector has been fully collectivized and state-owned.

In the industrial sectors, the state-owned enterprises (SOEs) have been instructed that they are now responsible for covering their own costs. They are also permitted to engage in international trade. This means that enterprises will no longer receive state subsidies (as happened in China and other socialist countries). Under the "military-first" politics, however, the military and defense industries will continue to enjoy a privileged position within the economy.

The idea of establishing special economic zones (SEZs) was first introduced in 1991 in the Rajn-Sonbong region in the northeast. A plan exists for promoting SEZs in other regions, such as outside Siuiju in the northwest or Kaesong across the demilitarized zone (DMZ) north of Seoul. But the experiment has not been successful so far for a variety of reasons. Geographic isolation, poor infrastructure, onerous rules, and mismanagement have contributed to the failure of the SEZs in the socialist Hermit Kingdom, as shown by the fiasco of the Sinuiju SEZ launched in 2002.[8]

These measures of limited economic reform in North Korea, unless they are well managed, are unlikely to succeed and are likely to create more losers than winners. The unintended consequences of the economic mishap will be the possibility of greater unrest.[9] With these socioeconomic changes, North Korea is also likely to move, as the economist Marcus Noland (2004) noted, from the realm of elite politics to a new era of an elite-mass politics.[10]

The last component of the reform strategy, that is, seeking aid from outside the country by "passing the hat," has worked up to a point, as shown by the UN WFP assistance to the famine-stricken population in the North. But the foreign assistance program has reached the point of diminishing returns as aid donor's fatigue has set in and as the lack of transparency and accountability in the aid-recipient country has become increasingly apparent. The DPRK's aid-seeking policy is also hampered by the Kim Jong Il regime's nuclear stalemate vis-à-vis the United States and the neighboring countries of Japan and South Korea.

In September 2002 the DPRK and Japan agreed, in principle, that Japan would provide a large sum of financial assistance to North Korea as part of the settlement of postcolonial claims. However, the negotiation on diplomatic normalization bogged down because of Tokyo's demand for further clarification, and Pyongyang's refusal to address issues of the North Korean abduction and release of twelve Japanese citizens.[11] So long as the North Korean nuclear stalemate persists and remains unsettled, there will be no further progress on the normalization talks between Tokyo and Pyongyang, and the DPRK will not be able to receive Japanese funds for domestic economic development.

Domestic Sources and Base of the Kim Jong Il Regime

What are the sources of system viability and regime dynamics in North Korea? Is it the leadership, ideology, or the institution that gives North Korean communism staying power? Alternatively, is the post–Kim Il Sung regime on the last leg of a tortuous journey, nearing eventual death and dismemberment as a political entity? North Korea has survived despite the adversity of economic failure and severe food shortages. Many prophecies of doom and collapse of the North Korean state under its leader Kim Jong Il have proven to be either inaccurate or misleading. The North Korean system and regime, in fact, have continued to survive after the Cold War and, according to some, even thrived beyond the expectations of many pundits and experts. The question is why? How do we account for the continuation of the failing state of the DPRK?

The Party-Military Nexus

The basis of Kim Jong Il's power in North Korea is his hold on the two key political institutions: the party and the military. The DPRK is a typical communist party-state and its ruling, monolithic, political party is called the Korean Workers' Party (KWP, Choson Nodong-dang), which was founded by Kim Il Sung (1912–1994) in 1946.[12] The military in North Korea is called the Korean People's Army (KPA, Choson Inmingun) and claims to have been founded on April 24, 1932, by Kim Il Sung at the tender age of twenty in order to fight against Japan as an anti-Japanese People's Liberation War. The current KWP leader is Kim Il Sung's son, Kim Jong Il, born in 1942, in a village outside Khabarovsk in the Soviet region of Siberia. At the time, his father was an officer of the Korean reconnaissance unit, attached to the Eighty-eighth Special Independent Brigade of the Soviet Red Army.[13]

In October 1997 Kim Jong Il became the top party leader in an unconventional manner. The established procedures would have required the KWP to call for a meeting of the Central Committee to elect its general secretary and to ratify this decision by the subsequent regularly scheduled party congress meeting. The KWP Charter stipulates, in Article 14 and section (a), that "the supreme leadership of party organization is as follows: (a) For the entire party, it is the congress; and between party congresses, it is the Central Committee elected by the party congresses" that are responsible for electing members of the collective leadership.

The KWP failed to convene its party congress to elect its collective leadership in 1997, however. In fact, the KWP congress has not been called into session for more than twenty-five years since the Sixth KWP Congress was held in 1980. At the 1980 meeting not only was Kim Il Sung reelected as the general secretary but also his son, Kim Jong Il, was elected as a new member of the KWP politburos (or the presidium). This party inner circle was led by his father and made Kim, the son, an official successor to the Great Leader Kim Il Sung.

The KWP was expected to hold a Central Committee plenary session to elect its general secretary. Kim Jong Il, however, became party general secretary in an unusual manner, because the KWP Central Committee (CC) and Central Military Commission (CMC) made a joint announcement on October 8, 1997, after a series of meetings of the representatives of party chapters held in each of the nine provinces and three major cities, as well as in the major government offices. It was by acclamation of the party cadres and the rank and file members throughout the country, rather than through the KWP CC or the KWP Congress, that a new "great leader" was chosen to lead the party. No election was held to choose the party's general secretary.

For more than three years, from July 1994, the time of his father's death, to October 1997, North Korea was ruled by Kim Jong Il as the supreme commander of the KPA. In December 1991 he had become a member of the KWP CMC. The rank and title of vice marshall of the KPA was bestowed upon Kim Jong Il despite the fact that he had not served in the military. He did not become chairman of the CMC, however, during this period. The speculation was that Kim declined to become the CMC chairman in deference to the memory of his deceased father who had held that post. The *North Korean Yearbook* published in December 1995 listed the supreme commander as the second highest office in the military commission, next to its chairman. The yearbooks published in 1996 and 1997, however, deleted the list of party and government hierarchies within the CMC.[14]

The result of all these political maneuvers is that as of 2005 Kim Jong Il rules the DPRK in his capacity as chairman of the National Defense Commission (NDC), which is a counterpart of the party's CMC. He became chairman of the National Defense Commission in April 1993. This suggests that the Kim Jong Il regime had been a long time in the making. As noted above, the father-son political succession was unveiled first at the Sixth KWP Congress in October 1980 when Kim Jong Il was elected to the party presidium. A 1998 study by Dae-Sook Suh traces the beginning of Kim's political ambition to as early as 1967.[15]

It was not until September 5, 1998, however, that the Kim Jong Il regime was officially inaugurated by the Tenth Supreme People's Assembly (SPA) on the state side that had met in its first session to adopt the new Socialist Constitution. Since April 1993 Kim Jong Il was already serving as the NDC chairman, a position that he considered to be the real seat of power. Hence, Kim decided to bypass the due process of election usually required to assume the ceremonial position of DPRK president. His father held the latter position until his death in 1994. Out of deference to his deceased father, the office of DPRK president was abolished in the new constitution.

According to the new constitution, the NDC is the "highest military leading organ of state power and an organ for general control over national defense" (Article 100). This led to a clarification by Kim Yong Nam, former foreign minister but newly elected chairman of the presidium of the SPA. According to him, "the office of NDC chairman is a very important post [and] is in charge of the whole of our political, military and economic capabilities and is the top post of the republic." This statement was made while Kim was delivering the decision of the KWP CC and CMC to propose the reelection of Kim Jong Il as NDC chairman during the SPA session. Since Kim Jong Il is known as a reclusive leader, who has been said to be shy in public, the protocol of representing the DPRK in its day-to-day relations with foreign countries was vested in the SPA Presidium in the absence of the office of DPRK president.

Ironically, North Korea is still ruled by its deceased founding leader, Kim Il Sung. The 1998 constitution says, in its preamble, that "the DPRK and the entire Korean people will uphold the great leader Comrade Kim Il Sung as the Eternal President of the Republic, (and also) defend and carry forward his ideas . . . [on] the *juche* revolution under the leadership of the Workers' Party of Korea." Clearly, Kim Jong Il is using his deceased father as a basis for building his own legitimacy of political rule. This is called the Yuhun Chongch'i (the politics of memorial or the rule of the willing by the ghost) of Kim Il Sung.

Kim Il Sung was born on April 15, 1912, the day that the *Titanic* sank while crossing the North Atlantic. His son Kim Jong Il succeeded the deceased leader officially on October 8, 1997, after a three-year-and-three-month-long period of national mourning. Kim Jong Il immediately proclaimed that the DPRK would adopt a new calendar system, marking 1912 as the first year of *juche* (self-reliance), the official ideology of North Korea that his father was credited with having created in 1955. Therefore, 2005 is year ninety-three of the juche reign and calendar system. Under these circumstances, many in the West have wondered whether the Kim Jong Il regime is a dynastic system and a hereditary monarchy in the making, or a variation thereof, needed to suit the unique conditions of the socialist Hermit Kingdom.

Is Juche Still the Reigning Ideology?

After the death of his father, Kim Jong Il took over the reins of North Korean politics. The primary means by which he prepared the way for his accession was his elaboration and expansion of juche theory. The domestic political basis of Kim Jong Il's power and reign in the post–Kim Il Sung era is his claim of inheritance as set forth in the ideology of juche, in addition to his control of the military and internal security forces.What is juche, and how and why does this mythology perpetuate itself in the land of Kim Il Sung? In what ways did Kim Jong Il modify the juche ideology to suit his own political ambition and as a regime survival strategy?

The Origins of Juche

In North Korea the ideology (juche) reigns over politics (which is manifest as dictatorship of the Suryong or Ryongdoja, i.e., the Great Leader). Initially North Korea had adopted Marxism-Leninism as its ruling philosophy when it proclaimed the establishment of the Democratic People's Republic of Korea (DPRK) on September 7, 1948. Marxism-Leninism was subsequently replaced by the so-called juche ideology, which it alleged was a creative application of Marxism-Leninism to suit the local condition that prevailed in North Korea. A constitutional revision in 1992 deleted reference to Marxism-Leninism. According to the 1992 Constitution (Article 3), "the Democratic People's Republic of Korea makes juche ideology, a revolutionary ideology with a people-centered view of the world that aims toward the realization of the independence of the masses, the guiding principle of its actions."[16] The 1998 Constitution goes further by saying in its preamble that "the DPRK is a socialist fatherland of juche, which embodies the idea of, and guidance by, the great leader Comrade Kim Il Sung."

The *North Korean Dictionary of Philosophy* published in Pyongyang defines juche ideology as "Kim Il Sung's revolutionary idea." The word *juche* was used for the first time by Kim Il Sung on December 28, 1955, when he made a speech entitled "On the Need to Repel Dogmatism and Formalism and to Establish Juche in Carrying Out Ideological Projects." His primary concern at that time was to consolidate his position of independence in reaction to the personality cult surrounding the Soviet leader Joseph Stalin and to the worsening Sino-Soviet ideological split. It was a vehicle for developing a personality cult of his own, and a means of defining North Korea's "independence" and "separateness" from both the Soviet Union and China, that juche became the reigning ideology of the DPRK.[17]

But North Korea began to use the term "juche ideology" more frequently after 1967. Kim Il Sung's report to the first session of the Fourth SPA on December 6, 1967, was called: "Let Us Materialize Our Self-Reliant, Independent and Self-Defensive Lines Completely." In his speech Kim said, "Our juche ideology refers to the most correct Marxism-Leninism-oriented guiding philosophy designed to carry out our revolution and construction."[18] Although oftentimes translated as "self-reliance," juche has become the catchword that could mean almost whatever the regime wanted it to mean, because, as Bruce Cumings noted, juche involves Korean identity and is thus inaccessible to non-Koreans.[19]

Not surprisingly, Kim Jong Il further expanded the concept of juche in the work he is said to have authored, *The Juche Idea*. According to this interpretation, the idea of juche or juche ideology consists mainly of two parts—the philosophical theory, which maintains that the masses are the masters of history and revolution, and the guiding principles, or the "Revolutionary View of the Leader," which asserts that "nonetheless the masses are not able to take up spontaneously any revolutionary course unless they are organized into revolutionary forces and are led by the *suryong* (the Leader)."[20]

The juche ideology, although created by Kim Il Sung, was, as Pyongyang claims, developed further by Kim Jong Il into what is said to be a man-centered philosophy. This claim has been part of the DPRK argument since the early 1970s and was used to justify a plan for Kim Jong Il's dynastic succession and to cement his status as an indisputable successor to his father. In the 1980s, North Korea maintained that Kim Jong Il developed the concept of the "Revolutionary View" and presented juche in a more theoretical and systematized form as his "Theory of the Immortal Sociopolitical Body."

According to this interpretation of the juche ideology, the *suryong*, the party, and the masses constituted what might be called an integrated trinity. As the party was an immortal sociopolitical body, so the *suryong* was said to be the brain (center) of this organic body. As the physical life was mortal, and given by one's natural parents, so the political life of the juche country was immortal and given by this sociopolitical body. Under this system the only thing that the masses were expected to do was to obey unconditionally the command of the *suryong*, because he was said to be the brain of the body politic. Bruce Cumings calls this interpretation of Kimilsungism the North Korean version of corporatism or the corporate state.[21]

Military-First Politics as the New Ideology?

The logic behind the Kim Jong Il regime's promotion of the "military-first" policy is twofold: first to compensate for the Kim regime's weakness in the face of dismal economic failure and food shortages and, second, to use the military as the basis for strengthening his authority to not only defend the DPRK from perceived external security threats but also to build a so-called *kangsong taeguk* (Strong and Prosperous Great Power). The term "military-first politics" first appeared in the *Rodong shinmun* (party organ) editorial on August 22, 1998. It was timed to coincide with Kim Jong Il's official succession to power on September 5, and the launching of the three-stage Taepodong missile across Japan on August 31. Pyongyang claims that the latter event was for the peaceful and scientific purpose of putting its Kwangmyongsong 1 satellite into orbit.

The most pressing problem facing Kim Jong Il was the possible collapse of the North Korean economy. But the regime called the economic difficulties a temporary setback due to adverse natural and man-made disasters, like the floods of 1995–1996 and the drought of 1997. According to the regime, the loss of trade partners in the former Soviet bloc countries of East Europe and the USSR was a more serious problem that could not be solved, a structural issue.[22] The regime continued to insist its economic management system, as founded by the late Kim Il Sung, did not need reform because the juche-oriented national economy was sound and correct in its policy.

This belief, however, is belied by reality. Since 1990 the North Korean economy has registered minus growth in real terms with an estimated gross national product (GNP) of $17.7 billion for 1997, according to an estimate by the Bank of Korea in Seoul. With the population estimated at 23.85 million in that year, the per capita GNP of North Korea was $741 in 1997, down from $1,064 in 1990. Government revenue for 1999 was also projected to be only 49 percent of the 1998 budget.[23]

From 1994 to 1998, two to three million people reportedly died of starvation and hunger-related illnesses, and the famines generated a range of social and political effects.[24] North Korea's grain needs are estimated at roughly 5 million metric tons. Since domestic production has fluctuated around the 2.5–3 million metric ton level in recent years, this leaves a 2–2.5 million metric ton gap that must be made up by either imports on commercial terms or foreign food assistance. North Korea refuses to use its limited foreign currency to purchase grain from the international market. Since 1995 North Korea has received humanitarian food assistance from abroad, including from the UN WFP. Without structural reform of its agricultural production and distribution, however, outside experts consider the DPRK unlikely to solve its food shortage problems in the foreseeable future.

The failure of the food rationing system resulted in the temporary breakdown of law and order in 1995–1996. The regime was not able to control roaming vagabonds in search of food. Since then, there has been a continuous flow of economic refugees who cross the northern border into China in search of food, as widely reported by the world media. Defectors from the North report dire conditions of poverty and starvation and practices of rampant corruption involving bribes and favors among privileged party members.

In an October 1996 address delivered by Kim Jong Il at a celebration of the fiftieth anniversary of the founding of Kimilsung University, Kim blamed the KWP for the breakdown of the food rationing system. In so doing, he tried to absolve himself and his deceased father of responsibility for the failed economy, including agriculture and food production. The text of this address was not intended for external distribution, but it was smuggled out of the country and subsequently appeared in a monthly magazine in Seoul.[25]

Pyongyang's poor economic performance is due in large part to an unbalanced development strategy. Excessive military spending and a focus on heavy industries like armament and ammunition factories no doubt drove the situation from bad to worse. North Korea's food emergency, likewise, reflects misguided economic policies, and food shortages will remain a chronic condition as long as these policies remain in place. International food aid has crowded out imports on commercial terms, according to some experts in recent testimony before the Congressional Human Rights Caucus, and now feeds perhaps a third of the population in North Korea. This raises moral and ethical questions, as noted by Noland: "While we are ethically obligated to feed starving North Koreans, we are not obligated to do so in ways that strengthen the existing political regime there" under the Kim Jong Il dictatorship.[26]

The three-year plan (1994–1996) that followed the disappointing third seven-year economic plan (1987–1993) adopted an "agriculture-first, light-industry first, and trade-first" policy, but the economic targets could not be achieved with insufficient investment. In 1998 this policy was replaced by the new "heavy-industry-first" policy, meaning arms buildup, like missile launchers, which can be used as an export commodity to earn valuable foreign currencies. With the Kim Jong Il regime at the helm since September 1998, the DPRK has chosen to promote a new developmental policy called "Building Kangsong Taeguk."

Foreign Relations and Building Kangsong Taeguk

The DPRK foreign policy, under Kim Jong Il, has remained "rational" in the sense of being coherent in its pursuit of a consistent set of policy objectives. The DPRK developmental task, as stipulated by the leadership, has also been one of turning the backward economy to confront the challenge of modernity by building what they call *kangsong taeguk*.[27] The style and emphasis of Kim Jong Il's promotion of foreign relations vis-à-vis the major powers and South Korea can, therefore, be considered as an extension of the regime's domestic politics.

Sadaechui Placed on Its Head?

Pyongyang's foreign policy objective has been to achieve diplomatic normalization with the United States and Japan, while relegating the Republic of Korea (ROK) to the sidelines.[28] The reason why progress has been slow in normalization talks with the United States and Japan, however, has to do with North Korea's nuclear brinkmanship and its self-righteous stance on Korean security and reunification issues.

Pyongyang's foreign policy, until the June 2000 summit meeting between Kim Dae Jung and Kim Jong Il, had been one of denigrating the legitimacy of the ROK. The reason why the post-summit relations continue to remain stagnant, however, is in part due to the realization by Pyongyang that, once economic exchanges and cooperation between the two Koreas were put into effect, North Korea would be no match for the dynamic economy of South Korea. There was also the perceived threat that the consequence of opening the door to the outside world would eventually lead to Pyongyang undergoing forced economic reform. Because of the possible negative fallout from an open-door policy, the ruling elites appear to have decided that they need more time for the regime to first do away with its autarkic economic policy of juche and juche ideology.

Despite Kim Jong Il's isolation and reclusiveness as a leader, the DPRK has demonstrated skill and sophistication in conducting its diplomacy. The regime has strategic goals and policies it wishes to carry out with efficiency and effectiveness. Pyongyang conducts its diplomatic negotiations with both adversaries and allies with tact and determination. It has proved time and again, as demonstrated by its negotiations with the United States on nuclear and other related issues, that its style of bargaining is not only tough but also governed by the rules of negotiating on the edge.[29] One has to assume that North Korean decisionmaking follows the rational choices of action and strategy, including the rules of mini-max (i.e., minimization of cost and risk and maximization of benefit and reward).[30]

Pyongyang also seems to have a clear-cut set of strategic objectives in conducting diplomatic negotiations and bargaining that rarely deviate from a set of preestablished strategic goals and plans.[31] The DPRK has rarely strayed, for instance, from its long-lasting policy goal of forcing U.S. troop withdrawal from the South. This policy is based on its strategic objective to realize Korean reunification on its own terms and by its own effort without interference from foreign powers.

The North Korean demand for direct negotiation with the United States to replace the Korean armistice agreement with a permanent peace treaty, for instance, is based on the strategic calculus of undermining the rationale for U.S. troop presence in the South. The call for U.S.-DPRK bilateral talks on the nuclear issue, following the George W. Bush administration's characterization of North Korea as an "Axis of Evil" country together with Iraq and Iran, was planned in such a way as to isolate South Korea and to weaken the U.S.-ROK alliance by creating a wedge between Seoul and Washington. In the past, Pyongyang relied on an "encircling" strategy against the South by "attempting diplomatic normalization with the United States and Japan on the one hand, and the recovery of friendly relations with China and Russia on the other."[32] Whether such a grand strategy for entrapment of South Korea will work out for Pyongyang will remain to be seen, as its success hinges upon the resumption of, and progress in, the U.S.-DPRK bilateral talks. In the post-Korean summit era since 2000, the North-South dialogue has continued to make slow but steady headway.

DPRK relations with China, until recently, were relatively low key and lacked the old warmth that had characterized them during the Cold War era. In 2003 Beijing hosted the U.S.–North Korea talks in March and the Six-Party Talks on North Korea's nuclear issue on August 28, 2003, involving the United States, South Korea, Japan, and Russia. This was followed by the second and third sessions of the Six-Party Talks, on February 25 and June 22, 2004, respectively, during which the countries did not succeed in attaining a breakthrough but kept the process moving by agreeing to meet again. DPRK relations with Russia were also cool and tepid despite Moscow's repeated efforts to improve ties with Pyongyang. This was because Moscow and Beijing decided to establish diplomatic relations with Seoul in 1990 and 1992, respectively, despite Pyongyang's objections. In September 1995 Moscow decided to scrap the thirty-five-year-old bilateral treaty of mutual defense and assistance with Pyongyang. However, in a move to recover its influence over North Korea, Moscow has recently begun to restore its balanced policy toward Seoul and Pyongyang.

Russia's president Vladimir Putin visited Pyongyang in July 2000, one month after the historic Korean summit meeting. One year later Kim Jong Il paid a return visit to Moscow by riding on the Trans-Siberian Railway. China also continues to exert its influence on the Kim Jong Il regime of North Korea as a fellow socialist country. Kim Jong Il paid an unannounced visit to President Jiang Zemin for consultation on the eve of the scheduled inter-Korean summit in June 2000. The Chinese leader, in turn, paid a reciprocal state visit to Pyongyang in September 2001. On April 18, 2004, Kim Jong Il made a three-day visit to Beijing again to consult with China's new leadership, including President Hu Jintao. Clearly, there has been increased diplomatic interaction and exchanges between Pyongyang and its erstwhile allies of China and new Russia in recent years.

North Korea's bargaining strategy in diplomacy, characterized by brinkmanship in the nuclear negotiation with the United States in 1992–1994, derives inspiration from its juche ideology, according to one observer. As Eberstadt put it, the idea of juche is like *sadaechui* turned on its head or upside down.[33] Although interesting, this notion of whether juche is the opposite of *sadaechui* is disputable at best. *Sadaechui* literally means diplomacy of the Choson dynasty practices of "Serving the Great and belittling the Self," while juche is the diplomatic orientation of self-reliance, not siding with either one of the allies and maintaining its independence during the Cold War years, especially on the Sino-Soviet disputes.

More recently, the DPRK in the name of seeking juche has come to exhibit the traditional Korean vices of seclusion and self-righteousness rather than the virtues of flexibility and pragmatism that modern diplomacy and statecraft would require. In North Korea today, "traditionalism still triumphs," so observed one eminent scholar: "A remarkable inwardness characterizes the society as a whole, betokening Korea's ancient label, 'the hermit kingdom,' and its contemporary amulet, Juche (self-reliance)."[34]

On February 12, 1997, the top North Korean leader Hwang Jang-yop sought defection to South Korea at the ROK consulate general's office in Beijing. Hwang said he wanted to defect to the South "to save the starving North Koreans and prevent a war being plotted by the North." In responding to the news of Hwang's defection, a spokesman for the North Korean Foreign Ministry noted: "Our stand is simple and clear. If he was kidnapped, we cannot tolerate it and we will take decisive countermeasures. If he sought asylum, it means that he is a renegade and therefore dismissed."

The fact that Hwang was one of the powerful secretaries of the Central Committee of the ruling KWP, in charge of Pyongyang's foreign policy, carries special meaning and significance. He is known to have been the framer of Kim Il Sung's juche ideology. Hwang had served as president of Kimilsung University and later as chairman of the SPA.[35] There was speculation at the time of his defection in 1997 that there would be domestic political fallout, in terms of political purges and realignment, as well as foreign policy implications from the shock waves generated by his actions. Actually, what transpired was not an upheaval in the North but a decision to gradually overcome diplomatic isolation by opening its door slightly to the world outside. Also, Hwang's presence in the South caused more of a political ripple in South Korea's domestic politics than in inter-Korean relations. Hwang's voice has been kept silent while Kim Dae Jung was promoting the Sunshine Policy toward the North. This ROK policy of silencing Hwang has continued under the Roh Moo Hyun administration since March 2003.[36]

In February 2000, Moscow and Pyongyang signed a treaty of "Friendship, Good Neighborliness, Mutual Trust and Cooperation," although the agreement seems to lack any specific provisions for mutual defense in the event of crisis. Between January 2000 and August 2001, the DPRK normalized diplomatic relations with Australia, Italy, the United Kingdom, the Netherlands, Belgium, Luxembourg, Canada, New Zealand, Germany, Spain, Greece, and the European Union. It also normalized diplomatic relations with such Asian countries as the Philippines, Thailand, and Indonesia.

Building Kangsung Taeguk as the Path to Modernization

The slogan of building *kangsong taeguk* is reminiscent of the imperial Japanese policy of "Fukoku Kyohei" (Enrich the State and Strengthen the Army) in the era preceding World War II and the policy of "Pukuk Kangbyong" during the Park Chung-hee years in the 1970s. Pursuing this policy of "enriching the state and strengthening the army" was conceived not only as a way of modernizing but also as the path toward modernity in both prewar Japan and South Korea's Third and Fourth Republics under the Park Chung-hee administration.

This slogan of building *kangsong taeguk* acquires significance when it is combined with the DPRK's continuous push toward building a nuclear capability and a missile delivery system. On August 31, 1998, just before the scheduled fiftieth anniversary celebration of the founding of the DPRK on September 7, North Korea surprised the world with its launching of a three-stage missile over Japan into the Pacific Ocean, which it claimed succeeded in putting an artificial satellite into orbit. A *Rodong shinmun* editorial on January 5, 1999, under the headline "Let Us Go All Out for a General Onward March to Build Kangsong Taeguk," urged, "Let us glorify this year as a great turning point in constructing a Kangsong Taeguk."[37]

Despite this claim of building *kangsong taeguk,* what the North requires to solve its failing economy is the introduction of an incentive system for the workers and farmers urging them to double their efforts for production and profit making. This is how China's socialist economy was able to reform. Deng Xiaoping introduced the responsibility system first in the rural area and then in the industrial sector of the economy. Unfortunately, the Kim Jong Il regime has refused so far to confront the problem head on by adopting structural reform of the stagnant economy, only tinkering with macroeconomic policy of price reform at the edge.[38]

An editorial in *Rodong shinmun*, on September 17, 1998, is a typical example of the self-righteous tone with which the DPRK adheres to the myth of juche ideology in economic management. The editorial insisted upon an "economic structure of our own style," stating, "We should be guarded against imperialists' plots to lure us to reforms and door-opening." Since "we have incessantly improved and still are improving economic management in our own style under the principle of juche, for us there is nothing to reform and open up anew."[39]

This is a far cry from the reform-oriented and pragmatic economic stance expected of the new Kim Jong Il regime. However, given the dismal picture of economic slowdown and food shortages in the North, the reality may force the Kim regime to learn a hard lesson by accommodating the new institutions and practices of doing business in the capitalist marketplace of the world economy.

The official opening of Kim Jong Il's era brought about a noticeable switch of emphasis in foreign economic policy. The new constitution stipulates that in the DPRK "the State and social cooperative organizations shall conduct foreign trade activities" (Article 36), and that "the State shall encourage institutions, enterprises or associations of the DPRK to establish and operate equity and contractual joint venture enterprises with corporations or individuals of foreign countries within a special economic zone" (Article 37). These constitutional provisions notwithstanding, the Rajin-Sonbong area's foreign trade zone is judged to be a failure. There are some privately operated stores permitted in North Korea, but the scale of their operation is so miniscule as to make little economic impact as compared with other market-oriented socialist economies like China. Since the July 2002 economic reform, North Korea has introduced the functions of a market economy, but the situation remains precarious at best with a rising inflationary spiral and the shortage of capital for investment.[40]

The lack of basic modern infrastructure has also kept foreign investment from moving into the foreign trade zone. North Korea's economic predicament on both domestic and foreign fronts is dismal, indeed. Yet, for political reasons, the regime is not prepared to abandon the socialist economic principles of management and self-reliance. The leadership is afraid of facing the so-called reform dilemma that will unleash popular demands for a better life once doors are open and reform measures are introduced. In the face of this reluctance, whether and how the planned Kaesong industrial parks and complex, enticing South Korean companies to build production facilities for re-exporting manufactured goods, will succeed also remains to be seen.[41]

In its foreign economic policy, North Korea is falling woefully short of its goals. Before the current stalemate set in the 1990s, North Korea's foreign trade steadily rose over the years, reaching $390 million in 1965, $1.91 billion in 1975, and $3.1 billion in 1985. However, this figure then began continually to fall, finally reaching $2.17 billion in 1997. The share of foreign trade in the GNP, which registered a high of 29.4 percent in 1975, steadily declined to 20.5 percent in 1985, to 12.6 percent in 1992, and to 10.0 percent in 1994.[42]

Since the collapse of the Soviet bloc, North Korea has traded mostly with China and other capitalist countries. In 1997, according to one estimate, North Korea's trade

Table 1.1

North Korea's Trade with China and Japan, 2001–2002 (unit: US$1,000)

Category		2001	2002	Rate (+/–) (%)
Trade with China	Export	166,797	270,863	
	Import	570,660	467,309	
	Total (A)	737,457	739,172	0.1
Trade with Japan	Export	225,618	230,155	
	Import	249,077	132,693	
	Total (B)	474,695	362,848	−23.6
(A + B)		1,212,152	1,101,020	−9.2

Source: World Trade Atlas, "Outlook on North Korea's Foreign Economic Relations in 2003." North Korean Foreign Economic Relations #22, Digital KOTRA, 2003.

with China was $656.3 million, or 30.1 percent of its total trade, while that with Japan totaled $489.3 million, representing 22.5 percent of the total. The comparable figures were 9.8 percent with Hong Kong, 5.2 percent with India, 3.9 percent with Russia, 4.0 percent each with Germany and Yemen, and 2.0 percent with France.[43]

North Korea's foreign trade, until 2002, had remained static or decreased steadily. Its trade with China and Japan, which comprised almost 50 percent of its foreign trade, decreased by more than $100 million in 2002 (see Table 1.1). Among the reasons for the decline were cuts in international support for North Korea, North Korea's lack of supply capability, and its inferior export competitiveness. All of these factors indicated that under the prevailing economic circumstances, there were limits to large-scale trade expansion through the unilateral efforts of North Korea.[44]

Since 2002, however, North Korea has pushed to attract foreign investment through special economic zones in an attempt to overcome its chronic financial difficulties, while trying to expand economic cooperation with neighboring countries. A number of special administrative areas were designated, for instance, by proclaiming the Sinuiju Special Administrative Region, in September, the Kumgang Mountain Special Tourism Zone, in October, and the Kaesong Industrial Zone, in November. As a result, the special economic zones in North Korea have increased from one to four, including the original Najin-Sonbong Free Trade and Investment Zone. What is noteworthy is that the Sinuiju administrative district was given special legislative, administrative, and juridical autonomy, thereby reducing at least in theory the possibility of the central government authorities' interference. The "Law on the Kaesong Industrial Zone" was also enacted, which states that South Korean companies are allowed to invest in North Korea.[45]

North Korea has also continued its foreign economic and diplomatic activities by exchanging economic envoys. Exchange of economic envoys with the countries belonging to the European Union, for instance, has continued, and with Russia, as indicated by high-level officials' cross visits, as well as economic envoys. North Korea has engaged in active exchanges with Southeast Asian countries. Economic cooperation discussions were in motion, for instance, between North Korea and Russia, especially with the Far East Russia. Areas covered included the Trans-Siberian-Trans-Korean railway (TSR-TKR) connection project, joint development of North Korea's minerals, Russian crude oil processing in North Korea, support for North Korea with electricity produced in the Far East, and joint lumber and agricultural cooperation in the region. The fact that the August 2002 summit between Chairman Kim Jong Il and President Putin was held in Vladivostok, in the Russian Far East, strongly illustrates the new trend.[46]

The nuclear standoff between North Korea and the United States, however, has delayed North Korea's ambitious foreign economic activities. Without substantive progress on the nuclear issue, North Korea is unlikely to obtain international support including the lifting of economic sanctions by the United States. It is not surprising, therefore, that foreign economic cooperation has come to a standstill and remained stagnant over the years, and so has the pattern of North Korean foreign trade with the West, including the EU member countries. North Korea's economic open-door policy has come up against a wall because of the failure so far to attain peaceful settlement over the North Korean nuclear weapons program.

Grand Strategy or Grand Illusion?

In its relationship with the outside world, the DPRK has consistently pursued a self-righteous and hard-line policy stance toward its neighbors near abroad and afar. In its external relations with China and the Soviet Union during the Cold War years, for example, Pyongyang subscribed to diplomacy of independence in the name of upholding juche vis-à-vis Moscow and Beijing, while taking hostile anti-Japanese and anti-American policy stance in the name of supporting the party lines of anti-imperialism and antimilitarism. This suggests that the Kim Jong Il regime might suffer from a kind of self-serving grand illusion or grand strategy that could be beyond its reach in most cases.

Nuclear Brinkmanship

Although the DPRK is a failing state economically, and its population is starving due to food shortages and the mismanagement of its economic resources, North Korea has an ambitious program of developing weapons of mass destruction (WMD). After expelling two on-site monitors from the International Atomic Energy Agency (IAEA), North Korea announced that it was restarting its nuclear fuel reprocessing laboratory that would supply weapons-grade plutonium. On September 27, 2004, the North Korean vice-minister of foreign affairs Choe Su-hon stated before the United Nations General Assembly that his country took necessary steps "to increase its self-defensive military power" and was successful in turning the 8,000 fuel rods into nuclear weapons.[47]

Once North Korea is allowed to attain its nuclear ambitions, the Korean peninsula will no longer be nuclear-free because nuclear-armed North Korea may force South Korea and Japan to eventually acquire their own nuclear weapons capability. In order to forestall such an eventuality, it seems imperative that all parties concerned, including the two Koreas and the major powers with an active interest in Korean security, begin to address ways of defusing the tensions and promoting confidence-building measures through arms control and disarmament.

North Korea blames the United States for its decision to restart their nuclear program, calling it an act of self-defense in reaction to U.S. aggression and its hostile policy toward the DPRK.[48] Its decisions were necessary, it argues, because President George W. Bush called North Korea a member of the "axis of evil," together with Iraq and Iran, and made threatening statements toward it, halting the delivery of much-needed fuel oil. Pyongyang also criticized the Bush administration for recruiting Russia and China to pressure North Korea, saying that the crisis could and should be solved by the United States and North Korea directly without outside interference and that the United States should also agree to sign a mutual nonaggression pact.[49]

Speaking to U.S. troops at Fort Hood, Texas, President Bush said, "In the case of North Korea, the world must continue to speak with one voice to turn that regime away from its nuclear ambitions."[50] Tensions between Washington and Pyongyang intensified in October 2002, when U.S. officials said North Korea had admitted to an American delegation visiting Pyongyang that it had maintained a clandestine nuclear weapons program of enriching uranium. Ironically, what began as a fact-finding mission to resume long-stalled talks with the reclusive Stalinist North Korea turned into unproductive and failed diplomacy.

In late December 2002, North Korea raised the stakes drastically by announcing that it would reopen a nuclear complex in Yongbyon that had been mothballed under the 1994 Geneva Agreed Framework that had prevented the DPRK from developing nuclear weapons. In exchange for this agreed nuclear moratorium in 1994, North Korea was to receive two light-water reactors (LWRs), constructed by an international consortium including South Korea, Japan, and the United States, and 500,000 tons of fuel oil annually until one of the two LWRs was ready and turned over to North Korea.[51] But the shipments of fuel oil were halted in December 2002 when Washington learned about Pyongyang's clandestine highly enriched uranium nuclear weapons program.

Pyongyang denied a U.S. State Department delegation's claim that North Korea had admitted the existence of a highly enriched uranium program. It added, however, that the DPRK had the "sovereign right to develop nuclear power for peaceful purposes" of generating electricity.[52] This nuclear dispute and brinkmanship by North Korea triggered a series of diplomatic moves and international countermeasures by the IAEA. Seoul dispatched envoys to Beijing and Moscow, respectively, to exchange views on how to stop Pyongyang from reactivating nuclear facilities, thereby forestalling the looming crisis associated with the DPRK threat to reprocess spent fuel rods into weapons-grade plutonium.

If the 8,000 fuel rods temporarily stored under the agreement were reprocessed, according to one analysis, the North could have enough plutonium to make three to six weapons within a month or two.[53] North Korea had already hinted that it would withdraw from the NPT regime that it had joined in 1985. It had once threatened to withdraw in 1993, but reversed its stance three months later after obtaining an agreement with the Clinton administration to defuse the nuclear standoff in June.

Not surprisingly, the IAEA called for an emergency meeting of its thirty-five-member governing council. The UN nuclear agency passed a resolution on January 6, 2003, condemning North Korea's latest efforts to resume its nuclear program and giving Pyongyang an opportunity to come back into compliance with international nonproliferation agreements that it had signed. The IAEA resolution "deplores in the strongest terms North Korea's unilateral acts to impede the functioning of containment and surveillance equipment at its nuclear facilities and the nuclear material contained therein."[54]

The IAEA called on North Korea "to cooperate urgently and fully" by following a series of steps, including meeting immediately with IAEA officials, slowing the reestablishment of surveillance and containment measures, and "giving up any nuclear weapons program expeditiously and in a verifiable manner." North Korea is given "one more chance to come into compliance," as the IAEA official added, and "unless the DPRK cooperates and cooperates fully with the agency, the matter will be referred to the Security Council."[55]

The initial U.S. position was to seek a "verifiable and visible" dismantling of North Korea's nuclear weapons program as the precondition for resuming talks with the DPRK. To defuse the escalation and confrontational atmosphere over the nuclear standoff, the trilateral coordination and oversight group held a meeting in Washington, DC, attended by high-ranking diplomats from its member countries of the United States, South Korea, and Japan. The two-day conference attendees agreed on a common negotiation strategy vis-à-vis the DPRK by seeking immediate dialogue with North Korea to address common and mutual concerns.[56]

In a statement of about eight hundred words, it was noted that "there is no security rationale for North Korea to possess nuclear weapons" and dialogue with North Korea was endorsed as a "useful vehicle for resolving serious issues." The U.S. delegation explained that the United States was "willing to talk to North Korea about how it will meet its obligations to the international community . . . [while stressing that] the United States will not provide quid pro quos to North Korea to live up to its existing obligations." President Bush also noted that he believes "diplomacy will work" and he had no intention of invading North Korea.[57]

Instead of seizing the opportunity for diplomatic settlement of its nuclear issue, Pyongyang continued to accuse the United States of spreading a "false rumor" about its nuclear program. "There is an increasing danger of a nuclear war on the Korean peninsula due to the U.S. criminal policy toward the DPRK," according to a statement released from Pyongyang's Korean Central News Agency (KCNA). "The U.S. is deliberately spreading a false rumor about the DPRK's 'nuclear issue,' in particular, in a bid to vitiate the atmosphere of inter-Korean reconciliation and unity and foster confrontation among Koreans," the statement insisted.[58] This accusation was followed by a bombshell, on January 10, that the DPRK was declaring "an automatic and immediate" withdrawal from the NPT and, one day later, that North Korea might end its self-imposed moratorium on ballistic missile tests.

Pyongyang defended the withdrawal decision on the grounds of safeguarding its sovereignty, dignity, and right to exist. It charged that the United States "instigated the IAEA to adopt another 'resolution' against the DPRK" and that "the NPT was being used as a tool for implementing the U.S. hostile policy toward the DPRK . . . aimed to disarm and destroy the DPRK by force." Insisting that its withdrawal was "a legitimate and self-defensive measure," the statement added that the DPRK had "no intention to produce nuclear weapons" and its "nuclear activities at this stage [would] be confined only to peaceful purposes, such as the production of electricity."[59]

Foreseeing the IAEA reporting on the matter to the UN Security Council for further action, the DPRK insisted that its withdrawal from the NPT was "totally free from the binding force of the safeguards accord with the IAEA under its Article 3." If the UN Security Council decided to impose sanctions against the DPRK withdrawal from the NPT, Pyongyang would consider such measures as tantamount to "an act of war" and as leading to "a holy war" and even "World War III."[60]

When the IAEA governing board voted, on February 12, to cite Pyongyang for defying UN nuclear safeguards, and to send the issue to the Security Council, Pyongyang accused the IAEA of being "America's lapdog" and urged it to investigate instead "the illegal U.S. behavior that brought a nuclear crisis to the Korean peninsula." Since North Korea had already withdrawn from the NPT in January, the DPRK claimed that it had no legal obligations associated with the IAEA safeguard, the official KCNA news agency insisted. It also noted that "discussing the nuclear issue through IAEA was an act of interference in internal affairs."[61] The U.S. move to entice the UN Security Council to deliberate on the IAEA report on North Korea's withdrawal from the NPT was tabled when Washington learned that Russia and China were inclined to oppose such a move by the Security Council.

Keeping the South on a Leash?

North Korea suffers from what may be called the "Trojan horse" paranoia that keeps it from joining the world by opening its doors to the outside. North Korea has a strong sense of national pride and self-righteousness that is associated, in part, with the official creed and ideology of juche. Basically, North Korea does not trust foreigners lest they take advantage of the weakness and vulnerability of the North. Some have compared self-imposed isolation of North Korea with the Choson dynasty practices of seclusion in the eighteenth and nineteenth centuries. This sense of skepticism and distrust toward the outside world was also part of the North Korean attitude and policy toward South Korea until recently. The June 2000 North-South Korean summit, however, restored a modicum of goodwill toward the Kim Dae Jung administration in the South, as well as his successor Roh Moo Hyun administration that is continuing the engagement policy toward North Korea. But this change may turn out to be short in duration and fluctuating over time with positive and negative messages emitted by Pyongyang's propaganda machine.

A series of measures undertaken by Pyongyang toward Seoul's "Sunshine" policy of engagement show that the North Korean regime is reinforcing its hardened position toward South Korea as part of an overall strategy of Korean reunification. The Mount Kumgang tourism project, started in 1998, provides an apt illustration of how and why South Korea is held on a leash by the North Korean strategy for survival. Set up in a remote region, without allowing contact with the local residents, it is characterized by some critics as a "barbed wire guided tour." That North Korea collects from each South Korean tourist a US$100 admission fee is an example of North Korean authorities' rent-seeking and free-rider behaviors.

North Korea is set to continue its policy and program of a socialist economy rather than adopt a new reform policy patterned after the Chinese model of market-socialism. North Korea's mindset as shown by the Kim Jong Il regime is basically alien to the notion of give and take in diplomacy, the rule of reciprocity that constitutes the norms and standards in international relations and diplomacy. This requires new strategy and policy toward North Korea by outside powers that go beyond the "Sunshine" policy of engagement. The Bush administration's policy of "hawk(ish) engagement" may have made this point clear when Bush condemned North Korea as part of the "axis of evil" that led to initial confusion among allies and enemies alike. There is a method to this seemingly shifting policy toward Pyongyang, as Victor Cha noted, because the Bush administration wants to engage Kim Jong Il for a very different reason: to set him up for a fall rather than a survival through brinkmanship.[62]

The North Korean state is often called *Yukyokdae Kukka* (or what Wada Haruki once called *Yugekitai Kokka*) or the Guerrilla Band Dynasty as its founding leader Kim Il Sung had constituted it before he became the DPRK leader in 1948.[63] As such, the North Koreans cannot relate to the norms and institutions of openness and reciprocal exchange. Instead, their rules and principles are based on a zero-sum game in which only one side can win. This is manifest in its brinkmanship strategy, a trademark of the DPRK's diplomatic negotiation and bargaining.

A variance of what is called "United Front Strategy" of the communist movement has underscored the DPRK strategy toward South Korea on the reunification issue. The Committee on Reunification of the Fatherland (CRF), for instance, is the political arm of the KWP responsible for waging campaigns toward South Korea. Even if the KWP general secretary Kim Jong Il allegedly said that the preamble of the KWP, in reference to communization with the South, was to be rewritten, it is unclear whether such pledges made during the visit to Pyongyang by the ROK newspaper delegation were ever to be carried out. Under this circumstance, South Korean domestic politics seems to be held on a leash by North Korea in the name of promoting reunification of the fatherland. The

DPRK policies toward the outside, including South Korea in the 1990s, for instance, can be examined as an illustration of this strategy of deception and brinkmanship.

Pyongyang's "Brinkmanship, if Provoked" strategy was evident during the time of the 1994 nuclear crisis on the Korean peninsula. Former U.S. president Jimmy Carter's "personal diplomacy," which took him to Pyongyang in June 1994 was instrumental in defusing the military showdown between the DPRK and the United States on the Korean peninsula. Pyongyang's "Encirclement, if Enemy Retreats or Hesitates" strategy was the modus operandi of North Korea's negotiation and bargaining diplomacy. This mode of operation was revealed especially during the Four-Party Peace Talks held six times in Geneva between 1996 and 1999, but with little tangible results in turning the Korean peninsula into a peace zone in Northeast Asia.

The Four-Party Peace Talks involved the United States, China, South Korea, and North Korea. ROK president Kim Young Sam proposed, and U.S. president Bill Clinton agreed, during their summit meeting in the Cheju Island in 1995, to launch this multilateral diplomatic forum to entice North Korea into measures of tension reduction on the Korean peninsula. The North Korean response to this proposal, however, was lukewarm from the very outset, and the process ultimately died. Lessons could be drawn from an analysis of the ways in which the Four-Party Talks ended in failure, if the ongoing Six-Party Talks in Beijing on North Korea's nuclear issue, first started in August 2003, are to bear the intended fruit. This topic is explored further in subsequent chapters, especially in chapter 12.

North Korea has steadfastly maintained the two-pronged approach and strategy for reunification, with peace slogans in one hand and a display of force and threat in the other. Pyongyang's sudden show of flexibility in the Four-Party Peace Talks in 1997, agreeing to have the third round of Talks after a long delay, was interpreted by Seoul and Washington as Pyongyang's desire to project a favorable peace-loving and peace-seeking image in the Korean peninsula. Kim Jong Il was interested in freeing his country from an international "rogue state" reputation now that it was actively seeking food assistance from the UN WFP. This tactical change, however, was designed more to fend off international pressure because North Korea had to skillfully balance the dual strategies of begging and brinkmanship. Had the Four-Party Peace Talks broken down again, North Korea would have faced strong criticism and suffered from the negative perceptions circulating within the international community.

In the subsequent Four-Party Peace Talks in Geneva, Pyongyang insisted that U.S. troop withdrawal from the South be an agenda item, which was not acceptable to the United States and the ROK. They argued that any troop withdrawal was strictly a bilateral issue between Seoul and Washington. As a way of breaking the stalemate, it was agreed that the fourth round of Talks would establish two separate subcommittees, including one on the status of U.S. troop presence in Korea. This subcommittee never materialized and the Four-Party Peace Talks became defunct soon thereafter. Pyongyang's "Encirclement, if the Enemy Hesitates" strategy was manifest by the DPRK negotiation strategy during the Four-Party Peace Talks in Geneva as a move to divide and conquer the adversaries.[64]

On the eve of the fifth and final round of Geneva Talks, the new ROK president Kim Dae Jung spoke, on April 6, 1999, and suggested that North Korea might not object to U.S. troops stationed in Korea as a peacekeeping force.[65] Kim Dae Jung asserted that, in the absence of U.S. forces in the region, Sino-Japanese military competition would arise, and this would not be in the common interest of either South or North Korea. He also added that Pyongyang's expression of such a view, in his opinion, was one of the positive reactions to his "Sunshine" policy initiative toward Kim Jong Il's North Korea.

This line of reasoning by the Kim Dae Jung administration became the key component of Seoul's approach to Pyongyang during the June 2000 Korean Summit in Pyongyang. Whether or not Pyongyang would modify its stand on the issue of U.S. troop withdrawal from the South, however, was never answered officially despite the subsequent claim by President Kim Dae Jung to the contrary.[66] So far, Seoul's preferred strategy has not been adopted by the Kim Jong Il regime.

Pyongyang's grand strategy, in short, has been to prevail and to win the war over the South in the long run. The DPRK was poised to launch a preemptive surprise attack on the South in a revolutionary war to unify the country by force, if necessary. This policy toward the South is something that was tried before but failed during the Korean War (1950–1953). For sometime thereafter, combat troops have been deployed along the DMZ facing the South. Pyongyang's military strategy has consistently been to create great turmoil in the South by launching simultaneous attacks on the front line and in the rear area in the early stages of a hypothetical war. The DPRK military operational strategy has been a quick strike to sweep the entire peninsula, with mechanized troops in tanks, armored vehicles, and self-propelled artillery. In addition to the regular forces, the North maintains special forces of 100,000 men, who could infiltrate by using underground tunnels, helicopters, speedboats, and submarines.[67]

This "Encirclement, if the Enemy Hesitates" strategy is also manifest in the United Front campaign of fostering antigovernment revolution and turmoil in the South. Because the DPRK's reunification policy is revolution oriented, so long as there is no fundamental change in this policy, no progress is likely to be made in inter-Korean relations. Pyongyang has been more interested in undermining the political stability in the South by sending espionage agents and commandos into the South. In the name of seeking greater national unity of the Korean people, Pyongyang has adhered to the revolutionary strategy of fostering antigovernment alliances in the South. This is the well-known United Front tactic that communist parties have relied on globally and is not compatible with the causes of building bridges of peace and cooperation between the two Koreas.

The "United Front," according to the North Korean *Dictionary of Political Terminology,* refers to "a political coalition of various political parties and social organizations as well as of individuals, formed for the purpose of opposing common enemies. . . . These tactics aim at isolating counter-revolutionary forces and nurturing auxiliary forces to assist the main revolutionary forces."[68] Prudence requires that the ROK government be vigilant toward the security threat from the North so long as these united front strategies and tactics continue to undermine the South and rally pro–North Korean elements in South Korea.

There is no indication, despite the June 2000 inter-Korean summit and its North-South declaration of June 15, that Kim Jong Il's North Korea has either modified or abandoned its reunification strategy and policy toward South Korea. Pyongyang's "revolutionary" reunification strategy, formulated in 1964, calls for the strengthening of the "three revolutionary capabilities: (1) creating a home base in the North to support all revolutionary activities in the South; (2) fostering strong revolutionary potentials in the South, which is the mainstay of the Korean revolution; and (3) nurturing the world progressive potential as supportive forces for the Korean revolution."[69] Because the presence of U.S. troops in South Korea poses an obstacle to its realization of this revolution-seeking strategy, Pyongyang continues to seek the withdrawal of U.S. ground troops from the South.

This strategy of Korean revolution, resorting to the use of force as necessary, has been upheld consistently as the KWP political line. This is counterbalanced with a peaceful coexistence strategy of Korean reunification. Pyongyang's reunification policy has been based on the formula of establishing the Confederal Republic of Koryo, first presented by Kim Il Sung in August 1960, and formally proposed by him on October 10, 1980. This formula was designed to allow two different ideologies and governments to coexist in one state as a transitional process toward an eventual unification.

Because there is a set of prerequisites that Pyongyang insists upon, the chance of this confederation or any others that North Korea harbors coming to fruition is rather low. Included in the list of North Korean demands are the abolition of anticommunist laws in South Korea; the guarantee to protect all political activities by all political organizations, including communist and pro–North Korean organizations, in the South; the "democratization" (meaning social democracy) of South Korean society; and the conclusion of a DPRK-U.S. peace treaty and the withdrawal of U.S. troops from the South.

The latest motion by the ruling Uri Party in the ROK National Assembly to abolish the anticommunist National Security Law following its electoral victory in the April 2004 parliamentary election, however, reflects the changing time and circumstance of Korea's new democracy consolidating itself. After considerable bickering in the National Assembly between the ruling party and opposition GNP, the Uri Party seems to have decided to incorporate most of the provisions in the National Security Law into existing criminal codes before voting on an outright abolition of the security law as a way of meeting the resistance by the opposition parties.[70]

The South Korean president Roh Moo Hyun delivered a controversial speech to a Los Angeles audience, on November 12, 2004, which Pyongyang would be pleased to hear. Roh called it "reasonable" for Pyongyang to develop "nuclear capabilities," which he said were "for defensive purposes." In a "stunningly naïve" and surprisingly unexpected manner Roh insisted that the Bush administration should "trust North Korea" and limit its range of solutions to "dialogue" on the North Korean nuclear standoff.[71] This major policy speech on North Korea by President Roh on foreign soil, sponsored by the civilian foreign policy group World Affairs Council in Los Angeles, one week before the planned U.S.-ROK summit talks during the Asia Pacific Economic Cooperation (APEC) economic summit in Santiago, Chile, generated an uproar and reactions both at home and abroad.[72]

The consensus of those interviewed indicated that President Roh seemed to place too much trust in North Korea to act rationally, and there was a sense of confusion about why he had made the speech.[73] Tokyo reacted with disbelief at Roh's comments with Japanese chief cabinet secretary Hiroyuki Hosoda saying he could not believe President Roh had made such a remark, although such remarks were often taken out of context in ways that were different from their original intention. The North Korean nuclear development, as far as Japan was concerned, "clearly posed a serious threat to the world's nonproliferation efforts and peace in the region and could never be tolerated."[74]

The U.S. State Department also released an official statement, saying that it believed Pyongyang's nuclear weapons posed a threat to U.S. allies and those nations friendly with the United States.[75] At the close of the APEC summit in Chile, President Bush said:

> Five APEC members are working to convince North Korea to abandon its pursuit of nuclear weapons, and I can report to you today, having visited with the other nations involved in that collaborative effort, that the will is strong that the effort is united and the message is clear to Mr. Kim Jong Il: Get rid of your nuclear weapons programs.[76]

It is obvious that during the face-to-face talks with President Bush, President Roh did not get his way and that the U.S. president succeeded in what has been described as "diplomatic kabuki."[77] Bush seems to have prevailed and his role was more a puppeteer than the other four at the kabuki show, where Kim Jong Il was one of the spectators in the audience along with members of the public. Another apt metaphor may be a strategic chess or ball game, where the next move or ball is now in Kim Jong Il's court at the Six-Party Beijing Talks.

What Does the Survival Mentality of the North Bode for Korean Reunification?

Despite this posturing, the North Korean regime continues to survive in part because of (a) its deeply embedded philosophy of juche, (b) the relative ease of political succession from father to son, and (c) its continued isolation, with a closed door to international communication and the free exchange of ideas. Recent international humanitarian aid has helped to limit starvation, but, ironically, it has also helped to shore up the regime by limiting local unrest. Recent threats have combined to help North Korea survive without needing seriously to confront the possibility of reunification by absorption. Reunification with the South could, by its very nature, threaten the continuation of the current regime and its fundamental philosophy. To date, dangling the olive branch of peaceful reunification has been more a mark of expediency than an indication of the willingness to participate in genuine negotiation with the South.

Reunification of North and South Korea by peaceful means is the official policy line adopted by both Seoul and Pyongyang in their July 4, 1972, joint communiqué on North-South Korean dialogue. Inter-Korean dialogue and negotiation on reunification were held subsequently, on and off, on numerous occasions, but failed to achieve a breakthrough in establishing a modus operandi for overcoming the stalemate between the two sides.

The June 2000 North-South Korean summit in Pyongyang, and its adoption of a five-points declaration, is no exception. Implementation of the North-South agreement terms, including the family reunion and economic cooperation, has failed to materialize beyond the first six months after June 15, 2000.[78] Changes in external circumstances, such as the Bush administration and the antiterrorism war in the wake of the September 11, 2001 attack is blamed by Pyongyang, but lack of trust and mutual confidence-building measures are the basic obstacles to institutionalizing the peace process on the Korean peninsula.

One can see the familiar pattern of inter-Korean dialogue and negotiation. The historic "Agreement on Reconciliation, Non-aggression, and Exchanges and Cooperation Between the North and the South," for instance, was signed on December 13, 1991, but it was not carried out successfully because of North Korea's unilateral boycotting of its implementation as well as the rivalry and deep-rooted mutual distrust and antagonism between the two sides.[79] The reality of the two hostile "regimes in contest" will make it difficult to realize the nationalistic aspiration of the Korean people toward reunification by peaceful means.[80]

In the absence of mutual trust and genuine reconciliation between the two sides, the Korean peninsula continues to remain the last Cold War frontier with its unsolved legacy. The subject of Korea's future and reunification, what can be done and whether it will be done, involves two separate questions. Whereas politics in theory relates to values, norms, and preferences, the question of practical politics also depends on facts, prejudices, and probabilities.

Instead of the scenario of Korean unification by peaceful means, through the modalities of inter-Korean dialogue, negotiation, and bargaining, the more likely scenario of Korean unification is either by default (as in Germany) or by forceful means (as in Vietnam or the likely scenario of China and Taiwan). However, the renewal of the Korean War is not likely under the present circumstance of economic globalization. When and if the opportunity arises, the conflict next time around will not be so much a repeat of the Korean War of 1950–1953 as a new and unexpected format for political experimentation that may have to do with a domestic backlash of economic globalization or a reversal in political democratization in the South as well as a military coup in the North or the death of the North Korean leader.

The North Korean succession of leadership issue will come to the fore again. Kim Jong Il has become a senior citizen following the celebration of his sixty-first birthday on February 16, 2003. When his father turned sixty-one thirty years ago, Kim Jong Il dedicated Pyongyang's Arch of Triumph. Upon his father's seventieth birthday, Pyongyang's Juche Tower was also presented to honor his father in an act of filial piety. Whether Kim Jong Il would embrace reunification by relinquishing his hold on power seems unlikely.

Yet the preparatory work for an eventual Korean reunification "by default" can and must continue. This will take place not only as part of a bilateral agenda between Seoul and Pyongyang, as the 2000 Korean summit has proven, but also as part of a multilateral agenda of cooperation and coordination between each of the two Koreas and the major powers with active interests in the Korean peninsula. The second and third sessions of the Six-Party Talks on North Korea's nuclear standoff met in Beijing, on February 25 and on June 22, 2004, respectively. If successful, the Six-Party Talks could be turned into a multilateral diplomatic forum and framework for addressing other pressing peace issues, including the settlement of the unfinished Korean War, in the days ahead.

The first three sessions of the Six-Party Talks did not succeed. This is why the fourth meeting is necessary in order to settle the question of keeping the Korean peninsula nuclear-free once and for all. The fourth session of the Six-Party Talks, planned for late September 2004, did not materialize because North Korea refused to attend the meeting on the grounds that the just-released disclosure of South Korea's nuclear experiments had "thrown up great hurdles," and it would not attend the scheduled meeting until questions are answered about South Korea and its nuclear testing.[81] North Korea also accused the United States of applying a double standard to North and South Korea, that is, tolerating nuclear experiments by the South, while demanding an end to nuclear programs in the North.[82]

To tame the ambitious nuclear weapons program of the North Korean leader, by turning the DPRK into a normal state that would emulate the Libyan and Iranian paths of adhering to international inspection, may take time and patience. The official policies of the major powers are to support the process of inter-Korean dialogue and negotiation. But the major powers are also posturing to make sure that their respective security interests are not compromised as a result. The evolving balance of power in the region will ultimately shape the form of Korea's reunification and its future.[83] In this sense, the past will be the prologue to the future of Korea.

Political Change and Future Prospects

North Korea suffers from what may be called the "Trojan horse" paranoia that has kept the Hermit Kingdom isolated from the outside world. North Korea has a strong sense of national pride and self-righteousness that is associated, in part, with the official creed of the juche ideology.

A series of policy measures undertaken by Pyongyang has reflected an overall strategy of coping with the outside world. North Korea is set to continue its policy focused on a self-centered national economy rather than adopting an open-door economic policy patterned after the Chinese model of market-socialism.

Basically, North Korea does not trust foreigners and outsiders, since they might take advantage of the weakness and vulnerability of the North. This sense of skepticism and distrust toward the outside world is also part of the North Korean attitude and policy toward South Korea. This is why North Korea pursued a strategy of divide and conquer in the South through its united front campaign involving an alliance with North Korean sympathizers and opposition political forces in the South during the 1990s, which has now been renewed somewhat by the Uri Party victory in the post-2004 National Assembly election era.[84]

This chapter has noted that primary concerns associated with regime survival have affected North Korea's foreign policy and its policy toward South Korea. In presenting this perspective on North Korea's policy and politics, we examine the question of what has sustained the DPRK regime despite adversity at home and abroad.

Existing studies have presented three prevailing scenarios for North Korea's future: (a) collapse and absorption (as happened in unified Germany); (b) successful reform in North Korea (as happened in post-Mao China); and (c) "muddling through" in which North Korea would make ad hoc, regime-preserving reforms that fall short of system transformation.[85] This chapter has proceeded from the premise that the DPRK under Kim Jong Il is more likely to "muddle through" than either to collapse or to undertake drastic economic reforms along the Chinese model.

Even if the DPRK has been able to make corrective adjustments to its political system, these adjustments are primarily at the edge, and the chances of saving the system through drastic reform do not appear likely at the time of this writing. Neither "hastening Korean reunification" via collapse, nor system transformation via wholesale internal reform, seems to be in the offing.[86] The construction of a new national identity for the Korean people has not been an easy or simple matter in this age of complex interdependence and globalization in which both South and North Korea are engaged to varying degrees of intensity.

Anthropologist Roy Grinker draws an alternative, more somber and dismal picture of Korea's future upon reunification. Based on his field surveys in the South, Grinker concludes that there exists what he calls a "disruption of Korean identity" and the failure of the Korean people to "mourn" the past resentment and loss of the unfinished Korean War between the two sides in the bygone era.[87] An obstacle to peace on the peninsula, Grinker argues, is the reality of South Korea becoming "a nation in which nearly all aspects of economic, political, and cultural identity are defined in opposition to North Korea." Such reasoning would also apply to the North Korean perception of the South. It is in this context that this volume examines the politics of North Korea's regime survival and foreign relations.

Finally, as for the prospect of DPRK political change in the immediate future, that is, in 2005, either the survival or the collapse of the Kim Jong Il regime seems to be in the offing. In the post–Kim Il Sung era a Second Republic has emerged under Kim Jong Il, as chapter 2 will argue. There are serious rumors and speculations, at the time of this writing in 2004, regarding the possible cracks appearing in North Korea's Second Republic under Kim Jong Il. The *New York Times* in its Japanese dispatch of November 22, 2004, entitled "Japanese Officials Warn of Fissures in North Korea," described the appearance of a poster referring to the North's belief in self-reliance that read:

> The Juche philosophy has made people slaves. It has created an absolutist, hereditary kingdom, rather than one where the people are the main players. The Kims, father and son, have made our people miserably poor and this country is now a global dropout that is far from being able to afford the meat, soup, tile-roofed houses, and silk clothes that Kim Il Sung promised us in 1957.[88]

Japan's ruling Liberal Democratic Party's acting secretary general Shinzo Abe was quoted by the *New York Times* as saying on Fuji Television on November 21 that "I think we should consider the possibility that a regime change may occur, and we need to start [developing] simulations of what we should do in such an event." The paper also cited an editor of the South Korean *Monthly Chosun* as saying: "China may be forming a fallback plan should Kim Jong Il prove incapable of reform or holding on to power. The scenario the Chinese are looking into is to create a buffer regime through North Korean defectors."[89]

There is still mystery surrounding the removed portraits of Kim Jong Il, which disappeared in the fall of 2004, from some hotels, meeting halls, and government buildings, as shown in the People's Culture Center in Pyongyang during the Second World Congress of Korean Studies in Pyongyang, August 4–5, 2004. The article went on to say that under this circumstance, "Mr. Kim might want to adopt a lower profile to avoid blame at home for North Korea's economic failures," and "to avoid coming into the cross-hairs of U.S. hawks."[90]

American Enterprise Institute senior fellow and Korea specialist Nicholas Eberstadt, in an essay entitled "Tear Down This Tyranny," has suggested a regime change in Pyongyang by warning that without a better government in Pyongyang the U.S. would face a more serious threat in the future, while presenting a five-point strategy to oust North Korean leader Kim Jong Il. The five points include defining success and failure for North Korea negotiations, increasing China's sense of responsibility for the North Korea issue, considering countermeasures for "appeasers" in South Korea, preparing nondiplomatic means for North Korea, and planning policy for a post-communist Korean peninsula.[91]

The preceding analyses of North Korea by Abe and Eberstadt led William Kristol, as chairman of the neocon think tank "Project for the New American Century," to fax a statement entitled "Toward Regime Change in North Korea" to political leaders and journalists in Washington, DC, on November 21, stressing the need for diplomatic strategies and simulations predicated on the collapse of the North Korean system. It also stressed that the issue of the North Korean regime was one of the most urgent of President Bush's second term in office to begin in January 2005.[92]

Whether these predicted changes in the North will result in collapse or survival of the Kim Jong Il regime, however, remains to be seen in the days ahead. Our primary task in the meantime will be to delve into the socialist Hermit Kingdom in an effort to shed the light of scholarship on what has been largely an impenetrable enigma. Escalating confrontation and the ongoing nuclear crisis will demand immediate attention. For the search for clues to understand and explain the process of change inside North Korea, we turn next to chapters that address the dynamic interaction among the forces that sustain the ongoing political and economic processes within North Korea.

Notes

1. See Kang and Rigoulot, *Aquariums of Pyongyang.*
2. Between 1995 and 2004, total international aid for North Korea, according to one source, was estimated at $2.19 billion. This figure includes $1.38 billion from the UN-led program known as the Consolidated Appeals Program (CAP), of which South Korea donated $383 million and the United States $644 million. This figure does not include about $290 million of estimated direct aid by China and Russia during the same period. South Korea has donated a total of $905 million in aid to North Korea since 1995, including its donation through the UN CAP. See "International Aid for North Korea Since 1995 Exceeds Two Billion U.S. Dollars," Global News Wire–Asia Africa Intelligence Wire, *BBC Monitoring International Reports*, November 15, 2004.
3. As for an analysis of the 2002 economic reform, see Chong, "Economic Reforms Under Way," 2–7; Noland, "Korea After Kim Jong-il," 46–57; Oh, "Changes in the North Korean Economy," 72–78; and Seliger, "Economic Reform in North Korea," 77–86.
4. Noland, "Korea After Kim Jong-il," 46–57.
5. Oh, "Changes in the North Korean Economy," 72–74. Unlike China and Vietnam in the 1980s, North Korea has yet to commit itself officially to market-oriented economic reforms.
6. Chong, "Economic Reforms Under Way," 3.
7. Noland, "Famine and Reform in North Korea," 47–48.
8. On obstacles and problems of North Korea's special economic zones, see Jung, Kim, and Kobayashi, *Confrontation and Innovation on the Korean Peninsula*, 34–59.
9. Noland, "Korea After Kim Jong-il," 49.
10. Ibid., 51.
11. Kim, "Japanese-North Korea Relations," 163–197.
12. Lee, *Korean Workers' Party*; Scalapino and Lee, *Communism in Korea.*
13. Snyder, *Kim Il-Song 1941–1948*, 31–32.
14. *Handbook on North Korea*, 7.
15. Suh and Lee, *North Korea After Kim Il Sung*, 18–21.
16. *Handbook on North Korea*, 11.
17. Reese, *Prospects for North Korea's Survival*, 16.
18. *Handbook on North Korea*, 73.
19. Cumings, *Korea's Place in the Sun*, 404.
20. *Handbook on North Korea*, 92–93.
21. Cumings, "Corporate State in North Korea," 197–230.
22. Eberstadt, *The End of North Korea*; Noland, *Avoiding the Apocalypse*; Oh and Hassig, *North Korea Through the Looking Glass.*
23. Korean Central News Agency, April 7, 1999.
24. Natsios, *Politics of Famine in North Korea.*
25. For coverage on Kim Jong Il's secret speech of December 7, 1996, delivered at the Kim

Il Sung University on the occasion of commemorating the fiftieth anniversary of its founding, see *Wolgan Chosun*, April 1997, 306, 317.

26. Noland, "Future of North Korea's Economic Reform," 73–90.

27. The term *kangsong taeguk* sounds like a two-headed monster: one the military and the other the economic agenda of state building. The word *kangsong* consists of two separate characters, meaning "strong" militarily and "prosperous" economically, respectively. Hence, Kim Jong Il's stated policy objective in development is to turn North Korea, which admittedly is militarily weak (or backward) into a "strong" and "powerful" country, while simultaneously turning an economically poor (or backward) state into a "prosperous" country. The word *taeguk* also consists of two characters, meaning "great" or "greater," and "country" or "nation," respectively.

28. Scalapino, *North Korea at a Crossroads*, 16.

29. Snyder, *Negotiating on the Edge*.

30. Aaron Kleiman, "North Korean Decision-Making and Rational Choice Theory," available at www.personal.umich.edu/~rtanter/F97PS472Papers/Kleiman.Aaron.

31. Oberdorfer, *The Two Koreas*; Sigal, *Disarming Strangers*.

32. Hong, "North Korea's Foreign Policy for National Security," 55–82.

33. Eberstadt, "Hastening Korean Reunification," 77–92.

34. Scalapino, *North Korea at a Crossroads*, 1.

35. Hwang, *Memoir*, 1.

36. Hwang's travel to the United States finally materialized in December 2003 when he appeared before the U.S. congressional hearings as a witness. His testimony moved Congress subsequently to enact the Human Right Act directed at North Korea, which became U.S. law when the Bush administration signed it in October 2004.

37. The term first appeared in an editorial of *Rodong shinmun* on August 22, 1998, two weeks before Kim Jong Il was to complete his succession to power on September 5, 1998, as the newly elected member of the Tenth Supreme People's Assembly.

38. Noland, "Korea After Kim Jong il," 46–57.

39. *Rodong shinmun*, September 17, 1998.

40. Chong, "Economic Reforms Under Way," 4–7.

41. On the economic analysis and effect of the Kaesong industrial complex, see Park, "An Analysis of Economic Effects," 40–50; Anthony Faiola, "A Capitalist Sprout in N. Korean Dust: Industrial Park to Broach Free Market," *Washington Post Foreign Service*, May 23, 2004: A18.

42. On the latest statistics regarding inter-Korean economic relations, see "Intra-Korean Trade Trend," North Korean Economy, *Digital KOTRA* (June 2004), available at www.kotra.or.kr.

43. A KOTRA-Korea Trade-Investment Promotion Agency survey, as cited in *Handbook of North Korea*, 33.

44. "Outlook on North Korea's Foreign Economic Relations in 2003," North Korean Foreign Economic Relations #22, *Digital KOTRA* (2003).

45. Kaesong Industrial Zone Law states, in Article 3, that "South Korean, overseas Korean, foreign corporate bodies and individuals and economic organizations can invest in the zone."

46. The heads of the two countries, during their summit meeting, agreed to continue their efforts to expand North Korea–Russian economic cooperation, including the expansion of the TKR–TSR connection project.

47. "North Korean Official Calls for End to USA's 'High-Handed Practices,'" Global News Wire–Asia Africa Intelligence Wire, *BBC Monitoring International Reports*, October 1, 2004.

48. Elizabeth Rosenthal, "North Korea Defends Decision to Restart Nuclear Program," *New York Times*, January 3, 2003.

49. Ibid.

50. "President Rallies Troops at Fort Hood," White House, January 3, 2003, 5, available at www.whitehouse.gov/news/releases/2003/01/20030103.html.

51. Kihl and Hays, *Peace and Security in Northeast Asia*.

52. David Sanger. "North Korea Says It Seeks to Develop Nuclear Arms," *New York Times*, June 10, 2003.

53. Pinkston and Lieggi, *North Korea's Nuclear Program*.

54. "Nuclear Agency Condemns North Korea," *CNN.com*, January 6, 2003.

55. Ibid.

56. Steven R. Weisman, "U.S., in a Shift, Is Willing to Talk with North Korea About A-Arms," *New York Times*, January 8, 2003.

57. Ibid.

58. "N. Korea Slams U.S. 'Criminal Policy,'" *CNN.com*, January 8, 2000.

59. Ibid.

60. Ibid.

61. "North Korea Accuses Nuke Agency of Meddling," Associated Press (Seoul), February 14, 2003.

62. Cha, "Korea's Place in the Axis," 79–92.

63. Buzo, *Guerilla Dynasty*; Wada, *Kita Chosen*.

64. On an analysis of the Four-Party Peace Talks, see Kwak, *The Four Powers and Korean Unification Strategies*.

65. "North Korea, First Admission of U.S. Troop Presence in the South: Remaining as Peace-Keeping Forces is Fine," *Digital Chosunilbo*, April 7, 1999, available at http://english.chosun.com.

66. Jane Perlez, "South Korean Says North Agrees U.S. Troops Should Stay," *New York Times*, September 11, 2000, A3.

67. Bermudez, *North Korean Special Forces*.

68. *Handbook on North Korea*, 128.

69. Ibid., 45.

70. "Times Change, So Why Not Laws?" *The Economist*, November 6, 2004.

71. For the text of President Roh Moo-Hyun's Los Angeles speech, see "Controversial Speech by Roh Moo-Hyun," November 15, 2004, available at www.nkzone.org/nkzone/entry/2004/11/controversial_s.php.

72. The opposition GNP, in a statement signed by all its lawmakers and adopted in an emergency caucus, said "We cannot but be stunned at the remarks," which "shake the international cooperation toward blocking" North Korea's nuclear ambition and "endanger the South Korea-U.S. alliance." The ruling Uri Party defended Roh's speech as an effort "to thwart a war" on the Korean peninsula. "The Ruling and Opposition Parties in War of Words Over Roh's Remarks," *Digital Chonsunilbo*, November 15, 2004.

73. "Roh Calls for U.S. to Guarantee N. Korea's Security," *Digital Chosunilbo*, November 14, 2004.

74. "Japanese Chief Cabinet Secretary Expresses Disbelief at Roh Comments," *Digital Chosunilbo*, November 17, 2004.

75. "U.S. State Department Refutes Roh Speech in LA," *Digital Chosunilbo*, November 17, 2004.

76. "President's Remarks at CEO Summit Closing Session," Casa Piedra, Santiago, Chile, Office of the Press Secretary, the White House, November 20, 2004.

77. Rebecca Mackinnon, "Diplomatic Kabuki . . . or Am I Missing Something?" *North Korea Zone*, November 20, 2004.

78. Kihl, "Overcoming the Cold War Legacy," 1–24.

79. Kihl, *Korea and the World*, 133–152.

80. Kihl, *Politics and Policies in Divided Korea*.

81. "N. Korea to Boycott Nuke Talks over S. Korea," UPI, September 16, 2004.

82. The real reason behind Pyongyang's decision to boycott the Six-Party Talks in September 2004 may have had more to do with the uncertain outcome of the U.S. presidential election on November 2, 2004, thinking that the defeat of the incumbent President George W. Bush might create a better strategic environment of negotiation for them.

83. Kihl, "The DPRK and Its Relations with the ROK," 123–144.

84. "Roh Appeals for Softer Bush Stance Toward N. Korea," *Korea Herald*, November 15, 2004; for the text of Roh's address, see "Controversial Speech by Roh Moo-Hyun," November 15, 2004, available at www.nkzone.org/nkzone/entry/2004/11/controversial_s.php.

85. Noland, *Avoiding the Apocalypse*; Pollack and Lee, *Preparing for Korean Unification*; Reese, *The Prospects for North Korea's Survival*.

86. Eberstadt, "Hastening Korean Reunification;" Eberstadt, *The End of North Korea*; Kim, *The North Korean System*; Noland, "Why North Korea Will Muddle Through."

87. Grinker, *Korea and Its Future*.

88. James Brooke, "Japanese Official Warns of Fissures in North Korea," *New York Times*, November 22, 2004, A3.

89. Ibid.

90. Ibid.

91. Eberstadt, "Tear Down This Tyranny," *Weekly Standard*, November 29, 2004.

92. "Hawks Push Regime Change in North Korea," Inter Press News Agency, November 22, 2004.

Part I

Domestic Politics and Political Economy

2

Emergence of the Second Republic

The Kim Regime Adapts to the Challenges of Modernity

Alexandre Y. Mansourov

Better, Merrier, More Hopeful Life?

Since the initiation of the political and socioeconomic reforms in the fall of 1998, life has been getting better in the Democratic People's Republic of Korea (DPRK). It has been an uphill battle with all the twists and turns accompanying a national transition from a highly centralized and overly militarized command-and-control economy to an increasingly decentralized market-oriented economy, from totalitarian to a neo-authoritarian political regime, from a totally closed *juche*-based (self-reliant) society preaching communist ideals to a gradually opening society rediscovering its traditional neo-Confucian roots and reviving postcolonial nationalism as its mass-mobilizing ideology.

Structural transition does pay off, slowly but inevitably. There are more visible signs of improvements in people's daily lives than ever before. More electric lights in many more public places, along the roads, and at residential homes are turned on for longer hours both in large cities and in small villages. More urban and rural buildings are repaired and have been given a facelift with fresh paint, new tile, and modern glass window packages. A construction boom is visible everywhere.[1] Significantly more vehicular traffic is observable in the streets, causing traffic jams and a surge in pedestrian and car accidents. As of December 2003, the number of large-scale district markets (over 500 registered private vendors) stood at thirty-eight, and is projected to grow to forty-two in the near future. Street vendors, both mobile and stationary, are everywhere, trading all kinds of daily necessities, snacks, baked chestnuts, sweet potatoes, soft drinks, household appliances, kitchenware, clothes, and what have you. The number of people engaged in small businesses has soared recently. In the juche corner of the "eurozone," euros, U.S. dollars, Japanese yen, Chinese yuan, and other hard currencies can be bought and sold at will without punishment in the streets and at the state-licensed exchange offices that begin to crowd out the black market currency traders. The Kim Il Sung University faculty revised economics textbooks before the beginning of a new school year in April 2004, in order to better reflect maximum profit-driven new economic realities.

Life is getting merrier, too. Restaurants, eateries, beer bars, and small cafés work day and night and are filled with increasingly well-to-do customers.[2] Bowling centers, public saunas, billiard parlors, and a handful of newly opened Internet cafés are crowded with enthusiastic patrons from all walks of life—from relaxing soldiers and workers, to respectable functionaries, to cigar-smoking new entrepreneurs. Attraction parks, mountain ski resorts, cinemas, and theaters are open for general public use and normal business again. Shopping and gawking at glitzy windows has become a favorite pastime for many urbanites,[3] and it is quite rewarding for those folks who actually have money to spend. Gambling, prostitution, and drug dealing are facts of new life, too.

Finally, life is getting more hopeful in the North. Transition toward a market economy creates new income opportunities, opens new career possibilities, allows for changes in lifestyle previously unthinkable but now quite within the reach of many entrepreneurial people, and begins to raise expectations about a better life in the future. There are plenty of losers, to be sure, but there are a few winners, too. Everyone has to adjust to new market realities for better or worse. New life conditions may cause despair and frustration among some, but they also can restore faith, form new desires, and generate optimism among others. Despite widely spread political apathy and lack of general public interest in politics and ideological campaigns, hope of a better individual future is back in North Korea. The country is finally awakening from a decade-long coma and pain inflicted by a dramatic severing of the umbilical cord connecting it with the communist womb of its procreators in the early 1990s.

Why is there progress, seeming or real, in North Korea today? The cynics assert that it is just a Potemkin village set up for outsiders to marvel at, where the real situation in the country is as bad as it has ever been. The economic determinists say that it is a recurrent phenomenon. Following a decade of steep macroeconomic decline, it is almost inevitable that there would be a cyclical uptick in the economy after it hit a transient bottom. That trend of protracted steep declines followed by short-lived upswings is likely to continue until the long wave of economic collapse is reversed by fundamental changes in the DPRK's economic system. They argue that more time is needed to ascertain that an even harder landing in the future will not follow the current gradual recovery.

In contrast, the optimists believe that the recent upturn in the economy is the long-awaited result of the socioeconomic reforms initiated by Kim Jong Il in the late 1990s. It proves that the current regime can change for the better and has the political will and the organizational capacity to steer the country out of its prolonged economic depression and social malaise into a brighter, more civilized future.

But some pessimistic critics credit most of the recent surge in economic activity to the burgeoning inter-Korean trade. They argue that North Korean nuclear blackmail finally began to pay off, after Pyongyang was able to drive a deep wedge in the U.S.-ROK alliance and compelled Seoul to expand its one-way transfer of resources from the South to the North amid the escalating nuclear crisis despite the U.S.-sponsored international campaign to isolate the communist regime.

Whatever the origins of the social and economic changes unfolding in North Korea—superficial cosmetics, developmental cycle, government policy adjustment, or stimulus from the external environment—everyone is affected positively or negatively by its predictable and unintended consequences, including the elite, the bureaucracy, and the masses. Individuals are forced to make new personal choices affecting the group dynamics and generating a new public context for combined social action. Emerging social chaos undermines the traditional value system, the rigid ruling ideology, divine personality cults, and previously rock-solid power hierarchies: they lose legitimacy, credibility, and mass appeal, and become fluid, porous, malleable, and transient. Incumbent gods and demigods enter the twilight zone as the rising leaders of the future prepare to challenge their rule.

How do various groups inside the "black box" of the juche elite cope with the ongoing structural transformation of the North Korean society? What are their long-term individual and group interests and corporate objectives, as well as short-term preferences, fears, and expectations, and how can one shape them? Who gets ahead in the interbureaucratic rivalries—and why—and how can one benefit from the emerging clashes of divergent bureaucratic interests and differences of organizational outputs? What forces shape the transition of the North Korean state by determining the pace, directions, and specific advances, and who controls what in that process, including veto power? What are the productive pressure points where one can exploit various sensitivities and vulnerabilities of the North Korean elites? These questions constitute the subject matter of this chapter.

Path Dependence, Critical Junctures, and Institutional Change

Institutions, both formal and informal, are the rules of the game that structure incentives in human exchange in a society and reduce uncertainty by providing a stable structure to everyday life. Institutions define and limit the set of an individual's choices. Institutional change shapes the way societies evolve through time. Institutions connect the past with the present and the future so that history is a largely incremental story of institutional evolution, a study of the evolution of collective incentives and constraints against human individualism and the problem of achieving cooperative solutions to collective problems. Lack of public information and external transparency in a closed society should not be mistaken for the lack of rules, procedures, formal organizations, informal influence networks, and hierarchies of authority that are always present and very clear to the internal actors themselves.[4]

The current form of political organization and policy decisionmaking process in

North Korea is derived from the opportunity set provided by traditional values, inherent administrative culture, and the domestic institutional structures that evolved sometimes incrementally, at times showing a great degree of stability, and at other times experiencing rapid discontinuous change. They reflect a mixture of traditional neo-Confucian influences, the imprint of the Japanese colonial rule and postliberation Soviet military occupation, the impact of the Korean War time experiences, the "self-reliant" postwar socialist reconstruction, and decay.

Traditional Korean political culture is characterized by the heavy influence of neo-Confucianism accentuated by the teachings of Zhu Xi, especially his emphasis on the so-called Three Basic Relationships between the father and the son, the state and the subject, and heaven and the ruler. That gave rise to such traditional aspects of Korean politics as paternalism and filial piety, state-centered consensual politics and autocratic political agenda setting, "government of men rather than government of laws," the exercise of the Mandate of Heaven, and authoritarian despotism. Nepotism, corruption, and factionalism were the inevitable by-products of rigid hierarchical sociopolitical structures that evolved in the Hermit Kingdom.

Policymaking process in traditional Korea was exclusively personalistic in nature. At the policy initiation stage, either concerned individuals submitted memorials to the throne, or the king solicited the opinions of eminent Confucian scholars, former ministers, and counselors, primarily at times of crises. Six administrative departments—the Civil Office, the War Office, the Revenues Office, the Punishment Office, the Public Works Office, and the Ceremony Office—were in charge of policy deliberation. It was the Defense Council in the sixteenth century and the State Council later on that was responsible for policy formulation and policy recommendations to the throne. The State Council usually consisted of less than fifty noblemen, including three supreme counselors, two royal personal assistants, six ministers, chief inspectors, military leaders, and some provincial governors.

Any policy recommendation made by the State Council was always based on unanimous consent. But often arm-twisting and political intrigue were used to arrive at that unanimity. Then, policy recommendations were submitted to the king for his approval. As a rule, the essence of all major foreign policy and national security decisions was to hand the issue to the Chinese Imperial Court for its own deliberation and final approval. It was only natural because Korea was, after all, a tributary state of the Middle Kingdom. That was the decisionmaking process followed by Korean rulers when they had to make up their minds about how to handle the shipwrecked Western sailors washed up on Korean shores or whether or not and how to normalize relations with Japan and other Western powers in the mid-nineteenth century.

The Japanese colonial rule that lasted for thirty-five years contributed heavily to the dislocation of the traditional Korean political system, its values, institutions, informal influence networks, and policymaking mechanisms. Although the Japanese-installed Government-General of Chosen was not empowered to deal with foreign policy matters, its impact on subsequent institutional development in Korea was enormous. For it was the Japanese who for the first time set up a modern, efficient bureaucracy in Korea, inculcated many of the postwar Korean administrative beliefs, and left behind thousands of Japanese-trained Korean administrators, managers, and officials after their forced and abrupt departure in August 1945.

The amalgamated communist party-state formed under Soviet tutelage after liberation, and cemented in the trials and tribulations under Kim Il Sung's leadership during and after the Korean War was a localized replica of the Soviet communist party-state system, exhibiting many features of the typical Stalinist political system and bureaucratic regime, emphasizing the one man–centered communist party monopoly rule, mass mobilization politics, repressive security apparatus, unanimity and centralism in policy decisionmaking.

Kim Il Sung founded a dynastic monarchy in the late 1940s, although officially he proclaimed the establishment of the Cabinet-based parliamentary republic in September 1948, which was later recast as a presidential republic in the course of the constitutional revision in 1972. For a long time, the President cum Great Leader relied on his personal secretariat to set national security priorities and formulate foreign policy goals. As the issues grew in complexity, he began to turn for advice and support to the other senior leaders of the North Korean government, most of whom were his former revolutionary comrades-in-arms. That collective consultative process was officially legitimized when the 1972 constitutional reform set up the Central People's Committee (CPC), consisting of the CPC Foreign Policy Commission and National Defense Commission, as the supreme national collective body responsible for the deliberation of foreign policy and national security issues. The Supreme People's Assembly and its Foreign Affairs Commission rubber stamped the CPC decisions, whereas the International Department of the Central Committee of the Korean Workers Party (KWP) coordinated, supervised, and controlled their implementation by various ministries and organizations under the Administrative Council, including the Ministry of Foreign Affairs, Ministry of National Defense and its subordinate organizations, Ministry of External Economic Affairs and External Economic Commission, Ministry of Foreign Trade, and many others.

From the late 1950s until the early 1990s, the essence of political life in the DPRK had been defined by the single-party rule of the KWP, Kim Il Sung's ruthless consolidation of personal power, and its gradual and unconditional transfer to his heir, the eldest son Kim Jong Il. Intraparty factional struggles served as a functional alternative to larger political and social conflicts and policy disputes. Factional purges and political reeducation in provincial exile were Kim Il Sung's weapon of choice in his quest for absolute power. The KWP imposed on the North Korean people the twin cults of personality of the Great Leader and Dear Leader, rooted in neo-Confucian familism and indigenous Korean shamanism, sprinkled with elements of Japanese emperor's colonial worship, shadowed by the overtones of evangelical Christianity, backed by the cults of benefactor Mao Zedong and Stalin, and buttressed by the Manchurian-born siege mentality of the North Korean elites. All decisionmaking processes were subject to the Kim Il Sung-led KWP Central Committee Politburo and Secretariat control through the unified juche party doctrine and ubiquitous party committee system, reinforced by the ever-vigilant and merciless state security apparatus.

Public opinion was negligible. But, informed elite opinion was somewhat important, especially when a major change of course (like the North-South détente in the early 1970s or the breakup of relations with the former Soviet Union in the early 1990s) was contemplated. Rigid ideological tenets, the overbearing burden of past propaganda, and bureaucratic inertia constricted the ability of the national leadership to initiate major strategic shifts in foreign and domestic policies with total disregard for the dominant elite opinions. New policy initiatives always had to be masqueraded as creative reinterpretations of existing juche policies and introduced into the public consciousness slowly and surreptitiously.

Kim Jong Il was designated as the Great Leader's heir apparent when he was thirty-one in 1973, despite vociferous opposition from his stepfamily and some of the Great Leader's older revolutionary comrades-in-arms, who were later purged thrice in 1973–1974, in 1976–1977,[5] and in 1986–1987. On the one hand, Kim Jong Il was promoted to top positions in the KWP—notably, the KWP Central Committee Secretary (September 1973), Politburo member (February 1974), and member of the Politburo Standing Committee (October 1980). In 1980, at the Sixth KWP Party Congress, Kim Jong Il appeared in public for the first time next to his father, Kim Il Sung: by showing up together with his son, Kim Il Sung officially presented Kim Jong Il to the world as his heir.

On the other hand, in order to guarantee smooth political succession, Kim Il Sung gradually transferred to his eldest son the control over the military, too, by appointing Kim Jong Il as the First Deputy Chairman of the National Defense Commission (NDC) in May 1990 and six months later as the Supreme Commander of the Korean People's Army (KPA). In April 1992, Kim Jong Il was awarded the rank of "Marshal of the Republic" (konghwaguk wonsu), which made him the second highest-ranking person in the KPA, next to his father who held the rank of "Grand Marshal" (tae wonsu). In April 1993, Kim Jong Il was promoted to the chairman of the National Defense Commission, following a constitutional revision transferring control over the KPA from the DPRK President (chusok) to the NDC Chairman. Once the Dear Leader began his ascent through the party leadership labyrinths and military command structures to the pinnacle of power in Pyongyang, political authority began to bifurcate, resulting in the formation of a duopoly of power of sorts, namely, two informal power hierarchies leading to the father and his son, respectively.

As an anointed successor and early disciple of traditional Korean neo-Confucian thought, Kim Jong Il feared and revered his father, as well as left all principal policy and strategy decisions for his final approval. When the Great Leader was still alive, the Dear Leader allegedly often felt frustrated at his inability to step into his father's shoes and was seen as an underperformer by many outsiders. Consequently, pent-up frustrations allegedly led to a decadent lifestyle, bouts of alcoholism, and chain smoking in the 1980s and early 1990s.

This notwithstanding, Kim Jong Il shied away from a unique opportunity to assume the reigns over his absolute monarchy on one humid day in the summer of 1986, when the Great Leader Kim Il Sung suffered a severe heart attack during his meeting with a delegation of Bulgarian Trade Unions, after which he went into a coma.[6] Two days later, on a rainy Saturday morning, Kim Jong Il hurriedly invited Soviet ambassador Nikolay M. Shubnikov to his marbled and gilded office on the party street in downtown Pyongyang. Visibly traumatized, the Dear Leader came out in person to greet the Ambassador, shook his hand firmly and, without beating about the bush, informed the Soviet envoy via a Korean interpreter that "the Great Leader is passing away from us," and that the "Politburo has decided to revive him for us." He said that "the catastrophe occurred two days before, and urgent medical assistance from Soviet cardiologists is badly needed." Then, he described in detail what had actually happened to Kim Il Sung and how Korean doctors attempted to reanimate him. What was surprising was the level of detail and Kim Jong Il's almost professional knowledge of all related medical terms and processes. Kim Jong Il went on to say that the DPRK government would not spare any resources and expenditures in order to save the Great Leader. At the end of the conversation, he shook the Ambassador's hand, warned him that besides the two of them only five other people from the inner circle of the supreme North Korean party and military leadership and Kim Il Sung's three personal doctors were privy to that information, and admonished him to earnestly safeguard the state secret.

Upon his return to the Soviet embassy, Ambassador Shubnikov composed a ciphered telegram addressed only to Mikhail Gorbachev, burned the handwritten minutes of the conversation, and personally dispatched it to Moscow. Just twelve hours later, an emergency aircraft arrived in Pyongyang from Moscow with fifteen leading Soviet cardiologists on board. The Soviet heart specialists were immediately transported by helicopter from the Sunan International Airport to Myohyangsan, where Kim Il Sung's comatose body was lying at one of his secluded magnificent residences. It took a total of forty-eight hours for these extraordinary medical miracle workers to bring Kim Il Sung back to life. They continued to monitor Kim Il Sung's health progress until his full recovery in the following month. In other words, Kim Jong Il's decisive action saved his father's life and cemented the dictator's trust in his son's judgment and confidence in his filial piety.

But, on July 8, 1994, Kim Jong Il chose to move on and launched a new era in Korean history when the court doctors were ordered to cease their efforts to bring the eighty-two-year-old Great Leader back to life. During the ensuing neotraditional three-year mourning period, key decisionmaking processes allegedly became more "informalized" and "privatized" by Kim Jong Il and his thirteen to fifteen closest family members and staff aides. Organizationally, the party grip on the formulation of domestic economic policy, national security and defense strategy, and foreign policy began to loosen, as party and state functions appeared to be increasingly delimited, and other domestic actors, especially the national security establishment, began to move to the forefront in the domestic policymaking process while some institutions suffered relative decline.

For instance, the elections for the Supreme People's Assembly, whose ninth term expired in the fall of 1995, were not held until July 1998, and it failed to convene for four years following Kim Il Sung's death. The KWP Central Committee and Politburo held no plenary meetings, party conferences, or congresses. The DPRK Administrative Council was all but invisible. The state presidency and the Central People's Committee, which had functioned as a "super-cabinet" of sorts since 1972, were not functioning. Natural attrition of the older "guerrilla fighter" generation rapidly progressed. Substantively, interpretation and implementation of the Great Leader's last will (*yuhun chongch'i*) amid aggravating domestic economic crisis and deteriorating international environment has been the raison d'etre of Kim Jong Il's rule ever since.

Kim Jong Il's Revolution from Above

In the tumultuous decade following Kim Il Sung's death on July 8, 1994, after initial shock and a three-year policymaking hiatus, Kim Jong Il finally took the plunge and introduced a major constitutional revision and government administration restructuring in September 1998, followed by the civil-military readjustment and advent of the army-first policy in 2000; launched a diplomatic "charm offensive" and actively pursued summit diplomacy in 2000–2004; as well as successfully pushed through controversial economic liberalization reforms in July 2002.

Fundamentally, the reorganization of the North Korean state seems to be designed to reduce its vulnerabilities to the challenges of modernity and pressures of globalization, while safeguarding the basic foundations of the North Korean political system (dictatorship of the proletariat, one-party rule by the KWP, Kim Jong Il's cult of personality, and absolute reign of the Kim clan), economic system (command and control economy, state ownership, isolation from world markets, and militarization of economic life), and ideological system (domination of the unified juche ideas), as well as guaranteeing the survival of Kim Jong Il's regime of absolute personal power.

Although Kim Il Sung's legacy remains largely intact and there is a great deal of continuity between the policies pursued by the father and the son, one should not overlook significant elements of change that have emerged in the past decade. The emerging neotraditionalist state under Kim Jong Il's absolute leadership appears to be built on three new building blocks, or three "neos"—political neo-authoritarianism, economic neocorporatism, and cultural neotraditionalism.

The North Korean political regime appears to be in transition from totalitarian dictatorship of the past to the "siloviki"-led authoritarianism (office holders who come from or are associated with the national security establishment, or the power-wielding institutions and organizations), characterized by increasingly contentious rule by Dear Leader Kim Jong Il, much more military intervention in politics and civil affairs, gradual separation of the KWP from the state and declining party influence on government affairs, increasing centralization of government bureaucracy at the center, as well as the loosening of central government control at the local level. This political transition is accompanied by gradual political "decompression," which manifests in a semblance of *glasnost* in domestic news media, especially in the coverage of external events, unorthodox language used in news reporting, a few unprecedented political rehabilitations, as well as unusual transparency in describing the government decisionmaking processes and thinking.

The stage for the emergence of politically neo-authoritarian elements was set forth at the First Session of the Tenth Supreme People's Assembly (SPA), which passed a new "Kim Jong Il era" Constitution. Kim Jong Il's constitution:

- abolished the institution of the President and Vice-President;
- diminished the powers and status of the Central People's Committee;
- made the National Defense Commission the supreme state organ defining national security and defense strategy, economic and political development strategies;
- appointed Kim Jong Il as the de facto supreme leader;
- made the president of the Presidium of the SPA a formal "head of state" (plus three vice-presidents and four "honorary vice-presidents");
- abolished the Administrative Council and instituted a Cabinet of Ministers composed mainly of the economic ministries, while all "power-related ministries" were subordinated directly to the NDC;
- legalized private ownership;
- curtailed KWP party rule and expanded the scope of religious freedoms in the DPRK.

In addition, in September 1998, Kim Jong Il's regime introduced a series of measures to reform government administration. Their principle objective was to reduce government expenditures in order to save money and increase government efficiency through greater centralization of functionally related government bureaucracies at the center and through the delegation of responsibilities to local actors. The solution was to create the so-called superministries and supercommissions under the newly established Cabinet of Ministers and to reduce the central government workforce by almost thirty percent in five years. The number of party functionaries in the workplace was reduced drastically. The result was a significant decrease in the central government and party's control over local governments and economic actors and noticeable reduction in government budget deficits.

Furthermore, the army-first policy (*songun chongch'i* or AFP) expanded dramatically the military roles in the North Korean society, economy, and politics. The "military sprawl" under army-first politics, army-first policy, army-first leadership, and army-first ideology made the Korean People's Army not only the military defender of the nation and the principal guarantor of regime survival but also an important economic actor in agriculture, infrastructure construction, research and development, professional education, arms sales and hard currency earnings; the major ideological educator, socializer of the youth, and the general backbone of the society; as well as the principal veto power in all policy deliberations.

The fact of the matter is that the national security establishment in the DPRK is neither monolithic nor uniform in their assessments of the challenges and opportunities facing the North Korean state, in their preferred crisis management strategies and policy prescriptions for dealing with the problems at hand. The basic goals that they seem to share are consolidation of their own power within new socioeconomic conditions, perpetuation of the ruling regime in one form or another, enhancement of the DPRK's external security, and preservation of the national sovereignty and statehood, and, perhaps, to a much lesser extent, improved public welfare, especially their own wealth.

It is noteworthy that the military and the state security apparatus do not always see eye to eye on the fundamental problems of state survival, regime adaptation, and Kim Jong Il's late modernization drive. Since the late 1990s, Kim Jong Il decided to elevate the role of the military in the DPRK's decisionmaking, by launching the Songun Era of military-first politics. That was a clear-cut victory for the reform-inclined KPA that has become the primary actor in all policymaking processes, whereas the more conservative state security apparatus was relegated to secondary status in restructuring the North Korean state and building a "very powerful and prosperous nation."

The advent of the Songun Era and the "strong and great nation" (*kangsong taeguk*) strategy, which both debuted in official propaganda in January 1999, is unlikely to have been a response to the so-called hostile foreign environment, because it was the time of emerging détente between the DPRK and the West and in inter-Korean relations. Nor is it likely to have been caused by the protracted economic crisis, because the country was already entering the period of economic stabilization of the late 1990s.

The most likely reason for the introduction of the military rule under the Songun slogans and initiation of the military-backed modernization drive in the land of juche was the defeat of the power challenge brought by the state security apparatus against Kim Jong Il's leadership in 1998. There is always some tension between the military and the state security establishment, as previous purges in the national security establishment in 1976–1977 and in 1987–1988 indicate. That tension was exposed again at the end of 1998, following the purge of the top leadership at the State Security Agency and other organizations within the intelligence and counterintelligence community, which ultimately gave an impetus to the ensuing rise of the Songun policy in the DPRK.

Reportedly, a number of key security officials began to pass negative judgments on Kim Jong Il's leadership in early 1998. Especially harsh in his criticisms was Full General Kim Yong Ryong, First Deputy Minister of the State Security Agency, who essentially acted as the minister of state security in the absence of the aging and ailing Minister Chon Mun Sop.[7] Kim Yong Ryong is rumored to have stated in private conversations that "our political system is sick," and that "we also can live well if we open and reform our country." Even Kwon Hui-Gyong, Director of Office 35 at the KWP Central Committee in charge of the South, which used to be called the Foreign Intelligence Analysis Department, who was personally close to Kim Jong Il, is alleged to have shared these critical views. Moreover, they are alleged to have asserted that they could "restore discipline," "create a new order," and "rectify the mistakes committed by the current leadership" through "internal reforms and external opening," like the former Soviet KGB chief and the secretary-general of the Communist Party of the Soviet Union, Yuri Andropov, hoped to do in the stagnant Soviet Union in 1983.

Obviously, it was a direct challenge to Kim Jong Il's leadership from the state security establishment. The Dear Leader chose to rely on the KPA to suppress the dissent within the ranks of the intelligence and counterintelligence community and throughout the society. Kim Yong Ryong and his close associates were accused of treason and bribery from the export-oriented enterprises under the control of the State Security Agency and were promptly executed. Kwon Hui Gyong, the DPRK hero, was accused of failing to "repatriate" Hwang Jang-yop and of embezzling state funds during his ambassadorship in Moscow and was exiled. In addition, Kim Jong-u, former chairman of the Committee on Promotion of Cooperation with Foreign Countries, and some other officials responsible for economic exchanges with the South were accused of illicit wealth accumulation and disappeared. Seo Kwan-Hui, the then KWP CC Secretary for Agriculture, was accused of undermining the party agricultural policy and starving the people and was executed. Even General Lee Bong-won, the army commander with close ties to the State Security Agency, was accused of espionage and disappeared in late 1998. Through these purges, Kim Jong Il successfully reimposed "discipline and personal loyalty" among the senior leadership, by "teaching them a painful lesson in obedience." No heresies would be tolerated, especially within the inner sanctum responsible for the North Korean regime security. More importantly, the Dear Leader dramatically curbed the unbridled ambitions of the state security apparatus to change the course of the country in accordance with their own vision. Instead, the ever-loyal KPA was given the green light to start the modernization of the nation on its Songun terms.

In Pyongyang, there is indeed a policymaking consensus that the status quo is no longer acceptable. Policymakers appear to agree that the DPRK is faced with a profound macroeconomic crisis and that a new structural adjustment strategy must be adopted to improve the economic situation. "Economic neocorporatism" constitutes the second major building block of the emerging neotraditionalist state in the DPRK. Building a "great, powerful, prosperous nation" is declared as the number one strategic goal of national economic development.

To that end, Kim Jong Il's regime introduced a number of important economic reforms, the "July 1, 2002, economic improvement measures." These included (1) partial liberalization of prices and wages in all sectors of the national economy; (2) elimination of rice subsidies and transformation of the farmers' markets into district markets, as well as the legalization of market sales of agricultural, industrial, and consumer goods; (3) government blessing for the complete monetarization of the economy, including the Public Distribution System, various social entitlements, and residential and industrial utilities services; (4) quasi-privatization of residential housing and farming lots; (5) official licensing of small private enterprises; (6) growing de facto privatization of medium-size state-owned enterprises (SOEs); (7) advancement of plans for the securitization of assets (chaebolization) of large state-owned combines; (8) termination of the bulk of state subsidies to the SOEs, introduction of self-accounting and profit-based systems for SOEs, movement from mandatory to indicative central planning at SOEs; (9) contracting with an overseas investment bank to draw up plans for national banking reform; and (10) innovative government debt financing through T-bond issuance.

Immediate socioeconomic consequences of these reforms appear to be mixed. On the positive side, the national economy has seen some rise in entrepreneurial activity and labor productivity; initial accumulation of private capital has begun; quasi-private markets are beginning to proliferate; some consumer shortages have been alleviated; and there seems to be less government control over the economy overall. On the negative side, predictably, the national currency lost much of its value, inflation skyrocketed, unemployment soared, and social polarization widened.

Among obvious winners from the recent economic reforms have been people with access to foreign currency, especially the half-Japanese/half-Koreans, people with relatives in China and South Korea, foreign trade professionals; the newly emerging nouveaux-riche (including domestic traders and landlords); and traditional economic power holders such as the "red directorate" at privatizing state-owned enterprises, the party apparatchiks and government officials involved in the licensing of economic activity and distribution of foreign aid. In addition, the young and middle-aged males residing in large cities, the export-oriented production workers, and professionals with indispensable skills such as the IT-related technicians seem to benefit more from the ongoing reforms than other strata of the general population.

As economic reforms deepen and social polarization widens, a list of apparent losers gets longer. The people who seem to suffer the most from the unfolding economic changes include military NCOs and enlisted service personnel, the elderly and disabled citizens, women (80 percent unemployed) and children, hinterlanders and some rural residents, most of the budgetary employees (teachers, doctors, administrative staff), as well as intellectuals and scientists.

Kim Jong Il's current program of economic neocorporatism seems to be moving away from absolute state control of the economy (statism), but not in the direction of greater economic liberalism, rather toward greater "corporate" control in the emerging quasi-market conditions. Today, North Korea is no longer a centrally planned economy. But, concurrent new economic institution building is lagging much behind.

Cultural neotraditionalism is the third building block of the emerging neotraditionalist state in North Korea. The "politics of filial piety" practiced by Kim Jong Il during the three-year mourning period facilitated the revival of "neo-Confucian" values in North Korean society. The regime renewed emphasis on symbolism (rather than rationalism) in ideological propaganda by introducing the juche era calendar (the first year of which is 1912) and the Sun Day of April 15, thereby propagating the myth of Tangun as the "founder of the Korean nation," as well as memorializing Kim Il Sung as the "eternal president" of the DPRK.

The government redoubled its efforts to encourage traditional Korean nationalism in its quest to become the leader in the inter-Korean process of shaping a common Korean national identity. Communist aspects of Juche ideology are toned down, whereas nationalist elements are increasingly emphasized. North Korea projects itself as the sole independent guardian of authentic "traditional Korean values, mores, and customs," and derides South Korea as a Westernized and Americanized "modern-day puppet of global imperialism." The state began to sponsor the revival of religions (both Christianity and Buddhism), especially in the countryside, unthinkable less than a decade ago. Especially noteworthy is Kim Jong Il's decision to allow the construction of the Russian Orthodox Chongbaek Cathedral in Pyongyang in June 2003.

Finally, the DPRK government launched "charm diplomacy" in the late 1990s, in order to break out of its international isolation, normalize relations with its former enemies, and attract foreign assistance for national recovery. In four years, Kim Jong Il had three summits with Russia's president Vladimir Putin, two summits with China's president Jiang Zemin and one summit with President Hu Jintao, a summit with the ROK president Kim Dae Jung, two summits with Japan's prime minister Junichiro Koizumi, and hosted the visiting U.S. secretary of state Madeleine Albright in Pyongyang. Despite the Bush administration's hardline policy toward North Korea, Pyongyang's "peace offensive" appears to be successful in breaking up the U.S.-led international coalition formed to coerce the DPRK to give up its nuclear programs at the Beijing Six-Party Talks and bears positive fruit in terms of driving a deep wedge in the U.S.-ROK alliance, as well as inserting painful splinters and mutual suspicions into the U.S.-Japan alliance and the U.S.-PRC strategic partnership.

Overall, Kim Jong Il has attempted to rebuild the North Korean state along neo-traditionalist lines and implement a relatively ambitious domestic modernization agenda, using the military as the primary driving force in restructuring and modernizing the North Korean economy using a market-based approach, reenergizing North Korean society, and consolidating the ruling elite under the slogans of the army-first policy with the goal of building a "prosperous, powerful, great nation." He was clearly driven by a self-preservation instinct, not Marxist-Leninist or juche ideology. His "new thinking" (*saesago pangsik*) developed within the normative, organizational, and personnel constraints imposed by his father's legacy against the background of worsening domestic legitimacy and performance crises during the trial years of the "arduous march" (*konanui haenggun*). It is very important to note that the strategic decision to initiate the modernization reforms was a military-backed decision. Without the support of the top military leaders, Kim Jong Il alone could not have made a strategic decision to launch economic reforms. He needed the military support for his catch-up modernization drive, and he got it.

Moreover, it is noteworthy that even after the eruption of the second nuclear crisis in October 2002, the socioeconomic reforms and political decompression were not reversed but further advanced, despite an increasingly hostile international environment and the nuclear stalemate with the United States. Such policy continuity can be construed either as a sign that the reforms are generating positive feedback and may be approaching the point of no return or that the national leadership may not necessarily have complete control over them and cannot help but swim along with the new social and macroeconomic processes and microeconomic behaviors originated in the late 1990s and formally legalized in July 2002.

In the past five years, the overwhelming process of late modernization of the North Korean state began to change the substance of North Korean politics, create new social and political divisions in North Korean society, expand policy issues, and propel new social forces, corporate concerns, and interest groups into the policymaking arena at the expense of the previously ubiquitous class struggle for the establishment of socialism with juche specifics under KWP leadership centered on the "party headquarters." The issues that are the most important for the increasingly pragmatic and nationalistic leadership in Pyongyang today are regime security and power succession, economic reforms and defense modernization, national reconciliation and southward expansion, and, last but not least, the anti-U.S. struggle and the peaceful resolution of the nuclear crisis.

Who Governs: The Hub-and-Spokes Model of Decisionmaking

The North Korean government is neither a monolith nor a "black box." It is a semi-privatized amorphous collection of rival immobile organizations and stovepiped bureaucracies that often act at cross purposes and are pressed hard and corrupted by the individual and group interests of competing clans, social and political forces vying for power, prestige, and wealth invested by the Dear Leader. North Korean policymakers are rational and very predictable, whether one likes or dislikes their actions.

Kim Jong Il is the absolute monarch presiding over a Byzantine court on the Taedong River. His family clan resides in the modern-day juche Constantinople, the Kim family-built capital of Pyongyang. It encompasses at least six immediately related families (1 + 2 + 3), all competing for the emperor's attention, devotion, and favors, and jockeying for position in the event of post–Kim Jong Il succession.

Although it may be hard to believe, the race for the successor mantle and the inheritance of the "party center" has already begun among the third-generation "top echelon" of the revolution in North Korea. The year 2004 has a threefold symbolic meaning in North Korean political history because it marks the fortieth anniversary of when Kim Jong Il began to work at the KWP Central Committee (in the Organizational Guidance Department and the Propaganda and Agitation Department), the thirtieth anniversary of his designation as the heir apparent to his father Kim Il Sung, and the tenth anniversary of his assumption of power after the Great Leader's death. As potential heirs to Kim Jong Il grow up and mature, they begin to develop their own bureaucratic attachments and personal loyalties. As their distinctive power bases consolidate and expand, their leadership ambitions tend to grow and legitimacy claims solidify. The battle orders of the future "estate fights" between the first-tier, second-tier, and third-tier families within the Kim clan are already shaping up, despite the urgent party calls for the elites to unite behind the "top echelon" of the revolution.

As the power succession struggle intensifies, the political regime tends to crack along the lines of personal loyalties and "estate inheritance." Some power-wielding organizations and interested outside parties may take a risk and choose to take sides up front, expecting higher returns in the future. Others may wait to see who comes out on top in the power struggle within the Kim's extended family clan, without locking onto any particular candidate in the absence of a clear vision of the future government in Pyongyang.

Five major political forces, affecting all spheres of North Korean life, namely, the national security establishment, the old guard, the technocrats, the local elites, and the "foreign wind," approach the extended family clan with their own visions for national development and policy recommendations on the burning issues of the day, and attempt with different degrees of success to penetrate and influence the Kim "family court" in order to ensure the representation of their corporate interests in national decisionmaking at the time of political succession.

These five "spokes" connect the hub of North Korean policymaking, the Dear Leader and Supreme Commander-in-Chief Kim Jong Il, with an "outer circle" of North Korean elites, the brain-feeding tubes at the center and in provinces, who constitute external shock absorbers and safeguard the regime from mass discontent.

Party membership serves as an entry ticket into this elite outer circle, but increasingly that is taken for granted and is no longer sufficient for the new nomenclature. Access to state assets, prestige, power, accumulation of private wealth, or government-licensing authority is a must to qualify for the new elite status. Among members of the same interest group, there may exist significant value differences on an ideological continuum ranging from conservative to liberal and from moderate to radical. But, different "spokes" tend to articulate and aggregate divergent strategic priorities and policy preferences among North Korean elites.

The National Security Establishment

The national security establishment represents the interests of the power-wielding bureaucracies, namely, the military (the KPA General Staff, the KPA General Political Department, the Ministry of People's Armed Forces, the Pyongyang Defense Command, the MPAF Security Command, etc.), the state security apparatus (the Ministry of People's Security, the State Security Agency, the Secret Service), the prosecutorial and court system (the Central Public Prosecutor's Office and the Central Court), the defense industry (the Second Economic Committee), and the nuclear establishment (the General Bureau of Atomic Energy, the Yongbyon Atomic Complex, etc.). They use the National Defense Commission as the supreme national power organ to dominate the policymaking agenda in Pyongyang.

The fact that North Korea is run predominantly by the military under a military-first policy does not mean that the country is hopeless, however, as the experience of the ROK led by General Park Chung-hee, who orchestrated the South Korean economic miracle, powerfully testifies. Revolution from above is one of the possible pathways for North Korean modernization. If economic reforms continue to bear positive results, following the July 2002 liberalization of prices and wages, Kim Jong Il is expected to initiate a gradual privatization of state-owned property. At that time, the Korean People's Army may become one of the leading actors in the North Korean privatization process, because the KPA generals control so many of the country's key economic assets.

Bearing in mind Kim Jong Il's recent fascination with General Park Chung-hee's military rule,[8] in the future, North Korea might develop a corporate state capitalist economy under authoritarian military leadership, when the KPA generals decide to exchange their military uniforms for key civilian management positions in major industrial combines and trading houses in the same way as their South Korean rivals did back in the 1960s.

The Old Guard

The "old guard" represents the views of Kim Il Sung's generation, and they are now in their eighties and early nineties, the dying breed of the anti-Japanese guerrilla fighters. Some of them still possess real power and influence, especially within the national security establishment, despite their delegation of responsibilities for day-to-day management of their respective ministries and agencies to their younger deputies. Others are relegated to nominal honorary positions, primarily at the Presidium of the Supreme People's Assembly, and the KWP Politburo and Central Committee.

Although some representatives of the old guard still occupy important positions at the Presidium of the Supreme People's Assembly, the 11th SPA in general is a relatively middle-aged, university-educated, civilian technocrat-dominated and professionally oriented expert-driven institution, composed of the North Korean intellectual elite with little military representation, despite the era of Songun politics. As a matter of fact, on August 3, 2003, out of 687 deputies, 340 deputies were elected for the first time, which means that 51 percent of the 10th SPA deputies were replaced with new people at the 11th SPA. Moreover, 52 percent of them are younger than the age of fifty, including fourteen SPA deputies, probably some of the offspring of the current DPRK leaders, who are younger than thirty-five. Such a drastic revamping and rejuvenation of the SPA deputy corps and top ranks of the Cabinet of Ministers has led some observers to brand the newly elected and appointed third-generation leaders of the DPRK as the "2003 group."

The Technocrats

The "technocrats," who tend to have technical backgrounds and have been exposed to overseas policy innovations, are traditionally located within the central economic apparatus, including the Cabinet of Ministers and various central economic ministries, agencies, and commissions, that have been loaded with younger economists. Some of the more senior technocrats may be conservative, but most of those beneath them tend to be rather pragmatic and progressive in their policy views. The technocrats also aggregate the views of the new entrepreneurs and corporate elites, especially the former "red directorate" from about a hundred of the most important industrial combines and commercial enterprises that constitute the backbone of the DPRK's industry, agriculture, and service sector, including banking, construction, and commerce.

It is noteworthy that in the past three decades, four out of five North Korean premiers come from the eastern littoral provinces (Kang Sung San and Yon Hyong Muk is from North Hamgyong, deceased Ri Jong-ok was from South Hamgyong, and Hong Song Nam is from Kangwon) and only deceased Ri Gun Mo comes from South Pyongan. They all attended Kim Il Sung University and studied abroad. Three former prime ministers—Kang Sung San, Hong Sung Nam, and Yon Hyong Muk—studied at the University of Prague in the 1950s. During their tenures at the helm of North Korean economic decisionmaking, they, arguably, advanced the ideas of the so-called Prague school in North Korean economic policymaking.

In contrast to technocrats, who tend to be rather pragmatic and progressive in their thinking, the leading ideologues of the current North Korean regime differ widely in their views from conservative to moderate-conservative to moderate-progressive to progressive. Some of them actually stand behind Kim Jong Il's call for "new thinking" and demonstrate some proclivity for innovative approaches and ideas, whereas others are still aligned with the old guard and are generally regarded as the guardians of the revolutionary traditions, proponents of conservative thinking, and defenders of the unified juche party line.

The Local Elites

The "local elites" represent the voices of the provincial and county administrative and party bosses, as well as local military commanders. These local officials have their own parochial interests and try to shield themselves from political winds in Pyongyang. These leaders are very sensitive to regional differences and local problems, which gives rise to provincial regionalism (*chibangjuui*), fueling the revival of traditional region-based factionalism at the center.

It is noteworthy that Kim Jong Il tries to maintain an even balance at the center between the party and military leaders who come from the Hamgyong and Pyongan provinces, that is, North Korea's own northerners and southerners. For instance, out of fifty-four of the most influential leaders in North Korea (some of whom are already deceased, to be sure), twenty-four were born in the Hamgyong provinces, twenty-three were born in the Pyongan provinces, including the capital area of Pyongyang, and seven were born overseas (four in Manchuria, two in South Korea, and one in Russia).

In general, there has always been latent animosity and competition for central power between the Hamgyong people and the Pyongan people. The Hamgyong people (often called "brambles" or "king brambles" in the DPRK) tend to be clever, competitive, and eager to get ahead. They are tough, realistic, and aggressive in pursuing their interests. The Pyongan people (often called "stingy" and "leftover straws"), especially those who come from the capital of Pyongyang, are regarded as lacking substance, being selfish, crafty, two-faced, and averse to hard work. They have a reputation for shiftiness and scheming, because of their proximity to the halls of power. The role of regionalism, especially the north-south differences, can no longer be ignored in the analysis of North Korean policymaking.

Local influences can also be felt within major national public organizations and their respective local chapters. Heads of the most influential national social organizations and federations are elected as members of the SPA Presidium, where they represent the interests of their corporate constituencies at the national level.

Foreign Winds

The "foreign winds" reflect the interests of various compatriot groups, including the Koreans of Chinese, Japanese, Russian, American, and South Korean origins. Also, they may be reflected in the parochial interests of the government officials who are responsible for specific neighboring countries in their official duties or are known to have expressed noticeable interest in certain countries and cultures. Origin, educational background, known policy preferences, and observable interactions with foreign counterparts (job description, participation in international talks, visits to foreign countries, visits to foreign embassies, reception of foreign delegations, etc.) are used as criteria for listing certain individuals in the foreign winds group. These people are scattered throughout the entire government and operate in the penumbras of larger and more powerful political forces. They may or may not lobby for certain domestic and foreign policies that are beneficial or detrimental with respect to the DPRK's relations with its neighboring countries.

The DPRK's neighboring powers, including the Republic of Korea, China, Russia, and Japan, try to use the carriers of "foreign wind" (sometimes regarded as the potential "fifth column" by regime hardliners) to penetrate the North Korean political system. They strive to advance their respective national interests through whatever transmission channels they can master, in order to access the Kim family court and exercise direct or indirect influence on Kim Jong Il's thinking about power, policy, and the future direction of the nation.

The Big Picture: Forward with or Without the Kim Regime?

Today, North Korea is a different country than it was when the Great Leader passed away a decade ago. It is in the midst of steady, albeit stealthy, structural changes affecting all areas of the national economy, politics, and society, as well as people from all walks of life; it is strengthening neo-authoritarian military rule and accelerating catch-up modernization reforms aimed against communist party rule and socialist economic stagnation.

The four pillars of the traditional political regime—fear, isolation, elite unity, and juche ideology—are beginning to show noticeable cracks and signs of erosion. First, there is less fear in a country where money is king and people can buy their way out of any trouble, even exiles to the mines and labor reeducation camps. Second, there is less isolation in a country where hundreds of thousands of citizens can go back and forth across its national borders like they do on the Korean-Chinese frontier, where tens of thousands of people use mobile phone services, can watch international television channels, and have access to the Internet, regardless of its censored content and government monitoring. Third, there is less elite unity when economic stimulus supplants party loyalty in motivating human behavior, when factionalism and interest group politics reemerge, and power rivalries (often fueled by external sources of revenue) intensify with a vengeance. Fourth, there is much less ideological influence left since the unified juche idea has become simply what Kim Jong Il says it is, when faith in the infallibility of the semidivine Dear Leader is broken and cults of personality are disparaged, when traditional religions are revived, and hope of a new beginning beyond the old gods begins to glimmer on the horizon.

Kim Jong Il took his country on a path of modernization and national reconciliation with the South, which can be either complimentary or potentially fraught with contradictions, difficulties, and dangers. The biggest challenge for him is to preserve his personal power and to safeguard the throne for his successors, while reforming his country and engaging the South.

All signs indicate that Kim Jong Il welcomes creeping privatization of public property by the principal state authorities, including the leaders of the armed forces and security services, senior party functionaries, and the "red directorate." If such socio-economic transition in a partially deindustrialized, re-ruralized, extremely atomized, and semifeudal North Korean society were to proceed without civil strife, one might expect the formation of privatized chaebol-like economic conglomerates on the ruins of the North Korean socialist economic edifice, with substantial government stakes in flagship industries. With time, the latter may well be able to attract South Korean investment in the cheap-labor-based export-oriented sectors, which could provide the stimulus for the long-term recovery of the North Korean economy. Such gradual economic reforms are unlikely to bring prosperity to the DPRK's working classes, but they may bring about a more decent life, at least by removing the daily threat of starvation. If in the process of change the absolute power of the Kim monarchy is to be eroded or curtailed, Kim Jong Il is unlikely to halt the process as long as his dynastic rule is assured of continuing survival.

In fifteen to twenty years, Kim Jong Il's heir (who is being considered for nomination now) is likely to inherit a very different country, possibly embarked on a military, government-sponsored capitalist development road and engulfed in close economic ties with the Republic of Korea. Far from being a bona fide democracy, a post–Kim Jong Il North Korea may well develop into a constitutional monarchy more acceptable to the international community.

If dynastic survival is the paramount strategic goal of the Kim family, then nothing can offer the Dear Leader a better model of dynastic perseverance in the face of tremendous adversity than the Chrysanthemum dynasty in Japan, which survived U.S. nuclear bombardment and military occupation in the 1940s and remains one of the symbols of Japanese national power and unity today.

It is no wonder that, despite traditional Korean-Japanese animosity, Kim Il Sung is said to have advised Kim Jong Il repeatedly to step back from the domestic political arena and economic policymaking and leave both to the party and government officials, while concentrating his energy on cultivating national military power, advancing the international interests of the DPRK, and acting as a symbol of national unity, sovereignty, and dignity before the North Korean people and the world. If Kim Jong Il succeeds in redefining and relegitimizing the constitutional space for his absolute monarchy through bold constitutional compromises, and insulates it from the political and economic processes pressuring North Korean society from inside and outside through radical administrative reforms without undermining its charismatic legitimacy, then he may be able to extend its life for more generations to come.

The wild card is the set of pressures and incentives presented by the international community in the years ahead and the possible reaction of the North Korean national security establishment to these changing external circumstances. If the continuous survival of the Kim Jong Il clan eventually becomes an obstacle and a serious threat to the preservation of the DPRK's national sovereignty and independence for whatever reason (for instance, the threat of the use of force against the regime is substantiated and becomes a "clear and present danger," or the increased possibility of Kim Jong Il's "sell out" with a "golden parachute" by striking a behind-the-scenes deal on reunification with the ROK leaders, or the uncontrolled escalation of internal civil and political strife fueled by foreign penetration), then one cannot exclude the possibility that the national security establishment, the primary guarantors and main beneficiaries of territorial integrity and the national sovereignty of the DPRK, may orchestrate a swift palace coup or another car crash accident against Kim Jong Il and his clan.

They have witnessed what the Gorbachev reforms did to the old Soviet Union, which is no more. They have observed the chaos and destruction that took place under the liberal democratic Boris Yeltsin regime in the new Russia. Neither alternative is acceptable to them. But the rise of previously unknown KGB foreign intelligence operative Vladimir Putin to take the helm of a sinking Russia unexpectedly as a result of the "Gray Colonels coup" inside the Kremlin, and his imposition on Russian chaos of a nationalistic militaristic bureaucratic regime, spearheading the state-capitalist development and restoring Russia's great power status, may well appeal to their imagination.

In order to preserve national sovereignty against the looming threat of Southern-led absorption and abolition of the North Korean state, fraught with the likely decapitation of the Northern security, military, and party elites, the North Korean national security establishment may decide to move forward without the Kim clan altogether. In the view of some, state survival and Kim regime survival may become incompatible if the nation were to move from the Gorbachev-like current liberalization re-forms to a Putin-style regime with restored order and stability, pursuing state-led modernization and defending its independent national identity from the South. In order to skip or leapfrog the "lost decade" of the Yeltsin era, with its destruction of state institutions and tremendous losses of state assets, the outright removal of the Kim regime may become the necessary evil for the die-hard defenders of the North Korean state.

Kim Jong Il is aware of the undercurrent threats to his regime and the many difficulties that lie ahead. He got the message when his closest confidant, Kim Yong Sun, was killed and his wife, Ko Young-Hee, was severely hurt in unprecedented car accidents on the almost trafficless roads, respectively, in June and October 2003. His state security chiefs, his bodyguards, his generals, his party entourage, his relatives, and their respective foreign connections all are suspect. Against such a troublesome background, it was unexpected that the DPRK Minister of Public Security General Choe Ryong-su was replaced with Army General Ju Sang Song in July 2004, less than a year into his tenure. This is a time of rising uncertainty in Pyongyang. The regime is evolving and slowly cracking. It is high time for foreign influence to start shaping the direction of future developments inside the Hermit Kingdom.

Notes

The views expressed in this article are personal views of the author, and they do not represent the official positions of the U.S. government, the U.S. Department of Defense, or the Asia-Pacific Center for Security Studies.

1. In 2003, a number of new construction material businesses with local and foreign private stakes were established in the vicinity of Pyongyang, including the Seungho Cement Factory on the Nam River, the Sangwon Cement Union Company opened on June 14, 2003, a Slate Factory based on a joint DPRK-PRC venture opened on November 25, 2003, a Chinese-financed $50 million joint venture glass factory, and others.

2. In 2003, several new modern food-processing companies with private local and foreign stakes were established in the vicinity of Pyongyang, including the Kangseo Mineral Water Processing Factory opened on October 21, 2003, the Cheongdan Basic Food Factory producing soy sauce and soybean paste opened on May 31, 2003, the Taedonggang Beer Brewery opened on November 29, 2002, in the Sadong district of Pyongyang, and others.

3. Among the new semiprivate businesses opened in 2003, one should note the Sinuiju Cosmetics Factory, the Pyongyang Cosmetics Factory, and the Seongyo Knitting Factory. All three are joint ventures with Chinese and Korean-Japanese stakes, selling to the local market.

4. North, *Institutions, Institutional Change*, 3–10.

5. The now deceased DPRK vice president and KWP CC secretary Kim Tong-gyu, who was the number-three man in the North Korean power hierarchy after Kim Il Sung and Kim Jong Il in the mid-1970s, launched an open critique of Kim Jong Il and his personnel management policy at the KWP CC Politburo meeting in June 1976. Kim Tong-gyu opposed rush dismissals of former guerrilla fighters from top government positions in favor of Kim Jong Il–appointed younger generation cadres in violation of the party discipline and party rules. Kim Tong-gyu also criticized the intraparty discrimination against people who come from the South and who have "complicated backgrounds." He proposed not to rush to designate Kim Jong Il as

the Great Leader's heir apparent, but to take time and prepare the popular masses for the succession slowly. Kim Tong-gyu was supported by Ryu Chang-shik, the KWP CC secretary in charge of South Korean affairs, but was opposed by the other Politburo members—O Chin-u, Kim Il, and Choe Hyun. In the end, Kim Il Sung intervened in the discussion and cooled down the debate for the time being. However, several months later, when Kim Tong-gyu raised his opposition to Kim Jong Il's succession again, he was accused of violating the "Ten Principles of Party Unity" and factionalism. Consequently, Kim Tong-gyu and Ryu Chang-shik were purged and sent to a political reeducation camp in South Hamgyong Province in late 1977; Chang Chon Hwan, deputy minister of people's defense, was exiled to Chagang Province; and thousands of lower-ranking party officials accused of factionalism were purged from the KWP and exiled to the countryside and ore mines in the special districts in North Hamgyong and Ryangrang Provinces.

6. The following account is based on the author's conversation with one of the Russian participants of the described events who asked not to be identified.

7. Chon Mun Sop passed away in late 1998.

8. On May 13, 2002, in Pyongyang, Kim Jong Il "warmly welcomed and had a cordial tête-à-tête conversation with Mrs. Park Keun-hye, General Park Chung-hee's daughter, for an hour, after which he gave a dinner in her honor." See Korean Central News Agency, Pyongyang, May 14, 2002.

3

Kim Jong Il's
Military-First Politics

Ilpyong J. Kim

The Democratic People's Republic of Korea (DPRK), which is commonly known as North Korea, has been transformed into a military-party state for the past decade since the death of Kim Il Sung in 1994. From 1994 to 2004 the new leadership of Kim Jong Il has successfully transformed North Korea from a party-state system to a military-first political system. During the Kim Il Sung period (1948–1994), the Korean Workers' Party (KWP) played the central role in North Korean politics. However, the role of the KWP has been gradually diminished while the role of the North Korean military in politics has rapidly increased under Kim Jong Il's leadership.

Kim Il Sung was the revolutionary leader during the Japanese colonial rule of Korea from 1910 to 1945 and the founder of the DPRK in 1948. He is well known to the outside world because of his anti-Japanese revolutionary activities in Manchuria and Siberia in the 1930s and 1940s and also was recognized as one of the leaders of the Korean independence movement when Koreans ardently supported independence from Japanese colonial rule. The independence movement of Koreans abroad has been widely researched and documented by Korean scholars as well as foreign experts. Moreover, biographical studies on Kim Il Sung (1912–1994) have been so polarized as either pro- or anti-Kim that an objective analysis of his rule in North Korea is scanty at best. However, the Western studies of Kim Il Sung agree in general that the senior Kim had revolutionary ideas and organizational skills in recruiting Korean exiles in China and Siberia to carry out the movement for the independence of Korea.

This chapter will attempt to conduct an objective analysis and interpretation of Kim Jong Il's military-first politics and contrast it with the juche politics of his father Kim Il Sung, originator of the juche ideology. Among the issues to be discussed in this chapter are the origin and development of the military-first politics of Kim Jong Il, the process of transition from the juche ideology of Kim Il Sung, and the impact of this change on the government and the economic structures of North Korea.

Historical Background

Kim Jong Il emerged as the supreme leader of North Korea when his father died in July 1994 at the age of eighty-two. The groundwork for his accession began early on. Upon his graduation from the university in Pyongyang in June 1964, he became a cadre in the Organization and Guidance Department of the Korean Workers' Party (KWP) Central Committee (CC). He rose quickly to chief of a section in its Cultural-Art Department in 1971. He was later promoted to candidate member of the Politburo and secretary in charge of organization, propaganda, and agitation for the KWP CC in 1973. His position as successor to his father, Kim Il Sung, was firmly established by the KWP CC session held in February 1974 and formalized at the Sixth Congress of the KWP in October 1980.

In May 1981, Kim Jong Il began his "practical leadership training" when he accompanied his father as he inspected the development projects in Myohyangsan region as well as other major industrial development projects. Moreover, Kim Jong Il authored the treatise entitled "On Juche Ideology" in March 1982, which further developed the philosophy into the political theory that would serve as the foundation for consolidating his leadership in various movements such as those dedicated to increasing industrial production, learning from hidden heroes, arming the entire membership of the KWP with the juche ideology, and starting the movement for abiding by the law in the 1980s.

In 1984 the junior Kim also provided leadership for the so-called August Third movement to step up production of people's consumer goods. At this time, the senior Kim and the junior Kim began to define the division of labor for providing leadership and guidance to the KWP in domestic and foreign affairs. Moreover, when the senior Kim prepared his lecture notes on "The Historical Experience of Building the Korean Workers' Party" on the occasion of its fortieth anniversary on May 31, 1986, he spoke of "the problems of succeeding the supreme leader's political position and responsibilities" and asserted that "in our Party, the succession issue of revolutionary work has been resolved satisfactorily." It was the reaffirmation of the widely known fact that Kim Jong Il was his successor.

Kim Jong Il began to have full control of the military when he was elected to the first vice chair of the reorganized National Defense Commission (NDC) in May 1990 at the First Plenary session of the Ninth Supreme People's Assembly (SPA). He was also elected to the post of the Supreme Commander of the North Korean armed forces on December 24, 1991, at the Nineteenth Plenary Session of the Sixth Central Committee of the Korean Workers' Party. After attaining the rank of marshal in the North Korean armed forces on April 20, 1992, Kim Jong Il was elected chairman of the National Defense on April 9, 1993. Thus, he was able to consolidate his power as he took control of the KWP, the DPRK government, and the Korean People's Army as the supreme leader with the blessings of his father.

Were there any challenges or opposition to Kim Jong Il's quick rise to succeed his father? It was obvious in the early 1970s that the succession of Kim Young Ju, Kim Il

Sung's younger brother, was supported by one faction of the senior cadres of the KWP CC. However, the forces supporting junior Kim quickly suppressed the attempt.

The junior Kim laid the groundwork to shift North Korean politics from the control of the KWP to military-first politics after he took over the NDC. It was reported in the North Korean press that Kim Jong Il presented a wristwatch to all military personnel on the occasion of the sixtieth anniversary of the founding of the North Korean People's Army on April 25, 1992. This story was an indication of how much Kim Jong Il valued the military personnel and paid them more attention than any other organized group in North Korea.[1]

Kim Jong Il was reelected as the NDC chairman at the tenth session of the SPA on September 5, 1998. The elections of the SPA members were held in July 1998. Thus, he was able to consolidate his power in the military as well as in the KWP when he was appointed party general secretary by the KWP in 1997, which empowered him to control the party structure and make state policy. When the tenth session of the SPA amended the North Korean constitution by abolishing the post of presidency and making Kim Il Sung the "eternal president" in 1998, Kim Jong Il became the supreme leader of the DPRK as the chairman of the National Defense Commission, a position that has functioned as the center of political power in North Korea ever since—the most powerful position in the government of the DPRK.

Currently, Kim holds the posts of marshal, general secretary of the KWP CC, chairman of the National Defense Commission, and supreme commander of the Korean People's Army. He is also a member of the Politburo of the KWP CC and the chairman of the KWP Central Military Committee. Thus, the question arises as to whether or not the position of chairman of the National Defense Commission is more powerful than the general secretary of the KWP. In the communist political system the general secretary of the communist party is traditionally most powerful, as is the case in China as well as in the former Soviet Union. It was also the case in North Korea prior to the constitutional amendment of 1998.[2]

The people and press in North Korea address Kim Jong Il as the chairman of the National Defense Commission instead of mentioning him as the general secretary of the Korean Workers Party. Kim himself directed the constitutional amendment on September 5, 1998, to make himself the chairman of the NDC, an action that a Japanese journalist called a military coup because the political system that was based on the political power of the KWP has been radically transformed into military-first politics.[3] It is the general practice in a socialist and communist party-state system that the socialist or communist party directs military affairs, meaning the military is subordinate to the ruling party. But the junior Kim has carried out what amounts to a military coup so that the military may rule the party. Under the Kim Jong Il regime, the military directs party affairs as the superior. In fact, the military is so powerful that it is above the state. The military has now become the supreme commander of the state, the party, and society, turning North Korea into a military garrison state.

Under the new constitution of the DPRK, the chairman of the NDC is the most powerful person in North Korea since Kim has consolidated the powers exercised by the party and the state organization. During the rule of Kim Il Sung, the chairman of the state and party central directed the political, economic, and social system. The National Defense Commission consists of all military leaders, either active or reserve, except for two civilians: Yon Hyung-mook, a former premier of the government, and Chon Byong-ho, a veteran party leader. Thus the leadership of North Korea has now been transformed into a military leadership system by promoting the military leaders above the party leaders. Cho Myong-rok, the first vice chairman of the NDC, was the seventh in ranking during the senior Kim period but was promoted to second to Kim Jong Il in his rank following the constitutional change. Most military leaders have now achieved higher rank and status than political leaders, a situation that never occurred under Kim Il Sung's leadership.

The Juche Ideology of Kim Il Sung

Because Kim Jong Il's military-first politics is based on his father's ruling ideology of juche, it may be necessary to discuss the origin and development of juche ideology. *The Dictionary of Philosophy* in North Korea defines juche ideology as "Kim Il Sung's revolutionary idea." The word *juche* was used for the first time on December 28, 1955, when the senior Kim made a speech entitled "On the Need to Repel Dogmatism and Formalism and to Establish Juche in Carrying Out Ideological Programs." However, North Korea actually began to use the term *juche ideology* after December 6, 1967, when Kim Il Sung gave a speech to the first session of the Fourth Supreme People's Assembly under the title "Let Us Materialize Our Self-Reliant, Independent, Self-Defensive Lines Completely," in which he said, "Our Juche ideology refers to the most correct Marxism-Leninism-oriented guiding philosophy designed to carry out our revolution and construction." Juche can be translated directly as "self-identity," but the idea of self-reliance is more appropriate in practice. Many Western analysts of North Korean politics in the 1960s concluded that the *juche ideology* was born as an independent and self-reliance ideology to cope with the Sino–Soviet conflict as it intensified.

North Korea claims that the origins of the juche ideology should be traced back to June 1930 when Kim Il Sung presided over a meeting of the "Down-with-Independence League" in Manchuria, and that it was further transformed into a theory of philosophy by Kim Jong Il. The DPRK constitution used to contain a phrase stipulating that juche, which is a creative application of Marxism-Leninism, must be upheld as the guiding principle of North Korean ideology. However, the word Marxism-Leninism was deleted from the constitution of 1992 in the aftermath of the collapse of the communist bloc of nations in Eastern Europe and the Soviet Union.

In the post–Kim Il Sung era, especially following junior Kim's succession as the KWP general secretary and the chairman of the National Defense Commission, the usage of the juche ideology gradually declined. It may have had something to do with the defection of Hwang Jang-yop who claimed that he was the originator of the juche ideology and that he had taught the juche philosophy to the junior Kim at Kim Il Sung

University in the 1960s.[4] Hwang Jang-yop, former secretary of the Korean Workers' Party Central Committee and professor of philosophy at Kim Il Sung University, who defected to South Korea in 1997, claimed that he had developed juche ideology under the direction of Kim Il Sung in the late 1950s.[5]

The juche ideology consists mainly of two parts—the philosophical theory, which maintains that the masses are the masters of history and revolution, and the guiding principle, or the "Revolutionary View of the Leader," which asserts that "nonetheless, the masses are not able to take up spontaneously any revolutionary courses unless they are organized into revolutionary forces and are led by the *Suryong* (great leader)." This is similar to what Mao Zedong called the mass-line approach during the revolutionary period of the 1930s and 1940s in China.[6] More recently, North Korea maintains that Kim Jong Il developed a more theoretical and systematic concept of the "Revolutionary View" and strengthened it during the 1980s in a treatise entitled "Theory of the Immortal Sociopolitical Body." In the treatise, he stressed that physical life, given by the parents, is mortal, but political life, which is immortal, is given by the Suryong (the brain or center of the body politic).

Beginning in 1998, due largely to the defection of Hwang Jang-yop, North Korea replaced juche with the doctrine of military-first politics. It is debatable whether or not the juche ideology is a theory of revolution as North Koreans claim it to be. It is rather a strategy of revolution in North Korea just as Maoism was a strategy of revolution rather than a theory of revolution in China. The transition from the juche ideology to military-first politics thus coincided with the peaceful transition of power from the father Kim Il Sung to the son Kim Jong Il with the blessings of a new revolutionary strategy developed by the successor.

When we compare the political system that Kim Jong Il created with that of Kim Il Sung, we find the fundamental change to be the increased military role in the political process. In the wake of the collapse of the communist system in the Soviet Union and Eastern Europe, coupled with the death of Kim Il Sung and the mounting economic crisis at home, it was inevitable that Kim Jong Il would search for a new strategy to overcome North Korea's unprecedented political and economic crisis. The junior Kim's solution to the problem was simply to upgrade the role of the military, gradually increasing their power in the 1990s following the death of his father. Since then, Kim Jong Il has attempted to militarize the whole of North Korean society by giving priority to the military, a process that has been termed military-first politics.

The Nature of Military-First Politics

The emergence of a dominant military-oriented strategy first appeared in an editorial of the KWP newspaper *Rodong Shinmun* (Workers' Daily) on April 7, 1997, under the headline, "There Is a Victory for Socialism in the Guns and Bombs of the People's Army." The editorial defined the military-oriented thinking as "the revolutionary philosophy to safeguard our own style of socialism under any circumstances," and credited the concept to Respected General Kim Jong Il. Though Kim Jong Il has never served in the military or had any experience of military training, he is regarded as the supreme military commander, and he routinely demonstrates the superior position in which he holds the army through frequent visits to the military units. Reflecting his military-oriented politics, for example, two-thirds of Kim Jong Il's public activities in 1997 were devoted to visiting the units of the Korean People's Army. It is also possible that the senior Kim's power relied upon the support of the old revolutionary cadres of the Korean Workers' Party but that the junior Kim does not trust them and increasingly relies upon the support of the younger generation of military commanders in the Korean People's Army.

The joint editorial of the KWP theoretical journal *Kulloja* (Worker) and the *Rodong Shinmun* on June 16, 1998, entitled "Our Party's Military-First Politics Will Inevitably Achieve Victory and Will Never Be Defeated," emphatically pointed out that "Military-First Politics is the leadership method under the principle of giving priority to the military and resolving the problems that may occur in the course of revolution and construction as well as establishing the military as the main body of the revolution in the course of achieving the total tasks of socialism."[7] In the editorial, "our party" was mentioned but it was not necessarily referring to the Korean Workers' Party as an organization but rather was clear that "our party" meant Kim Jong Il. Moreover, the editorial made it clear that "Military-First Politics was perceived as being able to resolve any problems that might occur in a revolution or reconstruction."[8]

As discussed, under the constitutional revision of September 5, 1998, the National Defense Commission (NDC) became the most powerful political organization headed by Kim Jong Il as its chairman. "The office of the Chairman of the National Defense Commission is a very important post: It is in charge of the whole of North Korea's political, military, and economic powers and is the top post of the republic," Presidium Chairman Kim Yong-nam said when he nominated Kim Jong Il as chairman of the NDC at the first session of the Tenth Supreme People's Assembly on September 5, 1998. The National Defense Commission's ranks at the time included First Vice Chairman Cho Myong-rok, Vice Chairmen Kim Il Chol and Li Yong-mu, and members Kim Yong-chun, Yon Hyong-muk, Li Ul-sol, Paek Hak-rim, Chon Byong-ho, and Kim Chol-man.

More recently, the first plenary session of the Eleventh Supreme People's Assembly on September 3, 2003, reelected Kim Jong Il for a third five-year term as the chairman of the NDC. The NDC is now composed of First Vice Chairman Cho Myong-rok, Vice Chairman Yon Hyong-muk, Vice Chairman Li Yong-mu, and five regular members who are Kim Yong-chun, Kim Il-chol, Chon Byong-ho, Choi Yong-su, and Paek Chae-bong. Apparently, Li Ul-sol and Paek Hak-rim were not reelected to the NDC due to their ages (both are in their eighties). They were replaced by the new generation of military leaders. Moreover, the former prime minister and economic expert Yon Hyong-muk was elected to serve as one of the vice chairmen, indicating that the economic leadership is being shifted from the KWP to the NDC and that the KWP would confine its leadership to the sphere of ideology and ideological training.

Kim Jong Il thus transformed the National Defense Commission into a command post of the ruling elite in North Korean politics. He might have learned from his experiences while working in the organizations of the KWP Central Committee that the old cadres, who were recruited and promoted by his father, continued to maintain their allegiance and loyalty to his father rather than to him. Moreover, following the defection of his former professor–mentor of juche ideology at Kim Il Sung University, Hwang Jang-yop, to South Korea in 1997, Kim Jong Il seemed to have lost confidence in the old cadres who had been associated with his father. Thus, he decided to make a transition from the juche ideology to military-first politics by transforming the National Defense Commission into the pivotal center of political power for ruling the 23 million people of North Korea.

It was not until October 20, 1998, that North Korea introduced the term "*songun-chongchi*" (military-first politics). The Supreme People's Assembly placed the office of the NDC chairman on the apex of North Korea's ruling elite. In June 1999 North Korea also began to develop theories to justify and propagate among the people the validity of military-first politics. In an editorial of the KWP newspaper *Rodong Shinmun* published on June 16, 1999, "Our Party's Policy of Giving Priority to the Army is Invincible," it was stressed that military-first politics is a cure-all in this era of ideological, military, and economic confrontation with the imperialists.

It also pointed out that Great Leader Kim Il Sung established an army before he inaugurated the party organization into the course of his revolutionary activities. "The socialist cause inevitably goes with a fierce face-off with imperialism, and the party's policy of giving priority to military affairs is instrumental in winning a victory in the serious ideological stand-off with imperialism," the editorial stressed. It continued to assert that, "giving priority to military affairs is not a mere tactical issue, but a strategic issue in close relations with the fate and future course of the revolution." This editorial was reprinted in *Kulloja* for wider circulation and discussion. Thus, the theoretical groundwork was laid in the late 1990s to meet the challenges of the most powerful forces of the United States and its allies in the twenty-first century.

Moreover, an editorial of *Rodong Shinmun* on December 21, 2001, went one step further to justify military-first politics. "The army-based policy of the Party embodies the Juche idea, the revolutionary doctrine for the defense and realization of the independence of the popular masses mirrors the lawful demands for the accomplishment of the socialist cause that is launched and pushed forward in a fierce confrontation with imperialists. Indeed, it is a political mode that makes it possible to carry to completion the cause of independence of the popular masses, the cause of socialism." This editorial was also carried in the December issue of *Kulloja* in 2001, saying that military-first politics alone can defend and protect the fatherland as it is faced with the most powerful military forces in South Korea.

What then is the hidden motive behind Kim Jong Il's military-first politics? During Kim Jong Il's four decades of work in the party organization, he discovered the party machine was becoming increasingly bureaucratic and losing its dynamism. He also witnessed the cadres who were aging lose their revolutionary zeal. They were unable to provide the dynamic and innovative leadership that the revolution and construction work required. He realized that corruption was rampant in the party organizations and the heretical behavior of the rank and file was out of control. Moreover, Kim Jong Il reached the conclusion that it was impossible for him to resolve the organizational problems of the KWP by simply revamping the party organizations or reshuffling the leadership positions of tired, aging cadres.

Therefore, when Kim Jong Il succeeded his father as the general secretary of the KWP and chairman of the National Defense Commission (NDC) in 1998, he launched the restructuring of the NDC by means of constitutional amendment, thereby placing the NDC above the KWP Central Committee that had, in the past, been the traditional power center. As Mao Zedong asserted, "political power grows out of the barrel of the gun." Kim Jong Il determined that political power should be derived from the support of the North Korean military forces. The military is better organized and better disciplined than the KWP and is comprised of a younger generation of North Korean society, unlike the KWP. Furthermore, the military men are patriotic and dedicated and willing to sacrifice their lives for the defense of the fatherland. In short, it was easier and more comfortable for Kim Jong Il to identify with the military rather than the KWP bureaucracy because the military was more responsive to his command than the party organizations.

Following Kim Il Sung's death on July 8, 1994, North Korea attempted to develop new slogans and ideology to reflect the new politics and new leadership. They tried the "Red Flag Ideology," which was designed to step up ideological indoctrination, and emphasized the "Politics of Benevolence and Virtue" to pave the way for Kim Jong Il to succeed his father. When the three-year mourning period ended in 1997, military-first politics emerged as the new slogan and ideology of North Korean politics under the leadership of Kim Jong Il. Military-first politics simply meant that the Korean Workers' Party, which controlled North Korea for almost four decades, would be replaced by the military. The KWP will be subordinate to and under the control of the North Korean military, which is headed by the junior Kim. North Korea is attempting to prevent the collapse of its socialist system in the aftermath of the breakdown of the communist system that swept through East Europe and eventually the Soviet Union in the early 1990s. In short, the choice of military-first politics has been put in place to avoid the upheavals of leadership change and suitably transform North Korean economic and political systems into more competitive vehicles for modern times by elevating younger generations to positions of power to ensure the continuity of Kim Jong Il's leadership.

Kangsong Taeguk *and Economic Reform*

The ultimate goal of military-first politics is to achieve a "Strong and Prosperous Great State" (kangsong taeguk) in order to cope with the security threat from the outside world, including the allied forces of the United States and South Korea, as well as the problems created by the collapse of the communist system in the former Soviet Union and Eastern Europe. Confronting the challenges posed by the powerful states in the South, Kim Jong Il had to build up a strong and prosperous nation just as neighboring Japan had achieved the status of powerful nation with the slogan "Fukoku Kyohei" (Rich Country with Strong Army) after the Meiji restoration in 1868. Moreover, although the southern part of Korea was lagging behind North Korea economically in the late 1940s and 1950s, the military coup of 1961 ushered in rapid economic development and industrialization that ultimately surpassed the North. Thus, the economic development model of a South Korean military revolution seems to have influenced Kim Jong Il and his followers to launch military-first politics as the means to achieve their goals.

The idea of constructing a strong and prosperous great state (kangsong taeguk) emerged early in 1998 when Kim Jong Il carried out "on-the-spot-inspections" through August 15, 1998. The KWP newspaper *Rodong Shinmun* published an article on the kangsong taeguk on August 22, 1998, widely circulating it as the slogan of the Kim Jong Il leadership. When North Korea succeeded in launching the satellite Kwangmyong No. 1 on August 31, 1998, Pyongyang began to propagandize it as the signal for moving toward its goal to achieve development through a strong ideology, a strong military, and a strong economy. Having a strong ideology means achieving the ideological unity of the party and revolutionary cadres, while a strong military state refers to the goal of victory in every battle, militarization of the entire population, and fortification of the whole nation by acquiring strong offensive and defensive capabilities as well as by repelling any attack launched by enemy forces. Having a strong economic state means revitalizing economic production to provide a self-reliant and prosperous economic life for everyone in the nation.

There are several reasons why North Korea decided to launch the slogan of a strong and prosperous great state. First, domestically they needed a new slogan that would give hope to the North Korean people on the occasion of Kim Jong Il's succession, opening the new era with a new generation. Second, externally North Korea intended to alleviate the misperception that it is on the verge of collapse, and to prove to the world that it is still strong and surviving despite the collapse of the socialist systems in other countries. Third, it was important that the North Korean system be seen as still viable and able to sustain itself for a long time under Kim Jong Il's leadership.

In his conversations with South Korean newspaper publishers in 2001, Kim Jong Il stressed that "My strength is derived from the military's strength. Without military strength nothing can be done. In our relations with foreign countries our strength grows out of that strength. "[9] From these statements we can surmise that Kim Jong Il maintains his political power and governing system on the basis of military power. The military has contributed to the survival of Kim Jong Il as the political leader, preventing the collapse of the North Korean state system. Kim's thinking is that the military is essential not only for the purpose of national defense but also for the maintenance of his power structure as well as the economic and social systems. In the former communist systems of Eastern Europe and Russia, the party organizations were plagued by power struggles or factional rivalries among their leaders. Kim Jong Il intends to transform such a traditional practice into a new system of controlling the ruling party by using the military's power. This is the essential feature of military-first politics in North Korea.

Economic reform has also been emphasized by the Kim Jong Il regime. A major economic reform program was launched on July 1, 2002, known as the July First Economic Management Improvement Measures (hereafter July 1 measures). A market economy was gradually introduced in 2003, opening the comprehensive market for general goods, which strengthened the private economic system in North Korea. Moreover, a private cultivation system was experimented with in the farmland of Hamkyong province in 2002 under the July First Economic Management Measures and was expanded to the entire nation by 2004. This system is similar to the Chinese model of the household responsibility system in agriculture by which farmers lease a certain portion of the collectively owned farmland to cultivate privately.

Under the system, the farmers will sell their excess produce on the free market after delivering their assigned quota of the crops from the leased farmland. The household responsibility system in China increased grain production more than twofold and some farmers became rich. In the past, North Korean peasants were allowed to plant vegetables on small plots around their houses and to sell them on the free market. Under the new lease system of state-owned land for private cultivation, it is estimated that the production of food grains has doubled. The private cultivation system will be expanded in 2005 to increase the production of food grains in North Korea, which is a drastic departure from the collective farm system that retarded them previously.

"The more I sell, the more money I make." This remark from a woman in her late thirties, who was running a sidewalk cart on the streets of Pyongyang, was quoted in the *New York Times* in October 2002, indicating the economic change that took place after the July 1 measures were introduced. Following more than a decade of isolation from the market-oriented economic reform in East Europe and Russia after the collapse of planned economic systems, North Korea is now beginning to carry out radical economic reform. Under the reform measure, North Korea instituted an overhaul of its rigid wage and pricing systems, increasing monthly wages 200-fold, from 110 North Korean won to 2,000 won. The July 1 measures allowed the application of the guiding principle of a market economy, that is, to depend on the free market's "invisible hand" to govern supply and demand, and a tighter application of a self-reliance accounting system for all business firms. In short, under these new measures the achievements of plants are weighed not by the quantity of goods they produce, but by the amount of their income. The more a company earns, the more it can pay to its employees.

North Korea has also transformed its farmers' market, in an effort to introduce more market functions in agriculture, which emerged spontaneously with government's tacit approval in the mid-1990s during the nation's serious food shortages. The farmers were permitted to sell their agricultural produce as well as manufactured goods and other commodities to expand the market economy to include rural society. The new measures also allow manufacturers to sell their products in the market, directly or indirectly, to help them recover operating costs. Thus, the July 1 Economic Management Improvement Measures have laid the groundwork for a market economy system in North Korea similar to the Chinese model of economic reform in the 1980s.

In the aftermath of his father's death, Kim Jong Il encountered enormous problems in the agricultural economy and North Korea suffered from an acute shortage of food grains due to the lack of food production incentives. Furthermore, three years of natural disasters like drought, famine, and flood in 1994–1997 led to an economic crisis. It was inevitable that Kim would turn to the military to maintain political order and resolve the economic problems of feeding the starving people (two million people were reported to have died due to the famine during this period). Under the circumstances, Kim Jong Il had no choice but to carry out the Chinese model of economic reform and open-door policy. The decline in economic output in the 1970s and 1980s was caused by structural problems, as well as mismanagement by the bureaucracy. To alleviate the economic crisis in the 1980s, North Korea attempted a piecemeal reform and opened its economy to foreign investment. Kim Jong Il took a trip to China in June 1983 to learn more about the Chinese model of structural reform and open-door policy. He was particularly interested in the Special Economic Zone in Shenzhen.

Upon his return from the China trip, Kim experimented with the Joint Venture Law in 1984 to solicit foreign investment and to improve relations with capitalist countries like the United States and Japan. However, his attempts to reform the economic system did not yield positive results due in large part to the opposition of an older generation of conservative cadres who resisted any change in the economic system or the adoption of a new policy to deal with a hostile international environment. As a result, efforts by capitalist countries to have joint venture enterprises in North Korea were stymied, while meager investments from Western European countries and the efforts of Korean residents in Japan did not bring in sufficient investment to enable North Korea to take off economically.

Following the collapse of the communist system and the end of the Cold War, North Korea introduced a reform program in December 1991 when the cabinet adopted reform bill no. 74, which established the Rajin-Sonbong Free Economic and Trade Zone and made Chongjin a free-trade port. These measures were similar to what China attempted in 1978 as a prelude to economic reform and their open-door policy. To facilitate such a reform program, North Korea adopted more than thirty new laws, including the Foreign Investment Law in 1992. In March 1993, a comprehensive plan for national reconstruction was proclaimed to support economic reform and an open-door policy. After the death of Kim Il Sung and the three-year mourning period (1994–1997), there were clear indications of policy changes in North Korea as it became evident that economic reform and opening to the outside world were the most urgent tasks of the new leadership of Kim Jong Il.

Following the announcement of Kim Jong Il's appointment to the post of the KWP general secretary on October 8, 1997, North Korea moved to establish private enterprises for the purpose of attracting foreign investment, introduced an independent accounting system in public enterprises, and expanded the Rajin-Sonbong Free Economic and Trade Zone. These measures were similar to the policies that the Chinese government implemented in the 1980s. However, debate in top policymaking circles did not end with implementation of these new measures. Faced with the challenges of the conservative generation of cadres, it was imperative for Kim Jong Il to transform the outdated juche ideology into military-first politics to avoid repeating the historical mistakes of his father.

Kim Jong Il has replaced most of the old guard with a younger generation of leadership in the KWP, the military, and the government structure, thereby paving the way for structural reform and an open-door policy. A number of changes have already taken place since 1998, such as the historic summit meeting with South Korean President Kim Dae Jung held from June 12 to 15, 2000, and the establishment of diplomatic relations with Australia, Canada, Italy, New Zealand, and other countries of the European Union. Kim Jong Il also made his third official visit to China in January 2001, and toured the industrial complex in Shanghai to learn more about the Chinese model of economic reform and its open-door policy. There is a clear indication that Kim is willing to open North Korea to the outside world for foreign investment and to restructure their outdated economic system in the twenty-first century.

North Korea developed the theory of military-first politics to reiterate that the driving force of the revolution is not the working class, but the army. This argument is a complete rejection of the classic Marxist theory of proletarian dictatorship. Furthermore, a *Rodong Shinmun* editorial on March 21, 2003, stressed that "The military-first idea means, in a word, the idea of giving priority to military affairs in all matters and the line and strategy and tactics of putting the army before the working class, as it calls for projecting the army as the pillar and main agent of the revolution." The lengthy editorial under the headline "The Military-First Idea Is an Invincible Banner for the Cause of Independence in Our Era" went on to emphasize that "This is a revolutionary idea in an era of fierce anti-imperialist struggle when imperialism has become extremely reactionary and militarized and revolutionary theory has reached a new, higher stage of development for human society as all countries and all nations work hard to build independent, powerful states."

Lessons of the Past

In the process of succeeding his father, Kim Jong Il encountered many problems, including the challenges of factional rivalries. The task of selecting a successor to a ruler in any country is an enormous responsibility for the decision makers. In a democratic society, the successor to the president or prime minister is usually decided by the electoral process. However, in a feudal society, the rule of the kingdom is hereditary and dynastic cycles determine who succeeds. Korea was no exception to the dynastic rule and has had a long history of dynastic cycles. The Chosen dynasty (1392–1910) was rampant with factional struggles among various groups vying for the throne. The recent history of Korea was so afflicted with factionalism that the

Chosun dynasty was greatly weakened and eventually fell under Japanese colonial rule. After thirty-five years of Japanese colonial rule, Korea was liberated at the end of World War II. However, it was divided into two halves, North and South Korea, at the thirty-eighth parallel. The power struggle to establish Kim Il Sung as the sole leader in North Korea took almost a decade, entailing a series of bitter factional infights.

When the North Korean Bureau of the Korean Communist Party was organized in October 1945 in North Korea, the first leader was not Kim Il Sung but Kim Yong-bom, a well-known revolutionary leader of the 1930s. However, the official history of North Korea recorded Kim Il Sung as the first chairman of the Organizational Committee of the North Korean Communist Party. In addition, the founding date of the organization was changed from October 13 to October 10, 1945. The North Korean Bureau recognized the fact that it was a branch of the Korean Communist Party Central Committee, the headquarters of which was located in Seoul until 1946 and headed by the anti-Japanese revolutionary Park Hon-young. Kim Il Sung served as the top leader of the government organization when he returned to North Korea from Manchuria in September 1945.

Kim Il Sung became chairman of the North Korean Provisional People's Committee (the People's Government) in August 1946 under the auspices of the Soviet military government, functioning as the head of the North Korean government. However, in August 1946 when the Sinmin-tang (New People's Party) and the North Korean Communist Party merged to create the North Korean Workers' Party under the direction of the Soviet Union, Kim Tu-bong, a well-known Korean linguist and revolutionary leader of Koreans in China became its chairman and Kim Il Sung served as the vice chairman. Kim Il Sung became premier of the DPRK in 1948 and the bona fide chairman of the Korean Workers' Party in June 1949 when the North Korean Workers' Party and the South Korean Workers' Party merged.[10]

In 1948 when the Supreme People's Committee (legislature) elected its Standing Committee (the cabinet of the government), Kim Tu-bong became its first chairman and functioned as head of state for ten years. The New Year's Message, which is comparable to the State of the Union message in the United States, was delivered by Kim Tu-bong, SPC Standing Committee chairman, not by Premier Kim Il Sung. Thus, Kim Tu-bong served as the nominal head of the state until he was purged in 1958. Although Kim Il Sung was premier and general secretary of the KWP, he did not achieve the top leadership position in North Korea until 1959. The senior Kim had gone through a decade of factional struggles to reach the status of supreme leader. The junior Kim learned from the lessons of history. He began to consolidate his power by expanding his ruling circle and eliminating potential opponents to his succession. In the process of consolidating his power, Kim Jong Il turned to the North Korean military, which was the most disciplined, dedicated, and loyal to him among the contending political groups in North Korea, including the Korean Workers' Party. The creation of military-first politics in North Korea was thus an invention of Kim Jong Il in order to reorganize the political institutions he inherited from his father so that he might effectively govern North Korea.

Recently, the South Korean press reported that Kim Jong Il has directed a broad reorganization of the KWP structure. As the chairman of the NDC as well as the general secretary of the KWP, Kim carried out the restructuring of the KWP in September and November of 2004 by purging his brother-in-law Chang Song-taek, second-highest cadre to Kim Jong Il in the KWP power hierarchy. It was reported that Chang was removed in February 2004 from his position as deputy director as the result of a conflict with Prime Minister Park Bong-ju, the head of the North Korean cabinet in charge of economic reform measures. However, it is generally accepted that Chang was purged because his political ambition began to displease Kim Jong Il. Chang was reported to have spread the rumor that he would succeed Kim Jong Il as the chairman of the NDC as well as the KWP general secretary. Moreover, Hwang Jang-yop, the highest-ranking member of North Korean leadership to defect to South Korea, publicly predicted in Seoul that Chang would succeed Kim Jong Il and no one would challenge him. Chang was thus purged from his leadership positions and charged with factionalism and rumor mongering to satisfy his personal ambitions.

Kim Jong Il is reported to have eliminated three bureaus of the secretariat of the KWP Central Committee, the top policymaking body in the nation. The secretariat is composed of twenty-two bureaus, each with separate responsibilities including selecting the cabinet members, reviewing economic policy, and formulating military policy. The bureaus in charge of military affairs, economic policy, and agricultural policy have been abolished in the restructuring process. It is plausible that the policymaking role of the KWP is greatly reduced following the restructuring and that the policymaking power of the NDC has been greatly enhanced. The reorganization resulted in the reassignment of 40 percent of the secretariat personnel because the economic policy review bureau is one of the largest groups in the KWP bureaucracy. This is the first major attempt by Kim Jong Il to restructure the KWP since the death of his father.

Some South Korean analysts of North Korean affairs have speculated that the military bureau of the KWP was abolished because Kim Jong Il wanted to eliminate KWP meddling in military affairs. In short, the party's policymaking power is greatly reduced, while the military role in policymaking has expanded enormously. It is also speculated that North Korea's economic and political systems will undergo further restructuring after Kim's birthday on February 16, 2005. Economic and agricultural policies of North Korea will be administered by the cabinet under the premier in order to implement the economic reforms that were introduced on July 1, 2002. Yon Hyong-muk, former prime minister and a veteran economic policymaker, has been appointed to the post of the vice chairman of the National Defense Commission, which is an indication that Kim will closely monitor economic reform as carried out by the cabinet.[11] The KWP will be in charge of the ideological sphere, while the government cabinet will be in charge of economic reform. It is the National Defense Commission that will provide the leadership for the operations of the KWP, the government cabinet, and the military.

Conclusion

Kim Jong Il created new slogans and institutions to replace such old ones as the juche ideology and the Korean Workers' Party of his father's generation. He had begun to transform the juche ideology into that of military-first politics in order to achieve a strong and prosperous great state (kangsong taeguk) for North Korea in the 1990s, when he was preparing to succeed his father as supreme leader. Kangsong Taeguk functions as the goal of a strategy of strong ideology, an indefatigable military, and a prosperous economy, while military-first politics functions as the tactics for reaching that goal.

Military-first politics, in essence, gives priority to the military as well as strengthening it to defend the nation during times of crisis. Following the death of Kim Il Sung in 1994, North Korea encountered various crises such as the succession problems, the economic crisis caused by drought, flood, famine, and structural issues, and the security crisis of defending itself from possible attack by hostile countries. The function of military-first politics was thus to cope with the external crisis posed by the collapse of other socialist systems as well as to alleviate domestic economic crisis and the factionalism among old cadres who had been entrenched in party and government organizations for the almost five decades of Kim Il Sung's rule. Military-first politics has enabled Kim Jong Il to consolidate his power by replacing the old cadres in the party, government, and military with a younger generation of military leaders. Through this new strategy, he has been able to pave the way for economic reform and an open-door policy.[12]

Having given the priority to its military to defend its national security, North Korea is preparing to launch a drastic reform program at home and open itself to the outside world in 2005. The year 2005 is the sixtieth anniversary of Korea's liberation from Japanese colonial rule and also the sixtieth anniversary of the founding of the Korean Workers' Party. Furthermore, the year 2005 is the tenth anniversary of the initiation of military-first politics by Kim Jong Il. The anniversary date of such important events in North Korea is usually celebrated with a special announcement of a political event or program. It is expected that 2005 will mark the reinforcement of military-first politics with particular emphasis on economic reform and an open-door policy in order to achieve their goal of kangsong taeguk.

Notes

1. The *Joong-Ang Daily News*, November 28, 2004.
2. For the text of "Socialist Constitution of the Democratic People's Republic of Korea," adopted on September 5, 1998, see Ilpyong J. Kim, *Historical Dictionary*, 147–173.
3. Shigemura, *Kita Chosen*.
4. Hwang, *Memoir*, and his second book entitled *Kaein eui Saengmyong bota guijoonghan Minjok eui Saengmyong* (The Nation's Life is More Important than the Individual's Life). Also see Park, "The Nature and Evolution of Juche Ideology," 9–18.
5. Hwang, *Memoir*.

6. Kim, Ilpyong J., *Politics of Chinese Communism*, particularly chapter 5 on "Mass Mobilization Policies and Organizational Techniques."

8. Shigemura, *Kita Chosen*, 74.

9. Shigemura, *Kita Chosen*.

10. Quoted in Shigemura, *Kita Chosen*, 75.

11. See more details in Scalapino and Lee, *Communism in Korea*; Suh, *Kim Il Sung*.

12. See the *JoongAng Daily*, December 8, 2004.

13. For a detailed analysis of military-first politics, see Chong, "Kim Jong-Il's Military-First Politics," 2–8; Chong, "North Korean Leadership After Kim Il-Sung," 2–9; Kim, Keun-sik, "Kim Jong Il Sidae Bukhanui Dang-Jeong-Gun Gwangye Byeonhwa" (The Change in North Korea's Party-Government-Military Relationship in the Kim Jong Il Era: The Implications of the Changes of the "Great Leader" [Suryong] System), 349–365; Kwon, "State Building in North Korea," 286–295; and Suh, "Military-First Politics of Kim Jong Il," 145–167.

$$\text{———— 4 ————}$$

Reconciling Nuclear Standoff and Economic Shortfalls

Pyongyang's Perspective

C. Kenneth Quinones

Perceptions of a problem define the context for its resolution. The same can be said about the persistent problem of nuclear proliferation in Northeast Asia. Nations with keen interest in the region—the two Koreas, China, Japan, Russia, and the United States—agree that nuclear proliferation on the peninsula, if not halted, will have a potentially devastating impact on their shared goal of peace and stability on the Korean peninsula and throughout the region. Since at least 1991, these nations have invested continuous effort in trying to prevent nuclear proliferation there, but their efforts have thus far failed.

A contributing factor may well be the persistent gap in the respective perceptions of the two primary antagonists, the United States and North Korea. As the title of this chapter implies, the Korean nuclear proliferation problem seems directly linked to North Korea's economic woes. Washington and Tokyo, more than Pyongyang, subscribe to this perception. The present and past U.S. administrations have sought to induce or coerce North Korea to give up its nuclear weapons activities and related materials in exchange for future prosperity.

Much to Washington's dismay, Pyongyang so far has rejected these overtures. Consequently, the problem persists. Here we assess North Korea's perception of the nuclear problem. Our aim is to better comprehend why a small, impoverished nation like North Korea would prefer to continue arming itself with weapons of mass destruction rather than voluntarily trade this pursuit for promises of prosperity.

Clashing Perceptions

Since 2001, the United States and Pyongyang have wrangled inconclusively over the cause of and solution to the proliferation problem. Washington sees the problem in terms of North Korea's past conduct, or misconduct, as viewed from Washington. Pyongyang counters that Washington's "hostile policy" toward it requires that it develop a "nuclear deterrence" in accordance with its "sovereign right" to defend itself. From these fundamental differences flow other contrary contributing factors that further complicate and continue to impede reaching a "peaceful diplomatic solution," both sides' avowed goal.

The Clinton and George W. Bush administrations defined the problem as an integral part of global nuclear proliferation. This emphasis on "global" diminishes regional geopolitical considerations. It reinforces Washington's conviction that any solution must preserve the global counterproliferation regime per U.S. priorities. Within this context, both U.S. administrations have labeled North Korea a "rogue" or "evil" nation because of its past noncompliance with previous commitments to bilateral and multilateral nuclear nonproliferation accords. Here both U.S. administrations have recited an impressive litany of North Korea's unfulfilled commitments: the 1991 Joint South-North Declaration on the Denuclearization of the Korean peninsula, the 1992 North Korean nuclear safeguards agreement with the International Atomic Energy Agency, and the 1994 U.S.-DPRK Agreed Framework, plus Pyongyang's withdrawal from the Treaty on the Non-proliferation of Nuclear Weapons (NPT).

Washington's solution has remained fundamentally unaltered since 1992, except for tactical differences between the Clinton and Bush administrations. Both administrations' perceptions of the nuclear problem identify economic considerations as the primary motive behind North Korea's nuclear ambitions. They see this impoverished and economically isolated nation as attempting to convert its "nuclear card" into an economic windfall so that the Kim Jong Il regime can survive and prosper. Given this perspective, both administrations have sought either to entice or coerce North Korea into giving up its nuclear ambitions.[1]

The preferred solution of the United States amply takes into consideration North Korea's economic concerns, but ignores the national security and domestic political concerns of Pyongyang's leadership. Until the gap narrows between the U.S. and North Korean perspectives, a diplomatic solution of the Korean peninsula's nuclear problem will remain elusive.

A Question of National Security

For North Korea, the nuclear problem is all encompassing. It affects national security, domestic political concerns, and pressing economic needs. Its ruler Supreme Commander Kim Jong Il prefers clear and persistent priorities in his policies. This is quite evident in his handling of the nuclear problem. First and foremost, it is a matter of national survival. Within this broad context, he pursues a policy and strategy consistent with the preferences of his primary political supporters, the North Korean People's Army. To ensure that they have access to the resources vital for securing the nation's defense, Kim must achieve economic revitalization.

Pyongyang, given its profound economic shortcomings, must yearn for the poten-

tial economic benefits that reconciliation with Washington offers, but of more immediate concern is countering Washington's "hostile" policy. This has been North Korea's
consistent claim and concern since the Korean War ended in a stalemate in 1953. Ever
since, it has alleged that U.S. conventional air, naval, and ground plus nuclear forces
in South Korea, Japan, and the western Pacific pose an imminent threat to its survival.
Further buttressing this threat, in Pyongyang's eyes, is Washington's refusal to normalize diplomatic relations and multiple layers of economic sanctions that impede its
efforts at economic revitalization.[2]

North Korea, however, has responded positively to overtures from the United States
only when the latter demonstrated sensitivity for Pyongyang's national security. For
example, the first Bush administration initiated in 1988 a cautious process aimed at
defusing North Korea's hostility, ending its isolation from the international community, and enticing it to forego its traditional coercive and occasionally belligerent
foreign policy. The effort acquired the nickname, "Modest Initiative." It offered North
Korea a modest package of diplomatic and economic inducements. They included
the opening of a diplomatic channel of communication and the opportunity for North
Korea to purchase "basic human needs" from the United States. But the icy bilateral
relationship did not begin to thaw until 1991, when President Bush told the United
Nations General Assembly on September 27, 1991:

> Last year, I cancelled U.S. plans to modernize our ground-launched nuclear weap-
> ons. . . . I am, therefore, directing the United States to eliminate its entire world-
> wide inventory of ground-launched short-range—that is theater—nuclear
> weapons. We will bring home and destroy all our nuclear artillery shells and
> short-range ballistic missile warheads.[3]

South Korean president Roh Tae Woo followed in November 1991 with a public
pledge intended to "initiate the resolution of the nuclear issues on the Korean peninsula." He promised that the Republic of Korea would "not manufacture, possess, store,
deploy or use nuclear weapons." He also promised that South Korea would "submit
to comprehensive international inspection of all nuclear-related activities and materials on its territory in compliance with the Nuclear Non-proliferation Treaty (NPT)
and with the nuclear safeguards agreement" it had concluded with the IAEA. The two
presidents' remarks opened the door to the December 1991 "Joint South-North Declaration of the Denuclearization of the Korean Peninsula." That declaration built upon
President Roh's unilateral pledges and set the stage for the two Koreas' subsequent
signing of their Agreement on Reconciliation, Non-aggression and Exchanges.[4]

Alas, this initial effort soon faltered, compelling the United States to engage
North Korea in direct negotiations that began in June 1993. Again, no progress was
made at the initial round of talks until the United States again demonstrated sensitivity for North Korea's security concerns. This led to the U.S.-DPRK Joint Statement of June 11, 1993. In this first ever joint statement between the two enemies,
they agreed to the principle of "assurances against the threat and use of force, in-

cluding nuclear weapons, and peace and security in a nuclear-free Korean Peninsula." In other words, in exchange for U.S. promises not to attack it, North Korea agreed to suspend its withdrawal from the NPT. This opened the door to the negotiations that eventually yielded the October 21, 1994, Agreed Framework. Similar security assurances appeared in the 1994 agreement and in the October 12, 2000, U.S.-DPRK Joint Communiqué issued when Kim Jong Il sent Vice Marshal Jo Myung Rok to Washington to represent him at the highest-level bilateral meeting between the two nations.

Revival of the "Hostile" Policy

Since 2001, North Korea has considered President George W. Bush's criticism of the Agreed Framework and increasingly critical rhetoric aimed at North Korea and its leadership as an intensification of Washington's "hostile" policy toward Pyongyang. The United States has been quick to dismiss North Korea's claims as unfounded. But to North Korea's leaders, the "hostile" policy of the United States is real. It is neither a propaganda motto nor a figment of the imagination. The allegation predates the presidency of George W. Bush by several decades.

North Korea repeatedly referred to U.S. "hostile policy" during the first nuclear crisis of 1993–1994. When the first round of U.S.-North Korea bilateral nuclear talks commenced on June 3, 1993, First Vice Minister of Foreign Affairs Kang Sok Ju declared:

> Our decision to withdraw from the Nuclear Non-proliferation Treaty is the consequential outcome of the policy pursued by the United States so far over the last four decades since the end of the Korea War, a **policy of hostility** against the Democratic People's Republic of Korea.

Kang went on to say in his opening remarks:

> The point of immediate priority is that the United States rescind (sic) its policy of strangling the DPRK and posing nuclear threat (sic) against the DPRK.[5]

Ten years later, North Korea was still citing U.S. hostile policy as the root cause of nuclear proliferation on the Korean peninsula. On October 25, 2002, two weeks after North Korea's apparent admission to having a clandestine highly enriched uranium (HEU) program, Pyongyang's Foreign Ministry spokesman stated:

> As far as the nuclear issue on the Korean Peninsula is concerned, it cropped up as the U.S. has massively stockpiled nuclear weapons in South Korea and its vicinity and threatened the DPRK, a small country, with those weapons for nearly half a century, pursuing **a hostile policy** toward it in accordance with the strategy for world supremacy.[6]

North Korean chief delegate to the UN General Assembly's 2004 session, Vice Minister Choe Su Hon, continued the same theme in his address to the assembly. He said that, "the nuclear issue is the product of the deep-rooted hostile policy on (sic) the DPRK pursued by the United States for more than half a century." Choe continued, "The nuclear deterrent of the DPRK constitutes a legitimate self-defensive means to counter ever-growing U.S. nuclear threat and aggression against the DPRK." He then claimed, "If the United States renounces practically its hostile policy on the DPRK including the cessation of nuclear threats, the DPRK also is willing to scrap its nuclear deterrent accordingly."

For North Korea, the "hostile policy" of the United States has and continues to be the cause of nuclear proliferation on the Korean peninsula. North Korea thus points to President George W. Bush's sometimes blunt criticism of North Korea's leadership and inclusion of North Korea in his "axis of evil" not as causes but as symptoms of the nuclear proliferation problem.[7]

Similar Concerns, Shared Solution

South Korea's admission in September 2004 of prior "small" violations of the NPT has further intensified North Korea's suspicions about the long-term objectives of South Korea and the United States. The South Korean government admitted to the International Atomic Energy Agency (IAEA) in August 2004 that a few "rogue" scientists had conducted "small" nuclear experiments in 1982 and 2000 that technically violated its nuclear safeguards commitments under the NPT. An official of President Kim Yong-sam's administration (1993–1998) claimed that a third such experiment had been conducted in 1993. All the experiments were small scale, but nuclear weapons related. IAEA director general Mohamed ElBaradei told the UN organization's board of directors on September 13 that the experiments were "a matter of serious concern" since they were not previously reported to the IAEA "as required by the ROK safeguards agreement."[8]

North Korea ambassador to the United Nations, Han Song-ryol, voiced Pyongyang's initial reaction to Seoul's admissions in an interview with South Korea's Yonhap News Agency on September 8. Han was quoted as having said that his government views South Korea's actions "in the context of an arms race in Northeast Asia." He added that Seoul's nuclear experiments were "a dangerous move that would accelerate a nuclear arms race in Northeast Asia."

Pyongyang's formal reaction followed on September 11 in a "Statement of the DPRK Foreign Ministry Spokesman." In this authoritative statement of policy, the spokesman said his government has a "strong suspicion that the disclosed experiments might be conducted at the instruction of the United States." He accused the United States of applying "a double standards (sic)" regarding the transfer of nuclear technology to its allies and has "connived at their faking up 'misinformation' about the DPRK on account of its ideology and system."

Seoul, like Pyongyang, shares two underlying motives for their respective nuclear activities. National interests drive both nations' foreign policy, and security tops their lists of national interests. Second, neither trusts the United States, but for different reasons. Pyongyang sees the United States as the primary threat to its survival. Seoul fears that the United States will withdraw from the Korean peninsula, exposing it to its primary enemy North Korea. For both Koreas, the solution is the same—develop a "self-reliant" defense that encompasses a nuclear weapons capability. This suggests that economic considerations are of secondary importance, even in Pyongyang.

Kim Jong Il's Political Considerations

Kim Jong Il is an authoritarian ruler. To remain in power, Kim must retain the confidence and loyalty of his domain's decisive political force, the Korean People's Army (KPA) and its generals. This is alluded to in Kim's preferred official titles, the Supreme Commander and Chairman of the National Defense Commission. In September 1998 when he formally stepped out of the shadow of his father, Kim Il Sung, and assumed leadership of North Korea, Kim Jong Il declared that he would create a "strong and great nation" (*kangsong taeguk*). This announcement coincided with the fiftieth anniversary of the DPRK's founding and the sixty-sixth anniversary of the KPA.

Kim Jong Il moved quickly to crystallize his close political association with the KPA. On September 5, 1998, the Supreme People's Assembly (SPA), North Korea's legislature, revised the constitution to name the National Defense Commission (NDC) as the government's foremost ruling body. Kim Jong Il was designated its chairman, and high-ranking military officials filled seven of its ten positions. Meanwhile, the number of military officials serving in the SPA had climbed from 62 in the previous session to 111 in the September 1998 session. Of these 111 generals, 75 were two-star generals or of higher rank. Between 1960 and 1994, the number of military officials in the SPA had averaged only about forty representatives.[9]

A further indication of Kim's efforts to align his civil administrative goals and priorities with those of his military was his institution of a joint Korean Workers' Party-Korean People's Army New Year's editorial. Prior to 1999, the nation's mass media ran an annual New Year's Day editorial on January 1, a practice Kim Jong Il's father had initiated. But beginning in 1999, the younger Kim authorized a joint editorial that set forth his policy priorities for the forthcoming year.

The 1999 editorial proclaimed the nation's foremost priority to be the building of a kangsong taeguk. The term was defined as "the combative slogan our Party and people should uphold. A socialist kangsong taeguk is a juche-oriented country that is dyed throughout with the ideas of Great Comrade Kim Jong Il." Its goal is to build "an impregnable fortress," because:

> The imperialists [i.e., the United States and its allies] are more viciously imposing politico-military pressures upon us and economic sanctions against us to squeeze our Republic to death. Under the imperialist siege, we should make our country

stronger ideologically and militarily, strengthen in every way our economic power, safeguard socialism of our own style, . . . Our general onward march to glorify this year as a turning point in building a *kangsong taeguk* is a requirement for shattering the imperialists' plot against our republic and safeguarding a socialism of our own style.[10]

The KPA was anointed the pillar of "a militarily strong socialist country and the foremost life-or-death unit safeguarding the *suryong* (Supreme Commander Kim Jong Il)." Kim called his policy *songun*, that is "military-first."

Strategic Choices

Kim Jong Il, at least two years before the 2001 change of presidential administration in the United States, had established national defense as his foremost goal. This was consistent with his father's views and the younger Kim's earlier writings. Within the context of his "military-first" priority, Kim listed his nation's economic development. Earlier, Kim is credited with having written:

> Victory or defeat in modern war depends largely on whether or not manpower and material resources necessary for the war effort are ensured for a long period. . . . Upholding the policy of building the economy and defence (sic) simultaneously, our (Korean Workers') Party has made good preparations both militarily and materially and built up both the front-line areas and home front to cope with war.[11]

In 1999, Kim Jong Il retained his priorities of defense first followed by economic development. He seems to have shifted primary responsibility for both, however, to his military. After all, it is the KPA that has had responsibility for sustaining North Korea's defense capability. Prior to the Soviet Union's collapse in 1991, this had required maintaining a close alliance with the Soviet Union. Soviet military assistance enabled the KPA to maintain at least parity with the combined conventional forces of South Korea and the United States. Equally important was the Soviet nuclear umbrella that matched the U.S. umbrella over South Korea. But the Soviet Union's collapse undermined North Korea's deterrence capability and exposed it to its worst enemies, South Korea and the United States.

By 1992, North Korea appears to have overhauled its military strategy. Lacking assistance from both the Soviet Union and China, and hard pressed economically at home, North Korea could ill afford to strive for parity with its enemies in conventional and nuclear weapons. In addition, the awesome display of superior conventional weapons technology by the United States during the 1991 Gulf War must have stunned North Korea's generals. Their massive and previously mighty array of Soviet-designed weaponry was identical to that which Iraq possessed at the time. Despite appearances, the U.S. military quickly and easily rendered such armaments impotent and obsolete. Lacking the technology, military assistance, and economic means to modernize its conventional forces, North Korea appears to have opted to develop a "self-reliant" nuclear deterrence capability.

The U.S.-North Korea nuclear negotiations and diplomatic agreement of 1994, however, appear to have at least stalled the North Korean military's pursuit of a nuclear capability. At that time, Kim Jong Il apparently opted to take full advantage of the diplomatic and economic benefits that the United States offered in exchange for halting his nuclear weapons program. The inducements were indeed attractive. They included two modern nuclear light water reactors, the phased normalization of bilateral diplomatic and economic relations with the United States, plus 500,000 metric tons of heavy fuel oil to generate electricity until the nuclear reactors began operation. Often overlooked, however, has been the equally important U.S. inducement regarding North Korea's security. The Clinton administration had given and repeatedly reaffirmed security assurances that the United States would not threaten to use either nuclear or conventional military force against North Korea.

Political Realities

Against this backdrop, and given Kim's prior commitments to his generals, one could hardly expect him to abruptly forego his "military-first" and "great and powerful nation" priorities to accommodate the demands of his foremost enemy, the United States. Since 2001, those demands have accented North Korea's unilateral disarmament of all weapons of mass destruction without any prior substantial concessions from the United States. Such a move by Kim would require that he trust his enemy not to attack his domain.

President George W. Bush's words and deeds since entering office have not been reassuring in this regard. He invaded Iraq to seek out and destroy its prior ruler's imagined arsenal of weapons of mass destruction. Bush has refused to grant North Korea security assurances as a first step toward possible further talks and eventual disarmament. Nor has Bush's reluctance to shelve his "military option" encouraged Kim to believe that the United States would not invade it once it has unilaterally disarmed.

Kim's reluctance to conform to Bush's demands most likely reflects such concerns. We cannot say for certain. But given North Korea's authoritarian government, it would seem safe to conjecture that Kim's concerns are accurately reflected in his mass media. Most obvious is that Kim does not trust Bush. Also, while Kim appears confident in his generals' loyalty to him, he may harbor reservations about their willingness, over the long term, to comply with the terms of a negotiated settlement, especially if it requires North Korea's total and unilateral disarmament.

Economic Realities

Kim Jong Il's reluctance to bow to the disarmament demands of the United States and its allies has imposed a tremendous burden on the North Korean people. They have had to endure starvation, disease, and poverty since he succeeded his father in 1994. North Korea avoided political turmoil and economic collapse in the 1990s. Arguably this was more because of the North Korean peoples' pervasive sense of self-discipline, intense work ethic, and combination of fear and national pride than the astuteness of Kim Jong Il's policies.

But Kim Jong Il's adroit foreign policy has enabled North Korea to sidestep the dilemma that the United States and it allies have confronted Pyongyang with since 1988. That dilemma was designed to confront him with a choice. He could exchange the end of his weapons of mass destruction programs for impressive economic inducements plus the normalization of diplomatic relations with the United States and Japan. Otherwise, his nation must continue to be denied normal diplomatic relations with the United States and Japan, remain under U.S. economic sanctions, barred from membership in international financial organizations like the Asian Development Bank (ADB), and denied the foreign direct investment that North Korea desperately needs to reinvigorate its economy and to modernize its industrial and transportation infrastructures, among other things.

Since 1995, the Kim Jong Il regime has successfully walked a tightrope between submitting to Washington's demands and falling into the pit of political and economic collapse. The most urgent need to avoid catastrophe was the acquisition of food for the starving population followed by the restoration of North Korea's agrarian sector. The regime also had to quickly acquire sufficient crude oil to quench the thirst of its military machine and industrial sector. Finally, to sustain access to food and fuel, the regime must modernize the nation's economic infrastructure. This requires modern technology and foreign investment. Kim Jong Il has tentatively accomplished the first two tasks regarding food and fuel, and is making some steady progress regarding technology, but the critical shortage of investment capital persists.[12]

Food

Kim Jong Il began restoration of his domain in the fall of 1995 by seeking humanitarian assistance from the international community. The response was prompt and generous as evident in Table 4.1.

Gains in food production have steadily reduced food aid needs. The annual estimated need, according to the World Food Program (WFP), has dropped from 1.145 million metric tons (M/T) in 1996 to 544,000 M/T in 2003. The amount of food aid North Korea received in 1996 amounted to 844,600 M/T, or about 16 percent of estimated total need. A poor harvest in 2001 increased the need for food aid to 1,370,000 M/T (27 percent of estimated grain consumption). The international community supplied 1,011,300 M/T of food aid, or 74 percent of this need. One year later, however, increased domestic production cut the food aid need by 37 percent to 512,000 M/T. By 2003, the estimated need for food aid had declined 40 percent to 544,000.

The UN Food and Agriculture Organization (FAO) and WFP reported at the end of November 2004 that North Korea's 2004 grain harvest exceeded that of the previous

Table 4.1

Total Food Aid to DPRK, 1995–2001 (unit: 1,000 metric tons [M/T])

	1996	1997	1998	1999	2000	2001	Total
Government	779.3	464.25	747.1	823.0	888.2	971.7	4,673,500
NGOs	65.2	185.6	260.1	26.0	48.9	39.6	625,400
Total	844.5	649.8	1,007.2	849.0	937.1	1,011.3	5,298,900

	Government (M/T)	Government (% total aid)	NGO (M/T)	Total food aid (M/T)	NGO (% total aid)
Donor					
USA	1,322,300	28.3	12,024	1,334,324	25.2
ROK	789,700	16.9	292,289	1,081,989	20.3
Japan	701,800	15.0	2,095	703,895	13.3
China	618,500	13.2	—	618,500	11.7
Subtotal	3,432,300	73.4	306,418	3,738,718	70.5
Region					
Europe	720,960	15.4	261,065	982,025	18.5
Middle East	370,150	7.9	—	370,150	7.0
South/ Southeast Asia	120,100	2.6	9,417	129,517	—
North America	29,800	0.6	48,500	78,300	—
Total food aid	4,673,310	99.9	625,400	5,298,710	

Sources: The above data were compiled from a variety of UN World Food Program (WFP) and UN Food and Agriculture (FAO) reports issued beginning in December 1995 and continuing to 2002. The WFP's Pyongyang Office's periodic "Situation Reports" and periodic reports of "Deliveries of Food Aid to the DPRK" were particularly helpful. Also invaluable was the annual "United Nations Consolidated Inter-Agency Appeal for Flood-Related Emergency, Humanitarian Assistance to the Democratic People's Republic of Korea," Geneva: U.N. Department of Humanitarian Affairs, 1996–2002. The author collected copies of the early reports, fall of 1995 through 1996, directly from the WFP's Pyongyang office. These materials are now difficult to obtain. Most other reports dating from 1997 are available at www.fao.org/waicent. This is the web site for the United Nations Food and Agriculture Organization's (FAO) World Agriculture Information Center (WAICENT) and serves as an archive of previously released FAO reports about agriculture and food production around the world. Additional information is available at www.reliefweb.org. An equally valuable source is the Pyongyang office of the UN Office of the Coordinator of Humanitarian Aid (OCHA). Although the office in the DPR Korea (North Korea) technically ceased operations in 2005 at the behest of the North Korean government, the UN World Food Program (WFP) office in Pyongyang continues to compile and issue monthly reports entitled "DPR Korea: Humanitarian Situation Bulletin." This report is distributed monthly via email. See ocha.dprk@wrf.org. Note that the MSN web searcher does not locate this address, but the Yahoo web searcher does.

Notes: These data were compiled primarily from World Food Program reports and publications, and ROK Ministry of Unification, *Promoting Peace and Cooperation: Five Years of the Kim Dae-jung Administration.* Seoul: Oh Sung Publishers, 2003, pp. 153–156. The data should not be considered exact, but a generally accurate reflection of most aid contributions.

The years listed in the above table are "harvest years," not calendar years. They run from October 1995 to the end of September 1996. Also, the amounts of food aid reflect the total amount delivered within the designated "harvest year," not the time frame that a government or other organization pledged food aid.

year by 2.9 percent. In 2004, rice production was up 5.6 percent over 2003, potato yield climbed 9 percent, while maize production was unchanged. North Korea's dependence on food aid continues to decline. Nevertheless, it will still need an estimated 497,000 M/T of grain for the period of 2004–2005. Of this amount, however, 170,000 M/T have already been pledged or are on hand as of November 2004.[13]

In 2004, North Korea will receive more food aid than it needs. The UN FAO estimated in the fall of 2003 that North Korea had a deficit of 944,000 metric tons of grain relative to production. But since then, grain aid to North Korea has exceeded this need. China has contributed an estimated 500,000 M/T, which reduced the deficit to 444,000 M/T. South Korea has begun delivering the 400,000 M/T it promised in June 2004, further cutting the deficit to 44,000 M/T. Russia's delivery of 35,000 M/T in July 2004 followed by the U.S. contribution of 50,000 M/T has erased the deficit.

Nevertheless, Japan and South Korea began delivering an additional 250,000 M/T tons in the fall of 2004. Japan in September 2004 began delivering 125,000 M/T of rice, half the amount it had pledged to give North Korea in June 2004. South Korea announced on October 23, 2004, that it would deliver 100,000 M/T of corn to North Korea. Since the U.S., Japanese, and South Korean contributions (275,000 M/T of grain) are being funneled through the World Fund Program (WFP), that UN agency will be able to use any surplus grain to repay the amounts of grain it had borrowed earlier from other nations' aid allocations.[14]

Sustainable Humanitarian Aid

Kim Jong Il also has successfully supplemented his meager capital investment resources by encouraging donor nations to shift their aid from food to other forms of assistance. As food aid needs have declined, donor organizations and governments have shifted to supplying fertilizers, farm equipment, and other essential inputs. The public health sector has also greatly benefited, and consequently, the health and welfare of the North Korea people have steadily improved.

South Korea

South Korea initially backed the U.S. strategy of confronting North Korea with a dilemma, but since 1998 its policies have drifted toward a more conciliatory posture. The Kim Dae Jung administration initiated this "drift" in 1998 by declaring its so-called sunshine policy that accented humanitarian and economic aid for North Korea in exchange for peaceful dialogue. While maintaining a resolute armed deterrence posture toward North Korea, President Kim sought to use aid to defuse Pyongyang's hostility and to move North Korea toward reconciliation. President Roh Moo Hyun, Kim's successor, has continued a similar strategy under the banner of "economic cooperation." Subsequent to the 1998 shift, Seoul has replaced Washington as the leading contributor of aid to North Korea. The trend in South Korea's aid is evident in Tables 4.1 and 4.2.

Table 4.2

South Korean Humanitarian Aid, 1995–2002 (unit: US$10,000)

	Government	Private	Total
1995	23,200	25	23,225
1996	305	155	460
1997	2,667	2,056	4,723
1998	1,100	2,085	3,185
1999	2,825	1,863	4,688
2000	7,863	3,513	11,376
2001	7,045	6,494	13,539
2002	8,375	5,117	13,492
Total	53,380	21,308	74,688

Source: ROK Ministry of Unification, *Promoting Peace and Cooperation* (Seoul: Ministry of Unification, 2003), p. 154; see also ROK Ministry of Unification, *Peace and Cooperation— White Paper on Korean Unification* (Seoul: Ministry of Unification, 2002), pp. 146–153.

Simultaneously, the nature of South Korea's humanitarian aid to North Korea has changed gradually since 1995. The aid initially emphasized food, but since 1999 it has become increasingly diverse. In 2001, South Korea provided the DPRK with US$135.39 million worth of aid, a 19 percent increase over 2000 according to the ROK Unification Ministry. Government aid totaled US$70.45 million, a 10.4 percent decrease from 2000. But South Korean civic organizations (NGOs) increased the value of their aid by 85 percent to $64.94 million. The government aid included 100,000 M/T of corn (delivered via the World Food Program), 200,000 M/T of fertilizer, and 1.5 million pairs of children's underwear, according the Unification Ministry. South Korea's 2001 aid to North Korea equaled about one-third of its total foreign aid to developing nations. These various shifts in the type of aid are reflected in Tables 4.2 and 4.3.[15]

China's Aid

As South Korea moved up to replace the United States as the second-largest aid donor to North Korea, China took over the number two position. China's 1992 normalization of relations with South Korea committed Beijing's Korean peninsula policy to sustaining balanced ties with both Koreas. North Korea, long China's favorite, initially resented China's changed stance. North Korea's declining economic fortunes combined with China's growing strategic concerns about North Korea's future helped to restore congenial bilateral relations by 1996. Concerned that the Kim Jong Il regime might collapse and create a power vacuum on its northeast border, China moved decisively to prevent this in order to forestall the possibility that the United States might assert its influence over the entire Korean peninsula.

Table 4.3

South Korean Humanitarian Aid by Type (unit: US$10,000)

Type of aid	1995	1996	1997	1998	1999	2000	2001	2002	Total
General[a]	23,225	455	4,329	2,891	565	1,434	6,067	4,174	43,140
% Total aid	0	99	92	91	12	13	45	31	58
Rural rehabilitation[b]	0	5	205	254	3,941	8,562	5,476	7,351	25,794
% Total aid	—	1	4	8	84	75	40	54	34
Public health[c]	0	0	189	40	182	1,380	1,996	1,967	5,754
% Total aid	—	—	4	1	4	12	15	15	8

Sources: ROK Ministry of Unification, *Promoting Peace and Cooperation* (Seoul: Ministry of Unification, 2003), p. 155; see also ROK Ministry of Unification, *Peace and Cooperation—White Paper on Korean Unification* (Seoul: Ministry of Unification, 2002), pp. 146–153.
[a]This category includes primarily food aid (rice, corn, wheat flour, and dried milk). Since 1999, it has also included fertilizer, seeds, and pesticides in addition to food aid.
[b]Rural rehabilitation activities include agricultural exchanges, farm and animal husbandry, model farms, farm machinery, and reforestation.
[c]Public health has concentrated on tuberculosis eradication conducted by South Korean NGOs and their foreign partners.

China's strategy to sustain North Korea is evident in the 1996 China-DPRK Agreement on Economic and Technical Exchange. Under this accord, China pledged to provide the DPRK each year beginning in 1997 and continuing to 2002: 500,000 M/T of food, 120,000 tons of crude oil, and 150,000 M/T of coal. These commodities were to be "paid for eventually" (and theoretically), but on an interest-free basis. A similar deal was struck in April 2002 when Kim Jong Il visited Beijing and Shanghai.[16]

In addition, China has provided North Korea the following "no-cost" aid:

- 1997: 170,000 M/T of rice
- 1998: 100,000 M/T food aid; 20,000 M/T of chemical fertilizer; and 80,000 M/T of oil
- 1999: 150,000 M/T food aid; 400,000 M/T of "cocus" (unknown food)
- 2000: 10,000 meters of cloth for student uniforms
- 2001: 15,000 M/T of light fuel oil and 579,000 M/T of crude oil
- 2002: 472,000 M/T of crude oil

European Commission Aid

The European Commission (EC), the European Union's (EU) executive body, initiated humanitarian aid to the DPRK in October 1995 and has continued its aid despite the chill in the EC's political relations with North Korea since 2002. The total value of the EC's aid to North Korea between 1995 and 2002 ranks it the third-largest donor behind South Korea and China. This puts the EC ahead of Japan, once the third-largest aid donor.

The EC began providing significant amounts of food aid in 1997. By 2001, this aid amounted to Euro 168 million and was delivered as follows:

- 106 million euros (including 6 million euros from European nongovernmental organizations (NGOs) sent bilaterally
- 50 million euros given to the World Food Program of which European NGOs distributed 12 million euros
- 11 million euros via seven European NGOs: CESVI (Italy), Concern, Children's Aid Direct, Action Contra la Faim, German Agro Action, Médecins Sans Frontières, and Triangle

The European Commission's Humanitarian Aid Office (ECHO) has coordinated these various aid activities. Between 1995 and 2000, it oversaw the distribution of 1.9 million metric tons of food aid worth US$85 million in the DPRK through the NGO-coordinated Food Aid Liaison Unit (FALU). ECHO also has annually funded several major public health projects. Since 2001, it has contributed more than 24 million euros for these projects, which include:

- a prosthesis factory
- an orthopedic hospital
- 12 county hospitals and a rural operating theater
- 12 nurseries and several cafeterias for children
- deworming and Vitamin A for 500,000 children and nutrients for 200,000 women who are either pregnant or of child-bearing age

In March and April 2003, the EC delivered 130,000 metric tons of urea fertilizer to the DPRK, plus an additional 46,000 M/T of wheat worth 9.5 million euros for children and pregnant and nursing women.[17]

Humanitarian Aid's Dollar Value

The value of all humanitarian aid that North Korea has and continues to receive is virtually impossible to estimate with any precision. Based on estimated values provided by UN organizations and various government organizations, Table 4.4 provides some indication. Between 1995 and 2002, the largest contributors gave North Korea an estimated $2 billion of food and other aid. Total contributions from other nations would increase this amount significantly.[18]

Speaking in humanitarian and political terms, this aid certainly prevented the deaths of hundreds of thousands of North Koreans from starvation and disease. Politically, it would be difficult to deny that the aid sustained the Kim regime's survival during a profound and pervasive public health crisis between 1995 and 2000. The extent to

Table 4.4

Value of Aid to North Korea, 1995–2002: Major Aid Donors (US$)

By rank	Official aid	Private aid	Total
1. United States	$620,000,000	N/A	N/A
2. South Korea	538,800,000	$208,000,000	$746,880,000
3. European Union	284,700,000	N/A	N/A
4. China[a]	270,000,000	N/A	N/A
5. Japan	256,500,000	N/A	N/A
Total aid	$1,9700,000,000	$208,000,000	$2,178,000,000

Sources: The above data were tabulated from the annual UN report entitled "United Nations Consolidated Inter-Agency Appeal for Flood-Related Emergency, Humanitarian Assistance to the Democratic People's Republic of Korea," Geneva: UN Department of Humanitarian Affairs, 1996–2002. The numbers should be seen as a generally accurate indication of each donor's contribution, but not taken as a precise figure of all contributions given the varying comprehensiveness of each government's and private donor's report to the UN office in Pyongyang.

[a]The amount of Chinese humanitarian aid appears smaller than the actual number, probably because it includes only the value of food aid from the central government but not provincial food aid and economic assistance in the form of crude oil and other basic commodities.

N/A = not available.

which the aid has altered the North Korean people's perception of the international community remains to be determined. As a consequence of the aid, North Korea now is a much more open and internationally accessible society than it was in 1995.

Fuel

Kim Jong Il's other critical need to avoid regime collapse is fossil fuel in the form of crude oil, natural gas, and coal. North Korea has no known significant reserves of oil and natural gas, but it does have substantial deposits of coal. North Korea encountered two "fuel shocks" between 1990 and 1995, one involving oil and the other coal.

The oil shock began in 1991 when one of its two major suppliers of crude oil, the Soviet Union, collapsed and its replacement Russia subsequently required cash payment for all such purchases. This ended Pyongyang's access to a major source of inexpensive oil. Soon afterward, China, North Korea's second major supplier of oil, began demanding cash payments. This seriously disrupted the flow of oil from China. The DPRK's total energy supply dropped from nearly 24 million M/T of oil equivalent in 1990 to a low of 14 million M/T in 1998. It then recovered to 15.7 million M/T in 2000. Crude oil imports dropped from 18.5 million barrels in 1990 to a low of 2.3 million barrels in 1999, but then began to increase, rising to 2.9 million barrels in 2000. (As a comparison, South Korea imported 894 million barrels of crude oil in 2000.) Coal production, about 70 percent of North Korea's energy supply, also fell from 16.6 million M/T of oil equivalents in 1990 to 9.3 million M/T in 1998, then rose to 11.2 million M/T in 2000.[19]

Table 4.5

China's Food and Oil Exports to the DPRK, 1991–1999
(unit: 10,000 metric tons)

| | DPRK food imports | | | DPRK oil imports | | |
	All	China	% of total	All	China	% of total
1991	129.0	30.3	23	189.0	110.0	58
1992	83.0	62.0	74	152.0	110.0	72
1993	109.3	74.0	67	136.0	105.5	77
1994	49.0	30.5	62	91.0	83.0	91
1995	96.2	15.3	15	110.0	102.0	92
1996	105.0	54.7	52	93.6	93.6	100
1997	163.0	86.7	53	110.6	50.6	45
1998	103.6	27.0	26	60.9	50.3	82
1999	107.0	N/A		31.7	N/A	
2000	N/A	N/A		N/A	N/A	
2001	N/A	N/A		N/A	579.0	
2002	N/A	N/A		N/A	472.0	

Sources: The above table summarizes data obtained from the following sources: Chinhung Trading Company, "North Korea's Overseas Trade" (Seoul, 2001); "Chinese Fuel, Grain Exports to North Korea Dwindle in 2002," *Vantage Point* (July 2003), p. 56; ROK Ministry of Unification, "Recent Trends in Sino-North Korean Economic Cooperation," July 19, 2004, available at www.unikorea.go.kr; Chin Yong-san, "China-DPRK Economic Ties—Impact on Life in DPRK Society," in *Proceedings of the 1st World Congress of Korean Studies* (Seoul: Academy of Korean Studies, 2002), vol. 2, pp. 972–981.
N/A = not available.

Pyongyang first sought to diversify its oil supply by turning to the Middle East and the United States. It attempted to trade missiles and missile technology for oil with Arab oil-producing nations, particularly Syria, Libya, and Iran. Also in the 1994 Agreed Framework deal with the United States, North Korea sought to partially solve its energy crisis by trading the end of its nuclear weapons program for two nuclear light water reactors and an annual supply of 500,000 metric tons of heavy fuel oil (HFO) from the United States. The supply of Middle East oil proved unreliable, at least in part because of declining demand for North Korea's aging and inaccurate missiles and associated technology. The HFO shipments from the United States were always delayed and finally discontinued in 2002 along with the nuclear power plants' construction.

China's assistance, however, proved decisive in addressing North Korea's oil needs, as indicated in Table 4.5.[20]

North Korea's other fuel crisis, the coal shock, occurred in 1995, when torrential rains flooded numerous coal mines. But even before the floods, coal production had suffered from deteriorating infrastructure. The inability to repair and replace aging mine machinery and supporting equipment was already undercutting productivity.

Here too China has assisted by supplementing North Korea's coal production with an annual supply of 150,000 M/T of coal. North Korea's coal production, according to government figures, has steadily increased since 2000. At the same time, North Korea has invested intense effort into increasing its hydroelectric production.

Investment Capital

Kim Jong Il's efforts to attract foreign investment have all fallen short of their avowed goals. The foremost impediments remain the poor investment environment in the DPRK, particularly the high risk of failure and poor chances of profit, and fundamental differences between North Korea's socialist economic system and that of the international economy. As in other areas, South Korea and China have been Pyongyang's leading sources of economic cooperation.[21]

North Korea has tried various devices, most notably free trade zones. These, however, have yielded marginal gains. For example, the Rajin-Sonbong Enterprise Zone in the country's northeast corner attracted US$650 million worth of contracts, but realized only US$120 million worth of investment by September 2000.

With great fanfare, the North Korean government announced the establishment of the Sinuiju Special Administrative Region on September 23, 2003. This special economic zone is to rise in North Korea's northwest corner on the border with China and serve as a magnet for Chinese capital investment. The government's goal is to attract US$150 billion in foreign investment over the next five years. But the project is off to a faltering start. No sooner had Pyongyang named Chinese businessman and Dutch citizen Yang Bin the project's director than the Chinese government arrested and imprisoned him for alleged tax fraud, among other things. A South Korean businessman briefly renewed hope for the zone in October 2002 when he claimed to have secured US$10 billion for Sinuiju, but his claim proved premature. The Sinuiju project remains suspended.[22]

The Kaesong Industrial Park seems destined for a much brighter and enduring fate. This joint South-North Korean project is under construction near the North Korean city of Kaesong. This small city is 60 kilometers (about 36 miles) north of Seoul and 170 kilometers (102 miles) south of Pyongyang. Conceived in 1998, the two governments agreed in 2000 to reconnect roads and railroads to facilitate the project's construction, and then commenced to do so in September 2000. Agreements on communications, customs clearance, and quarantine were finalized on December 8, 2002. On December 17, 2002, North and South Korea agreed to entrust the construction and project management to South Korea's Hyundai Asan and the Korea Land Corporation with an initial investment of US$185 million in the project's first phase.[23]

The project is envisioned as an exclusively joint South-North venture. South Korean firms will provide the investment capital, production facilities, and raw materials. North Korea will provide the land and labor. South Korea will pay the North US$16 million to lease the land (810 acres) for fifty years. South Korean firms will also pay the DPRK a corporate income tax of between 10 and 14 percent of gross profits. The minimum monthly wage for each North Korean worker, who is to work forty-eight hours per week, will be US$57.50, with annual increases of 5 percent. Plans call for 19,000 South Korean small and medium enterprises to operate in the park after nine years. They are projected to employ 725,000 North Koreans who will earn US$600 million.

The aim is to promote the economic integration of the two Korea's over the next decade and to train North Korean workers in advanced production skills in exchange for their lower labor cost. All goods produced in the zone will be returned to South Korea for export. As of July 2004, over 1,000 South Korean garment, footwear, and other small-sized firms have applied to locate in the park. To encourage investment in the park, South Korea's official Ex-Im (Export-Import) Bank announced in May 2004 that it would partially compensate South Korean firms for 50 percent of any losses caused by North Korean partners' bankruptcies or natural disasters.[24]

The South Korean tourism project at the Mt. Kumgang area in North Korea has been in financial difficulty since its start in 1998. The project was initiated by the now deceased Chong Chu-yong (Jung Ju-yong) who founded the Hyundai Group, one of Korea's first and formerly most successful multinational businesses. In private meetings with North Korean leader Kim Jong Il held in the fall of 1998 in Pyongyang, Chong agreed to pay North Korea a US$450,000 monthly fee for allowing the Hyundai group to facilitate South Korean visits to the scenic mountainous area on the north side of the demilitarized zone (DMZ) that has divided the Korean peninsula since the end of the Korean War in 1953. Chong's fifth son, Chong Mong-hun, took over the project after his father's death, but then the younger Chong committed suicide in 2002 when it became publicly known that he had passed US$500 million on behalf of the South Korean government to North Korea shortly before the 2000 summit between the leaders of North and South Korea.

Since the project began, almost 600,000 South Korean and foreign tourists have visited the area: 10,554 in 1998; 148,074 in 1999; 213,009 in 2000; 57,879 in 2001; and 84,727 in 2002. This has earned North Korea at least US$413 million as of the end of 2003. South Korean government subsidies keep the project alive. Also, the project has facilitated the opening of land and sea routes between the two Koreas. A one-year renovation of the Mt. Kumgang Resort Hotel was completed in June 2004.[25]

At the same time, China's contribution of direct investment in North Korea has remained much lower than North Korea's expectations. At the end of 1999, thirteen Chinese enterprises had invested US$2.727 million in North Korea. Two years later, in 2001, Chinese firms had invested only a total of US$3.95 million. Most of this investment has been in restaurants, mineral water production, fish farming, and some light industries. Despite repeated Chinese government efforts, the level of Chinese investment remains very low.

China redoubled its effort in 2004. In April 2004, the Beijing government promised to construct a modern, multimillion-dollar glass factory in Pyongyang. It also recruited potential Chinese investors for a special tour of North Korea in May 2004. While construction of the government-funded glass factory is progressing smoothly, the level of private Chinese investment in North Korea remains marginal.

China is assisting in other ways. Three times between 1996 and 2002, China supplied the DPRK with satellite equipment and other high-technology meteorological equipment. Since 2000, a continuing bilateral exchange program involving scientists facilitates the transfer of technology from China to North Korea. They have formed the "Morning-Panda Joint Venture Computer Company," which now assembles and manufactures components for personal computers. Cooperation extends to computer software design and production. Nevertheless, the accumulative impact of such cooperation remains very sporadic and limited.[26]

Reflections on the Future

On July 1, 2002, the DPRK government announced a set of economic reforms that subsequently has fueled a debate among North Korea "watchers" regarding their intent and potential consequences. Some have argued that the reforms will erode the DPRK's orthodox socialist economy and open the way for the emergence of a market economy. The DPRK government insists, however, that its goal is to improve and perpetuate its juche socialist economy.

South Korean economists at the Korea Development Institute (KDI) in Seoul believe that the DPRK's economic policies accent a dual approach to revitalization of the economy's industrial sector. The first is to mobilize domestic capital and labor. Toward this end, Pyongyang initiated "economic reforms" in 2002 aimed at reasserting central economic control over domestic commercial activities that evolved between 1995 and 2002. Second, North Korea since 1984 has aspired to develop "islands" of foreign investment in special trade and economic zones, beginning with the Najin-Sonbong project and the more recently begun Kaesong Industrial Park.[27]

Regardless of these reforms' eventual impact, North Korea inevitably must induce much larger amounts of foreign investment to reinvigorate its economy. Neither the continuing reforms nor the present level of foreign investment can modernize North Korea's economic infrastructure. In this regard, the North Korean regime must inevitably take the following steps if it is to avoid demise:

- End its "military-first" policy that channels the best and most of critically short resources to this commercially unproductive sector.
- Reorient the economy from putting the military sector first to expanding the industrial sector's capacity to compete in the international market and to earn foreign currency through trade.
- Take the necessary political steps to end U.S. economic sanctions to gain access to international financial institutions.
- Make the Korean peninsula a safer place for foreigner investors.

North Korea Today—Illusion or Reality?

Pyongyang and its inhabitants today present a profound contrast to the harsh reality of just five years ago. Sidewalks are crowded with well-fed, well-dressed, and clean people. Children again jump and run, cheer and shout. Streets are busy with cars, many more bicycles, and new buses and trolleys. Most of the lights are on at night and the air conditioning, at least in special facilities, runs all night. Restaurants are full of customers and serve ample helpings of food and drink. Many less appealing sights have disappeared. The once huge lines of commuters waiting to board a bus or trolley are gone, as are the armed police patrols that once controlled the crowds. There are fewer broken down vehicles, particularly trucks.

The present illusion of ample food and fuel in North Korea is not a consequence of sound economic and developmental policies. Rather, it is a result of nature's and the international community's compassion plus ample amounts of economic aid from China and South Korea and the international community's humanitarian aid. The value of the international community's humanitarian aid alone exceeded US$2 billion dollars between 1995 and 2001. During the same period, North Korea received at least an equal or greater amount of sustainable economic aid from China, South Korea, and the European Union.

Another very substantial contributing factor to North Korea's relative plenty in 2004 is Kim Jong Il's revival of his father's coercive strategy of squeezing aid from neighbors by threatening to do what they oppose. North Korea's resumption of its nuclear weapons development program, and reluctant participation in the Six-Party Talks aimed at halting such a program, has convinced China, South Korea, and, to a lesser extent, Japan to continue supplying North Korea crude oil, grain, hard currency, access to modern technology, and some investment capital. This, not economic reform or movement away from socialism toward capitalism, also contributes to North Korea's relative economic well-being today.

Behind the façade of today's plenty remains the reality that North Korea could abruptly fall back into a desperate situation.[28] If North Korea is to sustain today's apparent abundance, its leadership must be convinced to forgo its traditional coercive approach to the international community. Instead, it must shift to taking the necessary steps to earn respect and, through trade, the hard currency to pay for its imports of oil and grain. Otherwise, either nature will again wreck havoc on North Korea, or the possibility of war will continue to impede its economic development. The burden of success in this endeavor rests equally on the leadership of North Korea and on the international community, particularly Pyongyang's primary antagonist, the United States.

Unfortunately, the United States clings to the perception that North Korea's poverty is the genesis of its nuclear weapons programs. But North Korea's persistent refusal to trade bountiful economic inducements for an end to its nuclear ambitions argues against this perception. Instead, the United States and its ally Japan should recognize the reality that security concerns, not poverty, drive North Korea's defense strategy. Recognition of this fact combined with appropriate security assurances and economic incentives might better facilitate progress toward a peaceful diplomatic resolution of the Korean peninsula's nuclear programs. Otherwise, a second Korean War could wreck havoc again over not just the Korean peninsula, but much of Northeast Asia.

Notes

1. For the Clinton administration, see Quinones, "North Korea: From Containment to Engagement," 101–119. For the Bush administration see Quinones, "Dualism in the Bush Administration's North Korea Policy," 197–224.

2. Regarding North Korea's policy toward the United States, see "The United States in North Korea's Foreign Policy," in Koh, *North Korea and the World*. Seoul: Kyungnam University Press, 2004.

3. U.S. Department of State Dispatch 2, no. 39 (1992), 1–4.

4. Roh, "Declaration of Non-nuclear Korean Peninsula Peace Initiatives."

5. Kang Sok Ju, "Opening Remarks of First Vice Minister of Foreign Affairs Kang Sok Ju at the DPRK-U.S. Talks, New York, June 1993" (emphasis added).

6. Statement of the DPRK Foreign Ministry Spokesman, October 25, 2002, available at www.kcna.co.jp (emphasis added).

7. Choe Su Hon, DPRK vice minister of foreign affairs, "Statement by Head of the Delegation of the DPRK at the General Debate of the 59th Session of the UN General Assembly," September 27, 2004; press release text distributed by the DPRK Permanent Mission to the UN in New York.

8. Dafna Linzer and Joohee Cho, "South Korea Acknowledges Secret Nuclear Experiments," *Washington Post*, September 3, 2004; James Brooke, "South Koreans Repeat: We Have No Atom Bomb Program," *New York Times*, September 4, 2004; James Brooke, "South Korean Scientist Calls Uranium Test 'Academic,'" *New York Times*, September 7, 2004; Sang-hun Choe, "North Korea Warns of 'Nuclear Arms Race,'" Associated Press, September 8, 2004; Sang-hun Choe, "South Korea Extracted Plutonium in 1982," Associated Press, September 9, 2004; Mark Gorwitz, "The South Korean Laser Isotope Separation Experience," September 27, 2004, available at www.isis-online.org/publications/dprk/sklisword2.html; DPRK Foreign Ministry spokesman, "Statement on Issue of Uranium Enrichment in South Korea," Korea Central News Agency, September 11, 2004; Mohamed ElBaradei, IAEA director general, "Introductory Statement to the Board of Governors," September 13, 2004, available at www.iaea.org; "South Korea Conducted Defense-Oriented Plutonium Test: *Monthly Chosun*," *Chosun Ilbo*, see *Napsnet Daily Report*, September 16, 2004, 3.

9. Yang Ho-min, "North Korea Placed Officially Under Military Rule in 1998, 16–19; "Kim Jong Il Era Dawns with Military Status Enhanced"; "Two-Thirds of Tenth Term SPA Members Are Newcomers," 11; Kim Gye-dong, "North Korea's Military-First Politics and Anti-South Strategy," 9; Chong, "Military Rule in Full Swing," 2–9.

10. (North) Korea Central News Agency, January 2, 1999, available at www.korea-np.co.jp.

11. Ibid.

12. Chong, "Economic Programs and State Budget," 2–8; Chung, "The Prospects for Economic Reform in North Korea," 43–53.

13. UN Food and Agriculture Organization (UNFAO), "Annual DRPK Crop Assessments. 1995–2004"; "One Thousand Hectares of Fish Farms Built in 2001," 13.

14. "100,000 Tons of Corn to Be Sent to North," *Joongang Ilbo*, October 22, 2004.

15. ROK Ministry of Unification, *Promoting Peace and Cooperation:* 2003; "South Korea Sends US$135.39 Million in Aid," 57.

16. ROK Bank of Korea, National Statistics Office; ROK Ministry of Unification, "The North Korean Economy in 2002 and Its Prospects for 2003: A Comprehensive Review," April 25, 2002, available at www.unikorea.go.kr/en/northkorea/; ROK Ministry of Unification, "Recent Trends in Sino-North Korean Economic Cooperation," July 19, 2004, available at www.unikorea.go.kr; Chin, "China-DPRK Economic Ties," 978; Liu Ming, "China's Role in the Course of North Korea's Transition," Nautilus Institute, July 13, 2004, available at www.nautilus.org.

17. European Commission, "The EC–DPRK Country Strategy Paper, 2001–2004"; European Commission, "North Korea: Commission Approves euro 7.5 Million in Humanitarian Aid," EU Statement (May 14, 2003); Nam, "North Korea, European Union Caught in Nuke Issue," 10–12; "60,000 Tons of Fertilizer from EU Arrive in North Korea," 18.

18. Food aid data were compiled primarily from World Food Program annual reports and publications. ROK Ministry of Unification, *Promoting Peace and Cooperation*; Chin, "China-DPRK Economic Ties," 973 and 978.

19. Chinhung Trading Company, "North Korea's Overseas Trade" "Chinese Fuel, Grain Exports to North Korea Dwindle," 56; ROK Ministry of Unification, "Recent Trends in Sino-North Korean Economic Cooperation," July 19, 2004, available at www.unikorea.go.kr; Chin, "China-DPRK Economic Ties," 973.

20. See note 19; and "Five Foreign Firms Prospecting for Oil in North Korea," 57.

21. "North Korea Expands Foreign Investors' Share of Joint Venture," 57; Chong, "The Project of Issuing Public Bonds," 14–18; "State Bank to Cover Losses from Trade with North Korea," 57.

22. Kwak, "Sinuiju Special Administrative Region," 2–10; "North Korea Aims to Secure US$150 Billion Foreign Investment in Sinuiju," 57.

23. "Construction of Kaesong Industrial Park," 23–24; Park Suhk-sam, "An Analysis of Economic Effects," 40–50.

24. "State Bank to Cover Losses from Trade with North Korea," 57; "Korean Banks to Support Firms in North Korean Industrial Complex," 57.

25. "Civic Efforts on to Keep Inter-Korean Tour," 25–27; "Mt Kumgang Inn to Reopen After Renovations," 56; "Mt. Kumgang Attracts Over 530,000 Tourists," 57.

26. The data about China's investment in North Korea were compiled from the South Korean journal *Vantage Point*, discussions with the editorial staff of the Tokyo-based newspaper, *Chosen shimpo*, and articles distributed by the (North) Korea Central News Agency (KCNA). "China to Provide US$50 Million to Finance Glass Plant in North Korea," 56. These data are intended to be indicative of, and not a comprehensive listing of, all Chinese investment in North Korea.

27. Chong, "A Year After Radical Economic Reforms," 2–8; Luse and Jannuzi, *North Korea: Status Report on Nuclear Program*; "Manufactures Selling Consumer Goods on Markets," 28; Nam Kwang-sik, "North Korea Heading Toward Market Economy," 8–11; Nam Sung-wook, "Prospects for Pyongyang's Economic Reforms," 11–15; "Number of Pyongyang's Markets Increasing Rapidly," 29.

28. United Nations Environment Programme, *DPR Korea: State of the Environment 2003*.

5

North Korea's
Weapons of Mass Destruction

Larry A. Niksch

North Korea's weapons of mass destruction (WMDs) have been a subject of intense interest and scrutiny since 1989 when North Korea shut down an operating nuclear reactor long enough to have allowed for removal of spent nuclear fuel from the reactor and conversion of the spent fuel into weapons-grade plutonium for nuclear weapons. That scenario and subsequent scenarios always have contained a big "IF": if North Korea had the technological capabilities to carry out such a process. The U.S. intelligence community and the intelligence agencies of several other countries have employed considerable resources to learn whether or not North Korea has developed weapons of mass destruction (WMDs) and, if so, in what form and quantities. Such activities are carried out secretly, and information acquired is highly classified. However, intelligence agencies have revealed portions of their findings periodically, and assertive journalists have been able to obtain information from intelligence officials. Thus, there is substantial, though incomplete, unclassified information on North Korea's WMDs.

There are three categories of evidence for the existence of North Korea's WMDs. The first is evidence discerned through sensory detection: visual sound, odor, and so on. These include open facilities such as nuclear installations, missile tests and launch sites, and missile deployments. North Korea's conduct of tests also has been detected. These include missile tests by both North Korea and by other countries such as Pakistan and Iran, which have received missile technology and components from Pyongyang. Iran and Pakistan have tested models of North Korean missiles, in essence, surrogate testing. Another form of North Korean testing has been numerous explosive detonation tests apparently aimed at developing a detonation mechanism within an atomic bomb that can trigger a nuclear explosion. A very recent category of visual evidence was the material that North Korea showed to American nuclear expert Sigfried Heckler in January 2004. Heckler concluded that the material was weapons-grade plutonium. A second type of evidence comes from human sources. Russia has had access to important human intelligence sources in the form of ex-Soviet nuclear and missile technicians who found employment in North Korea after the collapse of the Soviet Union. Russian intelligence and defense ministry officials and publicized classified reports have described ex-Soviet nuclear and missile technicians as important sources of information. A secret report of the Russian Defense Ministry, compiled in October 1993, stated that nearly 160 Russian nuclear and missile scientists had worked in North Korea in the late 1980s and early 1990s and that there were nine nuclear scientists and seventeen missile specialists still in North Korea.[1] A "senior" military officer in the Russian Defense Ministry was quoted in 1994, saying "We know the details and actual conditions of the [nuclear] development program because we have interviewed scientists who came back from there." He stated that there were over one hundred Russian nuclear and missile experts in North Korea.[2] Writing in *Izvestia* on June 24, 1994, Yevgeniy Albats, a former member of a government commission that investigated the KGB and author of *The State Within the State: KGB and Its Hold on Russia*, described Soviet nuclear experts as one of the "organized information channels" available to Russian intelligence agencies in scrutinizing North Korea's nuclear program. Also, in 1994, the South Korean Ministry of Defense published a book on the North Korean nuclear issue, which stated that there were approximately two hundred scientists of the former Soviet Union "in charge of nuclear development." The Ministry repeated this estimate in October 2002.[3]

North Korean defectors are another source of information. A number of defectors have come from the military and communist party establishments. Some have claimed knowledge of the nuclear program. The reliability of defector testimony often is uncertain, and its credibility cannot be established until it is compared with information from other sources. Another human source of information is Pakistan's A.Q. Khan, the czar of Pakistan's nuclear program and nuclear proliferation activities with a number of countries. Khan reportedly has provided details of his dealings with North Korea, but "reportedly" is the key word here. Information about Khan's "confessions" has been secondhand, passed on by Pakistan officials to U.S. officials and then to the press. Khan has been kept in seclusion by Pakistani officials and has made no public pronouncements.

Documents represent another source of information. At least two kinds apparently exist. The first are documents describing Pakistan-North Korean WMD activities. However, little is known about these. The second are documents related to North Korea's overseas procurements of components and materials that likely would be used in a nuclear weapons program. North Korea has made such purchases or attempted to make purchases in Japan and a number of European countries. These activities have involved contracts, banking documents, and shipping documents. The Central Intelligence Agency and the U.S. Department of Energy are believed to have access to many of these documents.

The Plutonium Nuclear Program

North Korea's plutonium nuclear program has been at the center of the controversy over North Korea's nuclear intentions since the early 1990s. There has been a consensus among foreign intelligence agencies that Kim Jong Il has directed the nuclear programs since at least the late 1980s. This was documented specifically in a top-secret report on North Korea's nuclear program sent from the Soviet KGB to the Soviet Communist Party in February 1990. This report referred to "the North Korean leaders, specifically Kim Chong-il, who personally controls the said research."[4] According to later testimony by Vladimir Kryuchkov, then head of the KGB, Eduard Shevardnadze, the second-ranking Soviet Communist Party official, responded to the report by exclaiming "We must invite Kim Chong-il as soon as possible."[5] U.S. assessments at the time were similar, according to Clinton administration officials, namely, that "Kim Jong Il had been the day-to-day manager of the North's government and was deeply involved in using the nuclear weapons program to ensure Pyongyang's security and bolster its diplomacy."[6] A later assessment came from U. Kotlov, deputy director general of the Information Bureau of Russia's Ministry of Atomic Energy, who had participated in constructing the nuclear facilities at Yongbyon, North Korea's main nuclear center. Kotlov stated that "the nuclear development program rapidly expanded since the Kim Chong-il regime was established after the death of President Kim Il-song" and that "Kim Chong-il was accelerating his nuclear and missile development programs."[7]

Production of atomic bombs from such a program involves several steps: the operation of a plutonium nuclear reactor for sufficient time (at least one year) to produce sufficient nuclear fuel to extract nuclear-weapons-grade plutonium; the unloading of nuclear fuel from the reactor; the conversion of this expended nuclear fuel into weapons-grade plutonium in a plutonium reprocessing plant; the development of a design and triggering mechanism for an atomic bomb; and the assemblage of the atomic bomb with the weapons-grade plutonium. The issue for U.S. and other intelligence organs since the early 1990s has been the degree of progress North Korea has made in completing all of these steps. Judgments have not been easy, given North Korea's attempts to keep its program secret.

Hard information exists that North Korea has completed four of these steps. It clearly has the infrastructure to produce nuclear fuel and reprocess it into weapons-grade plutonium. A five-megawatt nuclear reactor and a plutonium reprocessing plant have been in operation since the 1980s. They have been visited by both U.S. officials and officials of the International Atomic Energy Agency. Second, North Korea shut down the reactor twice in 1989 and 1994; it apparently unloaded spent nuclear fuel from the reactor in 1989 and definitely did in 1994. A U.S. National Intelligence Estimate (NIE) of late 1993 concluded that North Korea had unloaded nuclear fuel from the reactor in 1989.[8] Russian intelligence and Defense Ministry estimates reached a similar conclusion. In May 1994, the North Koreans openly removed nuclear fuel from the five-megawatt reactor, approximately 8,000 fuel rods. These were placed in monitored storage under the 1994 U.S.-North Korean Agreed Framework; but in early 2003, North Korea removed the fuel rods from the storage site to an undisclosed location.

A third North Korea success appears to be the reprocessing of expended nuclear fuel into weapons-grade plutonium. North Korea kept this work secret for many years;

but in 2003, it began to claim that it had produced weapons-grade plutonium. In January 2004, North Korea invited staff members of the Senate Foreign Relations Committee and a private American group to the site of the reactor and reprocessing plant, Yongbyon. The U.S. private group included Dr. Sigfied Hecker, former director of the Los Alamos Nuclear Laboratories. There, North Korean officials showed Dr. Hecker material that he concluded was metallic weapons-grade plutonium. A report of the Senate Foreign Relations Committee staffers stated that North Korean technicians "demonstrated that they had the requisite facility, equipment, and technical expertise, and they appear to have the capacity to extract plutonium from the spent fuel rods and fabricate plutonium metal."[9] Interestingly, this finding of 2004 parallels reported U.S. intelligence findings going back to 1993. Both NBC News (December 28, 1993) and the journal, *Nucleonics Week*, of July 8 1993, cited U.S. intelligence sources that North Korea had converted plutonium from liquid to metal. Both reports noted that metallic plutonium can be used only to produce nuclear weapons.[10]

Thus, it appears that North Korea has had the technology to produce weapons-grade plutonium technology since at least the early 1990s. This leaves little doubt that North Korea has produced nuclear weapons-grade plutonium, but there is more uncertainty concerning the amount of plutonium North Korea has produced. There is consistency in U.S. and Russian intelligence estimates that North Korea likely produced a significant quantity of plutonium from the nuclear fuel rods removed from the five-megawatt reactor in 1989. The U.S. NIE of late 1993 estimated an amount of twelve kilograms, enough plutonium for one or two atomic bombs. Russian estimates reportedly cited a broader potential range, from seven to twenty-two kilograms, possibly enough for three to five atomic bombs. One of the Russian estimates reportedly came out of a top secret Russian interagency meeting on North Korea's nuclear program in December 1995.[11]

A fourth known step by North Korea is a program for over a decade to develop a triggering device for an atomic bomb. U.S., South Korean, and Russian intelligence agencies have detected numerous test explosions inside North Korea since the early 1980s. The secret Russian interagency meeting of December 1995 reportedly discussed about seventy high explosive tests during the 1991–1994 period and concluded that they were aimed at perfecting a trigger mechanism for atomic bombs. A CIA report to the Senate Intelligence Committee in August 2003 stated that North Korea had conducted numerous high explosive tests since 1980 intended to develop a nuclear trigger mechanism.[12] South Korean government experts voiced similar assessments in 2001 and 2003.

Beyond these four areas of certain or near certain knowledge, there lies key issues where considerable uncertainties exist: the production of atomic bombs from weapons-grade plutonium, how many bombs produced, the development of nuclear warheads that could be mounted on missiles, the acquisition by North Korea of plutonium from outside sources, especially the former Soviet Union, and nuclear technology transfers to other states. On some of these issues, U.S. intelligence agencies have drawn conclusions, but these clearly are more tentative than conclusions regarding the four known steps cited above.

U.S. intelligence estimates since the early 1990s have gone from possibilities to probabilities to certainties that North Korea has produced atomic bombs. The NIE of late December 1993 reportedly concluded that there was a "better than even chance" that North Korea had atomic bombs. Secretary of Defense William Perry asserted in April 1994, "We estimate they [North Korea] probably have the capability to convert that plutonium into bombs. We estimate they have had enough time by now to succeed in doing that."[13] An NIE of December 2001 reportedly was more certain that "North Korea has produced one, possibly two nuclear weapons."[14] The CIA report to the Senate Intelligence Committee in August 2003 stated the same conclusion and that North Korea "has validated the designs [of an atomic bomb] without conducting yield-producing nuclear tests."[15] U.S. officials, however, never have explained why these estimates have been raised from the probability range to the certainty range.

Perry's explanation of North Korea having "enough time" may be part of the U.S. assessment, especially the seven years between his statement in 1994 and the NIE of late 2001. This explanation is given credibility by the Russian assessments of the early 1990s, which credited North Korea with major advances toward the production of atomic bombs. The February 1990 memorandum by the Soviet KGB to the Soviet Communist Party Central Committee referred to "a reliable source" that "the development of the first atomic explosive device has been completed."[16] The head of the KGB at that time, Vladimir Kryuchkov, later explained that one of his immediate subordinates had prepared the document and that the "reliable source" was "a North Korean agent who was most reliable."[17] Russian officials later explained that the nuclear device of the 1990 memorandum needed further engineering and design to become an actual atomic bomb.[18] Russian assessments of 1993 and 1994 veered between concluding that North Korea had developed a "nuclear device" and a full-fledged atomic bomb. A Russian Defense Ministry report of October 1993 reportedly concluded that the development of an atomic bomb was in a "final stage"; but a senior officer of the ministry's Military Strategy Research Center, which drafted the report, was quoted as saying that "North Korea has already completed the development of a Hiroshima-type atomic bomb, and it is widely known among us that North Korea has at least one atomic bomb."[19] He cited information obtained from Russian nuclear scientists, who had returned to Russia from North Korea. Vladimir Kumachev, an official of the Russian government's Institute of National Security and Strategic Research, rendered a similar evaluation that "According to information we have received, North Korea has nuclear warheads."[20] However, Lt. General Gennady Yevstafiyev, Director-General of the Massive Destruction Weapons Control Bureau of the Russian Federal Intelligence Service, was quoted in January 1994 as casting doubt that North Korea had developed a full-scale atomic bomb. He stated that North Korea was "near success" in producing a nuclear weapon but had frozen the program because of international pressure and the financial burden.[21] However, even if his estimate was correct in January 1994, it seems clear that North Korea's decision in 1995 and 1996 to advance a secret uranium enrichment program also would have meant that North Korea was proceeding with the development of a plutonium bomb in secret.

High-level North Korean defectors also testified that they had been told that North Korea had developed atomic bombs. This included Hwang Jang-yop, the Communist Party's top ideologist who defected in 1997, Kim Duck-hong (who defected with Hwang), and Kang Myong-to, the son-in-law of North Korean Prime Minister Kang Song-san, who defected in 1994. These individuals cited information obtained from North Korean officials that North Korea possessed five atomic bombs. Secretary of Defense William Perry responded to Kang's testimony that U.S. intelligence estimates of one or two bombs would not be altered but that "we do take . . . seriously" Kang's claim, partly because if North Korea possessed more sophisticated technology than the United States believed, "they could make five bombs out of the amount of plutonium we estimate they have."[22]

Estimates of the number of North Korean atomic bombs changed dramatically in 2003 when North Korea removed 8,000 nuclear fuel rods from storage ponds, expelled IAEA officials who were monitoring the fuel rods under the 1994 U.S.-North Korean Agreed Framework, and claimed that reprocessing of the fuel rods into weapons-grade plutonium was underway. Until then, U.S., Russian, and South Korean assessments stipulated a likelihood of one or two atomic bombs. The CIA report to the Senate Intelligence Committee of August 2003 reportedly stated that North Korea had produced one or two nuclear weapons. However, North Korea's claim of reprocessing in 2003 began to produce higher U.S. estimates by the end of 2003 into 2004: three or four, then six to eight. The *Washington Post* reported in April 2004 that U.S. intelligence agencies were preparing a new NIE estimating that North Korea had at least eight nuclear weapons.[23] However, there is no indication of the evidence used by U.S. intelligence analysts in reaching these higher estimates. The *New York Times* quoted a senior Bush administration official in December 2003 as replying to a question about North Korea's production of new plutonium and atomic bombs that "I would mean both. But I can't be specific because I don't think we know."[24]

If the assessments that North Korea has produced an atomic bomb are correct, then the crucial question becomes "what kind of atomic weapon?" Or more specifically, has North Korea been able to advance from production of a large atomic bomb similar to the bombs dropped on Japan during World War II to a smaller, designed nuclear warhead capable of being mounted on North Korean missiles? The answer to this question is crucial, for development of nuclear warheads would give North Korea a much greater capability to strike at targets in Japan, including U.S. bases in Japan, and U.S. targets such as Guam, Hawaii, Alaska, and even the continental United States. On the other hand, if North Korea has only developed so-called fat bombs weighing several tons (the bomb dropped on Nagasaki weighed 4.9 tons), its delivery options would be extremely limited: by plane to targets only in South Korea or by ship to targets in Japan or, more remotely, the United States.

Since North Korea first flight-tested the intermediate-range Nodong missile in 1993, outside intelligence estimates have concluded that North Korea was working on nuclear warhead development. If the Russian estimates of development of a Hiroshima/Nagasaki-type atomic bomb in the early 1990s are correct, then North

Korea has had a decade to concentrate on the next stage of nuclear warhead development. North Korean detonation tests in the 1990s likely are explained by progress in the warhead development program. Experts point out the key to developing a smaller nuclear warhead, as compared to a "fat" atomic bomb, is to refine the explosives and the explosive detonator so that a smaller quantity of explosives could be used, thus significantly reducing the weight of the nuclear weapon.[25] A Russian Defense Ministry report of October 1993 stated that North Korea was developing a one to two megaton nuclear warhead for the Nodong.[26] Since then, assessments of North Korean progress have varied considerably. The Russian Defense Ministry report asserted that North Korea "is in the final stage of production" on nuclear warheads. However, U.S. intelligence officials reported in January 1994 that North Korea would have, at best, primitive atomic bombs weighing over 1,000 pounds; they said nothing about warhead development.[27] South Korean Defense Ministry and National Intelligence Service (NIS) assessments from 1996 through 2002 concluded that North Korea had not developed nuclear warheads and that any North Korean atomic bomb would be a "Nagasaki-class" fat bomb, weighing two to three tons. The CIA's report to the Senate Intelligence Committee of August 18, 2003, appeared to back up the South Korean assessment. It claimed that North Korea has produced one or two "simple fission-type nuclear weapons." U.S. officials used the "primitive" characterization on other occasions in 2003.

U.S. estimates in 2003, however, appeared to contain a contradiction. In contrast to these estimates of a "primitive" bomb, the Japanese press reported in June 2003 that U.S. State and Defense Department officials had claimed to Japanese counterparts that North Korea possessed the "technology to develop small nuclear warheads." North Korea, according to these officials, had downsized nuclear weapons to about one ton each—small enough to be carried by Nodong missiles. Japanese officials, however, stated that U.S. officials had offered no "confirmed information" to back up their claim.[28] Some U.S. analysts reportedly said at this time that North Korea might have received assistance from Pakistan in warhead development as part of the North Korea-Pakistan deal for exchanges of missile and nuclear technologies.[29]

Given the contradictory assessments and the absence of hard public evidence, the status of North Korea's nuclear warhead capability is perhaps the central uncertainty in evaluating North Korea's plutonium program. It may well be the central uncertainty within U.S. and other foreign intelligence agencies. Again, the answer to the question will have huge implications for future evaluations of the actual North Korean military threat to the United States and Japan.

A final area of considerable uncertainty is the question of whether North Korea has been able to acquire nuclear materials, including weapons-grade plutonium, from the former Soviet Union. Since the collapse of the USSR, there have been constant reports of the lack of security for facilities housing nuclear materials and unemployed or underpaid ex-Soviet nuclear scientists and technicians who might be willing to sell nuclear materials to foreign governments. It also is known that North Korea had established a formidable intelligence apparatus inside the Soviet Union that continued into the 1990s. A direct warning of North Korean interest in Soviet nuclear materials came in June 1994. The head of Russia's Counterintelligence Service (successor to the KGB) said at a press conference that North Korea's attempts to smuggle "components of nuclear arms production" from Russia caused his agency "special anxiety," and he cited the deportation of five North Koreans who tried to do so.[30] This was an extraordinary statement, given that the official position of the Russian government was and has been that Russian nuclear materials were secure against smuggling. Was the head of the Counterintelligence Service trying to send the United States a message that North Korea had acquired Soviet nuclear materials without violating the official position of his government? Two years earlier, Genardy Chuplin, deputy director of the Institute for Oriental Affairs of the Russian Academy of Sciences, cited KGB sources in *Moscow News* that North Korea had smuggled plutonium out of the former Soviet Union.[31] This issue has also been a near-taboo subject for U.S. officials since the early 1990s. They say they have no hard evidence that North Korea has smuggled nuclear materials from the former Soviet Union. One official, quoted in the *Washington Times* of July 5, 1994, asserted that "There is the possibility that things have gotten over the [Russia-North Korea] border without anybody being aware of it." Defector Kim Duck-hong asserted in a 1999 interview that: "Since the collapse of the Soviet Union, various kinds of things were shipped from Russia. We can naturally think plutonium was one of them."[32] Dr. Sin Song-taek of South Korea's Institute for Defense Analysis (a branch of the Defense Ministry), stated in an article in the *Weekly National Defense Forum* that "a lot of high-quality nuclear materials were leaked from Russia during the period from 1992 to 1994" and that North Korea might have acquired some of the leaked materials.[33] The most specific claim came in the German news magazine *Stern* in March 1993, which cited Russian Counterintelligence Service reports that North Korea had smuggled fifty-six kilograms of plutonium from Russia—enough for eight to ten atomic bombs.

The Uranium Enrichment Program

The United States first found evidence of a secret highly enriched uranium (HEU) program in North Korea in late 1998. A Department of Energy report drafted at the beginning of 1999 concluded that North Korea "is in the early stages of a uranium enrichment capability." The report allegedly was sent to senior officials throughout the Clinton administration. President Clinton, himself, hinted at this knowledge in his certification memorandum to Congress regarding North Korea on February 24, 2000. In it, he declined to certify that "North Korea is not seeking to develop or acquire the capability to enrich uranium."[34] At this time, too, defectors Hwang Jang-yop and Kim Tok-hong testified that they were told that North Korea had been receiving HEU technology from Pakistan since the mid-1990s.

The evidence obtained by the United States is mainly of two types. The first is evidence of North Korean procurements or attempted procurements overseas of components and materials that would be used in a uranium enrichment program. The

Energy Department report cited an attempt by a North Korean trading company to purchase "frequency converters" from a Japanese company; frequency converters are used in the operation of centrifuge machines, which refine natural uranium into highly enriched uranium. More such evidence flowed into U.S. intelligence agencies in 2000 and 2001. A CIA report apparently stated that "During the second half of 1999, Pyongyang sought to procure technology worldwide that could have applications in its nuclear program," particularly in research and development of an HEU program. Another CIA report covering the last six months of 2001 reportedly declared that "The North has been seeking centrifuge-related materials in large quantities to support a uranium enrichment program."[35] In April 2003, U.S., German, and Egyptian authorities stopped a ship about to enter the Suez Canal and seized 200 tons of aluminum tubing suitable for the vacuum casings of centrifuges, which North Korea had purchased in Germany.[36]

The second type of evidence came from Pakistan related to the activities of A. Q. Khan, the "Godfather" of Pakistan's uranium enrichment nuclear weapons program. Since the late 1990s, U.S. intelligence agencies have paid increasing attention to Khan's relations with North Korea, including his frequent visits to Pyongyang and the visits of North Koreans to the Khan Laboratories in Pakistan. In 2002, a North Korean payment of $75 million to the Khan Laboratories was reported.[37] The Pakistan Government's crackdown on Khan's activities in late 2003 brought forth new information in the form of a confession by Khan reported by Pakistani officials to U.S. counterparts. Khan reportedly described a cooperative relationship with North Korea going back to 1991. Pakistan supplied centrifuges and other components of a HEU program in exchange for North Korean missiles and missile technology. The $75 million payment likely was for a package of centrifuges, raw uranium fuel, and other components of an HEU program, similar to a package that Khan sold to Libya. Jim Hoagland, national security writer for the *Washington Post*, cited "sources" that said North Korea had obtained 2,000–3,000 centrifuges, a sufficient quantity to produce a uranium-based atomic bomb.[38] By 2004, reports concerning Iran's HEU program included allegations that Iran and North Korea were collaborating in assembling centrifuges at an underground facility inside North Korea.[39]

North Korea's payment of $75 million to the Khan Laboratories and the CIA reports of stepped-up procurements of centrifuges and other HEU components in 2000 and 2001 raise the issue of how North Korea, after ten years of steady economic decline, could afford such financial outlays. A big part of the answer are the huge cash payments that member companies of South Korea's Hyundai Group made to Kim Jong Il during this period. From 1999 into 2002, Hyundai Asan made about $600 million in payments to North Korea for the right to operate the Mt. Kumgang tourist project inside North Korea. On top of that, Hyundai companies made $500 million in secret payments to North Korea prior to South Korean President Kim Dae Jung's trip to Pyongyang in June 2000. The secret payments, directly demanded by Kim Jong Il and made literally days before the summit, were Kim Jong Il's price for agreeing to the summit. A later investigation by a South Korean special prosecutor found that the Kim Dae Jung administration was complicit in organizing and facilitating the secret payments. Estimates of North Korea's exports in 1999 and 2000 indicate that the Hyundai payments made up at least 30 percent of North Korea's foreign exchange earnings.

According to the findings of the special prosecutor and media reports, the Hyundai money went into bank accounts in different locations controlled by Bureau 39 of North Korea's Communist Party, which reportedly is controlled directly by Kim Jong Il. (The secret payments went into a Bureau 39 bank account in Macao.) Bureau 39's functions are known to include the expenditure of North Korea's foreign exchange resources for procurement overseas of components and materials for North Korea's weapons of mass destruction and missiles. It thus appears to be no coincidence that just as North Korea was accelerating its procurements for the HEU program, a substantial cash inflow from South Korea was going into the North Korean organization in charge of such purchases. South Korea paid for much of North Korea's secret uranium enrichment program.

While U.S. information on North Korean procurements appears to be solid, other key questions are uncertain or unknown. U.S. officials admit that they do not know whether North Korea has assembled the centrifuges and other components into an operating infrastructure to produce highly enriched uranium and atomic bombs from the HEU. They also state that they know little about the locations of HEU activities inside North Korea.[40] Moreover, other governments, particularly those of China and Russia, have challenged U.S. claims that North Korea has a secret HEU program. The Bush administration asserts that North Korean officials admitted to a HEU program during Assistant Secretary of State James Kelly's visit to Pyongyang in October 2002. North Korea vociferously has denied that it disclosed a HEU program, and the issue has been disputed hotly in the Six-Party Talks over North Korea's nuclear programs since April 2003. To the puzzlement of many, the Bush administration has refused to release any of its intelligence information concerning North Korean procurements in Europe and Japan. It has relied on A. Q. Khan's confession in its public assertions; but this "confession" is secondhand, reportedly given to U.S. officials by Pakistani officials who have interviewed Khan. U.S. officials reportedly have not had direct access to Khan.

At least partly as a result of these uncertainties, U.S. intelligence agencies have put out varying and changing estimates of when North Korea would be able to produce a uranium-based atomic bomb. In mid-2004, the Energy Department and the Defense Intelligence Agency reportedly were estimating a near-term bomb manufacture—the end of 2004. However, the CIA and the State Department's Bureau of Intelligence and Research reportedly were estimating 2006 or 2007. A CIA Factsheet of December 2002 stated that a North Korean centrifuge plant likely would be operational "as soon as mid-decade" and would produce enough HEU for two or more atomic bombs per year. Later, CIA officials expressed uncertainty over the status of a centrifuge plant.[41] In short, unless diplomacy produces a nuclear settlement that exposes the details of the HEU program, North Korea likely will be able to continue it in an extremely secretive atmosphere.

Chemical and Biological Weapons

For a number of years, the U.S. and South Korean governments have claimed that North Korea has chemical and biological weapons programs, and they have given estimates of these programs. These statements and estimates give no indication of the sources of this information. A Pentagon report on the North Korean military, released in September 2000, stated that North Korea had developed up to 5,000 metric tons of chemical munitions and had the capability to produce biological weapons, including anthrax, smallpox, the bubonic plague, and cholera. South Korean officials have cited chemical weapons plants inside North Korea and large-scale imports from Japan of chemical materials that could be used to produce chemical weapons. U.S. military officials reportedly believe that North Korean artillery forces along the demilitarized zone have chemical shells that could be fired by heavy artillery. There also are reports from the early 1990s that North Korea assisted Syria and Iran in developing chemical and biological weapons capabilities.[42]

Missiles

While most of North Korea's other WMD programs contain major elements of secrecy to the outside world, outsiders know much more about North Korea's missile programs. This is due to both the nature of missiles and to North Korea's use of its program. North Korea has tested missiles on a number of occasions. Other countries like Iran and Pakistan have had visible collaborative missile programs with North Korea (Iranian and Pakistani missile experts have attended North Korean missile tests), and they have tested missiles clearly modeled upon North Korean missiles. The deployments of North Korean missiles, by North Korea and Iran and Pakistan, also are visible to satellite intelligence gathering.

North Korea has achieved significant gains in its missile program, especially since it began to produce short-range missiles in the mid-1980s based on Soviet Scud missiles. Production of the Scud-B in 1984 was followed quickly by production of upgraded Scud-B models in 1987 and 1991. These missiles, the Hwasong-5 and Hwasong-6, extended the ranges of the Soviet Scud missiles considerably, so that they could reach the entirety of South Korea. North Korea mass produced the Hwasong missiles, numbering today an estimated three hundred to five hundred.[43]

The Scud program set the pattern for North Korea's accomplishments, especially the development of missiles with extended ranges. The next stage in developing new models based on the Scuds was a big one. In 1993, North Korea test-fired a missile into the Sea of Japan. Production ensued, over one hundred have been deployed, and the missiles and associated technology have been sold to Iran and Pakistan. These missiles, dubbed the Nodong, appear to be of intermediate range capability with a range of between 1,300 kilometers and 1,500 kilometers. The Nodongs thus have a range to reach targets throughout Japan.

Statements by South Korean and U.S. officials from September 2003 to September 2004 indicate that North Korea's efforts to develop intermediate-range missiles did not stop with the Nodong. The South Korean Defense Ministry reported in July 2004 that North Korea had developed a new intermediate-range ballistic missile with a range of 3,000 to 4,000 kilometers, far longer than the range of the Nodongs. A U.S. satellite reportedly detected ten of these missiles at launching sites.[44] Subsequent U.S. and South Korean statements described the new missile being based on the Soviet SS-N-6 submarine-borne missile. Assessments by U.S., South Korean, and nongovernment experts portrayed a missile with several greater capabilities than the Nodong. It could be launched from mobile launchers or from ships or submarines. It appears to have a greater accuracy than the Nodong. Its range would include the U.S. island of Guam, the site of major U.S. military facilities. Experts believe the missile is fully capable of carrying a nuclear warhead.[45]

The Scud and Nodong missiles all had a single-stage launch vehicle. But in 1998, North Korea test launched a multistage missile over Japan out into the Pacific Ocean. The first two launch stages functioned properly, but the third stage malfunctioned. Nevertheless, this missile, dubbed the Taepo-dong I, demonstrated that North Korea was developing long-range missiles with potential intercontinental capabilities. Since then, there have been reports and statements from U.S. intelligence officials that North Korea is developing a Taepo-dong II missile that could reach Alaska, Hawaii, and the U.S. west coast. The Taepo-dong II, however, has not been tested; North Korea declared a moratorium in September 1999 on testing long-range missiles, which remains in effect despite repeated North Korean threats to test. Actual Taepo-dong II missiles have not been cited by U.S. intelligence. Thus, there is a good deal more uncertainty about North Korean long-range missiles than there is concerning intermediate-range missiles.

The Nature of the North Korean WMD Threat

Ever since the nuclear issue first emerged in the early 1990s, there has been a near consensus in the American view that North Korea presents a major threat to U.S. security. The Clinton administration continually raised the scenario of an all-out war on the Korean peninsula that would inflict thousands of American casualties and force the United States to commit hundreds of thousands of troops to Korea. In his report of October 13, 1999, William Perry, the administration's special advisor on policy toward North Korea, stressed "the risk of a destructive war to the 37,000 American service personnel in Korea and the many more that would reinforce them." Republicans in Congress largely agreed. The November 1999 report of the North Korea Advisory Group to the Speaker of the House of Representatives asserted that North Korea's weapons of mass destruction "post a major threat to the United States and its allies" and that "North Korea maintains a potent armed force capable of undertaking a large-scale invasion of the ROK."[46] An important component of this near-consensus view has been that North Korea's development of WMDs has increased the overall North Korean threat.

However, much of the U.S. discussion of the North Korean threat has focused on the military destructiveness of WMDs. There has been much less discussion and consideration of WMDs in relation to North Korean political-strategic objectives. There also has been much less discussion of WMDs in relation to North Korea's total military capabilities—the areas in which options to use WMDs can be separated from North Korean conventional military forces and where they cannot be separated.

Using this context begins with North Korea's long-standing, priority political-strategic objective of taking over South Korea. Especially since the early 1970s, North Korea has employed a combination of military, political, and diplomatic strategies to weaken the South Korean state and weaken the alliance between South Korea and the United States. In the 1970s and 1980s, Kim Il Sung directed a massive buildup of offensive conventional military power along the demilitarized zone. U.S. assessments were that North Korea had the capability to launch a massive invasion across the demilitarized zone. U.S. war planning during that period focused on the issue of whether U.S. and South Korean forces could hold Seoul, thirty miles south of the demilitarized zone, in the face of such a North Korean onslaught. This view predominated much of the thinking and planning within the Clinton administration during the 1994 nuclear tensions with North Korea.

WMDs were thought to strengthen North Korean invasion capabilities. Scud missiles could be used against U.S. and South Korean military bases and ports of entry for U.S. troops dispatched to South Korea. The Scuds and North Korean artillery are believed to have chemical warheads and shells. Nuclear weapons could be used against U.S. bases in Japan and Guam; or North Korea could threaten to use nuclear weapons in order to deter the United States from reinforcing South Korea with thousands of U.S. troops.

These perceptions of North Korean invasion capabilities persisted into the twenty-first century, increasingly in contradiction to the facts of the situation. These facts were that North Korean conventional forces suffered a steady deterioration in the 1990s. The causes were the end of the supply of Soviet weaponry with the collapse of the Soviet Union and North Korea's own precipitous economic collapse. Despite dire warnings from U.S. officials and U.S. military commanders in Korea until 2003, a range of public evidence and reported U.S. and South Korean military estimates and intelligence findings pointed to a serious deterioration of North Korea's conventional arms in the following areas: increasingly obsolete weaponry, a major decline in military industry production, fuel shortages, lack of big-unit training, food shortages even for front-line troops, decline in the physical quality of troops, and deteriorating morale. Testimony from high-level North Korean defectors such as Hwang Jang-yop and Kim Tok-hong and other reports indicated that North Korean leaders were well aware of the deterioration.[47]

An objective conclusion from these factors is that North Korea no longer has the capability to launch a massive invasion across the DMZ into South Korea with any prospect of penetrating defenses north of Seoul. The invasion threat, so strong in the 1970s and 1980s, has become remote. Much is said of the destructive power of North

Korean artillery along the DMZ. However, this artillery is not a mobile, offensive asset and does not compensate for the deterioration of offensive assets such as tanks, infantry, and strike aircraft. The same is true of WMDs. North Korea's option to use WMDs in an invasion has become correspondingly remote as conventional capabilities have declined. WMDs cannot maintain this threat in the face of conventional force deterioration. In short, this element of WMD threat has declined progressively despite the strengthening of North Korea's WMD arsenals.

Another North Korean political-strategic objective—deterrence of a U.S. military attack—seemed to gain currency in the late 1990s into the new century. North Korea has charged for decades that the United States was planning to attack. Pyongyang constantly employs this accusation in its propaganda strategy, including its propaganda strategy in dealing with the Bush administration. Nevertheless, North Korean leaders appear to have developed real fear of a U.S. attack. They are aware that the Clinton administration considered a military strike at the North Korean nuclear complex of Yongbyon in 1994. North Korea reacted nervously to the 1999 U.S. unilateral attack on Serbia and even more so to the U.S. attack on Iraq in 2003. There were reports that Kim Jong Il spent the spring and summer of 2003 deep in underground military bunkers.

North Korea now emphasizes deterrence as a motive for its nuclear program. Since 2002, it has claimed openly that it is producing weapons-grade plutonium and has a "nuclear deterrent." This also appears to be a motive in the accelerating program to develop longer-range missiles that could hit targets on U.S. soil. Pyongyang, in fact, may be on the verge of creating a nuclear and missile arsenal sufficient to constitute a genuine deterrence to any U.S. consideration of launching an Iraq-like ground-air attack or a Serbia-like air attack on North Korea. Such a force would have to consist of a sufficient number of nuclear weapons, probably at least eight to ten; missiles capable of reaching at least Guam, Alaska, and Hawaii; and the warheading of nuclear weapons.

Deterrence would appear to constitute a political-strategic objective that is defensive and thus does not constitute the definition of a threat. However, that may not be a totally correct view of North Korea, given its aggressive actions outside its borders for many years. These include involvement in terrorism and proliferation of WMDs to other countries. Today, proliferation of WMDs constitutes an important North Korean political-strategic objective. Since the late 1980s, North Korea has sold missiles and missile technology to Iran, Pakistan, Yemen, Libya, and Syria. It reportedly has provided nuclear technology to Iran and chemical weapons to Iran and Syria. Proliferation of WMDs provides important political-strategic benefits to North Korea. Kim Jong Il is known to spend huge sums of the foreign currency (estimated at $100 million annually) earned from missiles sales for imports of luxury products, which he distributes to a broad swath of the North Korean civilian and military elite. This alleviates the impact of economic deterioration on the elite and thus buys their loyalty. North Korea also uses earnings from WMD sales and proliferation arrangements with other countries to secure components and technology for North Korea's nuclear programs. This was the basis for Pakistan supplying North Korea with HEU components and technology. Moreover, North Korean WMD proliferation also has contributed to destabilization of the Middle East. Iran is the foremost example of this. The intimate North Korean-Iranian military relationship has helped Iran develop long-range missiles that could reach Israel, and Iran now stands on the verge of producing nuclear weapons. If one accepts that North Korean leaders genuinely worry about U.S. military or other coercive actions against them, it then stands to reason that they judge that destabilizing the Middle East and complicating U.S. policies and commitments in that region provide an important strategic gain for North Korea. It appears to be no coincidence that as the United States became bogged down in Iraq in the second half of 2003 into 2004, North Korea became more assertive and defiant of the United States in the Six-Party Talks on the North Korean nuclear issue. Pyongyang's fear of a U.S. unilateral attack obviously receded, and Pyongyang saw a new opportunity for diplomatic advantage.

U.S. officials have stated that they have no evidence that North Korea has proliferated WMDs directly to terrorist groups. As of this writing, there is no evidence of North Korean links with Al Qaeda. However, North Korea has military links with governments and elements within governments that have links to Al Qaeda and other terrorist groups. North Korea has dealt intimately with the Pakistani intelligence services, which contain individuals and groups that support Al Qaeda and the Taliban. Elements of Iran's Revolutionary Guards and intelligence services also reportedly have ties to Al Qaeda. Syria supports an array of terrorist groups. In short, such governments and governmental elements could act as conduits for transferring North Korean WMDs to terrorist groups. North Korea has the kind of WMDs that Al Qaeda reportedly wants. Much speculation of this kind has centered on nuclear weapons and nuclear materials; but Al Qaeda reportedly is interested in securing chemical and biological weapons.

Proliferation of WMDs to either other governments or to terrorist groups appears to be the biggest threat from North Korea to U.S. interests and security—bigger than the threat of a North Korean attack on the United States and/or South Korea. North Korean acquisition of a nuclear deterrent could increase this danger, for a nuclear deterrent likely would breed North Korean confidence in dealing with the United States. If such confidence transforms into overconfidence, Pyongyang might be tempted to expand proliferation of WMDs to other governments or even directly provide WMDs to a terrorist group, especially chemical or biological weapons. Temptation to expand proliferation likely would grow under three conditions: (1) if a buyer offered North Korea a considerable amount of money; (2) if North Korea believed that it had a good prospect of not being discovered as the ultimate source of WMDs in the hands of a terrorist group; and (3) if North Korea had reasonable confidence that the United States would not retaliate militarily—such confidence likely would come from possessing a nuclear arsenal and missile delivery capabilities.

Political-strategic objectives govern North Korean diplomacy toward the United States and other countries. Pyongyang has long employed military threats as a key intimidation tactic in its diplomacy. North Korean strategy in the Six-Party Talks of

2003–2004 has contained the threat to develop nuclear weapons and openly display or test them. North Korea's intention is to isolate the United States in the talks, influence the other participating governments (South Korea, China, Japan, and Russia) to withhold support of U.S. proposals and positions and support North Korea's proposals, and thus make it more difficult for the United States to resort to coercive measures, such as economic sanctions and interdiction of North Korean trade, including WMD shipments. On the eve of the U.S. presidential election of 2004, North Korea had achieved considerable success in employing the WMD threat in the Six-Party Talks. The other governments have given little support to the settlement proposal the Bush administration proposed on June 23, 2004, and they seem to follow a stricture that "one should say or do nothing in the Talks that will offend North Korea." This alone appears to provide North Korea ample incentive to continue its priority of WMD development.

Is Elimination of WMDs Possible?

There is no certain answer to this question. However, it is certain that the road to elimination of North Korea's WMDs remains a long, arduous one after more than twelve years of negotiations, agreements, and promises. The current Six-Party Talks on the nuclear issue are stalemated, and the future of those talks does not appear optimistic. The Six-Party Talks also deal only with the nuclear issue, leaving missiles and chemical and biological weapons to some unclear fate.

North Korea's policies during the twelve plus years of diplomacy give no optimism that Pyongyang would give up these weapons. In examining the history of North Korea's actions during the Clinton administration, three things stand out related to the current situation. The first is that in the 1994 Agreed Framework, North Korea was unwilling to disclose its past nuclear activities, particularly reprocessing of plutonium; and it was unwilling to allow an inspections role for the International Atomic Energy Agency (IAEA) that it had agreed to in the 1992 North Korea-IAEA safeguards agreement. Both of those positions remain central to North Korea's negotiating position in the Six-Party Talks today. Second, the Agreed Framework represented a North Korean rejection of dismantlement of its nuclear installations with a clear timetable for the beginning and completion of dismantlement. This also represents North Korea's position today. The recently published book, *Going Critical: The First North Korean Nuclear Crisis*, by former Clinton administration officials (Joel Wit, Daniel Poneman, and former Ambassador Robert Gallucci), shows the striking similarities between North Korea's negotiating position and negotiating tactics in 1993 and 1994 and North Korea's position and tactics in the Six-Party Talks today. The third element of this history that stands out is that, at the very time North Korea signed the Agreed Framework in October 1994, it was cooperating with Pakistan in exchanging North Korean missiles and missile technology for Pakistani uranium enrichment technology—in violation of the Agreed Framework. The North Korea-Pakistan deal dates to at least December 1994 when Pakistan Prime Minister Benazir Bhutto traveled to North Korea. According to Pakistani officials and top North Korean defector, Hwang Jang-yop, the transfer of technology and components was underway fully by 1996–1997. The Clinton administration knew of it by at least late 1998. All of this, of course, was in the heyday of "good" relations between the Clinton administration and North Korea in the aftermath of the Agreed Framework, including a massive amount of U.S. food aid to North Korea.

The reflection of this history in North Korea's negotiating position and negotiating tactics in the Six-Party Talks was pointed out graphically in 2004 in North Korea's reaction to the Bush administration's settlement proposal presented at the talks on June 23, 2004. That proposal emphasized dismantlement of both the plutonium and uranium enrichment (HEU) programs, but it also offered reciprocal benefits to North Korea. During an initial three-month "preparatory period," North Korea would declare its nuclear facilities and materials, freeze their operation, and agree to effective international inspections, including a return of the IAEA. The specific measures of dismantlement also would be negotiated during this period. In return, North Korea would receive heavy oil from Japan and South Korea and a "provisional multilateral security assurance" from the United States and the other participants in the Six-Party Talks. The United States and North Korea would begin bilateral talks over U.S. economic sanctions and North Korea's inclusion on the U.S. list of terrorist-supporting countries. The participants in the talks also would begin a study of North Korea's energy needs. After North Korea completed dismantlement, it would receive a permanent security guarantee, and permanent solutions to its energy problems would be undertaken.

The Bush administration's proposal needed more detail, and some observers questioned whether the three-month "preparatory period" was a sufficient amount of time to complete the tasks outlined. Nevertheless, the proposal did contain basic principles necessary for dismantlement of North Korea's nuclear programs. That may be why North Korea embarked on a strategy in July 2004 to "kill" the June 23 proposal as a basis for future negotiations. Beginning with a North Korean Foreign Ministry statement of July 24, 2004, labeling it a "sham," North Korean propaganda organs launched an assault on the U.S. proposal. North Korea rejected negotiations over the U.S. proposal. By mid-August, North Korea was rejecting proposals to hold a new round of Six-Party Talks before the U.S. presidential election of November 2, 2004.[48]

Most analysis at the time stressed a North Korean intention to wait until the results of the U.S. presidential election were known. However, in seeking to kill the June 23 proposal as a basis for negotiations, Pyongyang also was seeking to advance its core proposal at the Six-Party Talks, described by North Korea as "reward for freeze." In denouncing the United States after July 24, 2002, North Korea repeatedly demanded that the United States and other participants to the Six-Party Talks accept a settlement based on a nuclear freeze. The freeze proposal would apply to the plutonium installations, but it did not address the 8,000 nuclear fuel rods that the North had removed from monitored storage in January 2003 or any plutonium and/or atomic bombs produced from the fuel rods. The reward-for-freeze proposal also omitted the HEU program, whose existence North Korea had vociferously denied since the summer of 2003. Verification would be a limited verification at best and would not include the IAEA. U.S. and Japanese concessions and benefits, the "reward," would be extensive, including a total security guarantee, removal of North Korea from the U.S. terrorist list, supply of electricity, several billion dollars in "compensation" from Japan, restoration of shipments of heavy oil, and an end to U.S. economic sanctions and U.S. interference in North Korea's economic relations with other countries (including missile sales). The reward-for-freeze proposal left dismantlement as a vague goal absent any timetable.

The only logical conclusion from this is that North Korea seeks a revised Agreed Framework from the Six-Party Talks. Its reward-for-freeze proposal would establish a nuclear freeze more limited than the freeze under the Agreed Framework. It demands more U.S. concessions and benefits than provided in the Agreed Framework. And again, the similarities between North Korea's position and even tactics in the Six-Party Talks and the diplomacy of 1993–1994 are striking.

Any progress toward elimination of North Korea's nuclear program would require moving North Korea off its negotiating position and tactics and gaining an ascendant position for U.S. proposals in a negotiating agenda. A first step would be to overwhelm North Korea with details in any U.S. settlement proposal—details regarding the dismantlement process, verification and inspection, and U.S. and allied reciprocal measures. This would create new difficulties for North Korea in any future kill strategy. A second step would be to secure support from the other participants in the Six-Party Talks for any detailed, comprehensive U.S. proposal and a willingness of these governments to pressure North Korea strongly to accept it as a basis for negotiations. This may not be easy. China, Russia, and South Korea offered no positive statements in support of the U.S. June 23 proposal despite earlier urgings that the Bush administration offer a proposal and despite the fact that the June 23 proposal was modeled after a proposal South Korea offered at the February 2004 Six-Party Talks. North Korea's kill strategy appeared to be based on Pyongyang's recognition in July 2004 that the other participating governments were not endorsing the June 23 proposal. Even after North Korea had put the kill strategy fully into effect, Beijing, Seoul, and Moscow issued no specific criticisms of North Korean behavior or its reward-for-freeze proposal. In late October 2004, the Chinese and South Korean foreign ministers publicly criticized U.S. diplomacy in the presence of the visiting U.S. Secretary of State, Colin Powell. Besides North Korea's commitment to a settlement based on a freeze rather than dismantlement, the United States also faces a fundamental obstacle in the apparent views of these governments that favor a return to a revised Agreed Framework as a settlement of the nuclear issue. Thus, a new or revised U.S. proposal likely will not be sufficient. It would have to be linked with strong U.S. diplomacy toward these governments, including pressure, and an effective propaganda campaign aimed at opinion in these countries in order to move them toward the U.S. position.

An effective propaganda campaign is a third and vital task for the United States. North Korea has waged an effective propaganda strategy in its Six-Party diplomacy. The Bush administration has had no defined propaganda strategy that would pressure

North Korea and influence opinion in the other participating countries in the Six-Party Talks. One sees little effort in U.S. "public diplomacy" to tear down the credibility of North Korea's reward-for-freeze proposal. The Bush administration had no follow-up strategy to advance and promote its proposal of June 23, 2004, even in the face of Pyongyang's kill strategy. Unless U.S. policy makers understand the peculiarly important role of propaganda in any diplomacy with North Korea, the United States will continue to suffer setbacks, as the Six-Party Talks have shown dramatically.

A fourth task for the United States is to produce more convincing evidence of North Korea's HEU program. This is necessary to strengthen U.S. negotiating proposals and also to counter North Korea's denial strategy regarding the HEU program, which Pyongyang instituted in its propaganda campaign after the August 2003 Six-Party meeting. The administration has tried to counter the denial strategy, first with its claim that North Korea admitted to the HEU program during Assistant Secretary of State James Kelly's visit to Pyongyang in October 2002, and second with the reported "confession" of A. Q. Khan, Pakistan's nuclear czar who dealt directly with North Korea. However, the dispute over the contents of the Kelly visit have constituted a U.S.-North Korean "he said–she said" argument. A. Q. Khan's so-called confession is only a reported confession, based on secondhand sources. U.S. intelligence agencies reportedly have considerable evidence of North Korean procurements or attempted procurements in a number of countries of materials and components that would be used in an HEU program. Many of these apparently are in the form of commercial and bank documents. It is baffling why the Bush administration did not publicize this evidence, especially after Chinese, Russian, and even South Korean officials voiced skepticism that an HEU program exists.

In conclusion, the road ahead is a long, arduous one. But the United States could do better to advance the prospects of a settlement, or at least bring the issue to a point of decision.

Notes

The views expressed are those of the author and do not necessarily represent the views of the Congressional Research Service.

1. Sergey Agafonov, "A Total of 160 Russian Nuclear Scientists and Missilemen Helped North Korea to Create a Nuclear Bomb," *Izvestia*, January 27, 1994, 1. Akira Kato, "North Korea Already Has Nuclear Weapons—Classified Document of the Russian Defense Ministry Obtained," *Shukan Bunshun* (Tokyo), January 27, 1994, 50–53. The Defense Ministry's report reportedly was titled "The Russian Federation's Basic Military and Political Concept on the Current Military Situation in the Asian and Pacific Region."

2. Akira Kato, "North Korea Already Has Nuclear Weapons—Classified Document of the Russian Defense Ministry Obtained," *Shukan Bunshun* (Tokyo), January 27, 1994, 50–53.

3. Park Chae-pom, "Defense Ministry Published Book on Nuclear Issue," *Seoul Sinmun*, October 24, 1994, 5. Yonhap News Agency (Seoul) report, October 17, 2002.

4. "KGB Document Reports DPRK Completed Nuclear-Bomb Development," *Argumenty i Fakty* (Moscow), March 1992, p. 8.

5. Akira Kato, "Russia's Confidential Documents on North Korea's Possession of Nuclear Weapons," *Bungei Shunju* (Tokyo), December 2002, 146–156.

6. Wit, Poneman, and Gallucci, *Going Critical*, 34.

7. Akira Kato, "Russia's Confidential Documents on North Korea's Possession of Nuclear Weapons," *Bungei Shunju* (Tokyo), December 2002, 146–156.

8. Stephen Engelberg and Michael R. Gordon, "Intelligence Study Says North Korea Has Nuclear Bomb," *New York Times*, December 26, 1993.

9. *North Korea: Status Report on Nuclear Program, Humanitarian Issues, and Economic Reforms*, A Staff Trip Report to the Committee on Foreign Relations, United States Senate. February 2004, 7.

10. The NBC News report cited "one prominent government intelligence agency" as the source of the information.

11. Yu Min, "Russian Report Claims DPRK Will Not Give Up Nuclear Program," *Seoul Sinmun*, January 5, 1996, 2.

12. David E. Sanger, "North Korea's Bomb: Untested But Ready, C.I.A. Concludes," *New York Times*, November 9, 2003, 4.

13. Yonhap News Agency report, April 21, 1994.

14. "U.S. Spies Convinced on Korean Bomb," 9.

15. Jim Wolf, "CIA Says North Korea Already Has 'Validated' Nuke," Reuters News Agency report, November 7, 2003.

16. "KGB Document Reports DPRK Completed Nuclear-Bomb Development," *Argumenty i Fakty* (Moscow), March 1992, 8.

17. Akira Kato, "Russia's Confidential Documents on North Korea's Possession of Nuclear Weapons," *Bungei Shunju* (Tokyo), December 2002, 146–156.

18. Margaret Shapiro, "1990 KGB Document Concluded North Korea Had 'Nuclear Device,'" *Washington Post*, June 25, 1994, A17.

19. Akira Kato, "North Korea Already Has Nuclear Weapons—Classified Document of the Russian Defense Ministry Obtained," *Shukan Bunshun*, January 27, 1994, 50–53.

20. Agence France Presse report, February 14, 1994.

21. Yonhap News Agency report, January 15, 1994.

22. Lee Keumhyun, "North Korea Has Five Nuclear Warheads, No Delivery System, Defector Says," *Washington Post*, July 28, 1994, A25.

23. Glenn Kessler, "North Korea Nuclear Estimate to Rise," *Washington Post*, April 28, 2004, A1. David E. Sanger, "Visitors See North Korea Nuclear Capacity," *New York Times*, January 11, 2004, 9.

24. David E. Sanger, "Bush Lauds China Leader as 'Partner' in Diplomacy," *New York Times*, December 10, 2003, A6.

25. Yutaka Ishiguro, Ikuko Higuchi, and Junichi Toyoura, "North Korea's Nuclear Threat Growing, Analysts Say," *The Daily Yomiuri*, June 21, 2003.

26. Akira Kato, "North Korea Already Has Nuclear Weapons—Classified Document of the Russian Defense Ministry Obtained," *Shukan Bunshun*, January 27, 1994, 50–53.

27. John J. Fialka, "Check of North Korea Nuclear Sites Won't Provide Comfort Clinton Wants," *Wall Street Journal*, January 31, 1994, A14.

28. Kyodo News Service report, June 20, 2003. "Japan Yet to Confirm DPRK Has Built Nuclear Warheads Small Enough for Missiles," *Mainichi Daily News*, June 20, 2003.

29. Sonny Efron, "North Korea Working on Missile Accuracy," *Los Angeles Times*, September 12, 2003, 2.

30. Ivan Shomov, "'Chuche' Rubric: Kim Il-song's Regime Increases Penetration Into Russia," *Segodnya* (Moscow), June 16, 1994, 1.

31. Memorandum by Rinn-Sup Shinn of the Congressional Research Service, May 1, 1992. Chuplin's assertions were also reported by *Chungang Ilbo* (Seoul), April 25, 1992.

32. Agence France Presse (Hong Kong) report, April 16, 1999.

33. Kim Min-sok "KIDA Worries About North Korea's Import of Nuclear Materials," *Joongang Ilbo,* May 4, 1999.

34. Bill Gertz, "Pyongyang Working to Make Fuel for Nukes," *Washington Times,* March 11, 1999, A1. Presidential Determination no. 2000–15 of February 24, 2000, *Federal Register,* March 1, 2000, 10931.

35. The two CIA reports were cited in Walter Pincus, "North Korea's Nuclear Plans Were No Secret," *Washington Post,* February 1, 2003, A1.

36. Barbara Slavin and John Diamond, "North Korean Nuclear Efforts Looking Less Threatening," *USA Today,* November 5, 2003, 18.

37. Danny Gittings, "Battling the Bribers," *Asian Wall Street Journal,* October 29, 2002, A11. "U.S. Sees Korean Nuclear Threat," 10.

38. Jim Hoagland, "Nuclear Deceit," *Washington Post,* November 10, 2002, B7.

39. FBIS (Foreign Broadcast Information Service) Report, March 10, 2004.

40. David E. Sanger, "U.S. Widens View of Pakistan Link to Korean Arms," *New York Times,* March 14, 2004, A1.

41. Glenn Kessler, "China Not Convinced of North Korean Uranium Effort," *Washington Post,* January 7, 2004, 16; Bill Gertz, "North Korea Can Build Nukes Right Now," *Washington Times,* November 22, 2002, A1; Slavin and Diamond, "North Korean Nuclear Efforts Looking Less Threatening," *USA Today,* November 5, 2003, 18.

42. Kim Kyoung-soo, "North Korea's CB Weapons Threat," 78; Park Tong-sam, "How Far Has the DPRK's Development of Strategic Weapons Come?" *Seoul Pukhan,* January 1999, 62–71. Park Tong-sam was with the South Korean Government's Agency for Defense Development.

43. Yun, "Long-range Missiles," 121–148.

44. Yu Yong-son, "North Korea Has Deployed Intermediate Range Ballistic Missiles," *Choson Ilbo,* July 7, 2004.

45. Feickert, *North Korean Ballistic Missile Threat,* 5–6.

46. Larry A. Niksch, "Sparring over North Korea: The Clinton Administration and Its Critics," presented at Workshop on North Korea After the Perry Report, sponsored by the Gaston Sigur Center for Asian Studies, George Washington University, March 3–4, 2000.

47. For a detailed analysis of North Korean conventional force deterioration, see Larry Niksch, "The Role of U.S. Troops in Korea," paper presented at the conference on U.S.–Korea Alliance: Continuity and Change sponsored by the International Council on Korean Studies and Institute 21 of *Dong-A Ilbo Daily,* August 22–24, 2003.

48. Larry A. Niksch, "North Korea's Kill Strategy Toward the U.S. June 23 Proposal: How It Happened and Why It Is Important," *PacNet,* Pacific Forum–CSIS, September 10, 2004.

6

North Korea's Economic Crisis, Reforms, and Policy Implications

Dick K. Nanto

The Democratic People's Republic of Korea faces a dilemma as its economy stagnates. The end of the Cold War negated its value as a surrogate fighter for the former Soviet Union and China and as a standard bearer for the international proletarian revolution. The country's leaders in Pyongyang have only limited options remaining as they have placed their nuclear weapons program on the bargaining table in exchange for economic assistance, security assurance, and normalization of relations with the United States, Japan, and South Korea.

The worst of North Korea's economic crisis seems to have passed, but the economy is still heavily dependent on foreign assistance to stave off starvation among a sizable proportion of its people. With just one bad harvest, another severe food crisis could ensue. About 40 percent of the population still suffers from malnutrition. Currently, Pyongyang's reforms along with better weather and steady supplies of food aid are enabling the country to bridge its shortfall between food production and basic human needs. However, donor fatigue and competing humanitarian needs in Africa and elsewhere are depressing current donation levels.

World interest in the moribund North Korea economy goes beyond the leverage that economic assistance provides in the current negotiations. The DPRK economy provides the financial and industrial resources for Pyongyang to develop its military, constitutes an important "push factor" for refugees seeking to flee the country, creates pressures for the country to trade in arms and illegal drugs, is tied to Pyongyang's program to develop nuclear energy and bombs, and creates instability that ultimately affects the economy of South Korea. The North Korean threat to sell nuclear weapons material is driven in part by its need to generate export earnings to pay for imports. The North's dismal economic conditions also foster forces of discontent that potentially could turn against the ruling regime of Kim Jong Il—especially if knowledge of the luxurious lifestyle of regime leaders spreads or if the poor economic performance hurts even Pyongyang's elite. The North Korean economy also is a target of various economic sanctions.

Information on the DPRK's economy is scanty and suspect. The closed nature of the country and the lack of a comprehensive data-gathering structure using modern economic concepts and a systematic reporting mechanism make quantitative assessments difficult. Still, sufficient information is available to provide a picture of North Korea that is clear enough to address different policy paths.

Overview of the DPRK Economy

The North Korean economy is one of the world's most isolated and bleak.[1] It was completely bypassed by the "economic miracles" of the past quarter century that brought modern economic growth and industrialization to South Korea, Taiwan, Singapore, and Hong Kong, as well as rapid growth and trade liberalization to China, Thailand, Malaysia, and other countries of Asia. The "Stalinist" North Korean economy can be characterized by state ownership of means of production, centralized economic planning and command, and an emphasis on military development. The economic system is designed to be self-reliant and closed. The irony of the situation is that the more closed the economy is, the poorer its performance and the more dependent the country becomes on the outside world just to survive.

Pyongyang has embarked on a series of reforms that may ease the economic pressures over the long term. In the near term, however, major portions of the North Korean population are surviving primarily through transfusions of food and other economic assistance from abroad.

During the 1990s, the inefficiencies of North Korea's centrally planned economy, especially its promotion of state-owned heavy industries, along with high military spending—as much as 30 percent of the GDP—joined with drought and floods to push the economy into crisis. In addition, the collapse of the Soviet Union meant the loss of Russian aid, export markets, and cheap oil. Annual trade with the former Soviet Union dropped from as much as $3 billion to the current $45 million.[2] This added to disastrous domestic economic conditions in North Korea. Food has been so scarce that North Korean youth are shorter than those in other East Asian nations.[3] Since 1998, the military reportedly has had to lower its minimum height requirement in order to garner sufficient new recruits. Life expectancy has been contracting. It has only been with the help of the United Nations World Food Program (WFP)—which has been feeding more than a quarter of North Korea's 22 million people—that chronic malnutrition has fallen from 62 percent in 1998 to about 42 percent in 2003, while the proportion of underweight children has dropped from 61 to 21 percent.[4]

The DPRK's gross national product in 2003 in purchasing power parity prices (PPP)—prices adjusted to international levels—has been estimated at $22.85 billion. This amounts to national income of about $1,000 per capita in PPP values or roughly the same level as that of Tajikistan, Rwanda, or Kenya and considerably lower than that of China ($3,920), Indonesia ($2,830), or Mongolia ($1,760), and dramatically lower than South Korea's $17,300 in PPP values or $8,910 at market prices.[5] A remarkable fact is that in the mid-

Figure 6.1 **Growth in Real GDP in the DPRK, 1990–2003**

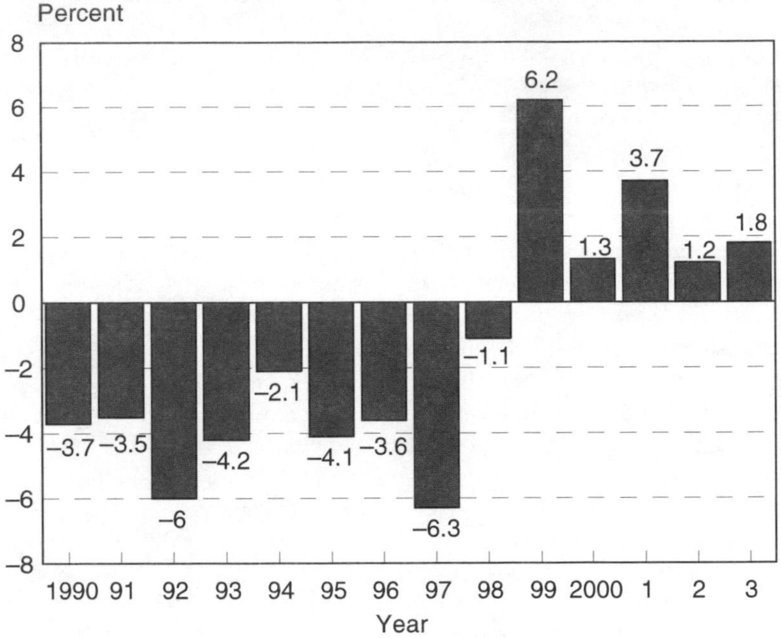

Percent

Source: Bank of Korea.

1970s, living standards were higher in North Korea than in China. Now, North Korea is far behind its rapidly growing neighbor to the west.

As shown in Figure 6.1, growth in estimated real gross domestic product (GDP) in the DPRK was negative for most of the 1990s before beginning to recover in 1999. In 2003, growth was just 1.8 percent, up slightly from 1.2 percent in 2002. In essence, the economy is expanding again but still is below its level in 1990. In 1990, per capita gross national income was estimated at $1,142. It dropped to $573 by 1998 but recovered moderately to $818 in 2003. Agricultural production is back at the 1992 level primarily because of better weather and imports of fertilizer from South Korea.

In this land of scarcity, consumer necessities have been rationed and used to reward party loyalists. Under Pyongyang's economic reforms, the government appears to be phasing out this system, but according to South Korean observers, North Korea classifies its citizens into three ranks and fifty-one categories based on their ideological orientation. The categories are then used to allocate rations for daily necessities, jobs, and housing.[6] According to the UN World Food Program, almost 70 percent of the population is still dependent on cereal distributions through the central Public Distribution System. In 2003, these rations amounted to only 250–380 grams per day or about half of the minimum daily energy requirements. Rural households have been able to supplement the meager rations by rearing livestock, growing gardens, and collecting wild foods, but urban families, particularly those in the inactive industrial zones of the north and northeast, have been the most deprived. (The WFP operates in 161 of 203 counties and districts in the DPRK covering about 85 percent of the civilian population. The WFP allows its food to be distributed only in those counties where monitoring is permitted.)[7]

The elite in North Korean society (party cadres who are leaders in the military and bureaucracy) have enjoyed privileges far above the reach of the average citizen. While starvation haunts the provinces, many of the privileged class live in Pyongyang (where provincial North Koreans cannot enter without special permission); some drive foreign cars, acquire imported home appliances, reside in apartments on a lower floor (so they do not have to climb too many stairs when the electricity is out), and buy imported food, medicines, and toiletries at special hard currency stores.[8] The elite have a strong vested interest in maintaining the current economic system, despite its problems. Their incomes originate from the treasury, from foreign investors (mostly South Korean), from remittances from ethnic Koreans in Japan (although these have been reduced), and from the country's shadowy trade in everything from missile technology to fake banknotes and narcotics.[9]

Economic Philosophy

The Pyongyang regime has pursued a policy of self-sufficiency and isolation from the world economy that they call *juche* or self-reliance. Juche goes beyond economics as it has been used since the 1950s to perpetuate power by the central government and to build an aura of the supernatural around the their supreme leaders Kim—both father and son.[10] The economic implications of juche have minimized international trade relations, discouraged foreign direct investment, and fostered what it considers to be core industries—mostly heavy manufacturing. While promoting such heavy industry, for most of the post–Korean War period, Pyongyang has emphasized the parallel development of military strength.

Current head of state, Kim Jong Il, however, has given the highest priority to the military. This places the army ahead of the working class for the first time in the history of North Korea's so-called revolutionary movement.[11] Under Kim Il Sung (Kim Jong Il's father), the juche ideology placed equal emphasis on political independence, self-defense, and economic self-support capabilities. Kim Jong Il, however, insists that North Korea can be a "country strong in ideology and economy" only when its military is strong.[12] The country, therefore, has been developing its industries within the context of a military-industrial complex with strong links between heavy industry and munitions production. Some of North Korea's munitions industries (manufacturing dual-use products) are virtually indistinguishable from those supplying civilians.[13]

When juche is combined with central planning, a command economy, and government ownership of the means of production, economic decisions that in a market economy would be made by private business and farmers have to go through a few elite in Pyongyang. These decision makers may or may not understand advances in agronomy or manufacturing and tend to be motivated by noneconomic factors, such as maintaining political power or avoiding blame for initiatives gone awry. Farming methods based partly on crop rotation or new varieties of rice, for example, may be viewed as too risky.[14] Foreign investment also is hindered partly because the regime abhors being "exploited" by capitalists who seek to make profits on their business ventures in the DPRK and partly because of their deep-seated mistrust of Westerners, Japanese, and South Koreans.

As with other isolationist economies in the contemporary world of globalization and interlinked societies, North Korea has been plagued with the negative effects of its attempts at self-sufficiency: technological obsolescence, uncompetitive exports, economic privation, and lack of foreign exchange. These difficulties, together with advice from China and the demise of the Stalinist economy in Russia, have compelled the Pyongyang regime to introduce some economic reforms, or what they refer to as "adjustments." To a large extent, they are adopting the Chinese sequencing with economic reforms preceding any political reforms while eschewing the Russian model of political reform preceding and concurrent with economic reforms.

Industrial Sectors

North Korea's industrial sectors are shifting rapidly. At the end of World War II, the DPRK represented the industrialized part of the Korean peninsula. Under Japanese colonialism, heavy industry, waterpower, and manufacturing were concentrated in the North, contrasted with the more agrarian South. Even in 1990, 49 percent of the North Korean economy was in mining, manufacturing, and construction, while 23 percent was in services (including government and utilities), and 27 percent in agriculture. In recent years, however, the DPRK's nonmilitary industries have almost collapsed. By 1997, mining, manufacturing, and construction had dropped from 49 percent to 32 percent of the economy but in 2003 had risen somewhat to 36 percent. In 2003, services had risen to 37 percent of the economy, while agriculture remained fairly constant at 27 percent (see Figure 6.2).

The drop in the share of manufacturing in GDP has come about largely because of the rapid decline in production from factories, not because of large absolute increases in services or agricultural production. Reports indicate that factories have been running at about 30 percent of their capacity. The economy lacks food for workers and raw materials, energy, and foreign currency to buy new equipment and import inputs into the manufacturing process.[15] Much industrial capital stock is nearly beyond repair as a result of years of underinvestment and shortages of spare parts. Recently, the government has emphasized earning hard currency, developing information technology, addressing power shortages, and attracting foreign aid, but it appears unwilling to do so in any way that jeopardizes its control. It has initiated some market-oriented reforms and allowed some liberalization that might bring new capital and production methods into its factories, but it is a long way from the reforms that have occurred in

Figure 6.2 **North Korea's Industrial Structure**

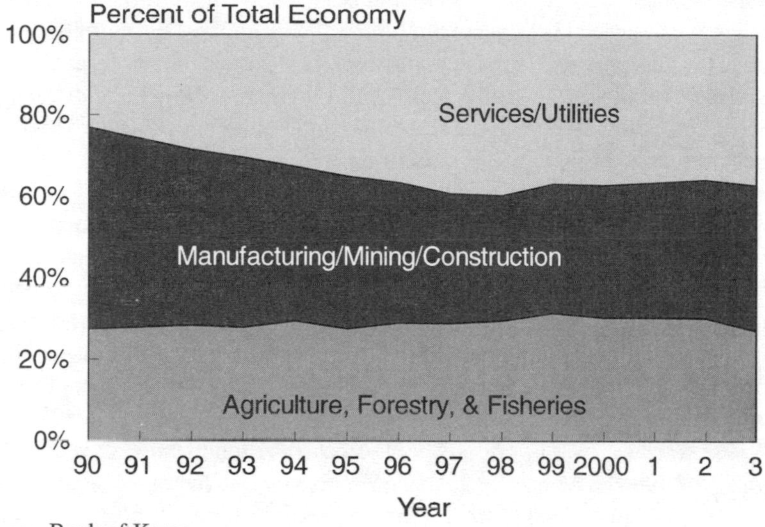

Source: Bank of Korea.

other socialist countries. As in other centrally planned economies, the most advanced industries in North Korea are associated with its military.

Pyongyang has been attempting to remedy its shortfall in electricity by purchasing surplus hydropower equipment from Russia and by repairing and upgrading its existing thermoelectric power stations built in Pyongyang and Pukchang through Soviet assistance in the 1950s. This resulted in increases in electricity production by 29 percent in 2002 and 21 percent in 2003. Still, at this rate, it will take until 2008 for the country to recover its 1989 production level.[16]

The DPRK's agricultural sector faces particularly dire straits. The economy depends heavily on collective farms that have been devastated by drought, lack of fertilizers and other inputs, antiquated farming methods, and a lack of incentives for private production. The UN WFP in cooperation with UNICEF cooperates with the DPRK government in local production of five different types of food for distribution. These include corn soya blend, rice milk blend, cereal milk blend, biscuits, and fortified noodles. The number of such factories has grown from one in 1999 to eighteen in 2003.[17] A report in 2003 from North Korea indicates that the situation along the border with China has deteriorated to the point that rates of starvation, disease, and even suicide were reaching a crisis point.[18] The situation would be worse without international food and other humanitarian aid.

Economic Reforms

On July 1, 2002, Pyongyang announced a series of economic reforms that some surmise may mark the beginning of the end of the Stalinist controls over the economy and the onset of more use of the market mechanism to make economic decisions, particularly production and consumer purchases. Although the government has dubbed the reforms as an "economic adjustment policy,"[19] the actions appear to be a desperate attempt to revive the moribund economy, similar to what was done in China. The reforms also dovetail with North Korea's "military-first" policy. As Kim Jong Il has given first priority to the military, the rest of the population has suffered. This, in turn, has raised pressures on Pyongyang to reform its economic system.

The adjustments feature an end to the rationing system for daily commodities (except for food), a huge increase in prices of essentials and in wages, a major devaluation of the currency (official exchange rate), abolishment of the foreign exchange coupon system, increased autonomy of enterprises, authorization to establish markets and other trading centers, and a limited opening of the economy to foreign investment. Prices still remain under centralized control but at levels closer to those existing in peasant (free) markets. North Korea has not abandoned the socialist planned economy, but it has been compelled to reform certain aspects of it.

Under the reforms, overall prices were increased by ten to twenty times. Government prices for many essential items, however, rose by much more. The price for rice rose by 550 times, for corn 471 times, for diesel oil 38 times, and for electricity 60 times. Wages also were raised but not enough to keep pace with skyrocketing consumer prices. Wages rose by eighteen times for laborers and twenty times for managers. Not all workers, however, received the promised wage increases. The price and wage reforms, moreover, caused households to face rampant consumer inflation, and many people ended up worse off financially than before the reforms.

In North Korean factories, reforms include greater control over prices, procurement, wages, and some incentives to increase profits in order to distribute them based on individual performance. The regime also wants to implement reforms in agriculture similar to those adopted in China (along the lines of the rural household contract system). In the mid-1990s, North Korea's agricultural work squads had already been reduced in size. Now they are moving toward family-oriented operations with farmers allowed to retain more of any production exceeding official targets.

Although small farmers' markets have long existed in North Korea, Pyongyang did not legalize such farmers' markets until June 2003. This followed the formal recognition of commercial transactions between individuals and the 1998 revision to the constitution that allowed individuals to keep profits earned through legitimate economic activities.[20] Now free markets and shopping centers that use currency, not ration coupons, are spreading. About three hundred such markets have opened with more than forty in Pyongyang alone. The Pyongyang Central Market is so crowded that a new, three-story supermarket had to be built. The Pyongyang No. 1 Department Store is now under Chinese management. Pyongyang's Tongil market with its lines of covered stalls stocked with items such as fruit, watches, foreign liquor, clothes, Chinese-made television sets, and beer from Singapore also is bustling with sellers and consumers, reminiscent of those in other Asian countries.[21]

Pyongyang's economic reforms are gradually spreading to agriculture. The farmer's markets and adjusted prices have provided real production incentives in agriculture. In 2003, food production reached 4.13 million tons—its highest level in recent years. In 2003, North Korea experimented with "information agriculture" on three farms in South Hwanghae province. Farmers used computers to survey the soil, choose crops, and determine types and quantities of fertilizers. On experimental plots, yields increased by 80 percent without use of chemical fertilizers. Similar experiments were tried in 2004 on one farm in each of the provinces across the country. If they are successful, the methods are to spread to the entire country. The hope—probably unrealistic—is that the economy can achieve self-sufficiency in food by 2008.[22]

The reforms also included opening certain areas to foreign investment. Under the Joint-Operation Act of 1984, over the next decade to 1994, there were 148 cases of foreign investment worth about $200 million into North Korea. Of these cases, 131 were from pro-North Korean residents of Japan. In 1991, Pyongyang opened the Rajin-Sonbong free trade zone and established the Foreigner Investment Act. By 1997, some eighty investments had totaled $1.4 million. Other areas receiving foreign investment include Nampo, Pyongyang, Kosung-gun, Shimpo, Wonsan, and Mt. Kumkang (a tourist destination). Foreign companies in North Korea include fifty South Korean companies including Hyundai, Daewoo, Tacchang, LG Electronics, Haeju, and G-Hanshin; Europe's DHL and ING Bank; Japan's Hohwa, Saga, and New Future Ltd. companies; Taiwan's JIAGE Ltd.; and the China Shimyang National Machinery Facility Sales Agency Corporation.[23] The UN Development Programme is promoting the Tumen River Valley Development Project that aims to develop business based on transit, tourism, and commissioned processing trade.[24]

Since 2000, the DPRK has attempted to emulate China's highly successful special economic zones (SEZs) (also referred to as free trade zones) by establishing the Sinuiju SEZ on the northwestern border with China along with the Kaesong SEZ along the border with South Korea. The development of the Sinuiju SEZ has been stymied because of Beijing's arrest of Chinese entrepreneur Yang Bin who was to head the project.

The Kaesong SEZ, however, is showing promise. It is being managed by Hyundai Asan and the Korea Land Corporation—a company especially created for this purpose. Located just across the demilitarized zone forty-three miles north of Seoul on the route to Pyongyang, this 810-acre SEZ aims to attract South Korean companies—particularly small and medium-sized enterprises—although the initial selection of companies for the pilot site has favored larger companies with arguably more growth potential and sound finances.[25]

Hyundai Asan and the Korea Land Corporation plan to attract about 850 companies and create 220,000 jobs for North Koreans. In 2003, more than three thousand South Korean companies bid for the initial three hundred available slots. The SEZ also should enable ROK industries to escape high South Korean labor costs and operate their labor-intensive manufacturing closer to home than in factories in China or Southeast Asia. For South Koreans, Kaesong has the added advantage of a common Korean language, proximity to Seoul, and no tariffs on the transfer of goods between South and North Korea. This SEZ also complements Seoul's push to become a business hub in Northeast Asia. Combined with the port of Inchon, the low-cost manufacturing base in Kaesong should contribute to the logistical and industrial aspects of this plan.[26] In September 2004, Hyundai Asan began a test operation of shuttle buses to run between Kaesong and Seoul with two round trips per day.[27] On June 30, 2004, a pilot complex at Kaesong was officially completed, and production is scheduled to begin in November.[28]

Pyongyang has been cooperating to facilitate the success of Kaesong by establishing a wage rate of about $57 per month for North Korean labor—about half that of China's $80 to $100 per month and about a tenth the level of wages in the ROK. Land also is relatively cheap at 45,455 won ($39) per square meter.[29] The ultimate success of Kaesong depends partly on the granting of most favored nation (normal trading relations) status by the United States. This would open the way for products originating in North Korea to be imported into the U.S. market at much lower tariff rates.

Some doubts have been expressed about whether or not the SEZs will work to transform the moribund North Korean economy in the same manner that they intensified the forces for reform in China. Much will depend on their success and whether Pyongyang will open the rest of the economy to global economic forces and allow market socialism to spread further to domestic agriculture, services, and industry. In the best case, the SEZs will become a microcosm of the workings of markets and demonstrate to Pyongyang the benefits that can accrue from transfers of technology, increased efficiency, and financial flows as a result of foreign direct investment in the economy. In the worst case, Pyongyang could view the SEZ companies as cattle with mad cow disease that can be temporarily milked of profits while being fed straw and kept corralled to ensure that they do not spread infectious ideas or methods across the SEZ fences. Whether SEZs become enclaves of productivity surrounded by antiquated and arteriosclerotic economic systems or whether they become models for market liberalization throughout the economy will determine to a major extent whether the North Korean economy emerges from the failures of its socialist legacy or remains a dualistic economy where the peasants suffer but the party members party on.

What is clear is that Kim Jong Il and his communist party leaders have not allowed the first round of capitalistic enclaves to flourish. Pyongyang has nearly stifled the experiments in the Najin-Songbong, Kumgangsan, and Sinuiju areas with its excessive restrictions and lengthy and complex approval processes. So far, rather than becoming a model for reform in the rest of the economy, Pyongyang seems to view these islands of globalization more as a means to extract funds from South Korean companies.

The spread of reforms and gradual economic recovery are having a multidimensional effect on the DPRK. First, they are assuring continual support of Kim Jong Il and his current policies. The country has stepped back from the precipice of economic collapse and chaos. Second, the reforms and gradual economic recovery can provide the resources for North Korea to continue its nuclear programs and maintain its heavy military spending. On the other hand, the reforms and economic recovery could be sowing the seeds of a new North Korea. If the forces of globalization penetrate into the DPRK economy, the country is likely to experience higher growth rates, a growing middle class, vested business interests in trade and international economic ties, freer information flows, and, ultimately, domestic pressures for more representative government. At some point, North Korea can emerge from its "Hermit Kingdom" status and rejoin the world with full diplomatic recognition, trade ties, membership in international financial organizations, and no need to engage in shadowy economic endeavors to feed its people. Whether this also creates a nation less dependent on a nuclear program to gain respect and to squeeze the purses of rich nations for economic assistance is yet to be determined.

International Trade

Despite North Korea's isolation and emphasis on juche, it does trade with other countries. The foreign economic sector plays an important role for Pyongyang in that it allows the country to import food, technology, and other merchandise that it is unable to produce in sufficient quantities at home. Because North Korea does not export enough to pay for its imports, it generates a deficit in reported merchandise trade that must be financed by other means. Pyongyang has to find sources of foreign exchange—other than from its overtly traded exports—to pay for the imports. North Korea's involvement in illicit or questionable economic activities, particularly illegal drug trade and sales of military equipment, seems to be an attempt to generate the foreign exchange necessary to fill this trade gap.[30]

Detailed data on the country's external economic relations suffer from reliability problems similar to those associated with the domestic economy. The foreign economic data on actual commercial transactions, however, tend to be the most accurate since they also are reported by trading partner countries and are compiled by the International Monetary Fund and the United Nations. Individual countries, for example, report on their imports from and exports to North Korea. These data, however, differ from North Korea's actual annual numbers because of the time lag in shipping (a product shipped from a country in late December of a year might not be recorded as arriving in North Korea until the following year), costs of freight and insurance (North Korean import data may be on a c.i.f. basis that includes insurance and freight charges that are not included in a country's export data), and differences in data-gathering methods, coverage, and reporting. Detailed and reliable data on trade in military equipment and illegal drugs also are notoriously difficult to obtain and to verify.

Another problem is political. South Korea considers trade with the North as inter-Korean trade, not foreign trade. The trade amounts it reports to the International Monetary Fund for its commercial transactions with the North are considerably lower than the amounts it reports as inter-Korean trade (available from the Korea Trade-Investment Promotion Agency [KOTRA]). The South Korean inter-Korean data also include more detail on nontransactional trade (mostly foreign aid) with North Korea. IMF data also differ somewhat from those reported by the United Nations. This chapter uses a combination of trade totals from the IMF, partner country data from the World Trade Atlas (subscription-based trade data), and intra-Korean trade from South Korea's KOTRA.

Table 6.1

Democratic People's Republic of Korea Merchandise Trade by Selected Trading Partner, 1994–2003 (US$ millions)

DPRK exports	1994	1996	1998	1999	2000	2001	2002	2003
World	1,039	1,201	965	892	995	1,047	1,274	1,330
China	181	69	51	42	37	167	271	395
Japan	328	291	219	203	257	226	234	174
S. Korea	176	182	92	122	152	176	272	289
Russia	44	347	8	7	8	15	10	3
Germany	57	32	24	20	20	21	26	15
DPRK imports	1994	1996	1998	1999	2000	2001	2002	2003
World	1,286	2,055	1,300	1,436	2,047	3,272	2,436	2,160
China	467	497	356	329	451	573	468	628
Japan	171	226	175	146	207	1,067	132	92
S. Korea	18	70	130	212	273	227	370	435
Russia	70	525	56	49	38	57	69	111
Germany	59	33	23	30	52	80	133	68
Balance of trade	−247	−854	−335	−544	−1,052	−2,225	−1,162	−830

Sources: South Korean data from Republic of Korea, KOTRA (Korea Trade-Investment Promotion Agency). Other data from the Organisation for Cooperation and Economic Development, *Direction of Trade Statistics*, Annual 2003 and Quarterly June 2004.
World total = OECD World – OECD Korea + KOTRA Intra-Korean Trade.

The DPRK's policy of juche, its suspicion of foreign countries, and the collapse of its industrial production, have resulted in a minimal level of commercial relations with other nations in the world. As shown in Table 6.1, in 2002 it exported $1,274 million in merchandise exports (up from $1,047 million in 2001) while importing $2,436 million (down from 2001 but up slightly from recent years), for a merchandise trade deficit of $1,162 million. Total exports in 2003 rose slightly to $1,330 million. After exports dropped in 1998, they have recovered considerably in recent years, although they are still quite a bit under their 1990 levels.[31]

North Korea's major trading partners have been China, Japan, South Korea, Russia, Germany, Brazil, India, Thailand, Singapore, and Hong Kong. As shown in Figure 6.3, North Korea's major import sources have been China, Japan, South Korea, Russia, and Germany. Thailand and India are also becoming major suppliers. Major imports by North Korea include machinery, minerals, plant products, and chemical products. In particular, imports of energy materials and foods reflect Pyongyang's attempts to remedy these fundamental shortages. Most recent increases in imports have been fuel imports from China, and food imports from various countries. Trade with Japan has been decreasing, while trade with South Korea has risen considerably.

Major export markets for the DPRK have been Japan and China with South Korea developing as a major market following the easing of relations (see Figure 6.4, p. 130).

Figure 6.3 **DPRK Imports by Major Source, 1994–2003** (in percentage shares)

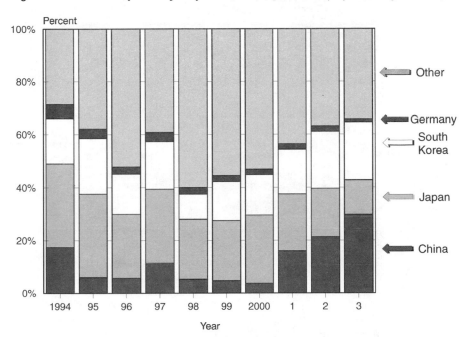

Sources: IMF, Direction of Trade Statistics, (South) Korea Trade-Investment Promotion Agency (KOTRA), and World Trade Atlas.

In Europe, Germany has been North Korea's major trading partner, and in Latin America, Brazil is developing as a market for North Korea's exports. In 2003, exports to Japan declined—due in part to friction over the DPRK's admitted abductions of Japanese citizens. North Korea's major exports include animal products, textiles, machinery, electronic products, and base metals.

A recent development has been North Korea's increase in exports of primary products (such as fish, shellfish, and agro-forest products) as well as mineral products (such as base metallic minerals). Pyongyang has imported aquaculture technology to increase production of cultivated fish and agricultural equipment to increase output of grains and livestock. It also has imported equipment for its coal and mineral mines. Some of this increased output is being sold abroad to generate foreign exchange to fund other imports.[32]

Meanwhile, traditional exports of textiles and electrical appliances have been declining. This reflects North Korea's unstable power supply, lack of raw materials and components imported from abroad, and the need to ship finished goods to China or another third country for final inspection. This diminishing ability of North Korea to provide a reliable manufacturing platform for the least complicated assembly operations does not bode well for the country's future ability to generate the exports necessary to balance its trade accounts. The quickest method of remedying this problem, of

Figure 6.4   **DPRK Exports by Major Market, 1994–2002** (in percentage shares)

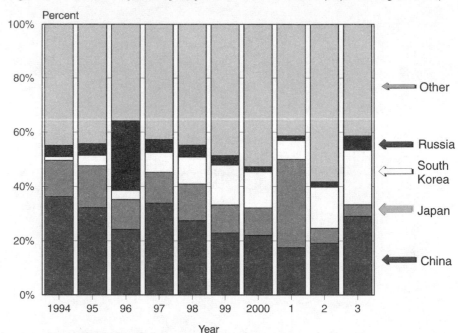

Sources: Data from IMF, Direction of Trade Statistics, World Trade Atlas, and (South) Korea Trade-Investment Promotion Agency (KOTRA).

course, is for trusted overseas manufacturers to establish production bases in the North Korean special economic zones.

Other Sources of Foreign Exchange

North Korea's $1 billion annual merchandise trade deficit implies that Pyongyang must be generating that amount in foreign exchange through some means—either legal or illegal. Legal means include borrowing, foreign investments, foreign aid, remittances from overseas Koreans, selling military equipment not reflected in trade data, and by selling services abroad. Illegal methods include the counterfeiting of hard currency, illegal sales of military equipment or technology, sales of illegal drugs, or by shipping illegal cargo between third countries. The country also can dip into what foreign exchange reserves it has available.

Legal Sources of Funds

North Korea is able to borrow on international capital markets. As of December 2003, the country had outstanding bank debt of $246 million (up from $167 million a year earlier). This is a relatively small amount, only $11 per capita. Of the total, $93 million had a maturity of one year or less, $9 million matured in over two years, and the rest had maturity undisclosed. The debts are owed to banks in Germany ($153 million—up from $50 billion in 2002), Italy ($28 million), France ($8 million), Austria ($5 million), and the United Kingdom ($4 million). Total liabilities to foreign banks increased by $79 million after declining by $86 million in 2002, and rising by $154 million in 2001 and by $7 million in 2000.[33]

International bond issues are not a major source of funds for North Korea. In May 2003, the country issued ten-year bonds—the first since 1950—but since its sovereign securities are not rated by major Western credit rating agencies, the issue has generated little interest on international financial markets and is aimed at domestic investors. Pyongyang claims that a million people have signed up to receive the bonds, but many speculate that the deductions from the salaries of North Korean purchasers in amounts equivalent to four months' wages to buy the bonds are not voluntary.[34]

Although North Korea is not a major recipient of foreign direct investment (FDI) or other foreign funds, in 1997 FDI inflows totaled $307.4 million. Inflows declined to $31 million in 1998, –$15 million in 1999, $5 million in 2000, –$24 million in 2001, and $12 million in 2002. In 2002, the stock of FDI in North Korea totaled $1,034 million.[35] North Korea's special economic zones, however, are attracting more foreign direct investment, but so far the actual inflows appear to have been fairly modest. South Korea's Hyundai Corporation, however, secretly paid North Korea nearly $500 million, partly in money borrowed from the South Korean government just a week before the two nations held a historic summit in June 2000. This was part of an estimated billion dollars or more Hyundai was to pay for exclusive rights to engage in seven major economic projects there.[36]

A major source of funding for imports into the DPRK has been foreign aid or direct government transfers. Both developmental and humanitarian aid and assistance under KEDO (Korean Peninsula Energy Development Organization, created under the 1994 Agreed Framework) to build two light water nuclear reactors and provide heavy fuel oil have enabled imports into North Korea without financing from Pyongyang. North Korea also receives funds in the form of official development assistance (ODA) from aid donor nations and organizations. As shown in Table 6.2, in 1999, the country received net ODA of $207 million in 1999, $78 million in 2000, $128 million in 2001, and $267 million in 2002. Over 2001–2002, the top donors of gross ODA were the United States, the European Commission, Germany, Arab Agencies, and the International Fund for Agricultural Development. South Korean aid to the North is not included in the ODA data.[37]

Since 2000, South Korean government assistance to North Korea has been running at around $80 million ($87.02 million in 2003). South Korean civilian organizations also provided $71 million in assistance to North Korea in 2003.[38] The United States also has provided food and energy aid to North Korea (much of which is not considered to be official development aid). Total U.S. assistance to the DPRK was $287 million in 1999, $139 million in 2000, $178 million in 2001, $173 million in

Table 6.2

North Korea: Total Receipts and Official Development Assistance by Major Source/Donor, 1999–2002 (US$ million)

	Total receipts net				Total ODA net			
	1999	2000	2001	2002	1999	2000	2001	2002
U.S.	146.3	1.6	0.3	131.2	146.3	1.6	0.3	131.2
Germany	−0.3	−2.4	34.1	35.0	2.9	1.5	27.0	33.2
France	0.7	28.4	12.8	−656.4	0.1	1.7	0.3	0.5
Australia	4.7	7.9	4.8	5.3	4.0	7.1	4.5	2.0
Norway	3.9	4.6	7.9	5.5	3.9	3.3	3.5	3.6
Sweden	4.4	3.5	3.4	4.3	4.4	3.5	3.4	4.3
Switzerland	−5.8	2.6	6.1	3.4	2.0	2.6	4.5	3.4
Mult. Agen.	35.6	48.3	68.1	78.1	35.6	48.3	67.2	77.1
of which EC	*16.9*	*25.0*	*40.3*	*61.2*	*16.9*	*25.0*	*40.3*	*61.2*
All donors	**156.6**	**39.9**	**190.9**	**−453.7**	**206.7**	**77.8**	**127.9**	**266.8**

Source: Organisation for Economic Cooperation and Development (OECD), *International Development Statistics*, online database.

Note: Data are from OECD members, multilateral agencies, and twelve other report nations not including South Korea, China, and Russia. Multilateral agencies include the UN, International Fund for Agricultural Development, Arab Agencies, and European Commission. EC = European Commission (excludes flows from EU member nations). Total receipts includes ODA + Other Official Flows + Private Flows.

2002, $27.8 million in 2003, and $26.1 million in 2004. Since 1995, the United States has provided the DPRK with $666.7 million in food aid and $403.7 million in energy assistance to the Korean Peninsula Energy Development Organization in exchange for North Korea's pledge to halt its existing nuclear program.[39] The United States also has paid North Korea to search for remains of American servicemen missing from the Korean War. In 2003, it paid $2.1 million to conduct four searches.[40]

The Organisation for Economic Cooperation and Development (OECD) compiles data on total financial flows to North Korea. These data include Official Development Assistance (foreign aid excluding that from South Korea) plus other official flows (export credits) and private flows (investments, bank and bond lending, and nongovernmental organization grants). As shown in Table 6.2, total net receipts by North Korea were $157 million in 1999, $40 million in 2000, and $191 million in 2001, and −$454 million in 2002. The negative flow was caused by a net outflow (probably a loan repayment) of $656 million to France. Preliminary data for 2003 indicate that the DPRK will again be losing more than it is gaining with total net receipts at −$2,024 million. This implies that Pyongyang is under considerable pressure to bring more outside financial resources into the country.

Another major source of income for certain North Korean families has been in remittances from overseas Koreans, particularly those who live in Japan.[41] Most of the ethnic Koreans in Japan either remained there after World War II or are their descendants. Some had been forcibly brought there to work in coal mines or factories during the fifty-year Japanese occupation of Korea. Currently, of the approximately 650,000 ethnic Koreans who live in Japan, an estimated 56,000 to 90,000 are from the North Korean area, and many are reported to be actively involved in supporting the Pyongyang regime. Ethnic Koreans born in Japan do not automatically receive Japanese citizenship. They work in a variety of businesses, but they face discrimination in Japanese society and are known for operating pachinko (pinball) parlors and other enterprises providing entertainment and nightlife as well as being involved with Japan's *yakuza* or gangsters. Many of these, as well as managers of North Korean-related credit unions, regularly send remittances to relatives or associates in North Korea. One unusual method of smuggling money to North Korea has been to hide 10,000 yen bills (worth roughly $90 each) under expensive melons (individually boxed) being shipped to Kim Jong Il as gifts.[42]

Given the decade of stagnation of the Japanese economy and rising tensions between Japan and North Korea, these remittances have apparently been declining. A 2003 Japanese newspaper report placed the amount at between $200 million and $600 million per year, but that figure could be exaggerated.[43] In testimony before parliament, Japan's finance minister stated that in Japan's fiscal year 2002, $34 million had been sent from Japan to North Korea through financial channels that required reports to the Japanese government.[44] A working estimate would be approximately $100 million per year in such remittances. Anecdotal evidence indicates that considerable amounts of currency from Japan are simply carried by individuals on ships and not reported. More than 1,000 North Korean freight vessels ply between North Korea and Japan each year. Japan, however, has tightened inspections of North Korean ships.

In summary, the DPRK's net total receipts plus remittances, aid and investments from South Korea, and special food and fuel assistance in connection with negotiations over Pyongyang's nuclear program, constitute most of the overt resource inflows that North Korea receives each year over and above its export earnings. These amount to perhaps a half billion dollars per year but can be offset by loan repayments. North Korea must finance the remainder of its trade deficit—which is approaching $1 billion—by other means.

Illegal or Questionable Sources of Funds

The DPRK's other means of generating foreign exchange include exports of military equipment, counterfeiting of currency, and trade in illegal substances. Data on North Korean sales of military equipment abroad are understandably murky, but the country is thought to have sold hundreds of ballistic missiles to Iran, Iraq, Syria, Pakistan, and other nations over the past decade to earn foreign currency.[45] The interdiction by Spain of an unmarked vessel in December 2002 containing North Korean–made parts for twelve to fifteen Scud missiles (valued at about $4 million each) bound for Yemen is one example of such arms sales.[46] In testimony before the House Committee on

International Relations, the Undersecretary of State for Arms Control and International Security pointed out that North Korea possesses Scud and Nodong missiles and is developing the Taepo-Dong 2. He stated that the country is by far the most aggressive proliferator of missiles and related technologies to countries of concern. The sales are one of the North's major sources of hard currency.[47] According to a U.S. military officer quoted in the Japanese press, North Korea exported $580 million worth of ballistic missiles to the Middle East in 2001.[48]

With respect to illegal drug trade, officials from the U.S. military command in Seoul reportedly said that North Korea is earning between $500 million and $1 billion annually from the narcotics trade.[49] North Korea is thought to produce more than forty tons of opium per year, which would make it the world's third-largest opium exporter and sixth-largest heroin exporter. The regime also is accused of trafficking in methamphetamine stimulants. U.S. counternarcotics officials are reported to have said that since 1976, there have been at least fifty arrests or drug seizures involving North Koreans in more than twenty countries. Japanese authorities say that nearly 50 percent of illegal drug imports into Japan come from North Korea.[50] According to the U.S. State Department, although such reports have not been conclusively verified by independent sources, defector statements have been consistent over years and occur in the context of regular narcotics seizures linked to North Korea. The U.S. State Department's *International Narcotics Control Strategy Report* for 2003 states that the quantity of information and quality of many reports "give credence to allegations of state sponsorship of drug production and trafficking that can not be ignored. It appears doubtful that large quantities of illicit narcotics could be produced in and/or trafficked through North Korea without high-level party and/or government involvement, if not state support."[51]

In a blatant incident in May 2003, the Australian navy and special forces commandeered a North Korean ship (*Pong Su*) off the country's southern coast that allegedly was moving 110 pounds of almost pure heroin valued at $50 million. The ship apparently picked up the heroin elsewhere in Asia and took a circuitous route to Australia.[52]

Allegations also have been made that North Korea engages in counterfeiting operations, particularly of US$100 notes. It is believed that the country earns $15 million to $20 million per year in counterfeiting.[53]

In the opinion of a North Korean expert at Seoul's Sejong Institute, "North Korea's economy had received a death sentence long ago, but it keeps afloat thanks to international aid and the country's trading in weapons and illicit goods."[54]

DPRK's Foreign Economic Relations

The United States, China, South Korea, Japan, and Russia each have different objectives in the current negotiations and standoff with the DPRK. On the economic front, each country is pursuing these objectives through a different mix of the above-mentioned carrots and sticks.

United States

The United States has taken the harshest policies with respect to the DPRK. U.S. policies include sanctions prohibiting certain trade with the North Korean economy, a ban on nonhumanitarian aid, prohibition on membership by the DPRK in international financial organizations (particularly the Asian Development Bank), and nondiplomatic recognition. North Korea does not have most favored nation trade status. This means that North Korean exports are subject to the relatively high tariffs existing before World War II in the United States. For example, women's blouses of wool or cotton carry a 90 percent import duty if from North Korea but 9 to 10 percent duty if from South Korea or most other nations without free trade agreements with the United States.

The United States, moreover, maintains various economic sanctions on North Korea because it is on the U.S. State Department list of state supporters of international terrorism, is considered a threat to national security, is a communist state, and it proliferates weapons of mass destruction. Travel to and trade with North Korea in other than certain dual-use goods are allowed if overarching requirements are met, and there are no restrictions on the amount of money Americans may spend in the DPRK. The sanctions related to the proliferation of weapons of mass destruction generally target the offending entities. North Korean assets in the United States frozen prior to June 19, 2000, remain frozen. North Korea is on the most restricted list of countries for U.S. exports (Country Group E) of items such as computers, software, national security-controlled items, items on the Commerce Control List, and service or repair of such items. Economic sanctions on North Korea, however, are essentially unilateral by the United States. Most other nations allow relatively free trade in nonsensitive goods with the DPRK.

The United States uses trade with and aid to North Korea as leverage and to send a message of disapproval for various activities by Pyongyang. In 2004, President George W. Bush signed the North Korean Human Rights Act (P.L. 108–333). Among other provisions, the act conditioned significant increases in U.S. support for humanitarian assistance upon substantial improvement in transparency, monitoring, and access to vulnerable populations throughout North Korea. The act also made nonhumanitarian assistance contingent upon North Korea's substantial progress in respecting basic human rights of its people, fully disclosing information on Japanese abductees, reforming North Korean prison and labor camps, and decriminalizing political expression and activity.

China

China is a long-time supporter of Pyongyang. It has extensive trade and ethnic ties with North Korea, but has, on occasion, used its economic clout to nudge Pyongyang more into line with its desires. For China, a North Korean economic collapse would spill across the border in several ways: first, with a flood of refugees into Northeast China; second, with a need for additional economic assistance; and third, it might create desperation in Pyongyang that could lead to additional sales of weaponry—including nuclear material or ballistic missiles—in exchange for badly needed cash. China's trade with the DPRK is small relative to its trade with South Korea. In 2003, China (excluding Hong Kong) imported $395 million from North Korea while exporting $628 million there. That placed the DPRK as fifty-sixth in China's ranking of countries both as a source of imports (less than from Equatorial Guinea or Romania) and a destination for exports (less than to Algeria or Burma).

Problems in Beijing's relations with the DPRK go beyond the threat that Pyongyang will trigger a nuclear arms race in Northeast Asia and that its ballistic missile testing will provide a fillip for a theater missile defense system with participation by Japan. The Chinese also appear exasperated at the slow pace of North Korea's economic reforms, at the growing economic and political rapport between Pyongyang and Taipei, at the unending flow of refugees across their common border, and at North Korea's cavalier attitude toward business. (China occasionally suspends shipments of humanitarian aid to the DPRK because Pyongyang regularly "forgets" to return Chinese railroad rolling stock.)[55] China, however, still wields enough clout to draw Pyongyang to the negotiating table and to insist that it learn more about and emulate China's economic reforms.

South Korea

Economic interchange has been a major tool for opening relations between North and South Korea. Seoul has a major stake in relations with the DPRK and the outcome of the current Six-Party Talks. It seeks a "soft landing" for the current standoff over the North's nuclear program—one that will lead to a lessening of tensions and steady integration of North Korea's economy into the global economic and financial system. As with other countries divided by ideology and a history of hostilities as "pawns" on the chessboard of the Cold War, the two halves of the peninsula face numerous issues to be resolved before they can normalize relations—let alone contemplate reunification.

South Korea has much to gain from a rapprochement with the North. Its strategy has been to use its economic leverage to open channels with the North Korean people while maintaining a credible military deterrent to overt hostile action by Pyongyang. South Korea recognizes that essentially it has won the Cold War on the Korean peninsula, but it recoils at the prospect of funding economic rehabilitation in the DPRK as was done by Germany in absorbing its eastern communist half. Seoul also recognizes that its economic ties are gradually shifting from reliance on the American market to greater integration with China, Japan, and other countries of Asia. Its labor costs are rising, and many of its companies are remaining competitive only by manufacturing in China and other low-wage markets. For them, the prospect of abundant cheap labor just a short distance to the north is appealing and perhaps less of a potential siren song than the lure of cheap labor in China. South Korean borrowers also have to pay an "instability premium" to lenders in international markets. A lessening of tensions with the North can translate into lower interest costs for corporations in the South. Since 1992, particularly under the Sunshine Policy of former South Korean President Kim Dae Jung and under the Policy for Peace and Prosperity of current President Roh Moo Hyun, Seoul has permitted its corporations to pursue business interests in North Korea.

Japan

For Japan, relations with the DPRK are delicate. Although the two nations have never established official diplomatic relations, they have maintained significant economic ties. Since the end of the Cold War and until recently, Japan was second only to China among North Korea's top trading partners. Bilateral trade has declined considerably since the 1980s, although this has been attributed primarily to the steep overall downturn of the North Korean economy as much as to the state of bilateral relations. Japan plays a key role in resolving the current stalemate over North Korea's nuclear program because Tokyo can provide considerable economic assistance to the country and reportedly is ready to write Pyongyang a large check as compensation for its fifty-year occupation once relations between the two countries are normalized. Japan's leaders recognize that the first use of a North Korean nuclear bomb would probably be on Tokyo,[56] and the two countries have struggled to resolve the issue of Japanese citizens abducted by North Korean agents in the 1970s and 1980s.

Although Japan is a major trading partner for the DPRK, the DPRK ranks ninetieth among the markets for Japan's exports (less than Slovenia or Kazakhstan) and fifty-seventh among sources of Japan's imports (less than Sri Lanka or Costa Rica). Japan's economic relations with North Korea extend beyond official trade. Japan has provided 766,000 metric tons of humanitarian food aid to the DPRK—mostly through the United Nations World Food Program. The pattern of Japanese aid reflects developments in the political relationship between Tokyo and Pyongyang; shipments began in 1995 and 1996 when relations warmed and were suspended after the Taepo-dong missile launch over Japan in 1998 and the spy ship incident in 2001.

Recent developments have dampened political and economic relations between the DPRK and Japan. Kim Jong Il's admission in Fall 2002 that North Korea abducted several Japanese nationals and the announced advancement of the North's nuclear weapons program have hardened public sentiment and official policy toward Pyongyang. Tokyo has intensified its monitoring of Chosen Soren, the ethnic North Korean organization in Japan, in an effort to stem support to the Pyongyang regime and also has imposed far more stringent inspections on sea links with North Korea.

Russia

Russian reforms and the end of the Cold War greatly reduced the priority of the DPRK in the strategy of Russian foreign policy. Following Soviet support of North Korea in the Korean War, the USSR provided assistance to Pyongyang that helped equip its military and create its heavy industrial sector. In 1998, at the peak of the bilateral relationship, about 60 percent of North Korea's trade was with the Soviet Union. Much of the trade was in raw materials and petroleum that Moscow provided to Pyongyang at concessional prices. Relations between the two cooled in the 1990s as Russia recognized South Korea, announced that trade with North Korea was to be conducted in hard currencies, and opted out of its bilateral defense agreement.[57]

Recently, overall relations between Russia and North Korea have been improving. Russia is upgrading its railway connections with North Korea and has been participating in an ambitious plan to build a trans-Korea railway. As is the case with China and South Korea, Russia is critical to North Korean security, since Russia shares a border with the DPRK, and Russian cooperation would be necessary to enforce any security guarantee. As fuel aid from abroad has decreased, moreover, North Korea has turned again toward Russia as a source of supply.

Still, the DPRK's trade with Russia lags behind what it has been in the past. In 2003, North Korea ranked 106th among Russia's sources of imports (below Jordan and Liechtenstein) and 65th in terms of markets for Russian exports (below Portugal and Lebanon). Russia, however, was North Korea's sixth largest trading partner.

Interests, Strategy, and Policy

In DPRK relations with the rest of the world, economic issues are part of grand strategy on both sides. The four legs of any grand strategy include economic, diplomatic, informational, and military means to accomplish goals and protect national interests. While the Six-Party Talks have focused on Pyongyang's nuclear program, the actual policies in place contain a large economic component. Existing policies and inducements are designed to compel Pyongyang to take certain positive actions or to deter it from pursuing specific negative policies—particularly the pursuit of nuclear weapons. In actual policy deliberations, diplomatic and military considerations play a leading role, but economic incentives and disincentives usually are the means short of war that actually can be used. This policy tool kit, using economics for compellence and deterrence, includes an assortment of carrots and sticks spanning a range of economic assistance, trade embargoes and sanctions, membership in international financial institutions, and longer-term co-opting of DPRK elites through trade, investments, and economic interests.

Although current policies with respect to the DPRK are still a work in progress, they have not deterred North Korea from continuing its nuclear weapons program, have not visibly weakened the Kim regime, have not eased tensions in the Korean peninsula, and seem not to have induced greater regard by Pyongyang for human rights or democracy. Economic sanctions have brought few concrete results. The sanctions have primarily been American and limited to a narrow range of products. North Korea continues to trade with other countries as well as to receive humanitarian food aid and limited foreign investment. The poor economic conditions in the DPRK also do not appear to have materially undermined the Kim regime. Experts consider internal dissident forces too weak and Kim's control over his military too strong for a domestic coup to occur.[58]

A basic strategic question for the United States is whether to move toward a South Korean style engagement policy in hopes that a more globalized North Korea will also be more responsible, realistic, and less a victim of its own propaganda about the intentions of the United States and other nations. The theory behind engagement is that it generates greater North Korean interest in and dependency upon international trade, investment, and greater interaction with the outside world. This not only gives North Koreans a stake in the global economy, but it raises living standards, increases knowledge and information flows, and eases pressures for refugees to emigrate. A more globalized North Korea also could weaken the hold by Pyongyang on the daily lives of citizens, reduce pressures to engage in illicit trade in order to cover its trade deficit, and diminish the need for Pyongyang to saber rattle in order to divert attention from its domestic problems.

On the opposite side of the engagement camp are those who propose a strangulation strategy in which other nations minimize interaction with and aid to the North Korean economy in the hope that the resulting economic chaos would weaken or topple the Kim regime—or at least reduce resources available to the military's nuclear program. Arguably, a more comprehensive sanctions regime would require a decision by the United Nations Security Council where support for such a proposal would likely be opposed by China, Russia, and France. Recent events have shown, moreover, that Pyongyang will simply allow its people to starve rather than shift resources from the military to the people. With the gradual improvement in weather and economic conditions, it now appears that the DPRK is actually edging back from the brink of economic disaster. A total breakdown seems unlikely as long as nations continue to provide the regime with trade opportunities and humanitarian assistance. Neither China nor South Korea would welcome a collapse of the North Korean economy and the chaos that could ensue.

Notes

Dick Nanto is a Specialist in Industry and Trade with the U.S. Congressional Research Service (CRS). Opinions in this paper do not necessarily reflect those of CRS, the Library of Congress, or the U.S. government.

1. For detail, see Noland, *Avoiding the Apocalypse*.
2. Mark Seddon,"The Land That Time Forgot," *The Guardian* (London), March 11, 2003, 2.
3. Julie Chao, "Economic Devastation Visible in Pyongyang. Korea Is Like a Land Time Forgot, and Crisis with U.S. Isn't Helping," *The Austin American Statesman*, May 3, 2003, A17.
4. Jonathan Watts, "Where Are You, Beloved General? In a Land Where Paranoia, Propaganda, and Poverty Are the Norm, an Albino Raccoon Reassures North Koreans That Good Times Are Ahead," *Mother Jones*, vol. 28, no. 3 (May 1, 2003), 52.
5. PPP figures are from U.S. Central Intelligence Agency, *World Factbook*. www.cia.gov.cia/publications/factbook. Gross national income at market prices for South Korea is from World Bank, *World Development Indicators 2003*. www.worldbank.org/data/wdi2005/index.html
6. "South Korea," Ministry of Unification, *North Korea Today*, August 14, 2001 (Internet edition).

7. United Nations, World Food Program, "Korea (DPR), Food Security: Overview," Updated July 23, 2004. http://www.wfp.org/country_brief/indexcountry.asp?country=408

8. Julie Chao, "Despite Oppression, Cracks Appear in North Korean Society. There's a Great Divide Between Regular and Elite Koreans in the 'Egalitarian' System," *The Austin American Statesman*, May 3, 2003, A18.

9. "Desperate Straits, Special Report (1)," *The Economist*, May 3, 2003.

10. See, for example: "Natural Wonders Prove Kim Jong Il's Divinity: North Korean Media,"Agence France Presse, May 3, 2003.

11. British Broadcasting Corporation, "North Korea: Paper Supports Leader Kim Jong Il's Military-First Ideology," April 26, 2003, reported by BBC from KNCA News Agency (Pyongyang).

12. Shigeki Toyama, "Expert on Kim Chong-il's 'Military-First Politics' South-North Issues," *Tokyo Gunji Kenkyu* (in Japanese, translated by Foreign Broadcast and Information Service), August 1, 2002, 108–117.

13. Woon-Suk Nam, "Guidelines of Economic Policies," Digital KOTRA, January 9, 2001. Available at http://crm.kotra.or.kr/eng/index.php3

14. Current experiments in agriculture are directed from Pyongyang with seven major tasks that include replacing chemical fertilizers with organic and microbial ones. "North Korea Eyes China as a Model for Development," *Yonhap News*, May 11, 2004.

15. "Former North Korean Professor Interviewed on Pyongyang's Economic Reform," *Choson Ilbo*, April 14, 2003. Translated and reported by BBC Worldwide Monitoring, April 18, 2003.

16. Jianyi Piao, "Two Years After the Japan-DPRK Pyongyang Declaration Was Issued: Will the North Korean Economy Collapse or Recover?" Original in Chinese. Translated and published in Japanese by Makoto Sasaki in *Tokyo Sekai Shuho*, September 28, 2004, 22–25. Translated into English by U.S. Foreign Broadcast and Information Service.

17. United Nations World Food Program, "Korea (DPR), WFP Activities," updated July 23, 2004. www.wfp.org

18. Rob Gifford, "North Korea" (audio report), National Public Radio Morning Edition, April 30, 2003. www.npr.org/templates/story/story.php?storyId=1247705.

19. Hong, "A Shift Toward Capitalism?" 93–106.

20. Chang-hyun Jeong, "Capitalist Experiments Seen Expanding into DPRK," *Joong Ang Ilbo*, October 19, 2003. Translated in CanKor #160 by Canada-DPR Korea e-clipping Service, April 13, 2004.

21. Lintner, "North Korea, Shop Till You Drop," 14–19; Lim and Chung, "Is North Korea Moving Toward a Market Economy?" 49–79.

22. Piao, Jianyi, "Two Years After the Japan–DPRK Pyongyang Declaration Was Issued: Will the North Korean Economy Collapse or Recover?" Original in Chinese. Translated and published in Japanese by Makoto Sasaki in *Tokyo Sekai Shuho*, September 28, 2004, 22–25. Translated into English by U.S. Foreign Broadcast and Information Service.

23. "North Korea, Status of Induced Foreign Capital," Digital KOTRA.

24. K. Park, "A Report on Visit to Rajin-Seonbong Region," Digital KOTRA, January 4, 2001.

25. Hye-min Pak and Chu-yun Hong, "Gaesong Site Draws Intense Competition," *Seoul Changang Ilbo*, August 30, 2004 (Internet version in English). www.fbis.gov

26. Jung, Yongsoo Kim, and Kobayashi, "North Korea's Special Economic Zones: Obstacles and Opportunities."

27. Ministry of Unification, "Approval for Operation of the Gaesong Industrial Complex Shuttle Buses," Press Release, September 16, 2004.

28. "North Korean Industrial Complex Made Ready for Seoul's Investment," *Yonhap* (News), June 30, 2004.

29. Hye-min Pak and Chu-yun Hong, "Gaesong Site Draws Intense Competition," *Seoul Changang Ilbo*, August 30, 2004 (Internet version in English). www.fbis.gov

30. Nicholas Eberstadt's statement, Hearing on Drugs, Counterfeiting, and Weapons Proliferation: The North Korean Connection, Subcommittee on Financial Management, the Budget, and International Security, U.S. Senate Committee on Governmental Affairs, May 20, 2003.

31. (South) Korea Trade-Investment Promotion Agency (KOTRA).

32. "North Korea's Foreign Trade in 2001," Digital KOTRA.

33. Bank for International Settlements, International Banking Statistics, Consolidated Foreign Claims of Reporting Banks on Individual Countries, Tables 8 and 9. The data are locational (reported by the country of location of bank not nationality of the parent bank). www.bis.org

34. Danny Gittings, "Kim Can't Kill the Free Market," *The Wall Street Journal (Brussels)*, May 30, 2003, A11.

35. United Nations Conference on Trade and Development, *World Investment Report, 2003*, Annex Table B, 251, 259.

36. Soo-min Seo, "Questions Linger Despite President's Statement," *Korea Times*, February 14, 2003; Michael Dorgan, "Secret Payment to North Korea Disclosed," *Knight Ridder*, January 30, 2003.

37. Organisation for Economic Cooperation and Development, "Aid and Debt Statistics," available at www.oecd.org.

38. Republic of Korea, Ministry of Unification, "Inter-Korean Relations on the Occasion of the 4th Anniversary of the June 15 Joint Declaration," June 18, 2004, 9. www.unikorea.go.kr/data/eng0102/000627/attach/eng0102_627A.pdf

39. Mark E. Manyin, *U.S. Assistance to North Korea: Fact Sheet*, U.S. Congressional Research Service Report RS21834, May 4, 2004.

40. "U.S. to Pay North Korea for MIA Search," Associated Press, July 15, 2003.

41. Emma Chanlett-Avery, *North Korean Supporters in Japan: Issues for U.S. Policy*, Congressional Research Service Report RL32137, November 7, 2003, 1.

42. "Melons Used to Smuggle Cash to N. Korea," *Japan Today News* (Online), January 1, 2003. www.japantoday.com/e/?content=shukan&id=161&page=13

43. "Remittance Law Reinterpreted Cash Transfers to Pyongyang May Be Suspended as Deterrent," *The Daily Yomiuri* (Tokyo), May 19, 2003, 1.

44. "Japanese Finance Minister Says 'At Least' 34m US Dollars Sent to North Korea," *Financial Times Information*, *Global News Wire—Asia Africa Intelligence Wire*, June 6, 2003.

45. Yoshiharu Asano, "North Korea Missile Exports Earned 580 Mil. Dollars in '01," *Daily Yomiuri*, May 13, 2003.

46. Jay Solomon, "U.S. Debates North Korean Exports," *Asian Wall Street Journal*, May 5, 2003, A1.

47. Testimony of John R. Bolton, Undersecretary for Arms Control and International Security, U.S. Department of State, U.S. House Committee on International Relations, June 4, 2003.

48. Yoshiharu Asano, "North Korea Missile Exports Earned 580 Mil. Dollars in '01," *Daily Yomiuri*, May 13, 2003; Brendan Pearson, "Illicit Boost for N. Korea Economy," *Australian Financial Review*, May 13, 2003, 12.

49. Richard C. Paddock and Barbara Demick, "North Korea's Growing Drug Trade Seen in Botched Heroin Delivery," *Washington Post*, May 21, 2003.

50. Ah-young Kim, "Halt North Korea's Drug Habit; a Narcotic State," *International Herald Tribune*, June 18, 2003, 8.

51. U.S. Department of State, *International Narcotics Control Strategy Report, 2003* (May 2004). www.state.gov/g/inl/rls/nrcrpt/2003

52. Doug Struck, "Heroin Trail Leads to North Korea," *Washington Post Foreign Service*, May 12, 2003, A01.

53. Yoshiharu Asano, "North Korea Missile Exports Earned 580 Mil. Dollars in '01," *Daily Yomiuri*, May 13, 2003.

54. Sang-Hun Choe, "North Korea Sees Sanctions Amid Tough Times," Associated Press Online, June 12, 2003. Accessed through Dialog, www.dialog.com/ (Subscription required).

55. Jane's Information Group, "China and Northeast Asia. External Affairs," *Jane's Sentinel Security Assessment*, October 27, 2003. http://online.janes.com/ (Subscription required).

56. Jane's Information Group, "Armed Forces, Korea, North," *Jane's Sentinel Security Assessment*, March 4, 2003. http://online.janes.com/ (Subscription required).

57. Stanislav Lunev, "New Era in Russian-North Korean Relations," August 23, 2000. Available at *Newsmax.com*.

58. Jane's Information Group, "Internal Affairs, Korea, North," *Jane's Sentinel Security Assessment*, June 10, 2003. http://online.janes.com/ (Subscription required).

Part II

The Politics of
Foreign Relations

7

U.S.–DPRK Relations in the Kim Jong Il Era

Robert A. Scalapino

The sudden, unexpected death of Kim Il Sung on July 8, 1994, came at a time of intensive negotiations between the United States and the DPRK, with the outcome still uncertain. Earlier, between 1989 and 1992, advances seemed to offer hope, both in North-South relations and with respect to U.S.-DPRK issues. Six rounds of high-level talks had taken place in Seoul and Pyongyang between ROK and DPRK officials, and on December 13, 1991, an Agreement on Reconciliation, Nonaggression, Exchanges, and Cooperation was signed, with an additional protocol on the denucle-arization of the Korean peninsula completed on the last day of that year.

Meanwhile, U.S.-DPRK talks had taken place in Beijing, starting in 1989, and on January 20, 1992, a meeting in New York between Arnold Kanter, undersecretary of state for political affairs, and Kim Yong Sun, Korean Workers Party Secretary for Political Affairs, constituted the highest-level meeting between the two nations to take place since the Korean War. Two weeks prior to this meeting, moreover, on January 7, the DPRK announced that it would join the International Atomic Energy Agency (IAEA) and allow monitoring of its declared nuclear facilities.

At the Beginning: The Post-1992 Crisis

Beginning in the last quarter of 1992, however, a series of setbacks occurred. IAEA discovered discrepancies in the North's records and demanded special inspections. The North-South Committee on Nuclear Issues ceased to operate. On March 12, 1993, moreover, the DPRK announced that it intended to withdraw from the Nuclear Non-Proliferation Treaty (NPT). Shortly thereafter, in June, U.S.-DPRK negotiations got under way in New York, with Assistant Secretary of State Robert Gallucci and Vice Minister of Foreign Affairs Kang Sok Ju leading their respective teams. The North agreed to suspend its withdrawal from the NPT, and two additional meetings were held in the course of the next five months. On February 18, 1994, the two parties announced an agreement to return to negotiations, with IAEA monitoring and inspections of nuclear facilities to continue. A short time later, however, the North began to unload fuel rods from its Yongbyon facility, and negotiations were suspended. President Clinton then sent Patriot missiles to South Korea and Secretary Perry took a tough stance, not ruling out a preventive military strike.

It was under these circumstances that, despite some reluctance on the part of the Clinton administration, Jimmy Carter made his trip to Pyongyang in June, meeting with Kim Il Sung. In addition to arranging for a summit meeting between Kim and ROK president Kim Young Sam, scheduled for July, Carter obtained from Kim a pledge that he would not expel IAEA inspectors and would freeze nuclear activities as long as efforts to resolve differences went forward via high-level negotiations.[1]

This was the situation as the Kim Jong Il era opened. In truth, however, the new era was cloaked in mystery. The new leader held only military positions initially, those of chairman of the National Defense Commission and Supreme Commander of the People's Army. These posts had been occupied before Kim Il Sung's death, in 1993, although the son had long been given training and responsibilities as President Kim's designated successor. Kim Jong Il's election as General Secretary of the Korean Workers' Party did not take place until October 1997, with the post of chairman of the National Defense Commission officially bestowed on him by the tenth Supreme People's Assembly in September 1998. The position of president was declared to be that of Kim Jong Il permanently.

In the opening years of the new era, the Korean Workers' Party virtually disappeared from view, with no evidence of an active politburo or secretariat. Moreover, Kim proved to be a highly reclusive figure in his initial years as leader, appearing in public only rarely. The one clear trend was the increased emphasis upon the military. At an early point, the Songun "military-first" policy was proclaimed, and Kim's appearances were almost exclusively with military leaders or at military installations. In addition, juche (self-reliance), a policy inherited from Kim Il Sung, continued to be the dominant ideological theme, although in practice, it had to be modified later due to the North's severe economic depression.[2]

In all probability, the tight bonds between the new leader and the military were instrumental in preserving stability during a period of severe distress. The view of many outsiders that the DPRK would collapse underestimated the power of Kim Jong Il's military alliance. However, this alliance was also conducive to placing a heavy emphasis on military-oriented issues: priorities for military support and their security concerns. Despite the growing economic crisis, a high proportion of the budget was devoted to military expenditures. Whether significant differences of opinion existed within the military over North Korea's foreign policies, most particularly, what course to take in relations with the United States has long been one of the uncertainties relating to this closed society. Kim Jong Il reportedly once remarked that there were differences among both his military and civilian advisors on this matter,[3] and it would be surprising if such were not the case. However, it must be assumed that the broad thrust within the military was toward toughness as was the case later in the U.S. Pentagon.

Given the circumstances, it was encouraging that negotiations continued between the DPRK and the United States after a brief lapse, and on October 21, the Agreed Framework (AF, or the Agreement) was approved by the two parties in Geneva.[4] The AF provided for a series of obligations, bilateral and multilateral. The United States accepted leadership of an international consortium that would finance and supply a light water reactor project with a total generating capacity of 2,000 megawatts by a target date of 2003. An effort would be made to conclude a supply contract with the DPRK within six months. Until completion of the first reactor unit, the United States would provide 500,000 tons of heavy fuel oil annually. Upon receiving U.S. assurances of the light water reactor construction and interim energy alternatives, the DPRK would agree to freeze its graphite moderated reactors and related facilities, and eventually dismantle them. The freeze would be fully implemented within one month of the signing of the agreement, and the IAEA would be permitted to monitor the freeze, with full access provided by the DPRK. Dismantlement would be finalized when the project was completed, and the United States and the DPRK would cooperate in finding a method to store the spent fuel during the construction of the project, subsequently disposing of it in a safe manner, one not involving reprocessing it in the DPRK.

Further, the two parties agreed to move toward full normalization of economic and political relations. Within three months, both parties would reduce barriers to trade and investment, including restrictions on telecom services and financial transactions. Liaison offices would be opened in the respective capitals and, as progress was made on issues of concern to both sides, the two nations would upgrade bilateral relations to official recognition. Both parties would also cooperate in building peace and security on a nuclear-free Korean peninsula. The United States would provide formal assurances to the DPRK against any military action by it. The DPRK would take steps to implement the North-South Joint Declaration on the Denuclearization of the Korean peninsula, and would engage in dialogue with the South. It would also remain a party to the NPT and allow implementation of its safeguards agreement under that treaty. Finally, when a sufficient portion of the project was completed, but before delivery of the key nuclear components, the DPRK would come into full compliance with its safeguards agreement with the IAEA, including taking all steps deemed necessary by the IAEA with regard to verifying the accuracy and completeness of its initial report on nuclear materials within the country.

Subsequently, President Clinton sent a letter to Kim Jong Il, pledging full support for the Agreement, and indicating that if the reactor project was not completed for reasons beyond the control of the DPRK, he would have the U.S. support the project as well as provide additional energy alternatives if required, after obtaining the approval of the U.S. Congress.[5]

After a lengthy period of uncertainty and recurrent crises, with the threat of conflict genuine, a hopeful new start had taken place. However, opinions in both the United States and the ROK remained sharply divided over such issues as the North's real intentions with respect to nuclear weaponry and the prospects for the success of the Agreed Framework. As early as 1993, U.S. intelligence sources had reported that the DPRK probably had one or two nuclear weapons. While this estimate was not based upon hard evidence, it received widespread attention. The broader issue that was to remain salient throughout the coming decade was whether the DPRK was truly prepared to give up its nuclear option. Given the rising fear of an American attack, especially after the events that unfolded in the early George W. Bush years, including the Iraq War, did the elite in the North, predominantly military, regard a nuclear deterrent as a necessity? This view might be buttressed by the fact that the maintenance of a massive 1.1 million-member military force was prohibitively expensive, and the North's conventional weapons were becoming progressively obsolete.

On the other hand, much evidence supported the thesis that threat was the only bargaining chip available to the DPRK, given its economic and political position. Among the salient threats, moreover, none was more potent than that of becoming a nuclear state. If sufficient compensation were given, both with respect to external threat reduction and economic-political support, would the DPRK not find it in its interest to abandon the nuclear option, especially given its concern over the rising economic-political costs and security risks? To date, this issue has not been resolved.

Meanwhile, in the period immediately after the initiation of the AF, various complexities and differences over issues slowed progress in implementing the Agreement. After extensive bilateral and three-party dialogues, on March 9, 1995, the United States, the ROK, and Japan signed an agreement creating the Korean Peninsula Energy Development Organization (KEDO), thereby formally inaugurating the light water reactor (LWR) program. The DPRK, however, immediately objected to the adoption of a South Korean prototype of LWR, and a compromise was reached only after strenuous three-week negotiations in Kuala Lumpur, with a June 12 agreement that further discussions on the LWR project would require DPRK talks with KEDO, not the United States. Subsequently, KEDO selected an ROK model LWR and made a South Korean firm the principal contractor, with the North accepting this decision. However, an agreement on a supply contract was not reached until December 15, with the issue of funding extras such as a port and an access road central. As 1995 ended, the cost of the project was rising and the time schedule was being lengthened.

In the succeeding years, the DPRK continued to face dire economic hardships, and required augmented aid. Its attitude toward the United States involved a combination of the expressed desire for improved relations and periodic brinkmanship accompanied by angry tirades. In 1996, the United States proposed a four-party dialogue involving the two Koreas, China, and the United States. The North, wanting only bilateral talks and adamantly opposed to the South being a party in any official dialogue, put forth certain stipulations including the removal of American forces from the Korean peninsula, and the proposal remained unfulfilled. In the following year, however, extensive discussions took place between the United States and the DPRK on missile deployment and sales along with negotiations on humanitarian assistance—now sizeable—and its monitoring. Moreover, visits by American officials and members of Congress to Pyongyang were matched by the visit of Vice Foreign Minister Kim Gye Gwan to Washington, the highest-ranking DPRK official to make such a trip. Further, the on-site groundbreaking ceremony for the KEDO project in Kumho took place in August. In December 1997, moreover, the Four-Party Talks opened in Geneva. It appeared that progress in U.S.-DPRK relations was being made, albeit, with periodic interruptions and denunciations.

Yet more negative trends lay ahead. On August 31, 1998, the North launched a Taepo-dong 1 missile with a 1,200 mile range that crossed over Japan, deeply disturbing both that nation and the United States. Moreover, bilateral talks between the United States and the DPRK as well as the Four-Party Talks failed to produce any results. The North began to complain bitterly that the LWR project was falling behind the established deadlines, and that the United States was late in providing its promised heavy oil. Dissatisfied with the U.S. response, the DPRK ceased the canning of spent nuclear fuel and threatened to reopen the Yongbyon facility.

An agreement was reached in September 1998 in renewed bilateral U.S.-DPRK talks that the United States would provide the promised fuel oil and that LWR construction would begin in November, in exchange for which the North would consider granting access to its underground facility and both bilateral and Four-Party Talks would continue in October. Yet no agreements were reached on the key issues, and despite Kim Dae Jung's Sunshine Policy, North-South relations as well as those between the United States and the DPRK were marked by multiple tensions.

Transition: From the Clinton to the Bush Administration

In November 1998, President Clinton created a North Korean Policy Review group headed by William J. Perry to undertake a thorough review of U.S. policies toward the DPRK and make recommendations. After extensive preparations including a trip to Pyongyang, Perry and his associates put forth a report, made public on October 12, 1999, recommending a comprehensive, two-path strategy.[6] In essence, the so-called Perry Process involved an effort to reduce U.S. pressures on the North that Pyongyang regarded as threatening in exchange for the elimination of the North's nuclear and long-range missile programs. If the North rejected this program, the United States should take steps to contain the North in multiple ways.

A month earlier, a reciprocal commitment known as the Berlin Agreement had been reached after bilateral U.S.-DPRK talks in which the United States agreed to lift certain economic sanctions in exchange for the North's pledge to forego the firing of a second Taepo-dong missile. In this period, the DPRK was working assiduously to improve its relations with both China and Russia. Relations with the ROK fluctuated, with a naval encounter in the West Sea temporarily disrupting progress, but with economic and cultural relations generally expanding. In this period, the United States, South Korea, and Japan had held frequent consultations under the label "Trilateral

Coordination and Oversight Group" (TCOG) in an effort to maintain the maximum possible unity in pursuing policies toward the DPRK.

This was the setting when President Kim Dae Jung made his trip to Pyongyang on June 13–15, 2000, for a summit meeting with Kim Jong Il.[7] The Joint Declaration that was issued at the summit, while lacking in specificity, seemed to augur improved economic and cultural relations between North and South, and served as a stimulant to the Clinton administration to move forward in its efforts to reach agreement with the DPRK on fundamental issues.

On June 19, immediately after the summit, the United States announced that it would begin an implementation of its September 1999 pledge to remove some of its economic sanctions against the North. Moreover, in less than a month, Secretary of State Madeleine Albright and DPRK Foreign Minister Pak Nam Sun held talks during the ARF Bangkok conference, and on October 9–12, a prestigious delegation headed by Vice-Marshal Jo Myong Rok visited Washington. A letter from Kim Jong Il to Clinton was presented, outlining the North's views, and at the end of the discussions, an agreement was reached to improve bilateral relations and support antiterrorist measures. The North Koreans wanted President Clinton to come to Pyongyang but it was finally agreed that Secretary Albright would make an initial visit to see whether sufficient agreement on the key issues could be reached to warrant a presidential visit.

The Albright trip took place less than two weeks later.[8] Her meeting with Kim Jong Il seemed productive. Kim agreed to controls over missile production, and an end to missile sales if compensation were made, since this was a key source of foreign currency. No additional firing of Taepo-dong missiles would be undertaken if South Korea made a similar pledge. Verification issues, however, would require further discussion.

Surprisingly, Kim asserted that given the end of the Cold War, American troops in South Korea played a stabilizing role.[9] As noted, he also asserted that there was an even split in his military on whether relations with the United States should be improved and, even in the foreign ministry, some opposed his decision to talk with Albright.

Kim indicated that, as for economic policies, he was interested in the Swedish or Thai models rather than that of China, another startling statement. Like other recent visitors, Albright found Kim to be intelligent and reasonably well informed, seemingly very interested in reaching agreements with the United States that would permit gradual normalization of relations.

A few weeks later, in November, U.S. and DPRK representatives met in Kuala Lumpur to discuss the key issues: the production, testing, deployment, and export of advanced missiles, including those already deployed; adherence to the Agreed Framework, including compliance with the pledge to refrain from nuclear activities; and full verification of these commitments. In exchange, the United States would arrange for civilian satellite launches for the North outside the country. The United States wanted a joint statement outlining the mutual obligations and, in addition, an exchange of confidential letters.

In the end, the Clinton visit did not take place. There were concerns that full agreement on the key issues would not be reached but, in addition, the President himself decided that the more crucial and immediate issue was to concentrate upon negotiations regarding the deeply troubled Palestinian-Israeli problem.[10] In essence, time ran out. The seeming advances of the last three months of 2000 came too late to permit a conclusion to the complex agreements that were required.

The Bush administration brought change, not continuity. Although the new secretary of state, Colin Powell, indicated at the outset that efforts would be made to continue the course pursued by the Clinton administration, he was quickly countermanded. Moreover, when Kim Dae Jung visited Washington in March 2001, Bush showed clear reservations about the Sunshine Policy, and indicated that the United States would undertake a thorough review of policies toward the DPRK before deciding upon a course of action.[11]

In early June, Bush proposed that three issues be discussed by the two parties: implementation of the AF, all issues relating to missiles, and conventional military policies. At this point, however, the DPRK was in an increasingly negative mood toward Washington, denouncing the Bush administration for its efforts to "suffocate, isolate and destroy" the North.[12] It called the newly designated missile defense program a policy "destroying the peace," and indicated that unless there was a change in attitude by the United States, it would not engage in negotiations.

During this period, the DPRK took measures on the international front that indicated a strong effort to strengthen its economic and strategic position. It reached out to the EU seeking an expansion of diplomatic relations with some success, and also indicated a desire to be more active in international and regional organizations. In addition, it made strenuous efforts to improve its relations with both China and Russia.

Meanwhile, the Bush administration displayed divisions of opinion with respect to the issue of North Korea.[13] The "hardliners," many in the Pentagon, favored minimal concessions and an effort to bring about a change in regime, primarily through economic and other sanctions. Support for a preventive military strike was slight, but the DPRK was being defined by this group as a rogue state, one to be carefully watched. Among these individuals, there was limited sympathy for negotiations. Moreover, the September 11, 2001, terrorist attacks resulted in a greatly increased emphasis upon the threat to American security from such external sources as North Korea. On the other hand, more moderate elements, many in the Department of State, urged continued efforts at negotiations, seeking a settlement of the admittedly difficult issues, so as to maintain rapport with our allies, the ROK and Japan, and with others, especially China, so vital to the peace and stability of the region.

U.S.-DPRK relations continued to languish in early 2002. President Bush's State of the Union speech in January listed the DPRK along with Iran and Iraq as a part of "the axis of evil," and subsequently indicated that he had no trust in Kim Jong Il. As expected, the North responded in vitriolic terms, and no positive actions were taken. In mid-2002, however, the DPRK took steps on the home front that augmented its need for a more expansive foreign policy. At the beginning of July, the government dramatically revised the price and wage system upward, adjusting the currency more closely with black market rates; state controlled rationing was abandoned, and the market system was significantly expanded, with the agrarian sector permitted greater freedom with respect to product distribution.[14] At last, the DPRK regime had begun to come to grips with the need to alter the old order if its faltering economic system was to be remedied. The initial results involved extensive inflation, but a new, seemingly irreversible course had been charted.

The implications for foreign policy were obvious. First, the economic importance of South Korea to the North was greatly enhanced, and within a brief period, negotiations with the Kim Dae Jung government on a wide range of measures, including expanded trade and investment, a new special economic zone, reopened rail and road lines, and more extensive cultural relations got underway. The United States also assumed increased economic importance, as the access to such agencies as the Asian Development Bank and International Monetary Fund became more significant.

New developments seemed temporarily stalled, however, when an incident in the Yellow Sea between the two Korean navies resulting in Northern casualties took place at the end of June. Once again, the North had transgressed the boundary line established in 1953 (which the North had refused to recognize). Yet on July 25, the DPRK officially expressed its regrets and urged that negotiations between North and South, the DPRK, and the United States, and the DPRK and Japan be reopened.

The Post-2002 Crisis: From Bilateral Negotiation to Six-Party Talks

A more serious issue soon emerged, on October 3–5, however. Assistant Secretary of State James Kelly held sessions with the North Koreans in Pyongyang, and presented to them evidence garnered from intelligence sources that the DPRK was engaged in a secret nuclear program in violation of the AF and its obligations under the Nuclear Non-Proliferation Treaty (NPT).[15] Kelly reported that Kang Suk Ju, the key DPRK negotiator, acknowledged that his country did have a highly enriched uranium (HEU) program under way. Outside observers were astonished. Subsequently, the DPRK government repeatedly insisted that there had been no admission of an HEU program, and that this charge was totally false. However, in many quarters, the program was believed to exist, and the United States toughened its stance.

For its part, the DPRK now argued that the United States was demanding that it surrender unconditionally, giving up all of its weaponry prior to any security guarantees. Further, it charged the United States with having violated the 1994 AF by delaying fulfillment of the pledge to construct the LWRs and being tardy in the delivery of heavy oil, thereby damaging the North's total economy. Pyongyang also asserted that by including the DPRK in "the axis of evil," the United States had made it vulnerable to a preemptive attack. Thus, it demanded a security assurance in the form of a non-aggression treaty between the United States and the DPRK as an immediate step.

The crisis worsened at the beginning of 2003. On January 10, the North announced its withdrawal from the NPT. This was followed by an announcement that its five-megawatt nuclear reactor in Yongbyon was being reactivated. In addition, another missile test took place, with a second test launched in March. To add to the complications, a U.S. reconnaissance airplane on the high seas off the East coast was intercepted by North Korean aircraft.

In turn, the United States was now demanding multilateral talks, insisting that the nuclear issue was a regional, not merely a bilateral issue. Further, it continued to assert that in accordance with the AF, the North must verifiably dismantle its nuclear installations. During this period, a readjustment of U.S. forces in the ROK, including the removal of troops from near the DMZ to the south of Seoul, prompted Pyongyang to allege that by removing its forces from the range of DPRK artillery, the United States was preparing for a preemptive strike. Unquestionably, the beginning of the war in Iraq worried North Korean authorities. It was reported that Kim Jong Il disappeared from public view for fifty days after the onset of the attack.

In the midst of a high level of tension, both parties issued moderating statements. On March 20, the U.S. ambassador to the ROK, Thomas Hubbard, asserted that the United States would be willing to have direct talks with the North in a multilateral context, and on April 12 the DPRK Foreign Ministry stated that it would not demand the placing of any given set of issues on the table if the United States would undertake "a bold switchover" in its policies to enable a resolution of the nuclear issue.

With China prodding both parties, especially North Korea, three-party talks took place in Beijing, April 23–25.[16] The dialogue did not produce any agreement other than an expressed willingness to meet again. The key issue unresolved was that of the sequence of events. The DPRK proposed that it would abandon its nuclear program if the United States provided security guarantees, economic assistance, and diplomatic recognition simultaneously. The United States, charging the North with employing blackmail tactics, insisted upon verifiable actions before any recompense.

In July, the North intensified its threat by proclaiming that it had reprocessed 8,000 spent nuclear fuel rods at Yongbyon, and had restarted its five-megawatt reactor. In turn, the United States obtained support from its Asian allies and China to put the nuclear issue before the UN Security Council if the DPRK did not participate in a multilateral dialogue. At this point, China increased its pressure on Pyongyang, and the North finally accepted Six-Party Talks, which took place on August 27–29.[17] The discussions were intense, and often recriminatory, but the key issues were clearly articulated, albeit, with no agreement secured. The North continued to dismiss any multilateral security guarantee as meaningless, ignoring the fact that a written agreement involving all six parties was more likely to be binding than a bilateral treaty that could be quickly discarded by a single party. The United States also insisted upon complete, verifiable, irreversible dismantlement (CVID), before major assistance would be forthcoming.

At this point, the DPRK raised the level of threat, asserting that if agreement could not be reached, it would conduct a nuclear test. Later, moreover, the North's vice foreign minister, Choe Su Hon, asserted that given the threats confronting it, the DPRK had no choice but to possess a nuclear deterrent. Although the reprocessed rods might be sufficient to produce six to eight nuclear weapons, opinions continued to differ over whether this was actually the North's aim or whether this and earlier statements were essentially an effort to raise the stakes in the bargaining process, without substance behind them. In any case, brinkmanship had now assumed more threatening proportions.

In October, President Bush set forth a new proposal at the Asia-Pacific Economic Cooperation meeting, stating that the United States and the other four nations who were party to the Six-Party Talks would provide a guarantee that none would attack the DPRK. After an initial rejection, the North stated that it would consider the Bush proposal if it were aimed at a package solution to the nuclear question based upon simultaneous action.[18]

The second round of the Six-Party Talks did not take place in Beijing until February 25–28, 2004. Both Kim Kye Gwan, head of the North Korean delegation, and James Kelly, head of the U.S. team, made conciliatory opening remarks, promising flexibility. Kelly asserted that after the North's nuclear program was dismantled, the United States and others would provide security guarantees to the DPRK as well as advance on all bilateral issues. The talks were generally less hostile than during the first round, and dealt with substantive issues in a detailed manner. They lasted one day longer than planned, and all parties publicly expressed satisfaction at their conclusion. An agreement was reached to continue with a third round, and in the interim, to set up working group meetings to prepare for the next session.[19]

At the same time, however, the key differences between the United States and the DPRK remained unresolved. The North insisted that it was willing to give up its nuclear weaponry, but only if the United States abandoned "its hostile policies" and provided compensation for such a move. The DPRK set forth a proposal based on stages of action, each requiring simultaneous responses on the part of the United States and the DPRK. At the end, the North's nuclear program would be totally dismantled, and the United States would have provided the necessary security, economic, and political compensation. The United States, on the other hand, demanded CVID of the nuclear program prior to meeting the DPRK demands. It also insisted that the enriched uranium program had to be acknowledged by the North and included in the dismantlement. At this point, the revelation that Pakistani scientist A.Q. Khan had transferred the equipment and technology required to produce uranium-based nuclear weapons beginning in the early 1980s added a new dimension to the earlier charges.[20] It reinforced the belief of those who felt that an enriched uranium program existed, a matter which the North continued to angrily deny.

South Korea also put forth a three-stage proposal, stating that when the North had frozen its nuclear facilities in a verifiable manner, it would provide fuel oil, with both China and Russia agreeing to join in that aid. The United States, while stating that its commitments would take place only after CVID, said it approved of the proposal.

Some two months after the close of the second Six-Party Talks, Selig Harrison had a series of discussions with key North Korean leaders in Pyongyang in which they set forth their views on the key matters, at least as they wanted them displayed publicly.[21] Kim Yong Nam, president of the Supreme People's Assembly, stated that he believed that Bush was not serious in resolving the nuclear issue, being preoccupied with Iran and the coming elections, and that his government could not accept CVID as a first requirement. He insisted that the DPRK wanted a nuclear-free Korean peninsula, and the only reason the North was developing nuclear weapons was to deter an American preemptive attack. Foreign Minister Paek Nam Sun asserted that the DPRK opposed all forms of terrorism, and would never transfer its nuclear material to others. Further, the North wanted and needed U.S. friendship. However, Kim Yong Nam stated that missile sales were essential in order to obtain foreign exchange.

The third round of Six-Party Talks subsequently took place in Beijing, June 23–25, 2004. On the opening day, James Kelly presented a new, more flexible proposal bearing some relation to the earlier South Korean plan. The DPRK would be given a preparatory time of up to three months to prepare for the dismantlement and removal of its nuclear programs. During this period, the North would provide a complete listing of its nuclear activities, including enriched uranium operations, and cease all such activities; permit the securing of all fissile material and the monitoring of all fuel rods; and permit the disabling of all nuclear weapons, weapon components, and key centrifuge parts. These actions would be subject to international verification.

During the initial period, the five nations involved in the talks with the North would provide a provisional pledge that there was no intention to invade or attack the DPRK. Further, China, South Korea, and Russia would provide heavy fuel oil. The United States would begin discussions with the DPRK on the reduction of economic sanctions and the removal of the North from the list of terrorist states. Once the nuclear program had been certified to have ended after full inspection by the IAEA, a formal multilateral security guarantee accompanied by economic and political advances in the U.S.-DPRK relationship could take place.[22] The term CVID was omitted from the proposal and the presentation.

While the DPRK response to the U.S. proposal was delayed in coming and its rejection less militant than in the past, the message was clear. The American plan, it was asserted, required their country to give up too much, too soon, and offered too little in return.[23] The North wanted the United States to participate in the fuel oil aid and in other forms of compensation from the outset. Its main theme was simultaneous moves by the two principal parties, symbolized by the phrases "words for words, actions for actions." Meanwhile, threat had been once again advanced with Kim Gye Gwan telling Kelly that if progress was not made, the DPRK might conduct a nuclear test. Yet while the third round of talks ended without agreement, a greater degree of flexibility had been shown, and the pledge was given by all parties for further negotiations. Some observers were hopeful.

At the beginning of July, only a week after the third Six-Party Talks were concluded, Secretary Powell met with Foreign Minister Paek Nam Sun during the course of the ARF meetings in Jakarta. Powell told Paek that there was now an opportunity for "concrete progress." Paek stated that the DPRK would not regard the United States as a "permanent enemy" if it now sought to improve bilateral relations. Yet he repeated the North's insistence upon "simultaneous actions."[24]

In the months that followed, however, several new issues emerged that presented additional obstacles. Congress passed a North Korea Human Rights Act, which was signed by the president in October. In essence, this legislation prohibited economic assistance other than humanitarian aid unless and until the DPRK corrected its abuses against human rights and religion. Not surprisingly, Pyongyang reacted to this event with fury.[25]

Another development was the revelation that in the early 1980s and also in 2000, South Korean scientists had produced a small amount of enriched uranium. While the IAEA subsequently determined that an insufficient amount for the production of a nuclear weapon had been produced, they initially criticized the Seoul government for not revealing the full details. The government insisted that these experiments had been conducted without its knowledge, and bore no relation to weapon production. From the time of the revelation, however, the DPRK began to demand that the issue be placed on the agenda along with its nuclear activities.[26]

At a fairly early point after the third Six-Party Talks ended, the DPRK began to drag its feet on attendance at a fourth session, originally scheduled for the end of September. It first withdrew from participation in working party talks, and then indicated that it saw no point in further talks unless the United States was prepared to abandon its "anti-DPRK policies." In late October, the DPRK outlined three requirements before it would return to the talks: the United States must drop its hostile policy; it must join economic aid programs for the North; and it must agree to discuss the ROK's "nuclear program."[27]

The scene was made more negative by name calling. President Bush in a Wisconsin campaign speech, referred to Kim Jong Il as a "tyrant." In response, the North Korean foreign ministry called Bush "an idiot," a "political imbecile," and "a tyrant who puts Hitler in the shade."[28]

The multination naval exercises off the coast of Japan, with a primary emphasis on deterring illegal activities, further antagonized the North, long accused of trafficking drugs, weapons, and other prescribed items. Thus, the fall months of 2004 were devoted to negativism, and September passed with no fourth round of talks in sight. Most observers were certain that despite statements by individuals like UN ambassador Han Song Ryol that it was a change of policy, not who was the American president that counted, Pyongyang was hopeful that Senator John Kerry would win the presidential election and a new start in the negotiations could commence. In all likelihood, the DPRK leadership was deeply disappointed in the election results, but while Kerry could have started with a relatively clean slate as far as rhetoric was concerned, any expectation that he would have advanced radically different proposals seems misguided. His principal proposal with regard to the North Korea issue, reiterated on several occasions, was that bilateral talks should take place. In point of fact, however, such talks had taken place repeatedly within the context of the multiparty framework and on the sideline of other multilateral meetings.

Conclusion and Prospects

In looking toward the future, it is important to keep in mind the complexities that dominate the scene today. First, U.S. past policies regarding North Korea have been handicapped by a lack of certainty regarding several crucial issues. Does the DPRK have nuclear weapons now and, if so, in what numbers? For many years, U.S. intelligence sources have stated that the North has one or two nuclear weapons, derived from enriched plutonium. More recently, it has been suggested that the number may have increased to six or eight as a result of the reprocessing of the stored nuclear fuel rods. Yet despite recent North Korean assertions that it has nuclear weapons, and some indications that a nuclear test may be in the offing, certainty with respect to whether it has deliverable weapons and in what quantity is not possible under current circumstances, given the paucity of verifiable intelligence.

Connected with this issue is the political question posed earlier, namely, is North Korea fully committed to becoming a nuclear state irrespective of the consequences, as some believe, given its deep fears, the costs of a large conventional force, and the desire for military options? Or is the nuclear program used principally as a bargaining chip, indeed, the sole bargaining chip that the North possesses, and hence, is it susceptible to being given up if the recompense is sufficient in the North's view? The latter position is that voiced repeatedly by North Korean leaders, but many question their credibility. Again, opinions in the United States and elsewhere are divided, with no side able to prove its case. This issue also relates to the question of whether time is on the side of the North, given its potential nuclear capacities, or in the light of the North's dire economic conditions, on the side of the United States?

In addition, another political question is of great significance. Are there serious differences of opinion regarding key policies relating to the United States within the North Korean elite? As noted, this has been suggested by Kim Jong Il himself, and it would be surprising if certain differences did not exist, given the complexity of the problems. Moreover, somewhat younger, better-educated individuals are replacing a number of the old military elite at the top of the DPRK power structure. Yet there is no evidence that such differences as may exist have shaken the regime or challenged the Dear Leader's power. This is another issue, however, that warrants continuous observation. In the meantime, there is little doubt that differences over policies toward North Korea within and outside the U.S. government exist now and for the foreseeable future, further complicating matters.

Looking to the future, two fundamental issues remain to be resolved, both of them complex and difficult to compromise. The first is verification. The United States has been willing to drop the term CVID, but with reason, given the background of events, it continues to insist upon complete and irreversible verification of the North's nuclear dismantlement in all of its facets, including HEU. The DPRK, sensing that at least some parties within the Bush administration aim at regime change, sees the nuclear issue as critical to its future and, hence, is unprepared to engage in full dismantlement prior to extensive security, economic, and political compensation.

This relates to the second fundamental issue, that of timing. Timing signifies the relationship of actions by one party to actions by the other. Should "simultaneous action" as advocated by the DPRK prevail, or should each stage of nuclear dismantlement be carefully verified, and only then result in certain corresponding actions by the United States, with complete U.S. security, economic, and political reciprocation awaiting the final, fully verified and guaranteed end of the North's nuclear program?

Making the resolution of these issues more difficult is the fact that there is a complete lack of trust in the other party on both sides. Thus, partial moves, subject to retreats, have been a part of the past scene, and may extend into the future. Up to this point, when frustrated by the United States, the DPRK has intensified its efforts to expand relations, especially economic relations, with the ROK, and also to keep both China and Russia acting favorably toward it. In reality, however, the North has no fully trustworthy allies. While China has strong reasons for not wanting to see the North collapse or a conflict to ensue, privately, it has been very unhappy with the North's reluctance to undertake major economic reforms and with its bizarre political system. Russia, while seeking to reenter the East Asia scene, including the Korean peninsula, as a major player, is not yet in position to be of great assistance and economically tilts toward the South for obvious reasons.

It can be argued, therefore, that despite certain gains in its relations with neighboring states, the DPRK has a very large stake in improving relations with the United States. If it feels a genuine security threat, as it has constantly insisted, there is only one route to its reduction, namely, an agreement with the United States. Moreover, if it pursues further economic reforms vigorously, it will need the assistance of international agencies in which the United States plays a powerful role. In addition, its legitimacy as a state would be significantly abetted by U.S. diplomatic recognition. Yet the North's past actions testify to the power of its military elite, and the military-first policy that is constantly reiterated must be restrained by the Dear Leader if greater flexibility is to ensue. There is also a challenge for the United States, namely, for it to show greater flexibility, given the hopes of Asian allies and colleagues. Unilateralism is a recipe for disaster. Thus, the importance of pursuing a multilateral course with dialogue regularized must be acknowledged by all parties.

Whatever the future, the critical issues are not likely to be resolved in one stroke, nor is the strongly negative cast to the U.S.-DPRK relationship likely to be quickly or easily removed. Yet the effort must be made and sustained if the peace and stability of Northeast Asia are to be advanced.

Notes

1. For broad perspectives on the late Kim Il Sung and early Kim Jong Il eras, including detailed accounts of U.S.-DPRK interaction, see Mazarr, *North Korea and the Bomb*; Oberdorfer, *The Two Koreas*; and Sigal, *Disarming Strangers*.

2. A perceptive evaluation of the military role in the DPRK is given in Oh and Hassig, *North Korea Through the Looking Glass*, especially chapter 5, 105–126.

3. According to Secretary Albright, Kim Jong Il told her that there was a fifty-fifty split within his military on whether or not to improve relations with the United States and that there were people in the foreign ministry who had opposed even his decision to talk to Albright and her associates. See Albright, *Madam Secretary*, 465.

4. For the text, see Council on Foreign Relations, *Success or Sellout?*

5. Council on Foreign Relations, *Success or Sellout?* See also Clinton, *My Life*, 624–625.

6. See Perry, *Review of U.S. Policy Toward North Korea*.

7. A contemporary appraisal is given by Samuel S. Kim, "North Korea in 2000," 12–29.

8. See Albright, *Madam Secretary*, 460–470.

9. Ibid., 465.

10. Clinton, *My Life*, 938. Clinton wrote that although Albright wanted him to make the trip to North Korea, believing that a missile agreement could be reached, he felt that a Middle East peace was close at hand. Arafat had assured him that he was eager for an agreement and urged him not to go to the DPRK.

11. For a general appraisal of the initial approaches to North Korea by the Bush administration, see Harnisch, "U.S.-North Korean Relations Under the Bush Administration," 856–882; see also Hong Nack Kim, "U.S.-North Korean Relations," 34–66. On Kim Dae Jung's Sunshine Policy, see Moon and Steinberg, *Kim Dae-jung Government and Sunshine Policy*.

12. Typical of the evaluations of U.S. policy toward it during this period is *Rodong Sinmun's* assertions as transmitted in "DPRK Urges U.S. to Change Its Hostile Korean Policy," *People's Korea*, September 27, 2003, 1.

13. For developments at the beginning of the Bush administration, see Scobell, "Grouching Korea, Hidden China," 343–368, and Campbell, "Bush's First 100 Days in Asia," 32.

14. See Nam, "North Korea Heading Toward Market Economy," 8–11, and Koh, "Dynamics of Inter-Korean Conflict," 422–441; Choong Yong Ahn, ed., *North Korea—Development Report 2002/03*.

15. An analysis of various facets of the DPRK nuclear program has been given by Philip C. Saunders, "Responses to a Nuclear North Korea," paper drafted on October 2, 2003; Soon-Jick Hong, "North Korean Nuclear Crisis," 23–38.

16. See Kyung-Ae Park, "North Korea in 2003," 139–146.

17. Kyung-Ae Park, "North Korea in 2003," 142–143. See also Kwak, "Solution to the North's Nuclear Weapons Problem," 2–8.

18. See "Pyongyang Proposes 'First-Phase Actions' for Settlement of Nuke Issue," *People's Korea*, December 13, 2003, 1, 4.

19. See Pan, "Solution for the Nuclear Issue of North Korea," 19–46. An insightful view into North Korean position is presented in Ambassador Li Gun, "Various Requisites for Resolving the Nuclear Question," *People's Korea*, February 28, 2004, 3–4.

20. Details are set forth in David E. Sanger, "U.S. Widens View of Pakistan Link to Korean Arms," *New York Times*, March 13, 2004, 1, 10.

21. Selig Harrison has presented his account of the interviews in "Inside North Korea: Leaders Open to Ending Nuclear Crisis," *Financial Times*, May 4, 2004, 3. Harrison has been a prolific writer on North Korea with works including *Korean Endgame: A Strategy for Reunification and U.S. Disengagement*. This was his eighth trip to the DPRK.

22. See James A. Kelly, "Dealing with North Korea's Nuclear Programs," a statement before the Senate Foreign Relations Committee, July 15, 2004.

23. For the DPRK perspective on the third Six-Party Talks, see "3rd Six-Way Talks Held—Propose (sic) of 'Reward for Freeze' Discussed as Basic Topic," *People's Korea*, June 26, 2004, 1, 4; see also Hu Xiao, "DPRK Says Proposals May Solve Nuclear Issue," *China Daily*, June 24, 2004, 1–2.

24. For accounts of the July 2 Powell-Paek meeting, see Christopher Marquin, "Powell Meets Foreign Minister of North Korea to Discuss Arms," *New York Times*, July 2, 2004, 1; "Peaceful Solution of Nuclear Issue of Korean Peninsula Discussed," *People's Korea*, July 17, 2004, 3; and "DPRK FM Dismisses U.S. 'Landmark Proposal,'" *People's Korea*, July 31, 2004, 2.

25. For example, "Pyongyang Denounces 'NK Human Rights Act' as Intended to Topple DPRK," *People's Korea*, October 16, 2004, 1, 4.

26. James Brooke, "North Korea Says Seoul's Nuclear Experiments Stoke Arms Race," *New York Times*, September 9, 2004, A7.

27. James Brooke, "North Korea Sets 3 Conditions for Returning to Nuclear Talks," *New York Times*, October 22, 2004, 1.

28. See "DPRK FM Spokesman Blasts Bush's Reckless Remarks," *People's Korea*, August 28, 2004, 2, and Andrew Ward and Song Jung-a, "North Korea Blames 'Idiot' Bush for Stall in Nuclear Talks," *Financial Times*, August 22, 2004, 1.

8

Japanese-North Korean Relations Under the Koizumi Government

Hong Nack Kim

Despite geographic proximity, cultural affinity, and historical ties, Japan and North Korea have had no diplomatic relations throughout the post–World War II era, largely because of the Cold War, which placed them on the opposite sides of the bipolar system. Since Japan and North Korea were in opposing camps during the Cold War, the bilateral relationship was inevitably affected by the East-West confrontation and conflict. Japan relied heavily on the United States for its national security and followed U.S. leadership closely in dealing with North Korea. Japanese-North Korean relations were also adversely affected by the confrontation and rivalry between North and South Korea during the Cold War era. As Japan normalized diplomatic relations with South Korea in 1965, while maintaining a policy of nonrecognition toward North Korea, Pyongyang regarded Japan as a hostile neighbor that attempted to side with South Korea against them.[1] There was little official contact between the two nations, only limited unofficial interaction.

In the aftermath of the collapse of the communist systems in the Soviet Union and Eastern Europe, Japan modified its policy toward North Korea as Moscow and Beijing established diplomatic ties with Seoul. To compete effectively with Moscow and Beijing, Tokyo also wanted to establish its diplomatic ties with both Koreas. North Korea complied quickly to Japan's overtures for rapprochement, for Pyongyang was shocked by the Soviet-South Korean summit meeting held in San Francisco in early June 1990. Another important factor was Pyongyang's desperate need to tap Japanese economic assistance for the purpose of revitalizing its sagging economy. On the basis of a joint declaration adopted by the leaders of Japan's ruling Liberal Democratic Party (LDP), the Japan Socialist Party, and the Korean Workers' Party on September 28, 1990, Tokyo and Pyongyang held eight rounds of normalization talks between January 1991 and November 1992.[2] However, due to a number of thorny issues, such as the scope and nature of

Japan's compensation to North Korea for the suffering inflicted on Koreans during Japan's colonial rule (1910–1945) and North Korea's flat denial of the abduction of Japanese nationals, the normalization talks were suspended. Although three additional rounds were held from April to October in 2000, the negotiations failed to resolve the compensation and abduction issues. North Korea persisted in its denial of any knowledge about the abduction issue, while refusing to accept the Japanese proposal to offer economic aid rather than reparations for Japan's wrongdoing during its colonial rule of Korea. In view of the uncompromising positions taken by both sides at the normalization talks, it became evident that the settlement of these thorny issues would require a high degree of political compromise between Tokyo and Pyongyang, probably as a package deal rather than a piecemeal approach.

Meanwhile, Japanese-North Korean relations were strained due to North Korea's attempts to develop missiles and nuclear weapons in the 1990s. Even though Pyongyang's nuclear program was frozen as a result of the signing of the Agreed Framework between the United States and North Korea in October 1994, Japan's suspicion about Pyongyang's ambition to develop weapons of mass destruction (WMDs) persisted. In August 1998, Japan was shocked by Pyongyang's launching of a ballistic missile (a Taepo-dong), which flew over Japanese airspace and fell into the Pacific Ocean. Japan was also deeply disturbed by North Korean spy ships' frequent intrusion into Japan's territorial waters.

It was against this background that the LDP-led coalition government headed by Prime Minister Koizumi Junichiro was inaugurated in April 2001. Although the Koizumi government's top priority was focused more on domestic economic reforms than foreign affairs, Koizumi surprised many by taking the bold initiative to visit Pyongyang for a summit meeting with Kim Jong Il twice between September 2002 and May 2004. Koizumi's historic first visit to Pyongyang aroused many expectations for the normalization of diplomatic relations between the two neighboring countries. However, such a hope was dashed due to a number of unexpected developments, particularly the revelation of North Korea's clandestine nuclear weapons program in violation of international agreements.[3] Apparently, Koizumi did not give up the idea of normalizing diplomatic ties with Pyongyang and surprised many Japanese again by making a second visit to Pyongyang to hold talks with Kim Jong Il on May 22, 2004. In the aftermath of the second Japan-North Korea summit meeting in Pyongyang, there is growing speculation that Koizumi is serious about normalizing relations with North Korea before the expiration of his tenure as prime minister in September 2006. It is the purpose of this chapter to examine Japanese-North Korean relations from the time of the inauguration of the new LDP-led coalition government headed by Prime Minister Koizumi in April 2001 to the present. It is a major contention of this chapter that in spite of Koizumi's desire to normalize diplomatic ties between Tokyo and Pyongyang, unless and until North Korea abandons its nuclear weapons program, it is quite unlikely that will occur.

Prelude to the 2002 Pyongyang Summit

Following the establishment of the Koizumi government, there was no immediate sign of improvement in Japanese-North Korean relations. Rather, the strain in these relations was exacerbated further by an incident involving an unidentified ship, suspected to be North Korea's, which was sunk by the Japanese Coast Guard following an exchange of gunfire on December 21, 2001. North Korea denied any knowledge of the sunken ship, but circumstantial evidence tended to indicate strongly it was a North Korean ship engaged in illegal activities. Subsequently, after recovering the sunken ship, Japanese officials formally identified it as a North Korean "spy ship."[4] In response to the incident, the North Korean Red Cross Society announced the decision to suspend its investigation and search for the "missing" (euphemism for "kidnapped") Japanese nationals toward the end of December 2001.

In the spring of 2002, Japanese-North Korean relations began to show some improvement following the talks between Japanese and North Korean Red Cross delegations in Beijing the end of April 2002, as the North Korean delegation promised to conduct a "serious investigation" into the "missing" Japanese. At another round of Red Cross talks in Pyongyang in mid-August 2002, North Koreans provided information for the first time concerning some "missing" Japanese, even though none of the eleven abductees on Tokyo's list was included. Meanwhile, North Korean officials told visiting Russian Foreign Minister Igor Ivanov in Pyongyang in July that they wished to open a dialogue with Japan and the United States "without any preconditions."[5] At the ASEAN Regional Forum meeting in Brunei in July 2002, Japanese Foreign Minister Kawaguchi Yoriko and her North Korean counterpart, Paek Nam Sun, agreed to hold a bilateral working-level meeting in August 2002.[6]

It was not until late that August that significant progress was made toward the resumption of the suspended Japanese-North Korean normalization talks. At bilateral director-general level talks in Pyongyang, Japan and North Korea agreed to deal "comprehensively" with various issues of mutual concern, including apologies and compensation for Japan's colonial rule of Korea, normalization of relations, and the "humanitarian problem" (i.e., the abduction issue).[7] At the meeting, Tanaka Hitoshi, director-general of the Japanese Foreign Ministry's Asian and Oceanian Affairs Bureau and his North Korean counterpart, Ma Chol-Su, were able to lay down the basic framework for a Japan-North Korea summit meeting by hammering out a compromise on the two thorny issues obstructing diplomatic normalization between Tokyo and Pyongyang: (1) the scope and nature of Japan's compensation to North Korea and (2) the abduction issue. First, reversing its previous position, Pyongyang indicated its willingness to accept Japan's economic aid instead of insisting on "reparations" on the compensation issue. Second, Pyongyang also hinted at its willingness to provide information concerning the "missing" Japanese. In return, Japan expressed its willingness to resume normalization talks with Pyongyang. Tanaka also delivered Prime Minister Koizumi's message to Kim Jong Il, promising to make serious efforts toward normalization and expressing the hope that Kim would do likewise. In reply,

Kim expressed his gratitude to Koizumi.[8] It was the first such exchange of messages between the two leaders.

Against this background, Japan announced on August 30, 2002, that Koizumi would visit North Korea on September 17 for a summit meeting with Kim Jong Il. Apparently, Koizumi's decision reflected his determination to normalize relations with North Korea, the only country with which Japan has not established diplomatic ties in the post–World War II era. Without normalizing diplomatic ties with North Korea, one of the few remaining issues stemming from Japan's defeat in World War II, Japan might not be able to compete effectively in Korea with other major powers such as China and Russia, which have established diplomatic ties with both North and South Korea. In addition, there was a strong feeling among some influential leaders of the Japan's ruling LDP and Foreign Ministry officials that the collapse (or "hard landing") of North Korea would not benefit North Korea's neighbors including Japan, for such a contingency could create enormous economic, political, and humanitarian problems for them.[9] In addition, there was a need for Japan to utilize the opportunity to pressure Pyongyang on security issues, such as missiles and nuclear weapons, and North Korean spy ships' frequent intrusions into Japanese waters. A successful resolution of the North Korean problem would not only be a major achievement for the Koizumi government but also boost the sagging popularity of the Koizumi government, which was losing popular support because of its inability to tackle the deepening economic recession.

For the Kim Jong Il regime, on the other hand, the settlement of the apology and compensation issues was clearly a top priority. North Korea was desperately in need of foreign economic assistance to cope with its deepening economic crisis. With its economy on the verge of collapse, it needed Japan's massive economic assistance in whatever form possible. This was why Pyongyang was indicating its willingness to make concessions on the compensation issue, to accept Japan's compensation in the form of economic assistance instead of insisting on reparations. Clearly, Pyongyang was also sorely in need of Japan's economic aid in order to ensure the successful implementation of an ambitious economic reform program announced on July 1, 2002. In addition, North Korea wanted to enlist Japan's goodwill and influence in improving Pyongyang's relations with the United States, which had become severely strained after the inauguration of the Bush administration in 2001.

The 2002 Pyongyang Summit

At the historic Japanese-North Korean summit held in Pyongyang on September 17, 2002, both sides gave ground on bilateral issues. Kim Jong Il acknowledged North Korea's responsibility for abducting Japanese nationals and offered an apology, pledging that such an incident would never be repeated. According to Kim, four of eleven Japanese citizens abducted by North Korea in the 1970s and 1980s were alive, but six others had died of illness or in natural disasters. One had never entered North Korea. In addition, the North Korean side provided information concerning three additional Japanese abductees who had not been on the original Japanese list: one was still alive, but the other two were dead. Thus, out of thirteen abductees, eight had died, while five were still alive. Koizumi demanded that North Korea continue its investigation into the cases, return those who were alive, and take measures to prevent such activities in the future. Kim pledged not to engage in such an act again, while revealing that Pyongyang had already punished those responsible.[10]

In a joint declaration released after the talks, the Japanese side voiced "deep regrets and a heartfelt apology" toward the people of North Korea. Concerning the outstanding issues related to the "lives and security of Japanese nationals," the North Korean side confirmed that it would take appropriate measures so that these incidents would "never happen again."[11] The two leaders agreed that Tokyo and Pyongyang should settle North Korea's demand for compensation for suffering inflicted on Koreans during Japan's colonial rule of Korea not through reparations but by economic cooperation involving Japanese grants and low-interest loans. Regarding the nuclear weapons issue, Kim promised to comply with "all related international agreements." In addition, Kim promised to extend North Korea's moratorium on missile testing beyond the previously pledged deadline of 2003. The two leaders confirmed the need to promote dialogue on security issues, including nuclear development and missiles. They agreed to make efforts to normalize their bilateral ties by resuming stalled bilateral normalization talks in October 2002. Although not included in the joint declaration, Kim Jong Il also pledged to prevent the recurrence of North Korean spy ships' intrusions into Japanese territorial waters.

The Koizumi-Kim summit meeting clearly achieved more than many Japanese had expected.[12] For the first time, Kim Jong Il had confessed and apologized for abducting Japanese nationals, promising to prevent a recurrence. At the same time, the Japanese side was greatly encouraged by North Korea's willingness to settle the compensation issue through economic cooperation rather than as reparations as Pyongyang had insisted in the past. As a result, the two major issues that had obstructed the progress of normalization talks between the two countries seemed to be close to resolution. The Pyongyang summit resuscitated the hope for the normalization of Japanese-North Korean diplomatic relations.[13]

According to a public opinion poll conducted by the *Mainichi Shimbun,* Koizumi's diplomatic initiative was supported by the Japanese. As for the resumption of normalization talks, 54 percent supported it. However, three-quarters of the respondents said Japan should not hurry to establish diplomatic ties with Pyongyang. The same poll also confirmed a dramatic rise in the popularity of Prime Minister Koizumi from 43 percent in August to 67 percent in the wake of the Pyongyang summit.[14] However, the reaction to Koizumi's visit to Pyongyang was not wholly positive but contained dangers of a backlash, as many Japanese were shocked to learn that eight out of thirteen abductees had died after being abducted to North Korea. There were angry reactions from the relatives of the victims, who resented Koizum's "hasty" decision to resume normalization talks without securing adequate information concerning the circumstances surrounding the deaths of the eight abductees or making necessary arrangements for the return of the surviving five and their families to Japan.

To placate enraged public opinion, Japan dispatched an official delegation to collect further information concerning the fate of the Japanese abductees. Pyongyang told the Japanese team that all eight had died from "illness and disasters" and had not been the victims of foul play. However, no credible explanation was given by North Korea to substantiate Pyongyang's claims. Japanese suspicions about the circumstances surrounding the deaths of the deceased abductees were deepened by Pyongyang's claim that seven of eight graves (together with remains) had been washed away in massive floods.[15] Furthermore, the same hospital issued death certificates to seven victims despite the North's claim that they died under diverse circumstances in several different provinces. As a result, relatives of the victims reacted angrily to what they branded as the details of a cruel hoax and more lies from the North Korean regime. They simply refused to believe the explanations offered. Under the circumstances, concerned Japanese demanded that Japan not normalize relations with North Korea unless or until the kidnapping issue was resolved satisfactorily.

As the anger of the victims' relatives and the sensational Japanese media reports showed no sign of abating, it became imperative for the Koizumi government to accommodate the demands of the victims' relatives. It promised to continue further investigation into the abduction cases in order to discover the truth about the deaths. At the same time, it had to work out an arrangement for the early return to Japan of the five surviving abductees from North Korea, as the relatives of these abductees were stepping up demands to bring them home. Through secret talks held between Tanaka Hitoshi and his North Korean counterpart, Ma Chol-Su, the Koizumi government was able to arrange for the five surviving abductees to return to Japan for a two-week visit, beginning October 15, 2002.[16] Apparently, North Korea decided to accept the Japanese request for the home visit to show its goodwill toward the resumption of normalization talks and to placate Japanese public opinion.

Following the arrival of the five abductees in Japan, Koizumi made it clear that their homecoming visit constituted the first step toward the resolution of the abduction issue. However, there still remained many outstanding issues requiring resolution, such as the return of family members of the returned abductees and a further probe into the cases of the other abductees who were reported to be dead.[17] Koizumi pledged that Japan would place top priority on dealing with the abduction issues in future negotiations with the promise that his government would help the returned abductees to bring their family members (e.g., children) left behind in North Korea to Japan. On October 24, Japan announced that it had decided to extend the stay of the five home-visiting abductees indefinitely so as to enable them to decide their future freely.[18]

Meanwhile, in addition to the abduction issue, Pyongyang's clandestine nuclear weapons program was shaping up as a major dispute in Japanese-North Korean relations. This revelation came during U.S. Assistant Secretary of State for Asia and Pacific Affairs James Kelly's visit to Pyongyang in early October 2002. The disclosure of the existence of a clandestine North Korean uranium-based nuclear weapons program in violation of several international agreements and treaties shocked Japanese leaders.

Coming barely a month after the signing of the "Japan-North Korea Pyongyang Declaration," in which Kim Jong Il had pledged to abide by all international agreements related to the nuclear issue, the exposure of the Pyongyang's secret nuclear weapons program clearly undermined Japan's confidence in North Korea's trustworthiness.[19]

At the APEC meeting at Los Cabos, Mexico, in late October 2002, jointly with the leaders of the United States and South Korea, Prime Minister Koizumi called on North Korea "to dismantle" its nuclear weapons program "in a prompt and verifiable manner" and to comply fully with its international commitments. Returning from the APEC meeting, Koizumi made it clear that Japan would strongly demand at the forthcoming Japanese-North Korean normalization talks that North Korea scrap its uranium-based nuclear weapons program immediately and comply with international agreements relevant to the nuclear issue as promised in the Pyongyang Declaration.[20] If North Korea would not comply favorably with such a request, Japan would neither normalize relations with Pyongyang nor offer economic assistance to the Communist regime.

At the twelfth round of Japanese-North Korean normalization talks, held in Kuala Lumpur, Malaysia, from October 29 to 30, 2002, it became evident that there was a wide chasm between Japan and North Korea on several key issues. First, the North Korean delegation headed by Ambassador Jong Tae-Hwa rejected Japan's demand for the settlement of the abduction issue, contending that it had been resolved at the Pyongyang summit on September 17 when Kim Jong Il offered an apology with a promise to prevent recurrences. Furthermore, North Korea insisted that it was cooperating with Japan in investigating details surrounding the deaths of the eight deceased abductees. North Korea also accused Japan of breaking its promise to return the five abductees to Pyongyang after a two-week home visit in Japan. It demanded that Japan keep its promise to pave the way for the resolution of the issue.[21] North Korea also rejected Japan's demand for the return of the families of the five abductees at an early date. In response, the Japanese delegation headed by Ambassador Suzuki Katsunari denounced Pyongyang's "criminal act of kidnapping."[22]

Regarding Pyongyang's uranium enrichment program, the Japanese delegation expressed strong concern over North Korea's nuclear weapons program, reminding Pyongyang of its international commitment and obligations and demanding that Pyongyang dismantle its nuclear program "in a prompt and verifiable manner."[23] However, North Korea rejected the demand, saying that it would resolve the nuclear issue through negotiations with the United States as Washington's "hostile policy" toward North Korea was at the root of the nuclear problem.

In response to North Korea's insistence that Tokyo and Pyongyang should discuss economic cooperation as a priority issue, Japan replied that economic aid would come only in the aftermath of the normalization of Tokyo-Pyongyang diplomatic relations. In short, Japan and North Korea failed to make any significant progress in resolving either the abduction or nuclear weapons issues during the twelfth round of normalization talks. Although the two sides agreed to hold high-level bilateral talks on security issues including Pyongyang's nuclear and missile development program, the twelfth round of talks adjourned without agreeing on a date for the next round.[24]

In the aftermath of the twelfth round of normalization talks, it became evident that relations between Japan and North Korea were stalemated. Japan decided to allow the five Japanese abductees to stay in Japan for good, despite Pyongyang's warning that it would not proceed with further negotiations unless the abductees were returned to North Korea. Japan was equally determined to secure concessions from Pyongyang not only for the permanent stay of the five abductees in Japan but also for the return of their families left behind in North Korea. In fact, because of enraged Japanese public opinion on the abduction issue, Tokyo made it clear to Pyongyang that return of the abductees' families to Japan was a precondition of resuming any further round of normalization talks.[25] In addition to the abduction issue, Pyongyang's adamant refusal to comply with the demands of Japan, the United States, and South Korea on the nuclear weapons program was casting serious doubts about any progress in Tokyo-Pyongyang relations.

The North Korean Nuclear Crisis

Japanese-North Korean relations deteriorated further as North Korea began to escalate tensions on the Korean peninsula by undertaking a series of provocative steps to reactivate the plutonium-based nuclear weapons program in Yongbyun in violation of several international agreements, including the 1994 Agreed Framework. On December 12, 2002, North Korea removed the seals and cameras installed by the IAEA to monitor the frozen facilities. When the IAEA demanded that Pyongyang restore the monitoring devices to their original positions, Pyongyang responded by expelling two IAEA inspectors stationed in North Korea. Furthermore, when the IAEA warned Pyongyang of the serious consequences of violating the Nuclear Non-Proliferation Treaty (NPT), Pyongyang announced its decision to withdraw from the treaty on January 10, 2003.

By the end of January, there were clear signs that North Korea was preparing for the swift reactivation of the Yongbyun nuclear facilities, which had been frozen since 1994 under the Agreed Framework. By late February, the United States confirmed that Pyongyang had reactivated its five-megawatt graphite-moderated nuclear reactor. Meanwhile, North Korea demanded a treaty of nonaggression with the United States as a prerequisite for the settlement of the crisis.

Against the backdrop of heightened tension on the Korean peninsula, the Koizumi government made it clear that Japan would work for the dismantling of North Korea's nuclear weapons program through a peaceful diplomatic approach, for too much pressure on the North could lead the Kim Jong Il regime to take unpredictable actions. Certainly, Japan wanted to avoid the renewal of war on the Korean peninsula, for Japan would be embroiled in the conflict either directly or indirectly in view of the existing security arrangement with the United States. Within the Japanese Ministry of Foreign Affairs (MOFA), opinions were divided regarding North Korea's intentions behind the nuclear standoff. The mainstream view of the ministry assumed that the North was trying to use its nuclear program as a diplomatic bargaining chip in negotiations with the United States.[26] They preferred to pursue a gradual, diplomatic approach to resolve the North Korean nuclear crisis. However, some in the MOFA and many in the Japan Defense Agency believed that North Korea was determined to develop nuclear weapons to ensure its security. Therefore, they would not support offering any major concessions (e.g., normalization of diplomatic ties, economic aid, etc.) to the North unless Pyongyang terminated its nuclear weapons program first.

In dealing with the North Korean nuclear crisis, Japan decided to cooperate fully with the United States, the guarantor of Japan's security under the U.S.-Japan security treaty of 1951. At the U.S.-Japan Security Consultative Committee's meeting in Washington on December 16, 2002, Japan and the United States urged North Korea to give up its nuclear weapons program in a "prompt and verifiable fashion."[27] In addition, they expressed "serious concern" over Pyongyang's ballistic missile programs and urged Pyongyang to terminate all missile-related activities. They also urged Pyongyang's full compliance with the Biological Weapons Convention and adherence to the Chemical Weapons Convention. Japan also indicated its willingness to support the U.S. plan to convene a multilateral forum on the North Korean nuclear issue. Such a move clearly irritated North Korea, which was demanding direct bilateral talks between Pyongyang and Washington.

North Korea's official media accused Japan of blindly following the United States in pursuing a hostile policy toward North Korea. For example, *Rodong Sinmun,* the official organ of the North Korean regime, charged that Japanese "right-wing forces" were committing wrongs by following Washington's hostile policy toward North Korea.[28] Furthermore, it declared that the Korean peninsula's nuclear issue "is not an issue for Japan to presumptuously act upon," for it is a "bilateral issue to be resolved between the U.S. and North Korea." It slammed the door on Japan by saying that "Japan is not a party concerned with the resolution of the Korean peninsula's nuclear issue and has no pretext or qualification to intervene."[29] In addition, it criticized Japan for using "various pretexts and excuses to shelve the liquidation of its past and deliberately slackened normalizing relations" with North Korea.

Because nuclear-armed North Korea with sophisticated ballistic missiles would pose a serious threat to Japan's security, Japanese Foreign Minister Kawaguchi made it clear in a major foreign policy speech delivered before the Japanese Diet in January 2003 that Japan would demand Pyongyang to abide by the Nuclear Non-Proliferation Treaty (NPT), "freeze" its nuclear facilities, and "abandon" all its nuclear weapons development programs.[30] In a related move, Deputy Chief Cabinet Secretary Abe Shinzo reiterated Japan's position that it would not resume normalization talks with North Korea unless Pyongyang would abide by international law and regulations. He added that "We cannot allow North Korea to arm itself with nuclear weapons."[31] In addition, Abe made it clear that Japan would not resume talks with North Korea unless Pyongyang let the families of the five surviving abductees return to Japan and give convincing replies to the set of some 150 questions concerning the eight dead abductees.

In the spring of 2003, North Korea escalated tensions further on the Korean peninsula by reactivating its five-megawatt graphite-moderated nuclear reactor at Yongbyun and test-fired an antiship missile on the eve of President Roh Moo Hyun's inauguration on February 25, 2003. Pyongyang continued to ratchet up its provocation by trying to intercept a U.S. reconnaissance plane and launching another antiship missile in early March. Clearly these developments aroused great concern on the part of the United States and its allies. Prime Minister Koizumi expressed his view that "the Pyongyang Declaration has been breached," partially if not in its entirety.[32] In a related move, in his testimony before a parliamentary standing committee, Chief Cabinet Secretary Fukuda Yasuo warned that Pyongyang's provocative acts had breached the spirit of the Pyongyang Declaration. He then warned North Korea that the test-firing of a long-range missile or the reprocessing of spent nuclear fuel for weapons-grade plutonium would constitute the "red line," the crossing of which would nullify the Pyongyang Declaration. Although Fukuda maintained that Pyongyang "has not crossed this line," he made it unmistakably clear that further provocation by North Korea could endanger the Pyongyang accord.[33]

Japan's Response to North Korea's Nuclear Threat

Japan's North Korea policy hardened in the aftermath of the trilateral (United States-North Korea-China) talks in Beijing in April 2003 as the talks ended without making progress in resolving the North Korean nuclear crisis. Although North Korea proposed the outline of a package deal, it was rejected by the United States, which demanded the dismantling of Pyongyang's nuclear weapons program before Washington would discuss reciprocal measures such as a security guarantee and economic assistance. Japan was clearly disturbed by the report quoting a North Korean delegate's assertion at the Beijing meeting that Pyongyang already possessed nuclear weapons and that it had nearly completed reprocessing of spent nuclear fuel into weapons-grade plutonium.

At the United States-Japan summit meeting, held at Crawford, Texas, in late May, both Bush and Koizumi declared their determination not to tolerate North Korea's nuclear weapons program and demanded that Pyongyang dismantle it in a verifiable manner. At the same time, Koizumi also declared that Japan would "crack down more vigorously" on illegal activities involving North Korea or pro-Pyongyang Korean supporters in Japan. The two leaders also agreed to take "tougher measures" in case of further escalation of the crisis by North Korea.[34] Following the summit meeting, Japan agreed to become one of eleven nations participating in the U.S.-led Proliferation Security Initiative (PSI), proposed by President Bush in May 2003 to interdict weapons of mass destruction shipments to and from countries like North Korea.

Starting in the spring of 2003, the Koizumi government began to expand safety inspections and searches for illicit contraband coming in from or shipped to North Korea. These measures were apparently adopted to cope with the growing suspicion and evidence that firms run by pro-Pyongyang Korean residents in Japan were providing North Korea with key parts for its missile and nuclear programs.[35] For example, in April, Japanese authorities filed criminal charges against Meishin, a trading company run by a pro-Pyongyang Korean resident in Japan that allegedly tried to ship North Korea electronic control devices that can be used in the production of strategic weapons. A shipment of the devices from Meishin was seized by Hong Kong customs officials at Japan's request. The shipment was reportedly destined for North Korea via Hong Kong and Thailand.[36]

Furthermore, in order to curtail the illicit trade of drugs and counterfeit currency from North Korea, Japan stepped up customs and safety inspections of North Korean ships entering Japanese ports. More than 70 percent of North Korean ships entering Japanese ports from January 2003 to August 2003 failed to meet the safety standards and were ordered to halt operations.[37] Japan also decided to require foreign ships to carry adequate insurance before being allowed to enter any Japanese port. According to the *Yomiuri Shimbun,* only 2.8 percent of North Korean ships entering Japanese ports in 2002 had the required insurance.[38] Apparently, strict inspections and other cumbersome requirements forced some North Korean ships to suspend or delay their scheduled visits to Japan in the summer of 2003. As a result, the number of North Korean ships making calls on Japanese ports dropped by 29 percent in 2003 as compared with 2002.[39] Pyongyang accused Japan of acting as the "shock brigade" for the U.S.-led "psychological warfare and blockade operation."[40]

Concurrently, the Koizumi government began to study measures to restrict trade with the North and the flow of remittances from pro-Pyongyang Korean residents. Reversing the previous tolerance of the pro-Pyongyang Korean resident association Chochongryon, Japan stepped up an investigation of the finances of the pro-Pyongyang organization and its affiliated credit unions beginning in 2001. Many of the credit unions affiliated with the Chochongryon became bankrupt as a result of mismanagement, embezzlement, and illicit funneling of sizable sums to North Korea.[41] Several of these credit unions were restructured under Japanese government supervision after being insolvent. The Chochongryon's financial predicament became more severe as several prefectural and local governments (e.g., the Tokyo Metropolitan government) decided not to accord tax-exempt status to the organization and affiliated Korean schools in Japan. Also, the organization's membership dwindled rapidly as many became disenchanted with the Kim Jong Il regime which now had an image that was severely tarnished as a result of massive starvation in the North as well as serious violation of international agreements and treaties such as the abduction of Japanese nationals by North Korean agents.

Reflecting the deterioration of Tokyo-Pyongyang relations, the volume of bilateral trade declined sharply in 2003. For example, the value of the two-way trade declined by 33.4 percent to 30.6 billion yen (or $255 million) in 2003 from 45.9 billion yen (or $383 million) in 2002.[42] Japan also considered revising its Foreign Exchange and Foreign Trade Law in an attempt to empower the Japanese government to impose economic sanctions unilaterally. If adopted, these measures would restrict trade with the North and the flow of remittances from pro-Pyongyang residents who were reported to have remitted to North Korea over several hundred million dollars annually in the early 1990s. Remittances are reported to have declined more recently (e.g., $85 million in 2002) due to economic conditions in Japan and the decline of the financial power of the Chochongryon.[43]

The Koizumi government also ruled out the possibility of providing any additional food aid to North Korea. Japan had been one of the largest donors to North Korea. Specifically, from June 1995 to October 2000, Japan provided 1,182,000 tons of food (mostly rice) aid to North Korea.[44] Most of the aid (valued at $1.45 billion) was sent to North Korea free of charge, while 350,000 tons were provided on a long-term loan basis. In the face of North Korea's unwillingness to give up its nuclear weapons program, the Koizumi government ruled out the possibility of extending additional food aid.

In order to cope with North Korea's nuclear and missile threat, Japan also adopted several important measures to beef up its military preparedness. Particularly disturbing to Japan were North Korea's ballistic missiles. North Korea was believed to have deployed over 150 Nodong missiles, capable of hitting Japan, with a range of over 1,300 kilometers. North Korea is also in the process of developing Taepo-dong long-range ballistic missiles that could reach Alaska and parts of the U.S. West Coast. In order to monitor the test firing of North Korean ballistic missiles, Japan successfully launched two spy satellites on March 28, 2003. In a related move, in December 2003, Japan decided to build an effective missile defense system (MDS). Starting in 2004, Japan began to procure and deploy PAC-3 (Patriot Advanced Capability) missiles and the SM-3 (Standard Missile) system to defend itself from North Korea's missiles. The land-based PAC-3 missile system is designed to shoot down enemy missiles shortly before they hit targets in Japan, while the SM-3 system, to be deployed aboard Aegis-equipped warships, is designed to intercept enemy missiles before they enter the earth's atmosphere. Japan will initially spend $1 billion to procure these advanced interceptor missiles and eventually plans to deploy a functionally layered antimissile defense system at a total cost of $7 billion by 2007.[45] To be sure, some hawkish Japanese leaders (e.g., Ishiba Shigeru, Director-General of the Japanese Defense Agency) have advocated the acquisition of cruise missiles (e.g., Tomahawk type) for possible preemptive strikes against North Korean missile sites in case of an imminent danger of attack from the North. According to Ishiba, if Japan were to wait until a North Korean missile was fired against Japan, it would be "too late."[46] Similar remarks were made by Prime Minister Koizumi on the eve of the Crawford, Texas, summit in May 2003.

In the summer of 2003, the Japanese parliament passed three "war contingency bills" that would give the Japanese government new powers to cope with armed attacks on Japan. Such contingency legislation had first been discussed among Japanese conservatives some forty years ago, but was shelved because of the possibility that it would violate Article 9 of the Japanese constitution. The threat posed by North Korea and international terrorism enabled the Koizumi government to win the support of the main opposition party, the Democratic Party of Japan (DPJ), for the enactment of this special legislation. Among other things, the new legislation would enable Japan to deploy the Self-Defense Forces (SDF) swiftly by suspending numerous restrictions hindering the effective mobilization and operation of the SDF.

By the winter of 2003, it was evident that the Japanese perceived North Korea as posing a greater threat to Japan's security than any other country. According to an opinion survey conducted by the *Mainichi Shimbun* in December 2003, over 50 percent of the respondents indicated that they regarded North Korea as a threat to Japan's security, while 24 percent regarded China as a threat.[47] Regarding the North Korean nuclear issue, 75 percent of the respondents believed there was no possibility of resolving the issue in 2004, while 5 percent believed in the possibility of making progress. Pertaining to Japan's food aid to North Korea, 64 percent maintained that Japan should suspend the aid to North Korea, while 26 percent supported offering such aid to the North.

Japan's Two-Track Approach

By the summer of 2003, it had become evident that Japan was placing its hope on the multilateral forum (i.e., the Six-Party Talks) to resolve the security issues relating to North Korea's nuclear and missile development by supporting the U.S. approach to these problems. Although there was no breakthrough at the Six-Party Talks involving the United States, China, Japan, Russia, and the two Koreas in Beijing in late August 2003, Japan was encouraged by the agreement reached at that meeting to continue a dialogue for the common objective of achieving a nuclear-free Korean peninsula.[48] In October, at the APEC meeting in Bangkok, Thailand, President Bush announced his willingness to offer North Korea a written security guarantee that would also be endorsed by other parties in the Six-Party Talks, provided that Pyongyang would dismantle its nuclear weapons program. North Korea indicated its willingness to "consider" the Bush proposal as part of a package solution to the nuclear issue. North Korea also announced its intention to attend the next round of Six-Party Talks in Beijing. However, there were substantial differences between the United States and North Korea with regard to the scope and nature of the package deal to be worked out at the multilateral forum. North Korea offered to "freeze" its nuclear program in return for a security guarantee, fuel, and other aid, while the United States demanded that North Korea agree to dismantle its nuclear weapons program in an irreversible and verifiable manner.

Concerning the issue of normalizing diplomatic ties between Tokyo and Pyongyang, Japan stressed at the Beijing meetings that the nuclear, missile, and abduction issues should be resolved comprehensively. Nevertheless, Japan decided to handle the abduction and other bilateral issues through direct bilateral talks with North Korea in parallel with the Six-Party Talks. On the sidelines of the Beijing talks in August 2003, Japan and North Korea held talks concerning the issues blocking the resumption of normalization talks. Japan demanded that North Korea allow the families of the five Japanese abductees to visit Japan. At the same time, it demanded information concerning the fate of ten other Japanese, including the eight abductees reported dead by Pyongyang. North Korea responded by repeating its accusation that Japan had broken its promise to send the five back to the North after what was supposed to be a temporary homecoming in October 2002. Nevertheless, they agreed to resolve these issues through further negotiations on the basis of the Pyongyang Declaration.[49]

On November 25, 2003, in his testimony before the lower house Budget Committee, Prime Minister Koizumi indicated his intention to consider imposing sanctions on North Korea if it continued to ignore Japan's demands on the abduction issue.[50] Koizumi also indicated his plan to take up the issue at the second round of the Six-Party Talks in Beijing. North Korea's response to these developments was clearly negative. According to Pyongyang's official Korean Central News Agency (KCNA), now that Tokyo insisted on taking up the abduction issue at the Beijing talks, North Korea would "never" accept Japan's participation in the forthcoming multilateral talks in Beijing. It also threatened not to take part in the talks if the abduction issue was going to be raised there.[51]

Against this background, a group of Japanese lawmakers led by Hirasawa Katsuei, an LDP Diet member, held talks with North Korean officials (including Ambassador Jong Tae-Hwa, who was in charge of normalization talks with Japan) on the abduction issue in Beijing in late December 2003. North Korean officials told Japanese lawmakers that Pyongyang was willing to send the family members of the five surviving abductees to Japan if they came to Pyongyang to meet their family members and return to Japan with them.[52] The North Korean offer was conveyed to the Koizumi government by Hirasawa. Apparently, the new offer aroused the interest of Foreign Minister Kawaguchi, who indicated Japan's willingness to negotiate with North Korea on the return of the abductees' family members, based on North Korea's reported offer.[53]

A breakthrough in the abduction issue became a necessity for the Koizumi government, as it became increasingly clear that more Japanese were concerned about the abduction issue than the North's nuclear weapons program. According to the public opinion survey conducted by the Japanese Cabinet Office in October and November 2003, 90 percent of the respondents said their main concern was the abduction issue, while 66 percent said they were concerned about North Korea's nuclear arms program.[54] Only 35 percent responded that they cared about the normalization of diplomatic ties between Japan and North Korea.

In mid-January 2004, a team of Japanese Foreign Ministry officials visited Pyongyang to take custody of two Japanese nationals detained by North Korea: one on a drug smuggling charge and the other for illegally entering North Korea. When these Japanese diplomats attempted to take up the abduction issue, North Korean officials reiterated their demand that Tokyo "keep its promise" and send back the five former abductees who had reneged on the promise to return to Pyongyang after a brief home visit. In February, another team of Japanese foreign ministry officials was dispatched to Pyongyang to explore the possibility of bringing family members of the five surviving abductees to Japan for family reunion. However, they were unable to make any progress toward resolving the issue. Nevertheless, the Koizumi government made it clear that it would continue to urge North Korea to resolve the issue of Japanese nationals abducted by the North and abandon its nuclear arms program in a verifiable and irreversible manner. According to Foreign Minister Kawaguchi, "issues concerning North Korea are on Japan's top diplomatic agenda" and Japan would continue to "seek a comprehensive resolution to such security issues as the abduction and North Korea's missile and nuclear developments."[55]

Meanwhile, in an attempt to pressure North Korea to come to terms on the nuclear and abduction issues, on February 9, 2004, the Japanese parliament passed an important bill revising the Foreign Exchange and Foreign Trade Control Law. The revised legislation empowers the Japanese government to impose unilateral economic sanctions on a country like North Korea without requiring a United Nations resolution or an international agreement mandating such actions. Under the new legislation, the Japanese government can ban cash remittances, restrict trade, freeze assets in Japan, and take other measures deemed necessary against a country that poses a threat to Japan's peace and security.[56] Although Koizumi maintained that his government was not considering immediate economic sanctions against North Korea, Chief Cabinet Secretary Fukuda Yasuo did not rule out possible sanctions in the future "if North Korea makes things worse."[57] North Korea's reactions to the revised legislation were negative. A spokesman for the North Korean Foreign Ministry denounced it as a "wanton violation" of the Pyongyang Declaration, warning that Japan would be responsible for "all consequences to be entailed by its foolish moves."[58]

To apply further pressure on North Korea, in the spring of 2004, lawmakers of the ruling parties (the LDP and the Komeito) introduced a bill to prohibit certain foreign ships from entering Japanese ports. The legislation was prompted by frustration among ruling party members about the lack of progress in resolving the issues of North Korea's nuclear program and the abduction at the second round of the Six-Party Talks in Beijing in February. The new legislation was designed to ban port calls by vessels from certain unfriendly countries for a limited period of time if the Cabinet determined such an action necessary to maintain Japan's peace and security. The bill clearly targeted North Korean ships suspected of being engaged in illicit activities, including the trafficking of drugs and counterfeit currencies and the transporting of equipment and parts used for the production of strategic weapons.[59] North Korea denounced the proposed bill as an "evil law" against North Korea.[60] Together with the revised Foreign Exchange and Foreign Trade Law, the enactment of the new legislation would clearly strengthen the Japanese government's ability to deal with the abduction issue as well as Pyongyang's nuclear weapons program by applying pressure, if necessary, on North Korea.

The 2004 Pyongyang Summit

As it became clear that Japan was taking preliminary steps toward the possible imposition of economic sanctions against North Korea, Pyongyang indicated a more flexible position on the abduction issue. At a secretly arranged meeting with former ruling LDP's Vice President Yamasaki Taku in Dalian, China, in early April 2004, North Korean Ambassador Jong Tae-Hwa indicated Pyongyang's willingness to allow a high ranking Japanese government official, instead of the five surviving abductees, to come to Pyongyang to pick up the eight family members. North Korea's new proposal was conveyed to Prime Minister Koizumi by Yamasaki a few days later. It was initially believed that the proposed mission could be carried out by a Cabinet member. However, Prime Minister Koizumi indicated that his visit to Pyongyang should not be ruled out as an option.[61] Koizumi's willingness to visit Pyongyang was not a real surprise to his colleagues, for he had indicated more than once his desire to normalize diplomatic relations with North Korea before the end of his tenure as the prime minister in 2006. In addition, Koizumi has been interested not only in enhancing Japan's international role commensurate with its economic power but also in playing a major role in dealing with the problem of peace and security on the Korean peninsula by normalizing Tokyo-Pyongyang relations.

At the bilateral talks held in Beijing in early May 2004, Japan and North Korea agreed on a plan for breaking the diplomatic stalemate over the abduction issue. Under the plan, Prime Minister Koizumi would visit Pyongyang to hold talks with Kim Jong Il and bring the families of five former abductees to Japan with him on his return. As a part of the agreement, Japan also indicated its willingness to resume diplomatic normalization talks, suspended in October 2002, and discuss humanitarian aid for North Korea if Pyongyang agreed to allow the family reunion in Japan and provided additional information about ten other Japanese abduction victims.[62]

On May 22, 2004, Koizumi visited Pyongyang to hold talks with Kim Jong Il. At the summit meeting, Kim agreed to allow the families of five former Japanese abductees to go to Japan for a family reunion. Regarding Japan's request for further information on the ten missing Japanese, including the eight who were reported to have died in North Korea, Kim promised Koizumi that a new investigation would be conducted. On the security issue, when Koizumi emphasized the importance of a comprehensive solution to pending issues, including Pyongyang's development of nuclear weapons and missiles, Kim reiterated North Korea's position that Pyongyang had to maintain a nuclear deterrent as a counterbalance to U.S. threat and pressure. Nevertheless, he stated that his goal was to achieve a non-nuclear Korean peninsula, and that Pyongyang's proposal for freezing its nuclear facilities in exchange for energy assistance and other compensation through the six-nation talks was a first step[63] in that direction. Kim reassured Koizumi that the North would maintain a moratorium on missile firing tests.

The second Koizumi-Kim summit meeting brought about diplomatic windfalls for North Korea. At the meeting, Koizumi promised Kim 250,000 tons of food and $10 million worth of medical assistance through international organizations.[64] In addition, the Japanese prime minister pledged that Japan would not invoke economic sanctions as long as North Korea observed the Pyongyang Declaration of September 17, 2002. During the ninety-minute meeting, the two leaders also agreed to hold working-level negotiations to seek the resumption of normalization talks between the two countries. In return, Pyongyang merely allowed five children of the repatriated abductees to go to Japan with the prime minister, while promising the remaining three family members of former abductee Soga Hitomi (i.e., her husband, Charles Jenkins, and two daughters) to have a family reunion at a third country to decide on their future destination. Jenkins, a U.S. army deserter, and his two daughters refused to go to Japan with Koizumi, fearing that he could be extradited to the United States.

According to an opinion survey conducted by the *Yomiuri Shimbun* on May 23, 63 percent of the respondents said they supported Koizumi's second visit to Pyongyang. However, 70 percent said they were not satisfied with the result of the summit talks in Pyongyang. Specifically, 56 percent of the respondents did not approve of Koizumi's pledge to provide North Korea with 250,000 tons of food and $10 million worth of medical assistance. Regarding North Korea's promise to reinvestigate the cases of ten missing Japanese, 64 percent of the respondents did not believe such an investigation would lead to discovering their whereabouts.[65] Thus, the poll indicated that, while giving Koizumi high marks for bringing home the family members of the five surviving abductees, most believed that Koizumi had paid too high a price. Even some conservative leaders of the ruling LDP criticized the prime minister for making easy compromises and concessions, such as his generous offer of humanitarian aid and his promise not to invoke economic sanctions against North Korea. Basically, they contended that Japan should not abandon such an important leverage in dealing with North Korea without securing Pyongyang's concessions on the nuclear weapons issue. Furthermore, Koizumi's critics expressed reservations about the plan to hold working-level negotiations for the resumption of normalization talks with North Korea.

To cope with these criticisms, Koizumi announced in the plenary session of the lower house of the Japanese Diet on May 25 that "normalization of relations cannot be achieved unless the abduction issue is resolved in a convincing manner and a comprehensive resolution is reached in other issues, such as North Korea's nuclear and missile development programs."[66] In an attempt to pressure North Korea to make concessions on the remaining issues, in June, the Japanese parliament enacted a new law to ban certain foreign ships from making port calls of Japan. It was designed to prohibit the entry of North Korean ships (e.g., the Mangyongbong-92) suspected of being engaged in illegal trafficking of money, drugs, counterfeit currencies, and transporting equipment and supplies from Japan for the production of strategic weapons in North Korea.[67]

In an apparent attempt to mollify Japanese public opinion, Pyongyang announced its decision to let Charles Jenkins and his two daughters meet Jenkin's wife, Soga Hitomi, a former abductee, in Jakarta, Indonesia, on July 9, 2004. North Korea has also announced its intention to repatriate four surviving Japanese Red Army members who had been living in North Korea after hijacking a Japanese passenger plane in 1970.[68] In the past, Pyongyang had rejected Tokyo's demand to repatriate them. These moves were clearly designed to improve North Korea's image in Japan so as to cultivate a better atmosphere for the resumption of normalization talks with Japan. It is also suspected that Pyongyang's prompt actions on the Soga's family reunion and the Japanese Red Army members' repatriation were designed to help Prime Minister Koizumi in the upper house elections of July 11, 2004. Clearly, Pyongyang was encouraged by Koizumi's professed intention to normalize Japanese-North Korean diplomatic relations under his leadership by 2006.[69]

In early August 2004, the Koizumi government announced its decision to ship the first half of the food aid and medical supplies to North Korea out of the humanitarian aid package promised by Koizumi at the Pyongyang summit in May. It would include 125,000 tons of food aid (worth $40 million) and $7 million in medical supplies to be distributed through international organizations.[70] It was designed to encourage Pyongyang to come up with reciprocal gestures of goodwill at the approaching bilateral working-level talks in Beijing. However, some in the Japanese ruling coalition led by the LDP expressed reservations about sending the aid, arguing that Tokyo should wait until Pyongyang produced some positive results in the ongoing investigation regarding the ten missing Japanese abductees.

On August 11–12, Japanese-North Korean working-level talks were held in Beijing. However, contrary to the Koizumi government's expectations, North Korea failed to provide any new information on the ten Japanese abductees in a "verbal interim report" presented at the meeting. In response to Japan's renewed call for scrapping North Korea's nuclear development program, North Korea's chief delegate simply promised to convey the message to relevant authorities in Pyongyang. Regarding the extradition of the four Red Army Faction members to Japan, Pyongyang's response was somewhat evasive, as it suggested that it was not opposed to their departure from the North but Tokyo should persuade them to return to Japan.[71] As there was no breakthrough in resolving either the abduction issue or Pyongyang's nuclear weapons program, the Koizumi government decided not to resume normalization talks anytime soon. As one senior Foreign Ministry official was quoted to have said, "Now's not the time to resume bilateral talks for the normalization of diplomatic ties."[72]

Conclusion

From the forgoing analysis, a few basic conclusions can be drawn: First, in dealing with North Korea, unlike many of his predecessors in the postwar era who closely followed U.S. policy and leadership, Prime Minister Koizumi has taken important initiatives toward North Korea, even at the risk of irritating the United States.[73] He is the first incumbent prime minister who has visited Pyongyang and held summit meetings with the North Korean leader twice in less than two years. Such a bold approach by Koizumi can be attributed to a number of factors. Apparently, it is his political ambition and desire to be recorded in history as the prime minister who has successfully settled one of the two major remaining issues stemming from Japan's defeat in World War II. He has revealed such a desire both privately and publicly. Also, Koizumi's foreign policy behavior toward North Korea reflects Japan's desire to play a greater role, one commensurate with its economic power, in the international political arena. Japan is frequently depicted as an economic giant but a political dwarf. Since the peace and security of the Korean peninsula are vital to Japan's own security, it is natural for Japan to take an active role in dealing with the current crisis triggered by

North Korea's attempts to develop nuclear weapons in violation of international agreements and treaties.

Second, the Koizumi government was successful in working out the "road map" for diplomatic normalization with North Korea during Prime Minister Koizumi's first visit to Pyongyang in September 2002. The two major obstacles (i.e., the abduction issue and the apologies and compensation) blocking the progress in normalization talks from 1991 to 2000 were largely resolved. However, North Korea's clumsy handling of the abductees' family reunion issue and its unwillingness to provide credible and exact details surrounding the deaths of eight Japanese abductees not only angered many Japanese but made it impossible for Tokyo to continue normalization talks. Through his second visit to Pyongyang in May 2004, Koizumi succeeded in bringing the family members of the surviving abductees from North Korea for a family reunion in Japan and Indonesia. However, the abduction controversy is by no means completely resolved, since Japan is still seeking the truth about the deaths of the eight Japanese who are reported to have died in North Korea plus information concerning two other missing Japanese suspected of having been abducted. Without resolving the thorny issue, the Koizumi government will not be able to normalize diplomatic ties with North Korea.

Third, the revelation of the existence of a clandestine nuclear enrichment program in clear violation of several international agreements has not only shocked the Japanese but also undermined the trustworthiness of the Kim Jong Il regime, which promised in the Pyongyang Declaration to comply with "all related international agreements" on nuclear issues on the Korean peninsula. Because the production and development of nuclear weapons by North Korea would pose a serious threat to Japan's security, Japan is determined to thwart Pyongyang's nuclear weapons program. If Pyongyang escalates tensions through testing its nuclear weapons or long-range missiles, Japan will most likely impose economic sanctions against North Korea and nullify the Pyongyang Declaration. It is essential for Pyongyang to abandon its nuclear weapons program if it is serious about normalizing diplomatic ties with Japan.

Fourth, North Korea's confrontational policy and provocative actions have strengthened not only negative perceptions of the Kim Jong Il regime on the part of many Japanese but also inadvertently advanced the political agenda of Japanese conservatives in favor of stronger Japanese defense preparedness and military capabilities. Because of the nuclear threat from North Korea, the Koizumi government has been able to enact several important laws, including new war contingency laws and the revised Foreign Exchange and Foreign Trade Control Law. Furthermore, to cope with North Korea's nuclear and missile threats, Japan is beefing up its defense preparedness by deploying an advanced missile defense system by 2007. In addition, there is a growing demand among Japanese conservatives that Japan amend Article 9 of the postwar constitution in order to make it possible for Japan to rearm fully.

Fifth, the primary concern of the Kim Jong Il regime in approaching normalization talks with Tokyo has been to secure massive economic assistance. However, Japan has made it clear that it is not going to normalize diplomatic ties with North

Korea unless Pyongyang dismantles its nuclear weapons program in a prompt and verifiable fashion. Unless and until the bilateral relationship is normalized, Japan will not offer economic aid to North Korea. Although the scale of Japan's aid to Pyongyang is yet to be determined through further negotiations, Pyongyang is reportedly seeking over $10 billion in economic assistance from Japan. If Pyongyang is serious about securing Japanese economic aid, it must fulfill the promises made in the Pyongyang Declaration of September 17, 2002, including its pledge on the nuclear issue. To be sure, Koizumi is still interested in resuming normalization talks with North Korea if Pyongyang complies with Tokyo's demands on the abduction and nuclear issues. However, in view of the fact that Koizumi's power within the LDP has been weakened as a result of the ruling party's poor showing in the upper house elections in July 2004, he is not in a position to make further concessions to North Korea for the sake of normalizing ties with North Korea. Under the circumstances, it is reasonable to conclude that unless North Korea agrees to dismantle its nuclear weapons program, it is virtually impossible for the Koizumi government to normalize diplomatic ties with North Korea. It remains to be seen if North Korea will abandon its nuclear weapons program in return for Japan's economic assistance and diplomatic recognition.

Notes

1. Hong Nack Kim, "Japan in North Korean Foreign Policy," 117.
2. For a detailed analysis, see Hong Nack Kim, "Japan and North Korea: Normalization Talks Between Pyongyang and Tokyo," 111–129.
3. Hong Nack Kim and Hammersmith, "Japanese-North Korean Relations," 611–616.
4. *New York Times*, October 5, 2002.
5. *Facts on File*, August 8, 2002, 606, available at www.factsonfile.com.
6. *Japan Times*, August 14, 2002.
7. *Japan Times*, August 27 and 31, and September 12, 2002.
8. Kyodo News Service, "Japan and N. Korea to Decide in September on Higher Talks," Japan Economic Newswire (hereafter *JEN*). See also, *Japan Times*, August 27, 2002.
9. Shigemura, *Saishin Kita Chosen Deta Bukku* (The Latest Data Book on North Korea), 230–234. See also, Katsumi Sato, "Tanaka Hitoshi wa naze hamen sarenainoka"(Why Has Hitoshi Tanaka Not Been Fired Yet?), *Shokun*, September 2003, p. 143.
10. *Japan Times*, September 18, 2002.
11. For a full text of the Japan-North Korea Pyongyang Declaration, see "Japan-DPRK Pyongyang Declaration," The Ministry of Foreign Affairs of Japan, Tokyo, September 17, 2002.
12. *Japan Times* (editorial), September 19, 2002.
13. Ibid.
14. *Mainichi Shimbun*, September 23, 2002.
15. For the report of the Japanese government investigation team on the fate of the Japanese abductees in North Korea, see "Kita Chosen ratchi jiken seifu hokoku sho," *Asahi Shimbun*, October 3, 2002. See also, *Facts on File*, October 3, 2002, 744, available at www.factsonfile.com.
16. *Daily Yomiuri*, October 11, 2002.
17. *Kyodo News Service*, October 15, 2002.
18. *New York Times*, October 25, 2002.
19. *Yomiuri Shimbun*, November 4, 2002.
20. Kyodo News Service, "Japan to Urge North Korea to Comply with Pyongyang Declaration," *JEN*, October 27, 2002.

21. *Yomiuri Shimbun*, October 30, 2002

22. Jiji Press Ticker Service, October 29, 2002.

23. Ibid.

24. *Japan Times*, October 31, 2002. See also *Nikkei Weekly*, November 5, 2002.

25. Kyodo News Service, "Top Japanese Diplomats in Beijing 'Apparently' in Touch with North Koreans," *JEN*, November 25, 2002.

26. Furukawa, "Japan's View of the Korea Crisis," 2–3.

27. Kyodo News Service, "Full Text of Joint Statement Issued after Japan-U.S. Security Talks," *JEN*, December 17, 2002.

28. "North Korean Paper Urges Japan to Drop Its 'Inborn U.S.-Toeing Policy," BBC Monitoring/BBC, Global News Wire–Asia African Intelligence Wire (hereafter BBC/AAIW), January 3, 2003.

29. "Japan Intervention in Nuclear Issue 'Ineffective'—North Korean Radio," BBC-AAIW, January 27, 2003.

30. Yukkio Ochi, "Japan to Continue Efforts Over N. Korea, Iraq," Kyodo News Service, *JEN*, January 31, 2003.

31. "Japanese Official Sees Hope in Resuming Dialogue with North Korea," BBC/AAIW, January 31, 2003.

32. "Japanese Premier Says North Korea Breaching Bilateral Deal," BBC/AAIW, March 3, 2003.

33. Junko Takahashi, "Tokyo May Kill Pyongyang Deal," *Japan Times*, March 20, 2003.

34. *Yomiuri Shimbun*, May 24 and 25, 2003.

35. *New York Times*, August 27, 2003.

36. *Facts on File*, June 12, 2003, 454, available at www.factsonfile.com.

37. Ibid.

38. *Yomiuri Shimbun*, June 20, 2003.

39. *Yomiuri Shimbun*, March 8, 2004.

40. *The Age* (Melbourne), June 25, 2003.

41. *Yomiuri Shimbun*, December 18, 2002.

42. [Nihon] Zaimusho, *Boeki Tokei* (Tokyo: Bureau of Customs, Ministry of Treasury). Monthly trade data on 2002 and 2003 are available at www.customs.go.jp/srch/indexe.htm.

43. *Daily Yomiuri*, March 5, 2003.

44. *Asahi Shimbun*, October 7, 2003.

45. *Yomiuri Shimbun*, June 22, 2003. See also *New York Times*, August 30, 2003.

46. *Yomiuri Shimbun*, February 13, 2003.

47. *Mainichi Shimbun*, January 5, 2004.

48. *Japan Times*, September 3, 2003.

49. Kyodo News Service, "Japan, North Korea Agree to Keep Discussing Abductions," *JEN*, August 29, 2003.

50. Kyodo News Agency, "Koizumi Eyes N. Korea Sanctions if Abduction Demands Not Met," *JEN*, November 25, 2003.

51. Kyodo News Agency, "Pyongyang Wants Japan Out of 6-State Talks, "*JEN*, November 20, 2003.

52. Jiji Press, "Japan Lawmakers Met with North Korea official," Jiji Press Ticket Service, December 25, 2003.

53. Kyodo News Agency, "Japan Ready to Negotiate N. Korea Offer on Abductees' Families," *JEN*, January 11, 2004.

54. *Japan Times*, January 11, 2004.

55. *Japan Times*, January 20, 2004.

56. *Yomiuri Shimbun*, January 30 and February 10, 2004.

57. "Japanese PM Rules Out Immediate Economic Sanctions Against North Korea," BBC/AAIW, January 27, 2004.

58. Xinhua News Agency, "DPRK Slashes Japan's Foreign Exchange Bill," January 31, 2004.

59. For a detailed analysis, see Chanlett-Avery, "North Korean Supporters in Japan," 4–5. See also Perl, "Drug Trafficking and North Korea," 1–13.

60. "North Korean Radio Denounces Japan's Bill Banning 'Specific Foreign Ships,'" BBC/ AAIW, March 31, 2004.

61. *Yomiuri Shimbun*, May 10, 2004.

62. *Mainichi Shimbun*, May 10, 2004.

63. *Yomiuri Shimbun*, May 23, 2004.

64. Ibid.

65. *Yomiuri Shumbun*, May 24, 2004.

66. *Asahi Shimbun*, May 26, 2004.

67. Kyodo News Service, "Japanese Parliament Enacts Law to Ban N. Korean Ships," *JEN*, June 14, 2004. See also, Chanlett-Avery, "North Korean Supporters in Japan."

68. *Asahi Shimbun*, July 7, 2004.

69. Nihon Keizai Shimbun, *The Nikkei Weekly*, July 5, 2004. See also Kyodo News Service, "Koizumi to Work Toward Normalizing N. Korea Ties in 1 Year," *JEN*, July 2, 2004.

70. Kyodo News Service, "Japan to Give N. Korea 5.2 Bil. Yen of Food, Medical Aid by Year-End," *JEN*, August 3, 2004.

71. *Yomiuri Shimbun*, August 13, 2004.

72. Ibid.

73. Rozman, "Japan's North Korea Initiative," 527–530.

9

Sino–North Korean Relations in the Post–Cold War World

Samuel S. Kim

In describing relations between the People's Republic of China (PRC or China) and the Democratic People's Republic of Korea (DPRK or North Korea), the term "bilateral" is somewhat of a misnomer. Since the end of the Cold War and the demise of global socialist ideology, Sino-North Korean relations have developed with a constant cyc toward both South Korca (ROK or Republic of Korea) and the United States. While the relationship between Beijing and Pyongyang remains a special one, its unique characteristics are now defined by China's use of its connections with the DPRK for the maintenance of domestic and "near-abroad" stability rather than for any grander ambitions.

When China looks at its 850–mile long (1,360 km) porous border with North Korea, it remembers the route by which imperial Japan launched its invasion of the Chinese mainland in the early twentieth century. It also recalls the U.S. intervention in the Korean War, when in late 1950 General Douglas MacArthur's forces crossed the 38th Parallel and approached the Chinese border. Since the fall of transnational communism, it is North Korea's potential implosion or explosion that is the focus of Chinese leaders and policy analysts. China is interested in protecting the enormous economic and political gains it made over the course of the 1990s, and one of the largest challenges to doing so comes in the form of its nominal ally and the potential for armed conflict that the U.S.-DPRK nuclear standoff brings to Northeast Asia.

North Korea's nuclear brinkmanship in 1993 and 1994—billed in the West as the first nuclear proliferation crisis of the post–Cold War era—became an instant security challenge for all the major players in Northeast Asian geopolitics. Even after the temporary resolution of that nuclear standoff during the Clinton administration, the possibility of implosion or explosion in North Korea seemed to have become more real than ever before. Today China is deeply involved in resolving the second U.S.-DPRK nuclear standoff, but it is constrained by the patterns of its historical relationship with North Korea and the contours of its relations with the United States and the ROK.

This chapter traces the checkered history of Sino–North Korean relations since the end of the Cold War with reference to three issue areas—political/diplomatic, military/security, and economic—in order to present some of the major goals motivating Chinese diplomacy in Northeast Asian geopolitics in general and in Korean peninsular affairs in particular, and in order to gain some insight into the possible future directions of the relationship. Because the triangular element of PRC-DPRK relations is crucial, the chapter begins with a discussion of the making of a triangular relationship.

Triangular Relations and Chinese Regional Goals

By fits and starts, Beijing's Korea policy evolved through several phases—from the familiar one-Korea (pro-Pyongyang) policy, to a one-Korea de jure/two-Koreas de facto policy, and finally to a policy of two-Koreas de facto and de jure. The decision to normalize relations with South Korea, finalized in August 1992, was the culmination of a process of balancing and adjusting post-Mao foreign policy to the logic of changing domestic, regional, and global situations.[1] This decision did not, however, imply a sudden end to the question of how China would relate to North Korea, the one and only country with which Beijing maintains its Cold War alliance pact, whether in name or in practice. Rather, it marked the beginning of a process of implementing the two-Koreas decision on a variety of issues over time. Since 1992, the main overall challenge has remained the same: how to translate China's preference for peninsular status-quo-cum-stability by maintaining a "special relationship" with Pyongyang while at the same time promoting and expanding "normal state relations" with Seoul.[2]

In the early 1990s, when the ROK and the PRC were realizing that they had more in common than they thought, Pyongyang was more or less sidelined. The odd man out, it was all too preoccupied in the 1980s and 1990s with the first-ever socialist dynastic succession at home and with the increasingly untenable quest for absolute one-Korea international legitimation. At the very moment when the DPRK might have followed China's cue to change its historical pattern of behavior and become more outward oriented, it instead continued to count on its rusty mutual defense pact with the PRC while whispering criticisms of the reform path that the post-Mao Chinese leadership was pursuing.

Perhaps because of the lack of change in Pyongyang's demeanor, after the normalization of relations with the ROK the PRC did not pursue a truly active geostrategic engagement as part of its approach to the Korean peninsula. Instead, it more or less followed Deng Xiaoping's foreign policy axiom of "hiding its light under a bushel," not placing itself on the front lines of the Korean conflict. Tellingly, this attitude was reserved specifically for the divided Korean peninsula; China was not pursuing such uninvolved diplomacy everywhere. Over the course of the 1990s, the PRC utilized bilateral and multilateral processes to resolve disputes along its long borders with Russia and the former Soviet republics. In 2001, it worked with Russia, Kazakhstan,

Kyrgyzstan, Tajikistan, and Uzbekistan to establish the Shanghai Cooperation Organization (SCO) as the official successor to an informal coordination mechanism that
had been in place since the mid-1990s; this was the first Chinese-initiated regional
multilateral security forum in Asia. Also in 2001, in its "state of the world message"
to the United Nations, Beijing described security for the first time as being increasingly globalized, indicating that the term "globalization" (*quanqiuhua*) had entered
Chinese strategic thinking as an "objective condition" or an "unstoppable trend" in
the world economy rather than as a manifestation of U.S. hegemony.[3] The Korean
peninsula, however, was treated more gingerly.

In the years since the turn of the millennium, Beijing has become more involved
on the Korean peninsula due to increasing economic benefits from trade with South
Korea, an increasing need to provide aid and support to North Korea for the sake of
staving off collapse, and the dangerous standoff between the United States and the
DPRK over the North Korean nuclear program. This involvement has emphasized
bilateral and multilateral approaches to dealing with North Korea and has led to
increased Chinese political cooperation with South Korea, Russia, and Japan. This
new proactive stance coheres with Beijing's strategic goals and demands.

In the post–Cold War era, China has taken an increasingly multilateral stance.
There has been a dramatic increase in Beijing's participation in UN-sponsored multilateral treaties and regimes. Beijing has furthermore undertaken a series of policy
shifts on a wide range of world-order issues, including arms control and disarmament, UN peacekeeping operations, global trade, human rights, and environmental
protection. Whereas in 1970 Beijing had signed about 10–20 percent of all arms control agreements it was eligible to sign, by 1996 this figure had jumped to 85–90
percent.[4] Much of this cooperative behavior had to do with China's determined drive
to be seen as a responsible great power.

In terms of grand strategic goals and trends in international conduct, China's
foreign policy forms a double triangulation: domestic, regional, and global levels
interact in the pursuit of three overarching demands and goals. The first goal is
economic development, with an eye to enhancing domestic stability and legitimacy.
The second is promotion of a peaceful and secure external environment free from
threats to China's sovereignty and in favor of territorial integrity in Asia. And the
third overarching goal is the cultivation of the PRC's status as a responsible great
power in world politics.[5]

In the context of the Korean peninsula, Beijing therefore seeks to achieve multiple
(and sometimes mutually competing) goals on several fronts, most of them focusing
on North Korea. These goals include maintaining peace and stability on the Korean
peninsula, promoting economic exchange and cooperation with South Korea, helping the North Korean regime survive, halting the flow of North Korean refugees into
Jilin Province, stopping the rise of ethnonationalism among ethnic Chinese-Koreans,
and enhancing China's influence in Korean affairs. These situation-specific objectives overlap with the three grand strategic goals; refugee flows, for instance, are a
threat both to continued economic development and to territorial sovereignty. From

this two-tiered set of goals, China's foreign policy wish list with respect to North Korea might be said to comprise at least five "no's": no instability, no collapse, no nukes, no refugees or defectors, and no conflict escalation.

When all is added up, China has been behaving as a largely conservative, status quo power, more satisfied with its born-again national status and security than at any time since the founding of the People's Republic in 1949. Therefore, when the various goals are given priority ranking, China is certainly more committed to the immediate challenge of maintaining stability than it is to pursuing the long-term objective of nuclear disarmament on the Korean peninsula. For the Chinese leadership and most Chinese strategic analysts, while the idea of a nuclear-free Korean peninsula is important, it is the survival of the North Korean regime and the reform of North Korea—what is often dubbed "Status Quo Plus"—that are China's greatest challenge and prime objective, respectively.[6] With this in mind, one can see how China's diplomatic initiatives, begun in 2003, have been not so much the result of North Korea's nuclear program as the result of the danger of Pyongyang being a possible target of aggressive military action by the United States, something that could destabilize the whole Northeast Asian region.

Political and Diplomatic Relations

In the early 1990s, Chinese foreign relations were in a state of disarray. Given the effect on Sino-DPRK relations of China's switch from a pro-DPRK policy to a two-Koreas policy, as well as the effect on Sino-American relations of the Tiananmen incident, Beijing commanded little geopolitical capital or leverage with either the United States or North Korea. And, in general, China still was feeling the fallout from the global collapse of communism. By the late 1990s, however, China's emergence as the world's fastest growing economy—and by 2004 as the world's third-largest trading power—had become manifest regionally and globally. In addition to this changed geoeconomic situation, the geopolitical situation shifted in such a way that Beijing and Pyongyang began to mend fences.

Beijing's relations with North Korea began to be renormalized in 1999, due in no small part to shared threat perceptions related to the U.S.-led war against Yugoslavia over Kosovo. Improvements in relations were made evident in a series of high-level political and diplomatic exchanges, including most notably the official state visit of Chinese President Jiang Zemin to Pyongyang in early September 2001. The Jiang-Kim summit followed on a decade of relations during which neither Jiang Zemin nor Kim Jong Il found it politically important or convenient to negotiate the short distance between Beijing and Pyongyang (an hour by plane) for a meeting. In contrast, there were many summit meetings between South Korean and Chinese leaders during the same period, including a visit to Seoul by all nine members of the Politburo Standing Committee of the Chinese Communist Party, the most powerful political institution in China.[7]

The NATO war against Yugoslavia followed upon other developments in the late

1990s—new Guidelines for U.S.-Japan Defense Cooperation and the growing U.S.-Japan cooperation in the development of a theater missile defense (TMD) system—that were threatening to China. When the U.S./NATO air war against Yugoslavia began, China protested on the grounds that the war would establish dangerous precedents of bypassing the UN Security Council in the name of U.S. neo-interventionism, of lowering the threshold for the use of force, and of replacing or trampling state sovereignty as the core principle of international relations. The accidental American bombing of the Chinese embassy in Belgrade also catalyzed Chinese public opinion against the war and U.S. military intervention. Kosovo was a turning point, according to one Chinese security analyst, because it caused "a shift in Chinese thinking on the matter of tolerance for U.S. forces in Asia. China now [felt] surrounded by the U.S.-Japan and U.S.-ROK alliances."[8] At the same time, the intervention in Kosovo triggered alarm in the DPRK and prompted Pyongyang to perceive the urgent need to restore and improve its diplomatic relations with Beijing and Moscow. In short, both Beijing and Pyongyang were sufficiently alarmed by the U.S. military operation to revive an allied relationship of strategic convenience.

To this end, Beijing sent Chinese foreign minister Tang Jiaxuan for a five-day visit to Pyongyang in April 1999. Two months later a fifty-member North Korean delegation, led by the Supreme People's Assembly (SPA) President Kim Yong Nam, made a high-profile state visit to China. This set the stage for Kim Jong Il to choose Beijing as the destination for his first-ever state visit, which occurred in late May 2000. Jiang Zemin then capped the renormalization process with his Fall 2001 visit to North Korea.

Even given rapprochement with North Korea, today China must still maintain a triangular relationship, balanced between both Korean states. As if determined to showcase this strategic balancing act, Beijing dispatched a delegation to each Korean state in October 2000, during the period of rapprochement with the DPRK. A military delegation went to Pyongyang, headed by Defense Minister Chi Haotian, to celebrate the fiftieth anniversary of China's entry into the Korean War—the "War to Resist America and Aid Korea," in Beijing's lingo—and to reaffirm Sino-DPRK military ties. Meanwhile, a civilian delegation went to Seoul, headed by Prime Minister Zhu Rongji, to elevate Sino-ROK relations from a "cooperative partnership" to a "full-scale cooperative partnership." Both meetings, however, were overshadowed by the presence in Pyongyang of U.S. secretary of state Madeleine Albright, who was holding a quasi-summit meeting with Kim Jong Il; Beijing was greatly surprised and even unnerved by the extent to which the U.S. diplomatic maneuver trumped its own delicate maneuvering.

President Jiang Zemin's three-day official visit to Pyongyang in September 2001 capped the flurry of renormalizing political and diplomatic exchanges and efforts that had begun in the spring of 1999. To put Jiang's state visit in historical and comparative perspective, Mao Zedong never visited the DPRK, Zhou Enlai made only two visits (1958 and 1970), Deng Xiaoping made three visits (1961, 1978, and 1982), and Jiang had made one earlier visit in 1990. Kim Il Sung, however, had paid more than ten official and unofficial visits to China. Obviously, Jiang's 2001 visit was meant to represent the formal mending of a relationship that had been troubled in the mid-1990s and to repay two successive visits by Kim Jong Il (to Beijing in May 2000 and to Shanghai in January 2001). Jiang, however, refused to acquiesce to North Korea on variations of the anti-U.S. declaration that had capped a Russo-DPRK summit one month earlier, a declaration condemning U.S. plans to withdraw from the Anti-Ballistic Missile Treaty, calling for the removal of U.S. troops from South Korea, and noting the benefits of combating hegemony and pursuing a multipolar world order. Clearly, there are limits to China's embrace of North Korea.

Military and Security Relations

In October 2000, during the period of renormalization, Beijing dispatched a high-powered military delegation to Pyongyang. Rather than a public pledge to defend the DPRK at any cost or under any circumstances, this was more likely another public demonstration and reminder of China's successful enactment, on the battlefield of the Korean War, of its national identity as a great power, where it defended itself against a menacing imperialist superpower and achieved an outcome that put China on the world map.[9] In this way, the visit symbolized the long history of military relations between North Korea and China, a history that began with the Korean War.

Part of the Korean War legacy for China and North Korea is the 1961 PRC-DPRK Treaty of Friendship, Cooperation, and Mutual Assistance. During the Cold War, Chinese leaders reiterated the immutability of their "militant friendship" with North Korea, as expressed in the text of the treaty. Both Premier Zhou Enlai and People's Liberation Army commander-in-chief Marshall Zhu De used the metaphor of neighbors "as close as lips to teeth" to delineate the strategic importance of Korea to China as a buffer state against hostile external powers.[10] Although the present-day Sino-DPRK relationship is not as close as it once was, neither Beijing nor Pyongyang has shown any interest in modifying the treaty. Unlike the 1961 Soviet-DPRK treaty, the PRC-DPRK treaty cannot be revised or abrogated without prior mutual agreement (Article 7).[11] Instead, the treaty is maintained by both sides partly as convenient fiction and partly as convenient fact.

In the immediate post–Cold War era, even after the establishment of PRC-ROK relations, visitations of Chinese and North Korean military delegations continued unabated, and in fact, mutual, high-level visits between China and North Korea accelerated greatly. These meetings and consultations suggested that the 1961 treaty was as relevant as ever. But then during Jiang Zemin's state visit to South Korea in 1995, following Kim Il Sung's death in July 1994, a Chinese Foreign Ministry spokesperson stated that the alliance did not commit Chinese troops to defending North Korea; Beijing wanted it known, if only informally, that it would not support Pyongyang if North Korea attacked South Korea.[12] While military contacts continued, they seemed mostly symbolic and ceremonial, not indicative of close strategic cooperation. Swinging the pendulum back toward the appearance of a functioning treaty, PRC ambassador to South Korea Wu Dawei vigorously asserted in January 1999—before the beginning of the NATO war against Yugoslavia—that the 1961 Treaty was alive and well and that there were no negotiations for revision in the works.

What seems most apparent about the China-DPRK alliance is that it now serves an ironic security function. Rather than providing security by speaking to the likelihood of one ally coming to the other's aid, it best provides security by allowing the PRC to work through consultations and monitoring to insure that the DPRK does not undertake rash or destabilizing actions. The alliance serves mostly as a mechanism for China to monitor its neighbor's unpredictable behavior and to retain some leverage over Pyongyang.

This leverage has been put to the test in the second U.S.-DPRK nuclear standoff that began in October 2002 and in which Beijing has chosen to play an uncharacteristically proactive conflict-management role. Indeed, Beijing's behavior since the start of the standoff reflects a changing strategic calculus on China's part and a reprioritization of competing interests and goals. At least until the end of 2002, China had maintained a "who me?" posture, trying hard to keep out of harm's way with a strategy of calculated ambiguity and equidistance. In the 1993–1994 U.S.-DPRK nuclear standoff, China tried to stay uninvolved, playing neither mediator nor peacemaker for fear it might get burned if something went wrong. China did threaten to veto any draft sanctions resolution in the UN Security Council at the time, which then enabled Pyongyang to obtain what it had been seeking from the beginning: direct bilateral negotiations with the United States. However, *Rodong Sinmun,* the official organ of the Korean Workers' Party (KWP), seemed determined to refute the notion that Beijing's behind-the-scenes diplomacy had anything to do with the Agreed Framework: "We held the talks independently with the United States on an independent footing, not relying on someone else's sympathy or advice, and the adoption of the DPRK-U.S. Agreed Framework is a fruition of our independent foreign policy, not someone's influence, with the United States finally accepting our proposal."[13] China seemed content to allow this fiction. Regardless of the credit due, Beijing viewed the 1994 U.S.-DPRK Agreed Framework as a window of opportunity for furthering its strategic goals, as Beijing hoped the agreement would improve economic conditions in North Korea, bolster the legitimacy of the Kim Jong Il regime, and enhance the general prospects of political stability.

When the DPRK revealed the existence of a highly enriched uranium (HEU) program to U.S. interlocutors in October 2002, China largely followed its initial instincts and downplayed the DPRK's intentions and capabilities. This reticent background posture, however, was short-lived, as China came to recognize the stark possibility that the United States and the DPRK might not come to any workable settlement on the nuclear issue without some form of third-party intervention.

In the first quarter of 2003, therefore, China launched into an unprecedented flurry of diplomacy, as if its New Year's resolution had been to see the nuclear standoff through to peaceful resolution. Having changed its demeanor, Beijing busied itself at long-distance diplomacy, meeting with North Korean officials sixty times and passing over fifty messages back and forth between Pyongyang and Washington.[14] In a surprising development, the PRC relaxed press freedoms with regard to North Korea; whereas on earlier occasions, problems related to North Korea were treated in the Chinese media with great discretion and sensitivity, since January 2003 the Chinese public has been provided with much more information and commentary.[15] Finally, Beijing successfully initiated and hosted, for the first time, a round of trilateral talks involving the United States, the DPRK, and China in Beijing in April 2003.[16] The PRC Foreign Ministry was very tight-lipped about the contents or outcomes of the trilateral talks. They acknowledged that the reemergence of the nuclear question had "resulted in the tension of the Korean peninsula and wide concern of the international community," and explained that "in order to facilitate its peaceful settlement, the Chinese side has invited the DPRK and the United States to have talks in Beijing."[17]

Despite or perhaps because of the inconclusive ending of the Three-Party Talks in Beijing, China's sudden burst of conflict-management activity in the form of jet-setting preventive diplomacy then accelerated. China recognized that it had to be the active third party bringing the two adversaries to the negotiating table. Taking the Iraq war as an indicator of the extremes to which the Bush administration was willing to go in pursuit of its announced ends, Beijing was spurred on to new levels in its mediation effort and, in July 2003, dispatched its top troubleshooter—Deputy Foreign Minister Dai Bingguo—to Moscow, Pyongyang, and Washington to seek ways of "finding common ground while preserving differences" (*qiutong cunyi*). The new Chinese president, Hu Jintao, reportedly selected and sent Dai to Pyongyang to carry a letter to Kim Jong Il in the official capacity of special envoy. In his letter, Hu is said to have made three key promises: (1) China would be willing to help resolve the crisis by mediating and facilitating negotiations with the greatest sincerity; (2) China would be willing to offer the DPRK greater economic aid than in previous years, although the letter did not mention specific numbers or amounts; and (3) China would be willing to persuade the United States to make a promise of nonaggression against the DPRK in exchange for the denuclearization of the Korean peninsula. In the course of a six-hour-long conversation, Kim Jong Il told Dai that he was willing to accept China's viewpoint and proposal to reopen talks with the United States in a multilateral setting while at the same time insisting that one-on-one negotiation would be his bottom line.[18]

The first round of Six-Party Talks was held in Beijing at the end of August 2003. In an analysis following the talks, the Hong Kong news media reported, "China succeeded in persuading the DPRK to join the Six-Party Talks. So being the organizer of the talks is in itself a winner."[19] From Beijing's longer-term perspective, the talks were said to have yielded agreement on four points: the Korean Peninsula must be denuclearized; this must be achieved peacefully; a "just, rational and integral" plan is necessary; and the parties will refrain from making any statement or taking any action that might escalate tension.[20] When it came to concrete discussions about the nuclear program, the United States insisted on "complete, verifiable, irreversible disarmament" (CVID), a seemingly non-negotiable stance that translated into an obvi-

Table 9.1

China's Trade with North Korea by Half-Year, 2001–2003 (unit: US$1,000)

	01–06/2001	7–12/2001 (% change)	1–6/2002 (% change)	7–12/2002 (% change)	1–6/2003 (% change)	7–12/2003 (% change)
Imports	24,655	142,142 (+468%)	103,904 (−27%)	166,959 (+61%)	107,764 (−36%)	287,782 (+168%)
Exports	284,124	286,536 (+1%)	221,131 (−23%)	246,178 (+11%)	270,064 (+10%)	357,931 (+33%)
Volume	308,779	428,678 (+39%)	325,035 (−24%)	413,137 (+21%)	377,828 (−8%)	645,713 (+71%)

Source: Chinese Customs Statistics and KOTRA (Korean Trade Association).

ous nonstarter for negotiations. Therefore, despite the rhetorical agreements, the talks did not yield any substantial positive steps toward resolution of the nuclear crisis, and the realization of future talks looked uncertain and contingent.

China had used both the carrot and the stick to bring about the first round of Six-Party Talks. As indicated by the change in Sino–North Korean trade between the first and second half of 2003, shown in Table 9.1, Beijing provided a substantial reward for Pyongyang's participation in the talks. After a mild decline in trade in the first half of 2003, which generally fit the levels of decline in previous years, Sino–North Korean trade soared in the second half of 2003 to heights that had not been seen in several years.

It took much additional Chinese cajoling and bribery to secure a second round of Six-Party Talks in February 2004. To obtain North Korean acquiescence to the talks, China offered some $50 million in new economic aid and energy assistance, including the construction of a glass factory in honor of Kim Jong Il's birthday.[21] The talks began with an auspicious two-and-a-half hour bilateral "side meeting" with U.S. and DPRK representatives but ended in embarrassment for China, when Pyongyang attempted to make some last-minute changes to what was to be the first joint statement of the Six-Party Talks. Without the televised joint communiqué that was planned, the closing ceremonies were delayed for several hours. Taking advantage of his dual role as the chairman of the Six-Party Talks and the head of the Chinese delegation, Vice Foreign Minister Wang Yi issued a cautious "Chairman's Statement."[22] In addition, Wang Yi stated that there was an "extreme lack of trust" between Washington and Pyongyang, indicating the distance the parties would have to travel in future talks.[23] But it appeared that China would be willing to walk that road with the two belligerent parties.

In the run-up to the third round of Six-Party Talks, China contacted Japan, the United States, South Korea, and North Korea repeatedly in a frantic effort to set timetables for working-level meetings and for the talks. In March 2004, Chinese foreign minister Li Zhaoxing visited Pyongyang, and South Korean foreign minister Ban Ki-moon traveled to Beijing. Then Kim Jong Il took a secret train trip to Beijing in April (his third trip to China in four years) to hold discussions with top Chinese leaders, including President Hu Jintao, Prime Minister Wen Jiabao, and former president Jiang Zemin. Jiang is said to have told Kim Jong Il that the United States was unlikely to invade the DPRK and that it would therefore be in Kim's interest to alter North Korea's hard-line stance.[24]

This persistence on the part of the PRC seemed to be paying some small dividends when the third round of Six-Party Talks, held in June 2004, opened with the United States suggesting a concrete albeit highly conditional proposal, according to which the other involved countries could provide energy aid as a positive incentive to North Korea in exchange for a nuclear freeze. While the news held some promise that the talks would make progress, and while the DPRK brought its own proposal for consideration (allegedly a demand for some 2.7 million tons of heavy fuel oil), in the end, "no substantive bargaining" occurred during the three-day talks.[25] This time, the United States rejected the issuance of a joint communiqué because so little headway had been made, and the Chinese vice foreign minister in his capacity as chairman of the Six-Party Talks and head of the Chinese delegation issued another "Chairman's Statement" declaring, *inter alia,* that "the parties stressed the need for a step-by-step process of 'words for words' and 'action for action' in search for a peaceful solution to the nuclear issue" and that they also "agreed in principle to hold the fourth round of the Six-Party Talks in Beijing by the end of September 2004."[26]

This fourth round of talks, however, was postponed. While some suggested that they would be resumed in early 2005 after the U.S. presidential election was over, others suggested that they would "not be held anytime soon, if at all ever again."[27] China blamed the dissolution of the talks on the mutual lack of trust between the DPRK and the United States. Several days after the postponement and in conjunction with the opening of the United Nations General Assembly session, the DPRK announced that it had weaponized all of its plutonium stores. Choe Su-hon, the DPRK's deputy foreign minister, said, "We have made clear that we have already reprocessed 8,000 wasted fuel rods and transformed them into arms."[28] China stood by North Korea and tried to deflect some of the negative fallout. PRC foreign minister Li Zhaoxing said, "I have never ever heard about such news. The official news I've gotten from the DPRK side seems not to be exactly the same as what you have heard about."[29]

The delays and failures of the talks should not be overly surprising; odds were against their quick success. In September 2003, Jack Pritchard, the Bush administration's former top negotiator with North Korea, offered a blunt assessment and sharp critique of the administration's hard-nosed policy toward North Korea, asserting that Pyongyang will not relinquish its nuclear weapons programs without more active U.S. engagement: "The idea that in a short period of time you can resolve this problem" in talks where diplomats from six countries sit down with twenty-four interpreters and try to make a deal without private consultations is "ludicrous."[30]

Even if agreement is not likely to come quickly, China clearly believes in the importance of keeping the negotiations in place. One clear catalyst for Beijing's hands-on, preventive diplomacy is growing security concerns about possible U.S. recklessness in trying to resolve the North Korean nuclear crisis through military means. Some Chinese analysts argue that the Bush administration is more interested in resolving the North Korean nuclear crisis with smart weapons than with dialogue and negotiations.[31] Despite a June 2000 decision by the Clinton administration to expunge the term "rogue state" from the U.S. foreign policy lexicon, presidential candidate George W. Bush continued to use the term "rogue state" to refer to North Korea, Iran, and Iraq. Bush also singled out Kim Jong Il by name in multiple stump speeches. Then in his January 2002 State of the Union Address, President Bush made an *ex cathedra* pronouncement that North Korea, Iran, and Iraq formed an "axis of evil," and in June 2002 he proclaimed the doctrine of preemptive war, which is more correctly described a doctrine of preventive war.[32] After a year of preparation, the United States invaded Iraq in March 2003, setting off alarm bells in both Beijing and Pyongyang to a degree that likely surpassed their reactions related to the Kosovo campaign of 1999, which itself had led to the renormalization of the PRC-DPRK relationship.

As U.S. behavior in the Middle East took on this threatening cast in 2002 and 2003, North Korea and the United States together undertook a series of actions ratcheting up the temperature in Northeast Asia. One month after Pyongyang's alleged confession of October 2002—the so-called mother of all confessions—about its secret HEU program, the United States imposed on the Korean Peninsula Energy Development Organization (KEDO) its unilateral decision to stop monthly heavy fuel oil shipments that were being made in partial accordance with the Agreed Framework. The supply of heavy fuel oil was, in fact, reportedly the only one of the four articles of the Agreed Framework that the United States has ever respected.[33]

Pyongyang responded to this interruption of its energy supply two weeks later by threatening to reactivate the Yongbyon nuclear plant and then removing International Atomic Energy Agency (IAEA) monitoring devices from the plant. In December 2002, U.S. defense secretary Donald Rumsfeld, in a display of disturbing braggadocio, warned North Korea not to try to take advantage of U.S. preoccupation with Iraq, since the United States was able and willing to fight and win two wars at the same time if necessary.[34] To intensify and accelerate the downward spiral, the DPRK expelled the remaining IAEA inspectors from the country, noted its intent to restart a nuclear processing plant, and then withdrew from the Nuclear Non-Proliferation Treaty (NPT).

In the Pentagon's Nuclear Posture Review of 2002, China and North Korea found themselves listed together as two of seven target countries. This was despite the fact that targeting of North Korea directly contradicted the 1994 U.S.-DPRK Agreed Framework, which declares that "the United States will provide formal assurances to the DPRK, against the threat or use of nuclear weapons by the United States." In addition, the review called for the development of small, "usable" nuclear weapons—in contravention of Article VI of the NPT.

Even as China was discovering itself to be the target of a new U.S. nuclear plan, it also was the target of a surprising new U.S. alliance initiative. In April 2003, particularly unnerving news reached Beijing that Rumsfeld had circulated a memorandum proposing that the United States ally itself with China to isolate and bring about a collapse of the North Korean regime.[35] China's "cooperative behavior"—to go along with America's regime-change strategy—became the litmus test for enhanced Sino-U.S. relations.

Given this set of provocations, Beijing developed the belief, also held by many North Korea experts, that Pyongyang's HEU program may have started as a hedge or a strategic "ace in the hole" but was then accelerated in response to the perceived ratcheting-up of hostility by the Bush administration. The logic of Beijing's proactive preventive diplomacy is to avert the crystallization of conditions under which Pyongyang could calculate lashing out—to preempt America's preventive strike, as it were—to be a rational course of action, even if ultimate victory were impossible.

As the Six-Party Talks continued in early 2004, the PRC's attitude toward the talks changed as a result of what it saw as U.S. provocation. China had come to reject the Bush administration's contention that North Korea had an HEU-based nuclear weapons program.[36] In the June run-up to the third round of Six-Party Talks, Chinese deputy foreign minister Zhou Wenzhong openly challenged Washington's repeated but conflated claims that North Korea had been trying to build HEU-based nuclear bombs, urging the Bush administration to stop using the allegations to hold up the talks. He said that the Bush administration should stop making charges about the HEU program unless it could offer more conclusive evidence. What is rather remarkable about this open disagreement with the Bush administration is how it was indicative of Beijing's growing frustration with the U.S. all-or-nothing CVID approach. While acknowledging that both the United States and the DPRK needed to compromise, China placed the burden more heavily on the United States. Zhou even admitted that Beijing was now edging closer to agreement with Pyongyang on the all-or-nothing nature of CVID and the problematic U.S. conflation of military and civilian nuclear programs.[37] Therefore, while the United States hoped to use China as an ally in the Six-Party Talks, the talks seem to have accomplished the opposite and driven the PRC to take the DPRK—or at least parts of its position—under the traditional Chinese wing.

Economic Relations

While analysts in the West often focus on China's rising military power and the size of its army, the greatest gains for the PRC over the past two decades have been economic. As early as 1991, the World Bank had singled out post-Mao China as having garnered an all-time global record by doubling per capita output in the shortest period (1977–1987).[38] GDP growth rate in the period from 1990 to 2001 was nearly four times the world average. In recent years, economic relations between China and South Korea have flourished. In 2000, China officially surpassed the United States as the most popular destination for South Korean foreign direct investment (FDI). In 2003, China emerged as South Korea's largest export market, and by mid-2004 China had surpassed the United States to become the largest trading partner of South Korea.

The percentage of North Korean foreign trade destined for China, on the other hand, has fluctuated greatly over the years. In the 1950s, anywhere from 25 to 60 percent of North Korean trade was with the PRC, involving around $100 million in annual absolute value. In the 1960s, 30 percent of DPRK trade was with China, until 1967, when the Cultural Revolution pushed the ratio to around 10 percent. In the mid-1970s, annual trade worth $300–600 million accounted for about 20 percent of North Korean trade, and although the value rose to $3–4 billion in the 1980s, the proportion declined to 10 to 20 percent. The post–Cold War relationship has been marked by a trend opposite to that of the 1980s: declining absolute value and increasing share. However, as indicated in table 9.2, the early years of the twenty-first century have seen sequential increases in Sino–North Korean trade, with the total level reaching over $1 billion in 2003 for the first time since the Cold War. This new level—an increase of 39 percent over the previous year—demonstrates the paradoxical effect of the second U.S.-DPRK nuclear standoff, which has accelerated Pyongyang's economic isolation due to the reinforced sanctions by Washington and Tokyo while simultaneously deepening North Korea's dependence on Beijing and Seoul for trade and aid.

As Table 9.2 also indicates, North Korea's trade deficits with China have been chronic and substantial, amounting to a cumulative total of $4.68 billion between 1990 and 2003—imports to the DPRK worth $6.7 billion and exports worth $2.1 billion. While China remained North Korea's largest trade partner in the 1990s in terms of total value, Beijing has allowed Pyongyang to run average annual deficits of almost $500 million since 1990. China's role in the DPRK's trade is even larger if barter transactions and aid are factored into these figures. Yet it is clearly not so large when compared to South Korea's trade with China, which in 2002 amounted to more than $41 billion—fifty-six times greater than that of North Korea—with a huge trade surplus for the ROK of about $10.3 billion.[39] In 2003, trade as a percentage of GDP was only 13 percent in the DPRK, whereas in the ROK it was 75 percent, and in the PRC—where the level has grown by twenty percentage points in five years—it was 65 percent.[40]

For the DPRK, the most critical challenge is survival in the post–Cold War, post-communist world of globalization, and its economic relations with China are motivated by this survival goal. To this end, Pyongyang seeks increasing amounts of aid as an external life-support system, hoping to avoid triggering a cataclysmic system collapse. During the long Cold War years, geopolitics and ideology combined to make it possible for Pyongyang to extract maximum economic, military, and security benefits from China and the Soviet Union and to claim that the North Korean system was a socialist success. Between 1948 and 1984, Moscow and Beijing supplied $2.2 billion and $900 million in aid, respectively, to North Korea.[41] But the so-called juche-based (self-reliant) economy, which lived in essence on disguised aid from the Soviet Union and China,[42] has been exposed as a mirage, and "our style of socialism" has proved a poor substitute for coping with deepening economic crisis. North Korea has earned a reputation, however, for employing "the power of the weak," creating and using crises to extract concessions to compensate for its growing domestic failings. China, more than any other country, has been the target of these appeals.

Table 9.2

China's Trade with North and South Korea (1990–2003) ($US million)

Year	Exports to North Korea	Imports from North Korea	Total North Korean-Chinese trade (balance)	Percent change in North Korean-Chinese trade	Exports to South Korea	Imports from South Korea	Total South Korean-Chinese trade (balance)	Percent change in South Korean-Chinese trade
1990	358	125	483 (+233)		2,268	1,553	3,821 (+715)	
1991	525	86	611 (+439)	+26	3,441	1,000	4,441 (+2,441)	+16
1992	541	155	696 (+386)	+14	3,725	2,650	6,375 (+1,075)	+43
1993	602	297	899 (+305)	+29	3,928	5,150	9,078 (−1,222)	+42
1994	424	199	624 (+225)	−31	5,462	6,200	11,660 (−740)	+28
1995	486	64	550 (+422)	−12	7,401	9,140	17,000 (−1,742)	+46
1996	497	68	565 (+429)	+3	8,539	11,377	19,916 (−2,838)	+17
1997	531	121	652 (+410)	+15	10,117	13,572	23,689 (−3,455)	+19
1998	355	57	413 (+298)	−37	6,484	11,944	18,428 (−5,460)	−22
1999	329	42	371 (+287)	−10	8,867	13,685	22,552 (−4,818)	+22
2000	451	37	488 (+414)	+31	12,799	18,455	31,254 (−5,656)	+39
2001	571	167	737 (+404)	+51	13,303	18,190	31,493 (−4,887)	+1
2002	467	271	738 (+196)	+0	17,400	23,754	41,154 (−6,354)	+31
2003	628	396	1,024 (+232)	+39	21,900	35,100	57,000 (−13,200)	+38

Sources: Ministry of Foreign Trade and Economic Relations, People's Republic of China at www.moftec.gov.cn/moftec/official/html/statistics_data/; 1996 Diplomatic White Paper Ministry of Foreign Affairs and Trade (MOFAT), Republic of Korea (ROK), p. 348; 1997 Diplomatic White Paper, MOFAT, ROK, pp. 396 and 400; 1998 Diplomatic White Paper, MOFAT, ROK, pp. 481 and 486; 2000 Diplomatic White Paper, MOFAT, ROK, p. 496; 2001 Diplomatic White Paper, MOFAT, ROK, p. 483; 2002 Diplomatic White Paper, MOFAT, ROK, p. 497; see www.mofat.go.kr.

North Korea's dependency on China for aid has grown unabated and has even intensified in the face of sanctions related to the nuclear standoff with the United States that began in October 2002. Although the exact amount of Chinese aid remains unknown, support for North Korea is generally estimated at one-quarter to one-third of China's overall foreign aid. Recent estimates of China's aid are in the range of 1 million tons of wheat and rice and 500,000 tons of heavy fuel oil per annum, accounting for 70–90 percent of North Korea's fuel imports and about one-third of its total food imports. With the cessation of America's heavy fuel oil delivery in November 2002, China's oil aid and exports may now be approaching nearly 100 percent of North Korea's energy imports.[43] In addition, the Chinese government has extended indirect aid by allowing private economic transactions between North Korean and Chinese companies in the border area, despite North Korea's mounting debt and the bankruptcy of many Chinese companies resulting from North Korean defaults on debts.

As described above, President Hu Jintao promised Kim Jong Il greater economic aid than in previous years as a way of enticing Pyongyang to the Six-Party Talks in late August 2003. It seems that each year Beijing has become more deeply involved in the politics of regime survival by providing more aid in a wider variety of forms: direct government-to-government aid, subsidized cross-border trade, and private barter transactions. In large part, China's aid is motivated by its fear of Korean refugee flows across the border into the PRC. As one senior Chinese leader said to a visiting U.S. scholar in the context of expressing China's opposition to any economic sanctions on North Korea, "We can either send food to North Korea or they will send refugees to us—either way, we feed them. It is more convenient to feed them in North Korea than in China."[44]

In the late 1990s, some 200,000–300,000 North Korean "food refugees" are reported to have used the porous Sino-DPRK border as a kind of revolving door each year, moving into and out of China in search of food.[45] Beginning at that time, more and more escapees tried to remain in China, waiting for improvement in the food situation at home. Otherwise, they have tried to head for other countries, usually South Korea. Estimates of the total number of North Korean refugees/defectors in China vary, ranging from 7,000–8,000 (according to the Chinese government) to 10,000–30,000 (per the South Korean government) to 300,000–400,000 (per South Korean human rights NGOs). In 2002, small groups of North Korean refugees began storming Western embassies in China in hopes of gaining asylum. Most refugees who have infiltrated the Canadian, German, Spanish, and South Korean embassies have found passage to South Korea through a third country. In order to avoid these sticky diplomatic situations and the gaze of international human rights monitoring agencies, the PRC sees it as in its interests to prevent or at least slow North Korean refugee flows through the provision of aid.

Paradoxically, Pyongyang's growing dependence on Beijing for economic and political survival has led to mutual distrust and resentment. Just as Mao demanded and resented Soviet aid for China's nuclear development, first Kim Il Sung and now Kim Jong Il have demanded but also resented Chinese aid. Indeed, Pyongyang's seeming inability to reconstruct its national identity in the face of a changing geopolitical context has engendered intense behind-the-scenes bargaining amid an atmosphere of mutual suspicion. In every high-level meeting between the two governments, North Korean requests for economic aid dominate the agenda.[46]

Beijing continues to provide this minimal, necessary survival aid in order to lessen the flow of refugees into China, to delay a potential North Korean collapse, and to enhance China's own leverage in both Pyongyang and Seoul. However, since the North Korean regime realizes that China's aid is given in Beijing's own self-interest, it has not greatly increased China's leverage with Pyongyang, to Beijing's growing chagrin and frustration. Chinese attempts to lessen aid to the DPRK—for instance, by requiring payment in hard currency for energy transfers in the early 1990s—have generally been unsuccessful.

The great hope for North Korea, from China's perspective, is that Pyongyang will choose to follow a reform path similar to that of the PRC under Deng Xiaoping. Despite the decision not to participate in the 1994 U.S.-DPRK Agreed Framework, China had thought that the AF would provide a window of opportunity for improving economic conditions in North Korea, bolstering the legitimacy of the Kim Jong Il regime, and enhancing the prospects of political stability. In addition, Beijing thought that the Agreed Framework would go some way in alleviating the dangerous imbalance of power between the two Koreas. However, the failure of the United States to fully implement the agreement meant that none of these dividends were realized. (China is not without blame either, since it refused to join KEDO, the multinational consortium for the implementation of the Agreed Framework, on the grounds that China "can be of greater help being outside than inside the KEDO." The PRC also blocked Taiwan's repeated offers to make financial contributions to KEDO.)

North Korea's experimentation with economic reform has been far from successful. The Rajin-Sonbong Free Economic and Trade Zone (FETZ), established in 1991, attracted, at most, $62 million over six years before investments tapered off.[47] Unlike China, which was able to attract $1.73 billion from about twenty-eight million overseas Chinese in the initial years of reform, the DPRK has not been successful in catalyzing substantial inflows of foreign direct investment.

China had much to do with the recent derailment of a second special economic zone, the Sinuiju Special Autonomous Region (SAR) in northern North Korea. Sinuiju was to have operated according to more market-based rules and was to have been a market-based complex of finance, trade, commerce, industry, technology, recreation, and tourism. But the Chinese saw it as the likely home of gambling, money laundering, and other illegal businesses; they did not want it on their border and therefore arrested Yang Bin, the Dutch-Chinese tycoon who had been designated the chief executive of Sinuiju. Because Beijing saw Sinuiju as a likely point of friction between itself and Pyongyang, it urged the North Korean regime in 1998 to relocate the SAR to the border with South Korea. Nonetheless, Pyongyang is pushing ahead with its opening, and Beijing likely will have to undertake new responsive measures to insure that the project takes on a desirable shape rather than a malignant one.[48]

Ultimately, China can only do so much to support North Korean reform. In political terms, if it pushes too hard, it runs the risk of alienating the Pyongyang regime. In economic terms, there are much larger gains to be reaped from pursuing economic relations with South Korea and with other market economies in East Asia. While

China's continued economic engagement with the DPRK speaks to the multiple roles of economic ties in international relations, the growing disparity between China's economic relations with the ROK and those with the DPRK indicates the true trajectory of Chinese political economy in Northeast Asia. While Sino-ROK trade and investment are clear components of a global economic order, Sino-DPRK economic relations are equally clear remnants of a Cold War ideological life-support system, one that has little place in the era of globalization.

Despite Pyongyang's general reluctance to engage in economic reform, however, Kim Jong Il did take the opportunity, during his state visit to China in May 2000, to acknowledge the significant achievements of China's socialist modernization program. This was the first time that the DPRK had praised China's turn away from the command economy. Then Kim Jong Il traveled to Shanghai in January 2001 to follow up on his May trip and to personally investigate "capitalism with Shanghai characteristics."[49] In light of recent price reforms in North Korea and the more or less constant need to raise the standard of living, the right type of cracks to encourage reform may be forming in the command economy.

Conclusion

North Korea seems at first glance like a textbook case of how most Chinese dynasties collapsed under the twin blows of *neiluan* (internal disorder) and *waihuan* (external calamity). Although Beijing's relations with Pyongyang have been in a process of renormalization since 1999, this is still a fragile relationship of strategic convenience fraught with subsurface tensions and asymmetries associated with mutual expectations, needs, and interests.

Despite the multiple external shocks and internal woes, North Korea has managed to defy all collapsist scenarios and predictions, as well as the classical realist axiom that "the strong do what they have the power to do and the weak accept what they have to accept." What explains this paradox? Part of the answer is a matter of geography—North Korea occupies China's strategic *cordon sanitaire* and exercises "the tyranny of proximity" for Beijing and Seoul, if not Tokyo and Washington. North Korea's place at the center of the strategic geopolitical crossroads of Northeast Asia has served rather well in bolstering Pyongyang's survival leverage strategy. Indeed, the single greatest challenge confronting Beijing may be not the strength but the power in weakness of post–Kim Il Sung North Korea.

Accordingly, Beijing will continue to invest the minimum necessary political and economic capital in its difficult relationship with Pyongyang in order to avert regime collapse or another armed conflict on the peninsula. For its own geoeconomic and geopolitical interests, Beijing has played a positive conflict-management role in Korean affairs not only by providing necessary if not sufficient (in Pyongyang's eyes) diplomatic and economic support to the DPRK, but also by making it clear to Seoul, Washington, and Tokyo that it is in the common interest to promote the peaceful coexistence of the two Korean states in order to avoid having to cope with the turmoil, chaos, and probable mass exodus of refugees that would follow in the wake of regime collapse in the North.

China's interaction with the two Koreas and other parties of interest in Northeast Asian geopolitics leads in more ways, in more depth and complexity, and in more areas than ever before to another paradox. China remains in some respects an incomplete great power because of growing domestic security, legitimation, and environmental deficits even as its capacity to initiate or implement consistent policies toward the two Koreas is increasingly constrained by the norms and practices of important domestic groups, by Northeast Asian regional and global regimes, and by the United States. Like it or not, China's two-Koreas policy cannot be contained in a state-to-state bilateral context, as an increasing number and variety of actors or interests must be taken into account. Growing complexity, density, and multilateralization have placed inordinate pressure on the Chinese foreign policy system to develop more effective coordinating mechanisms to monitor and supervise what is really going on.

Although commanding a rather unique position as the only major power that maintains a good relationship with both Koreas, Beijing has the daunting task of managing the primal reality that China and Korea remain the last two Cold War legacies of divided polity. Given the growing chasm between the two halves of Korea, any scenario of Korean reunification poses implications for China's own unification drive. Although Beijing stresses the fundamental differences between the Chinese and Korean cases, the two-Korea policy can only underscore that the two Chinas are going their separate ways as well.

China is arguably now a more influential player in reshaping the future of the Korean peninsula than at any time since the Korean War, and more so than any other peripheral power. Despite this unique position of influence, however, the future of North Korea is not for China to make or unmake. China can help or hinder North Korea in taking one system-rescuing approach instead of another, but in the end, no external power can determine North Korea's future. Only time will tell whether post–Kim Il Sung North Korea can ride out its economic difficulties by means of such a tenuous external life-support system without forfeiting its juche identity and without a sudden crash landing.

Notes

1. For a detailed analysis, see Samuel S. Kim, "The Making of China's Korea Policy in the Era of Reform," 371–408.

2. Song, "Lengzhan hou DongbeiYa anquan xingshe de bianhua" (Changes in the Post–Cold War Northeast Asian Security Situation), 37.

3. Pang Zhongying, "China's International Status and Foreign Strategy After the Cold War," May 5, 2002, in Foreign Broadcast Information Service (FBIS) document FBIS-CHI-2002–0506. See also Samuel S. Kim, "China's Path to Great Power Status," 35–75.

4. Swaine and Johnston, "China and Arms Control Institutions," 101.

5. For analysis along this line, see Wang, "Mianxiang ershi shiji de Zhongguo waijiao" (China's Diplomacy for the Twenty-First Century), 18–27.

6. See Scobell, *China and North Korea*, 14; and Shambaugh, "China and the Korean Peninsula," 55.

7. Taeho Kim, "Strategic Relations Between Beijing and Pyongyang," 306–308.

8. Quoted in McVadon, "China's Goals and Strategies for the Korean Peninsula," 170.

9. See Erick Eckholm, "Celebrating Korea's War Even as Peace Seems Near," *New York Times*, October 26, 2000, A4.

10. Lampton and Ewing, *The U.S.-China Relationship*, 45, and Spurr, *Enter the Dragon*, 62–63.

11. For the Chinese and Korean texts of the treaty, see Liu and Yang, *Zhongguo dui Chaoxian he Hanguo zhengci wenjian huibian (1958–1962)* (A Collection of Documents on China's Policy Toward the Democratic People's Republic of Korea and the Republic of Korea [1958–1962]), 1279–1280; and Li, *PukHan–Chungkuk Kwankyae 1945–2000* (DPRK-PRC Relations, 1945–2000), 318–320.

12. *Korea Times*, November 16, 1995, available at http://times.hankooki.com.

13. *Rodong Sinmun* (Workers' Daily) (Pyongyang), December 1, 1994.

14. John Pomfret, "China Urges N. Korea Dialogue," *Washington Post*, April 4, 2003, A16.

15. See Wang Jisi, "China's Changing Role in Asia," Atlantic Council of the United States Occasional Paper, January 2004.

16. The DPRK insisted that the talks were bilateral, between itself and the United States, while the United States and the PRC toed the line that they were trilateral. Ambassador Charles Pritchard, "Six Party Talks and the Prospect for Resolving the Nuclear Crisis" (presentation to Contemporary Korean Affairs Seminar at Columbia University, April 1, 2004).

17. PRC Foreign Ministry Spokesperson Kong Quan, press conference, April 24, 2003, available at www.fmprc.gov.cn/eng/xwfw/2510/2511/t22747.htm.

18. See Zong Hairen (pseudonym), "Hu Jintao Writes to Kim Jong-il to Open Door to Six-Party Talks," *Hong Kong Hsin Pao* (Hong Kong Economic Journal), August 28, 2003, translated in FBIS-CHI-2003–0828, August 29, 2003.

19. Wang Dejun, "Special Dispatch: The Results of the Six-Party Talks Are Better Than Expected," *Hong Kong Ta Kung Pao*, August 29, 2003, translated in FBIS-CHI-2003–0829.

20. Ibid.

21. Edward Cody and Anthony Faiola, "N. Korea's Kim Reportedly in China for Talks," *Washington Post*, April 20, 2004, A13.

22. Snyder, "Can China Unstick the Korean Nuclear Standoff?" 98.

23. Philip P. Pan, Glenn Kessler, and Fred Barbash, "N. Korea, U.S. 'Difficulties' Remain as Talks End," *Washington Post*, February 28, 2004. Elsewhere the word "extreme" has been translated as "complete"; see BBC News, "No Breakthrough in N. Korea Talks," February 28, 2004, available at http://news.bbc.co.uk/2/hi/asia-pacific/3494790.stm.

24. Audra Ang, "Report: China Urges Softer N. Korea Line," *Washington Post*, April 20, 2004. Others attributed a similar statement to President Hu Jintao; see Ryu Jin, "China Tells NK to Negotiate with U.S.," *Korea Times*, April 20, 2004.

25. Joseph Kahn, "U.S. Reports Scant Progress in Talks with North Korea," *New York Times*, June 26, 2004, and "N. Korea Asks for Energy Aid Worth 2 Mil. Kilowatts of Electricity," *Kyodo News*, June 24, 2004.

26. For the full English text of the Chairman's Statement, see *People's Daily Online*, June 28, 2004, at http://english.peopledaily.com.cn/200406/26/eng20040626_147642.html.

27. James Brooke, "6–Nation North Korean Nuclear Talks in Doubt," *New York Times*, September 26, 2004. The quotation was attributed to Kenneth Quinones, former director of the DPRK affairs office for the U.S. State Department. See also "U.S. Officials See No N. Korea Talks Before U.S. Vote," Reuters, September 29, 2004.

28. Anna Fifield and Guy Dinmore, "N. Korea Says It 'Weaponised' Spent Plutonium," *Financial Times*, September 29, 2004.

29. "Chinese Minister Doubtful on N. Korea Nuclear Claim," Reuters, September 29, 2004.

30. Quoted in Sonni Efron, "Ex-Envoy Faults U.S. on N. Korea," *Los Angeles Times*, September 10, 2003; see also Peter Slevin, "Former Envoy Presses North Korea Dialogue," *Washington Post*, September 9, 2003, A19.

31. See, for example, Shiping Tang, "What China Should Do About North Korea," *Asia Times*, April 18, 2003.

32. See Joseph Wheatley, "The Bush Administration's Preemption Doctrine: One Year Later," *Journal for Strategic Threat Analysis and Response*, available at www.istar.upenn.edu/research/JSTAR%20Article%20–%20Joseph%20Wheatley.pdf; and Richard Falk, "Will the Empire Be Fascist?" Transnational Foundation for Peace and Future Research, March 24, 2003, available at www.transnational.org/forum/meet/2003/Falk_FascistEmpire.html.

33. James Dao, "Bush Administration Halts Payments to Send Oil to North Korea," *New York Times*, November 14, 2002.

34. Anwar Iqbal, "Rumsfeld Warns N. Korea: U.S. Can Fight," United Press International, December 23, 2002.

35. David E. Sanger, "Aftereffects: Nuclear Standoff, Administration Divided Over North Korea," *New York Times*, April 21, 2003, 15; and David Rennie, "Rumsfeld Calls for Regime Change in North Korea," *Daily Telegraph* (London), April 22, 2003.

36. See Glenn Kessler, "Chinese Not Convinced of North Korean Uranium Effort," *Washington Post*, January 7, 2004, A16; and George Gedda, "China, U.S. Differ Over N. Korean Weapons," Associated Press, February 6, 2004.

37. Joseph Kahn and Susan Chira, "Chinese Official Challenges U.S. Stance on North Korea," *New York Times*, June 9, 2004, A12. It should be noted in this connection that there is a big difference between HEU ambitions and HEU capabilities. There is little doubt that Pyongyang has blueprints for HEU weapons, but it does not have the specialized material let alone the components and the independent power stations capable of delivering the constant supply of electricity necessary for operating thousands of gas centrifuges. See International Institute for Strategic Studies (IISS), *North Korea's Weapons Programmes*, 39–42.

38. World Bank, *World Development Report 1991*, 12.

39. See Economist Intelligence Unit, *Country Report: South Korea*, September 2003, 5.

40. The DPRK statistic comes from Bank of Korea, "Gross Domestic Product of North Korea in 2003," available at www.bok.or.kr/contents_admin/info_admin/eng/home/press/pressre/info/GDPNK2003.pdf, and author's calculations. PRC and ROK statistics are from the World Bank's *World Development Indicators*.

41. Hwang, *The Korean Economies*, Table 5.4.

42. According to Soviet economist N. Bahanova, Soviet aid was responsible for the construction of more than seventy facilities producing over one-fourth of the North Korean gross industrial output. See *Pravda*, August 6, 1990, in FBIS/Soviet Union, August 10, 1990, 10.

43. Shambaugh, "China and the Korean Peninsula," 46.

44. Quoted in Lampton and Ewing, *The U.S.-China Relationship*, 70.

45. Shim, "A Crack in the Wall," 11, and Natsios, *The Politics of Famine in North Korea*.

46. You, "China and North Korea," 389–390.

47. *ChoongAng Ilbo* (Seoul), January 29, 2001.

48. Liu, "China and the North Korean Crisis," 370–372.

49. Chanda, "Kim Flirts with Chinese Reform," 26.

10

Russo-North Korean Relations Under Kim Jong Il

Peggy Falkenheim Meyer

Since he became president of Russia, Vladimir Putin has played an active role on the Korean peninsula, pursuing ties with both North and South Korea. Putin's engagement with both Korean states has contributed to a perception by some that Russia could play an influential role in helping to resolve the second North Korean nuclear crisis that began in October 2002 when a North Korean official admitted that his country has been pursuing a secret uranium enrichment program.

What policy has Russia adopted in response to this crisis and how influential has it been? The short answer is that Russia wishes to play a role in resolving the crisis to reaffirm its status as a great power and to protect its security and economic interests. Moscow has proclaimed its strong opposition to North Korea's possession of nuclear weapons. But it has more in common with Seoul, Beijing, and to a certain extent with Tokyo, in its analysis of the roots of the problem and the best strategy to deal with it, than it has with the George W. Bush administration in Washington.

Although Moscow has participated in multilateral negotiations to resolve the crisis, its influence so far has been limited. Washington, Beijing, Seoul, and even Tokyo are likely to have more influence over the outcome than will Moscow. They have more to offer North Korea, which is looking for diplomatic recognition and security guarantees from Washington and promises of continued food, energy, and other financial aid to keep the bankrupt Pyongyang regime afloat.

Russia has energy resources that could be used by North Korea to compensate for the light water reactors that were supposed to be provided under the now defunct KEDO (Korean Energy Development Organization) program. But their provision will depend on resolution of the crisis and funding from other countries.

A Brief Overview of Russia's Past Policy

One persistent goal of Russia's policy toward the Korean peninsula has been to be accepted as an influential participant in efforts to resolve contentious issues and problems. Moscow wants a seat at the table to have its status as a great power recognized.

In the late Gorbachev period, Soviet leaders believed that their country had a special role to play on the Korean peninsula because it was the only major power that had diplomatic relations with both Koreas. In the early 1990s, after the dissolution of the USSR, there was growing awareness in Moscow that Russia's influence over Korean affairs had declined precipitously. Gorbachev's September 1990 establishment of diplomatic relations with South Korea, and the subsequent decision to end fuel and other subsidies to the North produced a serious estrangement between Moscow and Pyongyang.

North Korean officials were further angered by Russia's decision to reinterpret the 1961 Soviet-Democratic People's Republic of Korea (DPRK) Treaty of Friendship, Cooperation, and Mutual Assistance to make it clear that Russia would help defend North Korea only if it were the victim of an unprovoked attack. Before this reinterpretation, Moscow was obliged by the treaty's terms to defend the DPRK at any time it was involved in a war.

Yeltsin's reform-minded, Western-oriented government was annoyed by evidence that Pyongyang had backed the August 1991 foiled conservative coup against Gorbachev. There were even suggestions that the early Yeltsin regime was not interested in improving Russian relations with North Korea because they expected the regime to soon collapse.

Growing tensions between Moscow and Pyongyang reduced Russia's importance to Seoul. Whereas the late Gorbachev rapprochement with South Korea was motivated on the Soviet side primarily by economic incentives, Seoul primarily was interested in using Moscow as an avenue for influence over Pyongyang. Once it became clear that Russia had lost its influence in North Korea, Seoul was much less interested in Moscow. Another reason for South Korean disenchantment was Russia's failure to begin repaying a US$1.47 billion debt, money it owed Seoul for a loan extended in the late Gorbachev period. After an initial period of euphoria, South Korea's business community quickly became disenchanted with the prospects for profitable economic ties with Russia and the Russian Far East.

By the time of the first North Korean nuclear crisis in 1993–1994, the limits on Russian influence over the Korean peninsula were clear. Moscow tried to play a role in resolving this crisis by proposing the convening of an eight-party conference comprising representatives of the two Koreas, the United States, China, Japan, Russia, the United Nations (UN), and the International Atomic Energy Agency (IAEA). However, this proposal met with a negative response.

Russia played little or no role in the process leading to the October 1994 Agreed Framework between the United States and the DPRK. According to the terms of this agreement, North Korea pledged to freeze its plutonium reprocessing program in return for a promise of external fuel aid and help in building two proliferation-resistant light water reactors.

Russia did not become a member of KEDO, the body established by the United

States, the Republic of Korea (ROK), Japan, and the European Union (EU) to implement this agreement. KEDO did not accept Russia's offer to provide the light water reactors promised North Korea even though Pyongyang would have preferred Russian reactors to the South Korean reactors it was forced to accept. Not surprisingly, KEDO insisted on South Korean reactors both because Seoul was paying most of the cost and because North Korea would be forced to accept a major South Korean project and South Korean engineers and technicians on its soil.

Russian officials were upset by their country's exclusion from the Four-Party Talks focusing on inter-Korean issues. These talks began in 1996 with the participation of the two Koreas, the United States, and China. On numerous occasions, Moscow, sometimes with the backing of Tokyo, proposed expanding the Four-Party Talks to a six-party format that would include Russia and Japan. But this proposal was not accepted.

Starting around 1995–1996, Russia made a serious effort to improve its relations with North Korea in order to regain some of its lost influence on the Korean peninsula. This move to a more balanced policy toward the two Koreas was facilitated by the death of Kim Il Sung in 1994 and his replacement as top North Korean leader, albeit not as president, by his son Kim Jong Il.[1] This policy change was encouraged by the January 1996 appointment of Evgenii Primakov as Russia's foreign minister to replace Andrei Kozyrev. In contrast to his pro-Western predecessor, Primakov supported a more balanced foreign policy with greater emphasis on establishing and maintaining good relations with states in Asia and the Middle East, and with former Soviet states, as well as with the United States and its allies.

Moscow agreed to negotiate a new friendship treaty with Pyongyang to replace the 1961 Soviet-North Korean treaty that was allowed to elapse in 1996. In March 1999, Deputy Foreign Minister Grigori Karasin visited Pyongyang and initialed the Treaty of Friendship, Good Neighborliness, and Cooperation. In contrast to the 1961 treaty, this new treaty did not include a Russian security guarantee to North Korea. It committed Moscow and Pyongyang only to contact each other in the event of a crisis.[2]

Putin's Korea Policy

A new phase in Russian foreign policy began when Vladimir Putin succeeded Boris Yeltsin as acting president in December 1999 and then in March 2000 as Russia's second elected president. There is significant continuity between the foreign policy conducted by Yeltsin in his second term and Putin's foreign policy. However, Putin's policy often appears to be quite different because his good physical and psychological health enables him to pursue a much more activist foreign policy.

Putin has tried to improve Russia's relations with the United States and West Europe while at the same time actively courting former Soviet states, China, and so-called rogue states including Iran and North Korea. These states have been courted in part for economic reasons and in part because a multidirectional foreign policy is seen as giving an economically and militarily weak Russia greater perceived importance and leverage in world affairs.

Domestic politics also plays a role. Russia's top leaders, previously Yeltsin and now Putin, may understand that Russian national interests require the maintenance of good relations with the United States, the new post-Cold War global hegemon. A high proportion of Russia's economic ties are with Europe and the United States. However, a significant portion of the Russian foreign policy elite both within and outside official circles is viscerally anti-Western, retaining attitudes left over from Soviet days. This anti-Western bias at times may affect Russia's policy toward issues such as North Korea.

When all of this is put together, what emerges is a foreign policy that often appears incoherent and even contradictory. In both the domestic and foreign policy realms, Putin has been described as someone who tries to be all things to all people—as someone who tailors his message to the specific audience at hand.

One reflection of Putin's increased activism is his three summit meetings with Kim Jong Il. The first meeting took place in Pyongyang in July 2000 shortly before Putin's participation in the Okinawa G-8 summit. During this visit, the first ever by a Soviet or Russian head of state, Putin and Kim Jong Il signed the Treaty on Friendship, Good Neighborliness, and Cooperation that was negotiated and initialed near the end of Yeltsin's presidential term. A second outcome of this meeting was Kim Jong Il's supposed agreement to abandon North Korea's long-range missile program in return for a pledge that another country would launch two or three satellites for the DPRK.

When Putin arrived at the G-8 summit with this promise in hand, the Russian president attracted much more media attention than was warranted by Russia's relatively weak economic position. Subsequently, it was reported that Kim Jong Il was only joking when he offered to give up North Korea's missile program.

This interpretation of Kim's remarks has been disputed in a recent article by Georgi Toloraya, deputy director-general of the First Asian Department of Russia's Foreign Ministry. Toloraya claims that Kim Jong Il informed South Korean journalists in August 2000 that he had told Putin "we will not develop missiles if the U.S. would agree to launch satellites for us." He then mentioned the irony of the situation, observing that the United States or Japan would never seriously take him up on his offer. According to Toloraya, Kim's use of the word "irony" was later misinterpreted as "joke" by hostile media.[3]

The second summit between Putin and Kim Jong Il took place during midsummer of 2001 in Moscow. During this summit and the third summit in August 2002 in Vladivostok, Putin focused on promoting economic projects linking Russia with the Korean peninsula. In particular, he touted a plan to reconnect the railroad between the two Koreas and to link it to the Trans-Siberian railroad. Putin hopes to capture a large share of the Asia-Europe freight that would otherwise go to China. Just before he met Kim Jong Il in Vladivostok, Putin told Russian Far East officials, "If we do not link the railways here, it will be done anyway, in a different place, through the territory of our esteemed and dearly beloved neighbor, the People's Republic of China."[4]

Putin went on to warn that "Russia's far east and parts of the trans-Siberian will simply not see those freights."[5] Putin also promoted a project to build a natural gas pipeline from East Siberia through the Korean peninsula.

Although Putin's three summits with Kim Jong Il received more attention, his administration did not neglect relations with South Korea. During a February 2001 summit with then South Korean president Kim Dae Jung in Seoul, Putin promoted the railroad and other economic cooperation projects.

Putin and other Russian officials expressed strong support for Kim Dae Jung's "sunshine policy" aimed at improving relations with the North. One rationale for this policy is an assumption that the sudden collapse of North Korea would place too heavy a burden on the South, which would have to absorb the high cost of reforming the North's economy. For this reason, Kim Dae Jung prefers a long-term, gradual process to allow time for reform of the North's economy and an improvement in relations between the two Koreas. Russian officials and scholars have applauded what they perceive as a process of inter-Korean reconciliation that began during the historic June 2000 summit in Pyongyang between the presidents of the two Koreas.

Besides these contacts at the national level, officials in the Russian Far East have extensive ties with North Korea. North Korean workers have been welcomed to the Russian Far East, which has experienced a significant demographic decline since the USSR fell apart. This region needs more working age residents to sustain its economy. There are approximately 10,000 North Koreans in the Russian Far East working in forestry, agriculture, and construction.[6] Following a policy dating back to the Soviet period, Pyongyang annually sends North Korean workers to harvest timber in the Russian Far East. Their labor helps to pay off Pyongyang's US$5.5 billion Soviet-era debt. North Koreans under short-term contracts work at jobs in agriculture and construction and also moonlight in these sectors. Returning from an October 2003 trip to North Korea, Sergei Darkin, governor of Russia's Maritime Territory (Primorye), noted that currently 1,400 North Koreans work in Primorye and that number could be doubled by the following year. He stressed that there was a particular need for North Korean workers in agriculture. Only 30 percent of available fields were being cultivated because of a shortage of labor.[7] The head of Primorye's migration department, Viktor Plotnikov, announced in January 2004 that the quota for North Korean workers had been increased from 2,000 to 2,500.[8]

Russia's Response to the 2002–2004 North Korean Nuclear Crisis

Putin's more active policy on the Korean peninsula contributed to a perception by some that Russia could play an influential role in helping to resolve the second North Korean nuclear crisis. This crisis began in October 2002 when a high-level North Korean official acknowledged the validity of a U.S. allegation that his country had a secret uranium enrichment program. This program was a violation of the October 1994 Agreed Framework between the DPRK and the United States. Although the Agreed Framework's main focus was a freeze on North Korea's plutonium reprocess-

ing program, it contained a clause confirming the validity of the 1992 denuclearization agreement between North and South Korea in which they foreswore uranium
enrichment programs. The crisis was escalated by Pyongyang's subsequent renunciation of the Agreed Framework, removal of the seals and monitoring cameras from its
nuclear reactors at Yongbyon, expulsion of IAEA inspectors, withdrawal from the
Nuclear Non-Proliferation Treaty (NPT), reopening of its plutonium reprocessing
facility, and proclamations on several occasions that it possessed nuclear weapons
and that it had completed the reprocessing of all the spent fuel rods removed from
their casing at Yongbyon.[9]

After the crisis began, the Putin administration was asked to help mediate it. During a January 2003 visit to Moscow, South Korea's deputy foreign minister, Kim
Dang-Kyung, asked Moscow to help mediate the crisis. Kim observed: "Russia has
long-standing and unique ties with North Korea and so provides an effective channel
for dialogue with Pyongyang."[10] A South Korean military officer visiting the Russian
Far East asked for Russia's help to build trust and to promote cooperation between
the armed forces of North and South Korea.[11] At a January 2003 summit with Putin,
Japan's prime minister Koizumi Junichiro observed that Russia "holds strong influence over North Korea" and "has a perspective on North Korea that Japan does not
have."[12] The director-general of the IAEA, Mohamed ElBaradei, said that Russia
could play a leading role as a mediator and applauded Moscow's decision to perform
this function.[13]

Gaining a Place at the Table and Ensuring a Peaceful Resolution

Russia has been eager to participate in the efforts to resolve the North Korean nuclear
crisis in order to pursue its own interests and objectives. One important goal is to use
the North Korean nuclear crisis as an opportunity to restore Russia's great power
status by playing an important role in its resolution.

Another, arguably even more important, objective is to avoid the outbreak of armed
conflict on the Korean peninsula which could create massive instability and threaten
the Russian Far East if nuclear radiation or refugees poured over the border. Although
Russia's border with North Korea is much shorter than the Chinese-North Korean
border, Russian officials still worry about a massive inflow of refugees over land or
by boat into the Russian Far East.

Economic Motives

Russian and Western analysts have suggested that another reason why Moscow wants
to help resolve the nuclear crisis is that it impedes the process of inter-Korean reconciliation from which Russia hopes to derive economic benefits.[14] Projects linking
North Korea with the sparsely populated Russian Far East can help support that region's
economic development, reducing its vulnerability to China. Provision of Russian electricity or natural gas to North Korea could bring financial gain to Russia and, at the

same time, help resolve the nuclear crisis by enabling North Korea to meet some of its energy needs from sources other than nuclear power.[15]

Three prospective natural gas projects have been discussed: one that would bring natural gas from Irkutsk, another from Sakha, and a third from Sakhalin. At the time the crisis began, negotiations were taking place for a large pipeline project to send natural gas from the Kovyktinskoe field in Irkutsk province through China to South Korea. One of the routes under consideration would have gone from China through North Korea to South Korea. It was envisaged that North Korea would receive free natural gas as a pipeline transit fee.

It now seems less likely that Irkutsk gas will flow to North Korea even if the North Korean nuclear crisis is resolved. In November 2003, the results of a three-year feasibility study were announced by the South Korean, Russian, and Chinese companies negotiating the terms of the Kovyktinskoe project. Tentative agreement was reached on a pipeline route that would go from Irkutsk through China to Dalian and then under the Yellow Sea (West Sea) to Pyongtaek near Seoul, bypassing North Korea. This route was preferred because it was more financially viable and because it would not give North Korea control over the supply of gas to South Korea. However, the possibility of a route transiting North Korea was not entirely closed off. It was anticipated that the final decision would be made in late March 2004 by the South Korean government. It was suggested that Seoul still might prefer a route transiting North Korea as part of the resolution of the nuclear crisis.[16]

More recently, the prospects for early implementation of this project have become dimmer. Russia's state pipeline monopoly, Gazprom, has asserted its right to control this project.[17] Gazprom has suggested reserving Kovykta natural gas for domestic use and providing China and South Korea with gas from the still undeveloped Chayandinskoye gas field in Sakha.[18] Gazprom has suggested changing the Kovykta pipeline route from one that would pass through China and then under the Yellow Sea to South Korea to one that would pass through Khabarovsk and Nakhodka. A KOGAS (Korea Gas Corp.) official has indicated that the proposed new, costlier route does not make economic sense.[19]

Another more promising option is to provide North and South Korea with gas from Sakhalin. Seoul has proposed to Washington that their two countries should provide natural gas from Sakhalin to North Korea as a condition for Pyongyang's agreement to scrap its nuclear program. North Korea would receive natural gas at a subsidized price. South Korea would pay the market price. ExxonMobil now is building a gas pipeline from Sakhalin to Khabarovsk. It would cost approximately US$3.5 billion to build an extension from Khabarovsk to North and South Korea.[20]

North Korea's energy needs could be met more quickly by electricity from the Russian Far East. A proposed electric transmission line has been touted as an alternative to the light water reactors promised under the 1994 Agreed Framework that the Bush administration now is determined to block.[21] However, a report by Victor Minakov, director general of the Far Eastern office of Russia's UES (United Energy Systems) has made it clear that this project still is in an early stage of development.

What is being considered is construction of a 500-kilovolt, 380-kilometer transmission line linking Vladivostok with Chongjin in the northern part of North Korea. Before construction could begin, a feasibility study would have to show that there is an adequate volume of North Korean demand backed by an ability to pay. The feasibility study would have to demonstrate how the project would comply with strict ecological standards, since the projected route traverses several national parks and nature reserves.[22] Ongoing discussions among Russia, North Korea, and South Korea envisage extending the proposed transmission line to South Korea in a second stage.[23]

Russia and North Korea are discussing a project to renovate the wide-track railroad leading from Russia to the North Korean port of Rajin (also spelled Najin). Under the proposed project, Russia would renovate and rent port facilities in Rajin. These facilities would supplement the cargo handling capacity of Russian Far East ports, which are working at full capacity. Later, this renovated rail crossing could become part of a new route connecting the inter-Korean railroad to the Trans-Siberian. Also under consideration is a plan to renovate an oil refinery at Rajin which is closer to Vladivostok than an existing Russian oil refinery. Sergei Darkin, governor of Russia's Maritime Territory (Primorye), has suggested that the main obstacle to realization of these railroad, port, and oil refinery projects is not the nuclear crisis but the need to secure bank guarantees for investment.[24]

Counterproliferation

Another Russian concern is counterproliferation of weapons of mass destruction. On numerous occasions, Putin has expressed strong condemnation of North Korea's nuclear program. He has called on Pyongyang to abandon it. When Putin met with China's outgoing president Jiang Zemin in Beijing in early December 2002, their summit statement expressed the importance of preserving "the non-nuclear status of the Korean peninsula and the regime of non-proliferation of weapons of mass destruction."[25] At their January 2003 summit, Putin and Koizumi expressed "disappointment and profound concern" regarding Pyongyang's decision to withdraw from the NPT. When Pyongyang announced in January 2003 that it was withdrawing from the NPT, the Russian Foreign Ministry issued a statement expressing "deep concern."[26] At the June 2003 G-8 summit in Evian, France, Putin joined the other G-8 leaders in urging North Korea "to visibly, verifiably and irreversibly dismantle any nuclear weapons programs."[27]

The Putin regime's strong opposition to North Korea's nuclear program is not just rhetoric. It reflects a consistent position dating back to the late Soviet period. In 1965, the USSR exported a two-megawatt IRT-2000 research reactor to North Korea and trained North Korean nuclear scientists, thereby enabling Pyongyang to start a nuclear program. By the 1980s, however, Moscow insisted that Pyongyang sign the NPT before it would agree to further cooperation with North Korea. After 1985 when Pyongyang signed this treaty, the USSR agreed to build a nuclear power station in North Korea. However, when Pyongyang announced its intention to withdraw from the NPT, Moscow froze nuclear cooperation with the North and refused to ship the VVER-440 reactors intended for use in the station.[28]

U.S. intelligence officials recently reported that in the early 1990s, Russia's Foreign Intelligence Service cooperated with the U.S. Central Intelligence Agency (CIA) to monitor North Korea's nuclear program. According to a January 2003 *New York Times* report, Russian intelligence officials agreed to install U.S. equipment in the Russian embassy in Pyongyang to detect North Korean efforts to reprocess nuclear fuel and turn it into plutonium. The validity of this report was denied by Boris Labusov, a spokesperson for Russia's Foreign Intelligence Service. In an interview with the Interfax News Agency, Labusov said that the report was "inconsistent with reality."[29] Lobusov's denial is not all that credible. It is possible that Russia's intelligence service cooperated with the CIA but now does not want its cooperation made public.

Moscow has placed restrictions on the transfer of nuclear technology and nuclear weapons matériel to North Korea. Weapons scientists have been stopped from boarding flights to Pyongyang or encouraged to return home from North Korea. Illegal weapons exports have been seized at the border.

Despite these restrictions, some Russian nuclear scientists are believed to be working in North Korea, and some restricted arms and weapons matériel have reached North Korea from Russia. There is a danger that North Korean nationals working in the criminalized Russian Far East could become involved in smuggling nuclear materiel or technology.[30] Russian companies reportedly have been among the suppliers of North Korea's nuclear program. But U.S. officials believe that the technology provided by them is less crucial than technology provided by Pakistan.[31]

Russian Leverage

To achieve its objectives in North Korea, Russia would like to play a role in resolving the nuclear crisis. But its leverage over Pyongyang is limited because it does not provide the large-scale economic assistance needed to help the North Korean regime survive.[32] Russia's annual bilateral trade with North Korea now is approximately US$115 million, far less than North Korea's annual trade with South Korea or China. If the crisis is resolved, Russia may become more important as a provider of electricity or natural gas to North Korea. However, realization of these projects, especially the more expensive ones, may depend on funding from South Korea and other external sources.

By many accounts, Beijing has been the main provider of fuel and food assistance to North Korea. China continues to provide North Korea with fuel oil, but the exact amount is not made public. Beijing has used its control over credit and essential resources as a lever to pressure Pyongyang. China cut off fuel oil shipments to North Korea for a few days in March 2003 to pressure Pyongyang to attend a trilateral U.S.-China-North Korea meeting in Beijing the following month. The PRC's March 2004 announcement that it would provide US$50 million for a glass factory near Pyongyang was described as a reward for Pyongyang's participation in the February 2004 Six-Party Talks.[33]

Japan also is a more important current and prospective source of funding for North Korea than is Russia. Remittances sent by Koreans living in Japan have been a major source of funding for North Korea. Recently, Japan has taken some steps to reduce this transfer of funds. But substantial sums continue to flow, much of it in illegal transfers from pachinko parlors and credit unions associated with Japan's Korean community. Pyongyang considers Japan to be an attractive prospective source of official credits and private investment.[34]

Until the fall of 2002, the United States under the terms of the Agreed Framework provided North Korea annually with 500 metric tons of fuel oil. In October 2002, KEDO members decided to stop these shipments in retaliation for North Korea's cheating on its obligations under the Agreed Framework. Between 1995 and the end of 2003, the United States provided nearly two million metric tons of food aid to North Korea through the World Food Program.[35]

Russia's Mediation Role

Given its limited leverage, what kind of mediation role can Russia play? Russian specialists have acknowledged that Russia lacks China's economic leverage over Pyongyang and that China, not Russia, has been playing a proactive role in resolving the North Korean nuclear crisis. Still, some Russian analysts believe that Russia has influence because it enjoys the trust of both Washington and Pyongyang, which it can use to help broker a compromise. Danil Kobiakov of the PIR Center for Policy Studies described Russia's role as an "impartial intermediary" between the "extreme positions" of Pyongyang and Washington. Sergei Kasyanov of the Institute of World Economy and International Relations in Moscow, suggested that Russia as a country "above the fray" and as "the only participant which can be trusted by all sides" could play a role by endorsing "guarantees of another country if the parties don't trust each other."[36] Aleksandr Vorontsov, director of the North Korea section of the Institute of Oriental Studies in Moscow, said that Russia was conducting "whisper diplomacy" to help resolve the crisis, using "the good personal relationships and channels of close association between Russian and North Korean leaders."[37]

Russia has tried to play a mediating role in the crisis. So far, its efforts have not been successful. Moscow's ability to mediate the crisis is impeded by its limited leverage and by Pyongyang's desire to deal directly with Washington and not through a mediator. When Russian first deputy foreign minister Aleksandr Losyukov visited Pyongyang in January 2003 to hold talks with Kim Jong Il, he tried to assuage North Korean sensitivities by avoiding the use of the word "mediator." Instead, he affirmed that the aim of his mission was to "promote dialogue between the United States and North Korea."[38]

Another obstacle to Moscow playing a more influential role is Russian officials' analysis of the roots of the crisis and the strategy they have advocated to resolve it. While Moscow has adopted a position between those of North Korea and the United States, Russian officials have been inclined to put a good deal of the blame for the crisis on the Bush administration and to advocate solutions that are not acceptable to Washington. Referring to Washington's new doctrine of military preemption and Bush's January 2002 speech designating North Korea as part of an "axis of evil," Russia's deputy foreign minister Georgi Mamedov suggested that "such statements may aggravate the situation and don't facilitate constructive solution of the nonproliferation issues."[39] Washington is seen as partly to blame because of its slow implementation of commitments made in the October 1994 Agreed Framework.[40] Russia's atomic energy minister, Aleksandr Rumyantsev, blamed the deterioration of relations between Washington and Pyongyang on KEDO's failure to build the two promised light water reactors.[41]

The tough policy of the Bush administration is portrayed by some Russians as increasing the incentive for North Korea to acquire nuclear weapons. Russian intelligence officials reportedly believe that officials in Pyongyang are tempted to test a nuclear device, because if they do so, the United States will not dare to attack North Korea the way it attacked Iraq.[42] Yevgeniy Bazhanov, vice-principal of the Russian Foreign Ministry's Diplomatic Academy, has argued that harsh U.S. treatment increases the incentive for North Korea to acquire nuclear weapons.[43]

Russian officials have suggested that North Korea does not present a grave danger to the world. At the late October 2002 Asia-Pacific Economic Cooperation (APEC) meeting in Cabo San Lucas, Mexico, then Russian prime minister M. Kasyanov, who was attending in place of Putin, stated: "We do not have any evidence and proof that North Korea holds any threat."[44] Yevgeny Volk, director of the Heritage Foundation's Moscow branch, told Agence France-Presse in January 2003, that in his view, Pyongyang's decision to expel IAEA monitors and to restart its Yongbyon nuclear complex was a bluff designed to extract large-scale Western aid.[45] In a June 2003 interview with the BBC, Putin remarked: "North Korea is now in such a state that I do not have any reasons to believe that this country has any aggressive intentions."[46]

Some Russian officials and policy advisers have expressed doubts that North Korea possesses any usable nuclear weapons. According to Mikhail Titarenko, director of the Russian Academy Sciences' Institute of Far Eastern Studies, neither Russia nor the United States has reliable information that North Korea has nuclear weapons. Although North Korea has uranium and plutonium, it lacks the technology to build a bomb. Even if Pyongyang has two nuclear shells as the United States claims, Titarenko argues that this does not mean that North Korea has nuclear weapons, because it has not carried out any nuclear tests.[47] Rumyantsev, on more than one occasion, has expressed doubts that Pyongyang possesses any nuclear weapons.[48] While agreeing that North Korea currently does not possess nuclear weapons, Russia's intelligence community has suggested that Pyongyang may have one or two nuclear devices ready for detonation.[49]

Russian observers argue that a harsh approach to North Korea is likely to backfire. They have urged the adoption of a more conciliatory policy. In a January 2003 interview, Deputy Foreign Minister Losyukov warned against speaking "in the language of ultimatums and strict demands." He advocated a more "delicate" approach.[50] Perceiving a harsh approach as counterproductive, Bazhanov maintained that dialogue, moves toward diplomatic recognition of North Korea, and development of links with it would promote North Korean reform and its opening up to the outside world and would reduce the incentive for Pyongyang to acquire nuclear weapons.[51]

Moscow opposes the use of force to resolve the crisis. Russian officials have expressed strong support for a peaceful, negotiated solution, a position backed by China and South Korea, two of North Korea's other neighbors.[52]

Reflecting these perceptions, the package proposal that Losyukov presented to Pyongyang in January 2003 contained terms that were unacceptable to Washington. According to Toloraya, the proposal envisaged about a dozen synchronized steps. Initially, North Korea would freeze its nuclear program in return for U.S. readiness to resume fuel deliveries. In the next stage, Pyongyang and Washington would discuss the current status of the Agreed Framework and decide what to do with it. Subsequently, North Korea and the United States would exchange lists of concerns and demands. Possibly with the help of Russia and China and perhaps also of South Korea and Japan, Washington and Pyongyang would decide what was reasonable and what was not, what was worth pursuing now and what should be left to the future. The bottom line, according to Toloraya, was that Pyongyang would have to renounce nuclear weapons and return to the NPT, and Washington would have to give firm guarantees that it would not infringe on North Korea's sovereignty and security.[53]

Losyukov's proposal was perceived in Washington as too favorable to North Korea. Washington was demanding the complete, irreversible, and verifiable dismantlement of North Korea's nuclear program and also an end to its missile program and a reduction in its conventional forces. The Bush administration was insisting that these demands be met before it would consider extending security guarantees or other benefits to Pyongyang.

Losyukov's open-ended mediation proposal came under fire in Russia as well. Vladimir Lukin, a Duma deputy and former ambassador to Washington, suggested in an analytical program on Russian television that if this package proposal was accepted, the lessons to rogue states could be very dangerous. Lukin warned that it could set off a chain reaction by states trying to solve their problems by blackmailing big countries.[54] A June 2003 article in Kommersant warned that Russia's talk about multilateral guarantees sent the wrong signal to Pyongyang, encouraging it to intensify its nuclear blackmail.[55]

In the months after Losyukov's failed mediation effort, Moscow opposed the imposition of economic sanctions. Russian officials believed that sanctions could destabilize North Korea with negative effects on the region. Sanctions might even lead to war. When the IAEA Board of Governors voted in February 2003 to refer the Korean nuclear question to the UN Security Council, Moscow abstained, although Beijing supported the resolution.

Subsequently, both Moscow and Beijing have opposed UN Security Council consideration of the Korean nuclear crisis. They have done their best to delay this process. When the Security Council considered the Korean problem in April 2003, the resolution proposed by Washington was watered down in large part due to resistance by China and Russia.[56] In July 2003, Moscow along with Beijing and Seoul again resisted efforts by the United States, Britain, and France to bring the North Korean issue before the UN Security Council. Russia's deputy permanent representative to the United Nations, Gennadi Gatloy, argued that it was "premature" to bring the North Korean issue before the Security Council.[57] There have been hints, however, that Russia may drop its opposition to sanctions if North Korea develops nuclear weapons.[58]

Putin and other Russian officials and policy analysts have stressed the importance of providing Pyongyang with security guarantees. During his June 20, 2003, press conference, Putin affirmed his support for a nuclear-free Korean peninsula and then stated:

> We think that this matter should be settled through negotiations that take into account the legitimate interests and concerns of North Korea. We should not back North Korea into a corner and aggravate the situation. If North Korea has concerns over its security and is worried that someone might try to attack it, then we should provide it with security guarantees.[59]

Moscow's call for security guarantees has been backed by Beijing and Seoul.

In the spring and late summer of 2003, it appeared that Russia was going to play a very minor role in resolving the North Korean nuclear crisis. In April, Beijing hosted trilateral talks among the United States, North Korea, and China to discuss the nuclear crisis. The trilateral format allowed Washington to pretend that Pyongyang had conceded to its demand for multilateral, rather than bilateral talks. A statement by China's ambassador to South Korea in advance of the talks indicating that his country would play the role of host, referee, or middleman[60] was intended to assuage Pyongyang, which previously had insisted that it would agree only to bilateral talks with Washington.

Although Russian officials were disappointed that their country was excluded from these talks, they said that the fact that talks were taking place was more important than the format. It is likely that their expression of support was sincere.

Unfortunately, the Beijing talks did not produce a positive result. A North Korean representative announced in the middle of the talks that his country already possessed nuclear weapons and might test or export them. This announcement upset Beijing, which had convened the talks with the aim of persuading Pyongyang to renounce its nuclear program.

In this period, Russian comments on the nuclear crisis reflected a heightened sense of urgency. There was growing concern that the seemingly unbridgeable gap between the North Korean and U.S. positions might lead to war. Losyukov announced that civil defense officials in the Russian Far East had been ordered to make emergency preparations in case hostilities broke out on the Korean peninsula and radioactive fallout or refugees spilled over onto Russian territory.[61]

China, Russia, and other countries made a concerted effort to bring North Korea back to the bargaining table. There was speculation about what form the negotiations would take. At least publicly, North Korea was still insisting that it would agree only to bilateral talks with the United States. Washington was holding out for a multilateral format.

Until the end of July, the most frequent speculation was that a new round of trilateral talks would be held in Beijing with the participation of the United States, North Korea, and China. When U.S. officials spoke about their preference for multilateral talks with more than three participants, they usually mentioned their desire to include South Korea and Japan and sometimes added "and possibly Russia."

It thus seemed likely that the next round of talks on the North Korean nuclear crisis and possibly future rounds might exclude Russia. This perception changed dramatically in late July when North Korea's ambassador to Russia, Pak Ui Chun, said that Pyongyang had agreed to multilateral talks to discuss the crisis with the participation of six countries including North Korea, the United States, China, South Korea, Japan, and Russia.[62]

One can only speculate as to why Pyongyang agreed to multilateral talks and insisted on the inclusion of Russia. The unexpectedly fast U.S. victory in Iraq and North Korea's deteriorating economic situation may have alarmed its leaders. Pyongyang may have insisted on Russia's inclusion in the talks to make it more likely that there would be one more country supporting its position on contentious issues.

Pyongyang may feel more affinity with the Putin administration than with Beijing. There have been growing strains between Pyongyang and China's pragmatic leaders. Reportedly, Pyongyang resents China's efforts to pressure it to return to the negotiating table and to rejoin the NPT.[63] Some Chinese analysts feel that Pyongyang, even more than Washington, is responsible for the nuclear crisis. They note that North Korea's nuclear program predates the Bush administration.[64] One source even suggested that Pyongyang initially proposed holding the Six-Party Talks in Moscow, not Beijing. However, the Putin administration refused out of concern that accepting Pyongyang's proposal could hurt Russia's relations with China.[65]

In the weeks leading up to the August 2003 Six-Party Talks, Moscow and Beijing stressed the importance of providing Pyongyang with security guarantees.[66] Russia and China offered to provide their own guarantees of North Korea's security. But Pyongyang rebuffed their offer insisting that it would be satisfied only by a security guarantee from the United States. Washington refused Pyongyang's demand that it sign a nonaggression treaty to be ratified by the Senate. But U.S. secretary of state Colin Powell suggested that if Pyongyang agreed to the complete, verifiable, and irreversible dismantlement of its nuclear program, then Washington might be willing to provide it with some written security guarantees, albeit not in the form of a treaty.

When the Six-Party Talks were held in Beijing in late August 2003, the stark differences between the U.S. and North Korean positions were highlighted. Pyongyang proposed a package settlement that envisaged North Korean dismantlement of its nuclear program but only after Washington provided security guarantees and economic assistance. Washington reiterated its demand for the complete, irreversible, and verifiable dismantlement of North Korea's nuclear program. Bush administration officials hinted that some reward might be offered to North Korea if it took these steps. But they were unwilling to promise anything concrete to avoid the appearance that they were succumbing to blackmail.

At the talks, Russia adopted a position that suggested the need for compromise by both Pyongyang and Washington. Russia's representative, Losyukov, called for denuclearization of the Korean peninsula. At the same time, he stressed the need for the United States to provide security guarantees and financial aid as a condition for North Korea's agreement to dismantle its nuclear program.

Losyukov claimed that North Korea's delegate at the six-party conference had announced that his country did not possess nuclear weapons and had "no plans to develop them." This assertion was disputed by delegates from the United States, South Korea, and Japan who said that North Korea's delegate, Deputy Foreign Minister Kim Yong Il, had made no such statement.[67]

After the August 2003 Six-Party Talks, Putin urged North Korea not to take any provocative steps that might aggravate the crisis. This message was in a personal letter from Putin that Konstantin Pulikovsky, Putin's representative in the Russian Far East, delivered to Kim Jong Il.[68] Responding to Pyongyang's veiled threats that it might test a nuclear weapon, Russian deputy foreign minister Yury Fedotov demanded an end to "statements and actions that would complicate the negotiated resolution of the problem."[69]

Russian officials supported Beijing's efforts in the fall of 2003 and early 2004 to persuade Pyongyang to return to the negotiating table. In the end, these efforts were successful. In February 2004, a new round of Six-Party Talks was held in Beijing. Just before the talks began, the chief Russian delegate, Deputy Foreign Minister Aleksandr Losyukov, proposed a "package solution" to the nuclear crisis. This package solution envisaged Pyongyang abandoning its military nuclear program in exchange for security guarantees and assurances of noninterference by Washington. Losyukov expressed understanding both of the concern by the United States and other countries about North Korea's nuclear programs and of North Korea's desire for firm security guarantees and for the creation of "normal conditions" for its socioeconomic development.[70]

Losyukov described demands that North Korea eliminate its nuclear programs all at once as "unrealistic." He maintained that it was more "realistic and productive" to move toward dismantling North Korea's nuclear programs "step by step" while "simultaneously exercising active control."[71]

At the February 2004 Six-Party Talks, Russia, China, and South Korea offered to give energy aid to North Korea if it froze its nuclear programs and allowed international inspections to verify the freeze.[72] However, there was a significant difference between what Seoul was demanding as a condition for this aid and what was demanded by Moscow and Beijing. Seoul was insisting that North Korea must freeze all its nuclear programs, plutonium, and uranium, civilian as well as nuclear. The freeze must be soon followed by dismantlement.[73]

Seoul's position was in line with Washington, which maintained that Pyongyang did not have a nuclear program for the production of electricity. Pyongyang's new demand that it be allowed to keep a civilian nuclear program was rejected by Washington because it might make it easier for North Korea to resume an arms program.[74] Losyukov, by contrast, stated that Russia and China were "in the first place interested in the elimination of Pyongyang's nuclear arms program." He described North Korea's "civilian nuclear research" as an "intricate affair, because North Korea is not a participant in the non-proliferation regime and not liable to IAEA rules."[75]

Russia's ambassador to South Korea, Teymuraz Ramishvili, took a position that was even less critical of Pyongyang. Ramishvili linked Pyongyang's desire to have a nuclear program for peaceful purposes to KEDO's failure to fulfill its promise to build light water reactors. He argued that if KEDO fulfilled its pledge to provide North Korea with light water reactors, then the international community would be able to make a stronger case that North Korea should give up its peaceful nuclear program.[76]

While Losyukov did not deny Washington's assertion that North Korea had a uranium enrichment program in addition to its plutonium-processing program, he did not explicitly acknowledge it either. Losyukov asserted that it was anticipated before the Six-Party Talks that one purpose of them would be to clarify exactly what types of nuclear programs North Korea possessed. But this clarification never took place.[77]

After the talks had ended, Losyukov said that they had achieved "modest results." He cited the decision to establish working groups as one of their main achievements.[78] Losyukov expressed disappointment with what he described as a rather tough U.S. reaction to Pyongyang's promise to freeze its nuclear program. He urged Washington to adopt a more accommodating posture and to meet Pyongyang halfway.[79] Losyukov warned that if the nuclear issue were not resolved, mistrust could grow, aggravating the situation on the Korean peninsula.[80]

In late May 2004, Moscow agreed to join the Proliferation Security Initiative, a U.S.-led effort to intercept the transit of missiles and materials usable for the manufacture of weapons of mass destruction.[81] Previously, Russia had refused to join this initiative on the grounds that it encouraged states to act without UN Security Council sanction.[82]

At the June 2004, G-8 summit in Sea Island, Georgia, Putin supported a statement claiming that North Korea had both plutonium reprocessing and uranium enrichment programs. The statement called on North Korea "to dismantle all of its nuclear weapons-related programs in a complete, verifiable, and irreversible manner."[83] One Russian critic, Aleksandr Zhebin, lambasted Putin's action. Zhebin claimed that if North Korea admitted that it has a uranium enrichment program, it would open itself up to intrusive inspections of all its underground facilities. These inspections would help prepare the way for an attack on North Korea by a new U.S.-led "coalition of the willing."[84]

Russia's decision to join the Proliferation Security Initiative and support for the Sea Island summit statement seemed to bring it closer to Washington. However, continued sharp differences with the Bush administration were reflected by Russia's position at and following the third round of Six-Party Talks that were held in late June 2004 in Beijing. Russia's new foreign minister, Sergei Lavrov, repeatedly has affirmed that he considers Pyongyang's "freeze for compensation" proposal a reasonable first step toward the ultimate goal of denuclearization of the Korean peninsula. Lavrov has supported Pyongyang's demand for a security guarantee and for substantial economic compensation, including energy aid, in return for a freeze. In sharp contradiction to Washington's policy, Lavrov has made it clear that Russia supports North Korea's right to maintain a nuclear program for peaceful purposes so long as Pyongyang rejoins the NPT and allows IAEA inspections.[85] In mid-July 2004, Aleksandr Alekseyev, the new leader of Russia's delegation to the Six-Party Talks,[86] proclaimed that it is better to avoid disputes about whether or not North Korea has a uranium enrichment program. Alekseyev observed that the six-party working group would need time to draw up a list of weapons-related nuclear facilities to be frozen. He noted Pyongyang's objection to the three-month deadline suggested by Washington.[87]

Prospects and Conclusions

Russia has a large stake in the outcome of the North Korean nuclear crisis. If it is not resolved peacefully, Russia's interests will suffer. There will be an increased chance of instability and armed conflict in a neighboring country. If Pyongyang develops nuclear weapons, there will be a greater incentive for Japan and South Korea to do the same.

A resolution of the crisis could bring economic benefits to Russia by facilitating projects to provide North Korea with Russian electricity and natural gas. If these projects are successfully implemented, they could help develop the Russian Far East, making it less vulnerable to outside domination by China or any other country.

Despite its stake in the outcome, Russia's ability to influence Washington and Pyongyang is at best limited. Washington has relaxed its previously rigid position toward the North Korean nuclear issues by agreeing to a step-by-step resolution of the problem. But this change has occurred more in response to pressure from Seoul, Tokyo, and Beijing, than to pressure from Moscow.

Pyongyang has advocated Moscow's participation in the Six-Party Talks. However, it is doubtful that Pyongyang is willing to listen to Moscow on issues where it feels its survival is at stake. Putin and other Russian leaders have made it clear that they are opposed to North Korea's development of nuclear weapons. If North Korean leaders strongly believe that they need nuclear weapons not only as a bargaining chip but also as a deterrent, then they are not likely to abandon their nuclear program. At the very least, Pyongyang will want to preserve some ambiguity, so it will resist Washington's demands for a complete and verifiable end to its nuclear program.

Although Russia's influence over the North Korean nuclear crisis has been quite limited, so far it has avoided extensive damage to its relations with Washington and Pyongyang. Before the outbreak of the crisis, the Putin regime was pursuing a contradictory foreign policy. Putin was pushing to improve Russia's relations with the United

States and West Europe, while at the same time courting Pyongyang and other so-called rogue states.

In the case of North Korea, Putin was able to get away with this policy while this issue was not at the center of global attention. However, once the North Korean nuclear crisis erupted, there was a risk that U.S.-Russian relations would be badly damaged if Moscow opposed the Bush administration's hard-line position. Some analysts expressed concern that Moscow's failure to support Washington would further hurt the post–September 11 U.S.-Russian rapprochement that already was badly undermined by Moscow's opposition to the U.S. war in Iraq.

Although Moscow has adopted a position toward the North Korean nuclear crisis that is substantially different from that of Washington, the damage to U.S.-Russian relations so far has been limited. Moscow has opposed economic sanctions. It has encouraged the United States to offer security guarantees and financial aid to North Korea as a condition for its renunciation of nuclear weapons. But it has not been alone in advocating these views. Beijing and Seoul and, to a certain extent, Tokyo have opposed the Bush administration's hard-line position.

At times, Moscow has been more inclined than Beijing to place the blame for the crisis on Washington. But it has been able to get away with this criticism because of its limited role. Beijing's more active role has won it the ire of Pyongyang, inducing North Korea to support greater Russian involvement in negotiations to resolve the crisis.

In the 1990s, Russia was excluded from the negotiations resolving the nuclear crisis and from the subsequent Four-Party Talks. This time Russia has a seat at the table, reaffirming its great power ambitions even though its influence so far has been limited.

Notes

1. Toloraya, "President Putin's Korean Policy," 37.

2. Joo and Kwak, "Military Relations Between Russia and North Korea," 305–306. The contents of this treaty suggest that it is wrong to describe Russia as an ally of North Korea, as some analysts continue to do. Its timing shows that it was a Yeltsin initiative endorsed by Putin, not a change in policy initiated by Russia's second president.

3. Toloraya, "President Putin's Korean Policy," 40, n. 7.

4. James Brooke, "Putin Greets North Korean Leader on Russia's Pacific Coast," *New York Times*, August 23, 2002.

5. Rafael Behr, "Moscow Juggles to Help Solve Korean Crisis," *Financial Times*, January 7, 2003, in Johnson's Russia List (JRL), no. 7007, January 7, 2003.

6. Henry Meyer, "AFP Reports on Plight of North Korean's [sic] Working in Russian Far East," Agence France-Presse (AFP), January 23, 2004, in Foreign Broadcast Information Service, *Daily Report (FBIS: DR)*, January 23, 2004.

7. Alyona Sokolova, "Darkin Talks Business with North Korea," October 8, 2003, available at http://vn.vladnews.ru.

8. Meyer, "AFP Reports on Plight." On December 11, 2003, James Brooke reported in the *New York Times* that Primorye decided to admit as many as 5,000 North Korean workers on labor contracts.

9. Laney and Shaplen, "How to Deal with North Korea," 16–30; David E. Sanger, "North Korea Says It Now Possesses Nuclear Arsenal," *New York Times*, April 25, 2003; David E. Sanger, "North Korea Says It Seeks to Develop Nuclear Arms," *New York Times*, June 10, 2003; Don Kirk, "Report of North Koreans' Claim on Nuclear Rods Appears in South," *New York Times*, July 13, 2003.

10. Behr, "Moscow Juggles to Help Solve Korean Crisis."

11. Boris Savelyev, "Head of South Korean Military Delegation to Russia Promotes Broader Ties," *ITAR-TASS*, February 19, 2003, in *FBIS: DR*, February 19, 2003.

12. BBC, January 10, 2003.

13. Sergei Borisov, "Russia: Peacemaker on the Korean Peninsula?" *Transitions Online*, January 19, 2003, in JRL, no. 7026, January 21, 2003.

14. See, for example: "Russian Senate Speaker in Seoul Discusses North Korea," *ITAR-TASS*, February 24, 2003, in *FBIS: DR*, February 24, 2003; Ferguson, "A Chilly Fall for U.S.-Russia Relations."

15. "ROK's Yonhap: Pipeline Project Seen as Alternative to Reactor Project in N.K.," *Yonhap*, February 27, 2003 in *FBIS: DR*, February 27, 2003.

16. "ROK Report: Russian-PRC-ROK Natural Gas Pipeline 'May Not Run Through' DPRK," *Yonhap*, November 8, 2003, in *FBIS: DR*, November 8, 2003; Kim Sung-jin, "Russia-China-Korea Gas Pipeline May Detour NK," *Korea Times*, November 11, 2003, available at http://times.hankooki.com.

17. Gazprom always had an influence, but its role in this process is even greater now as a consequence of a recent broad reorganization of the Russian energy sector aimed at increasing the power of Gazprom and other companies closely allied with the Putin regime.

18. "Russia Wants to Change Gas Pipeline Route," *Mosnews*, April 2, 2004, available at www.mosnews.com/money/2004/04/02/chinapipeline.shtml.

19. "ROK Report," *Yonhap*, June 8, 2004, in *FBIS: DR*, June 8, 2004. The KOGAS official suggested that Gazprom may have proposed a change in the pipeline route as a bargaining tactic to gain leverage in ongoing negotiations with Chinese and South Korean companies over the price of Kovykta gas (ibid.). However, other sources have suggested that the proposed route change is part of a broader scheme by Gazprom to bring the pipeline closer to gas fields that Gazprom wants to develop. See, for example, Vladimir Todres, Bloomberg online, "Oil Major Considers Sharing Pipeline," *Moscow Times*, May 7, 2004, available at www.themoscowtimes.com/stories/2004/05/07/045–print.html.

20. "ROK's Yonhap: S. Korea Proposes Gas Supply Option to U.S. on N.K. Nuke Issue," *Yonhap*, January 18, 2003, in *FBIS: DR*, January 18, 2003; "Gas for Nukes Proposal Gains Momentum," *Korea Times*, July 13, 2004, in *Napsnet Daily Report*, July 13, 2004, available at www.nautilus.org/napsnet/dr/0407/JUL1304.html#contents/; James Brooke, "Russia Wants to Supply Energy to North Korea," *New York Times*, July 4, 2004.

21. "America as Russia's Strategic Ally," *Nezavisimaya gazeta*, October 29, 2003, in *Center for Defense Information (CDI) Russia Weekly*, no. 280, October 31, 2003.

22. Victor N. Minakov, "Transmission Line Project Linking the Russian Far East with the DPRK (Chongjin)," (paper presented at Energy Forum, Niigata, Japan, February 2004), available at www.nautilus.org/aesnet/Minakov_Niigata_2004_Peport.pdf.

23. "Power Transmission Line Project," *Vostokenergo*, November 4, 2003, available at www.vostok-energo.ru/5675/.

24. Sokolova, "Darkin Talks Business with North Korea"; James Brooke, "Building Ties with North Korea," *New York Times*, December 11, 2003. Brooke suggests that Russia will insist on acquiring ownership stakes in renovated facilities or a guaranteed stream of revenue.

25. Damien McElroy, "N. Korea Told to Quit N-Weapons Program," *Daily Telegraph*, reprinted in the *Vancouver Sun*, December 3, 2002.

26. Seth Mydans, "North Korea Assailed for Withdrawing from Arms Treaty," *New York Times*, January 10, 2003.

27. "G8 Countries Talk Tough on N. Korea, Iran Nuclear Programs," Associated Press, June 2, 2003, available at http://morningstar.com.

28. Pavel Felgenhauer, "Multipolar Nuclear Nightmare," *Moscow Times*, October 24, 2002, in *CDI Russia Weekly*, no. 228, October 25, 2002.

29. "Russians Say Times Report Is Untrue," *New York Times*, January 22, 2003.

30. James Clay Moltz, "Russian Nuclear Regionalism: Emerging Local Influences over Far Eastern Facilities," *National Bureau of Asian Research Analysis*, 11, no. 4 (December 2000), 35–57, available at www.nbr.org/publications/analysis/pdf/vol11no.4.pdf.

31. Elisabeth Bumiller, "Bush Sees North Korean Nuclear Effort as Different from Iraq's," *New York Times*, October 22, 2002.

32. AFP, January 9, 2003.

33. "China to Provide US$50 Mil to Finance Glass Plant in N. Korea," *Yonhap*, March 2, 2004, in *FBIS: DR*, March 2, 2004.

34. Gurtov, "Common Security in North Korea," 405.

35. "Ensuring a North Korean Peninsula Free of Nuclear Weapons," James Kelly, assistant secretary of state for East Asian and Pacific affairs, Remarks to the Research Conference-North Korea: Towards a New International Engagement Framework, February 13, 2004. Available at www.nautilus.org/DPRKbriefingbook/multilateralTalks/Kelly_NKChanceforRedemption.html.

36. Henry Meyer, "AFP: Russia Bids for Discreet Mediator's Role in N. Korean Nuclear Crisis," AFP, February 26, 2004, in *FBIS: DR*, February 26, 2004.

37. Chiang Ping, "Russian Experts on 2d Round of Six-Party Talks," *Ta Kung Pao*, February 22, 2004, in *FBIS: DR*, February 22, 2004.

38. Borisov, "Russia: Peacemaker on the Korean Peninsula?"

39. Bumiller, "Bush Sees North Korean Nuclear Effort as Different from Iraq's."

40. Behr, "Moscow Juggles to Help Solve Korean Crisis."

41. Laney and Shaplen, "How to Deal with North Korea."

42. Felgenhauer, "Multipolar Nuclear Nightmare."

43. "Russian Expert Urges Softly-Softly Approach to North Korea," *BBC Monitoring*, December 25, 2002, in *CDI Russia Weekly*, no. 237, December 27, 2002.

44. Tim Weiner, "3 Nations Put Pressure on North Korea," *New York Times*, October 27, 2002.

45. "Russia Left in the Dark Over N. Korean Crisis: Analysts," AFP, January 9, 2003, in *CDI Russia Weekly*, no. 239, January 10, 2003.

46. Sergei Blagov, "Russia's Lost Korean Opportunity," *Asia Times*, June 25, 2003, in *CDI Russia Weekly*, no. 263, June 27, 2003.

47. "Russia to Participate in North Korean Nuclear Arms Talks," *pravda.ru*, August 4, 2003, available at http://newsfromrussia.com.

48. "No Evidence DPRK Has Nuclear Bomb: Russian Minister," *People's Daily*, July 15, 2003, in *Napsnet Daily Report*, July 22, 2003, available at www.nautilus.org/archives/napsnet/dr/0307/JUL22–03.html#contents/.

49. Pavel Felgenhauer, "Iraq Is Not Like Chechnya," *Moscow Times*, July 24, 2003, in *CDI Russia Weekly*, no. 266, July 25, 2003.

50. Borisov, "Russia: Peacemaker on the Korean Peninsula?"

51. "Russian Expert Urges Softly-Softly Approach to North Korea," *BBC Monitoring*, December 25, 2002, in *CDI Russia Weekly*, no. 237, December 27, 2002.

52. Japanese officials largely share this view. However, at one point, Prime Minister Koizumi warned that Japan may resort to "other measures" if diplomacy fails. "Other measures" is seen as a code word for the use of force or the imposition of economic sanctions.

53. Toloraya, "President Putin's Korean Policy," 49.

54. Borisov, "Russia: Peacemaker on the Korean Peninsula?"

55. Blagov, "Russia's Lost Korean Opportunity."

56. Associated Press, April 26, 2003.

57. Felicity Barringer and David E. Sanger, "Delay by U.N. on Rebuking North Korea Is Urged," *New York Times*, July 3, 2003. An ROK foreign ministry spokesperson denied that his country opposed UN Security Council consideration of the North Korean nuclear issue. He said that Seoul had rejected U.S. proposals for the UN to intervene because the timing was not right. ("South Korea Denies Rift with US," AFP, July 30, 2003, in *Napsnet Daily Report*, July 30, 2003.)

58. "Russia Says It Could Back Sanctions Against North Korea," Reuters, in *Napsnet Daily Report*, April 11, 2003, available at www.nautilus.org/archives/napsnet/dr/0304/APR11.html#item10/.

59. Text in Johnson's Russia List, no. 7233, June 21, 2003.

60. Don Kirk, "South Korea Aide Sees Long Road Ahead in Talks with North," *New York Times*, April 18, 2003.

61. Michael Wines, "Warning to North Korea on Nuclear Arms," *New York Times*, April 12, 2003; "FBIS Media Analysis: 24 July: Russian Media Fan Fears of U.S. Attack on North Korea," *FBIS: DR*, July 24, 2003.

62. *Napsnet Daily Report*, July 31, 2003. Perhaps not coincidentally, just a few days before this announcement, U.S. Undersecretary of State John Bolton, at a press conference in Beijing, strongly supported Russia's participation in multilateral talks ("U.S. Official Expands on View That Russia Can Help with North Korea Dispute," *Interfax*, July 28, 2003, in *FBIS: DR*, July 28, 2003).

63. Alexandre Mansourov, "Giving Lip Service with an Attitude: North Korea's China/Debate," *DPRK Briefing Book-Special Report*, available at www.nautilus.org.

64. "US-PRC-DPRK Talks: Russia Has Trump Card to Play," *Hong Kong Hsin Pao*, April 24–25, 2003, in *FBIS: DR*, April 25, 2003.

65. "North Proposed Russia to Hold Six-Way Talks," September 9, 2003, available at http://english.donga.com/srv/service.php3?biid=2003091079068/.

66. In early August 2003, Russia's deputy foreign minister Yuriy Fedotov stressed the importance of providing Pyongyang with security guarantees and economic aid in return for a guarantee that North Korea's nuclear program is totally peaceful ("Russia: North Korea Sets No Conditions on Talks," *New York Times*, August 7, 2003).

67. "Russian Deputy Minister Warns Breakdown of North Korea Talks Could Lead to 'Hot Conflict,'" *ITAR-TASS*, August 27, 2003, in *FBIS: DR*, August 27, 2003; Andrei Kirillov, "Conflicting Reports on NK Talks," *Moscow News*, September 3–9, 2003, in *CDI Russia Weekly*, no. 272, September 3, 2003; "North Korea Rejects US Charge on Enriched Uranium," AFP, August 27, 2003, in *Napsnet Daily Report*, August 28, 2003, available at www.nautilus.org/archives/napsnet/dr/0308/AUG28–03.html#contents/.

68. Pulikovsky was in Pyongyang to attend the September 9, 2003, fifty-fifth anniversary celebrations of the founding of the North Korean regime ("North Korea Agrees in Principle to Six-Way Talks in November," AFP, September 12, 2003, in *Napsnet Daily Report*, September 12, 2003, available at www.nautilus.org/archives/napsnet/dr/0309/SEP12–03.html#contents/).

69. "Tokyo, Moscow Turn on DPRK over Nuclear Test Threat," AFP, October 17, 2003, in *Napsnet Daily Report*, October 17, 2003, available at www.nautilus.org/archives/napsnet/dr/0310/OCT17–03.html#contents/.

70. Aleksandr Zyuzin and Alexei Morozov, "Russia Calls for Package Solution to N. Korea Issue," *ITAR-TASS*, February 23, 2004, in *FBIS: DR*, February 23, 2004.

71. Andrey Kirillov, Aleksey Morozov, and Vladimir Pavlov, "Russia: Deputy FM Says Unrealistic to Demand DPRK Immediately Drop Nuclear Program," *ITAR-TASS*, February 26, 2004, in *FBIS: DR*, February 26, 2004.

72. "Russian Ambassador Says 6-Way Talks Failed to 'Meet Expectations,' Made 'Some Progress,'" *Yonhap*, March 4, 2004, in *FBIS: DR*, March 4, 2004.

73. "Seoul to Propose Three Conditions for Accepting DPRK Freeze Offer," *Yonhap*, Feb-

ruary 20, 2004, in *FBIS: DR*, February 20, 2004; Jack Kim, "The U.S., South Korea and Japan Insist that Any Solution to the Nuclear Dispute Address the Uranium Enrichment Program," Reuters, February 23, 2004, in *Napsnet Daily Report*, February 23, 2004, available at www.nautilus.org/archives/napsnet/dr/0402/FEB23–04.html#contents/.

74. Joseph Kahn, "Nuclear Talks Seem Mired in Discord," *New York Times*, February 27, 2004.

75. Alexander Zyuzin and Alexei Morozov, "Russian Deputy FM Comments on Results of Six Party Talks," *ITAR-TASS*, February 26, 2004, in *FBIS: DR*, February 26, 2004.

76. "Russian Ambassador: 'NK Has Right to Nuclear Development,' " *Korea Times*, March 4, 2004, in *Napsnet Daily Report*, March 4, 2004, available at www.nautilus.org/archives/napsnet/dr/0403/MAR04–04.html#contents/.

77. "Ambiguities Remain on North Korea's Nuclear Programme-Russian Envoy," *ITAR-TASS*, February 28, 2004, in *FBIS: DR*, February 28, 2004.

78. "Losyukov Says Six Parties Reach Consensus on Necessity of Establishing Working Groups," Xinhua, February 28, 2004, in *FBIS: DR*, February 28, 2004; "N. Korea Talks End with Deep Divisions Laid Bare," Reuters, February 28, 2004.

79. Aleksandr Zyuzin and Vera Pavlova, "Russia: Deputy FM Says US Takes Tough Stance at Korean Nuclear Talks," *ITAR-TASS*, February 28, 2004, in *FBIS: DR*, February 28, 2004.

80. "Russia Warns of Worsening N. Korea Situation-Tass," Reuters, February 29, 2004.

81. See several articles in *CDI Russia Weekly*, no. 309, June 4, 2004.

82. "U.S. Lobbies Russia to Join Campaign Against Illicit Arms Shipments," AFP, January 29, 2004, in *CDI Russia Weekly*, no. 291, January 30, 2004.

83. "Summit Document: G8 Action Plan on Nonproliferation: Sea Island, June 9, 2004," available at www.g7.utoronto.ca/summit/2004seaisland/nonproliferation.html.

84. Aleksandr Zhebin, "Nuclear Impasse for 'Coalition of the Willing.' Moscow Drifting in Washington's Direction," *Nezavisimaya gazeta*, June 23, 2004, in *FBIS: DR*, June 23, 2004. Zhebin is head of the Institute for the Far East's Center for Korean Studies under the Russian Academy of Sciences.

85. See, for example, Vitaly Kuchkin, *ITAR-TASS*, June 28, 2004, in *FBIS: DR*, June 28, 2004; *ITAR-TASS*, July 6, 2004, in *FBIS: DR*, July 6, 2004.

86. Alekseyev led Russia's delegation to the June 2004 Six-Party Talks. The former delegation head, Losyukov, now is Russia's ambassador to Japan.

87. Valery Agarkov, *ITAR-TASS*, July 14, 2004, in *FBIS: DR*, July 14, 2004.

— 11 —

North Korea–South Korea
Relations in the Kim Jong Il Era

Seongji Woo

Following Kim Il Sung's death in July 1994, Kim Jong Il has risen as the new leader of North Korea and has ruled the North for a decade. For him and his people as well as for outside observers, it has been a rough ten years. The country presiding over the northern half of the peninsula has suffered natural disasters, alliance breakdowns, mass starvation, and intermittent sparring with South Korea. Defying many pundits' predictions of the early demise of the Stalinist regime due to its isolation and inefficiency, the Democratic People's Republic of Korea is muddling through economic hardship internally and international pressure externally. Kim Jong Il nurtures the fear of a U.S. attack on his people to keep them vigilant, and uses the juche (self-reliance) ideology that he and his father jointly created to cement popular cohesion.

The bilateral relationship between Pyongyang and Seoul under Kim Jong Il is developing under a very different context from the one that existed under Kim Il Sung. Economically, North Korea is too weak to compete with South Korea, which has an economy that is more than thirty times larger than the North's.[1] Yet, even with a defunct economy, North Korea possesses a rather formidable military might that is aging rapidly. Given that Pyongyang has no chance of winning a conventional arms race against its rich counterpart, it is determined to arm itself with unconventional weapons, an aim that is vehemently opposed by the United States. Chairman Kim Jong Il will doggedly uphold his nuclear and missile programs for as long as possible because they provide the safety valve for the North Korean regime's survival.

For Pyongyang, regime survival is its utmost objective. Its imminent task is not to export revolution to the South, but to buy the time in which it can rebuild its physical strength in order to compete successfully with Seoul. Until the balance of power is restored between the two Koreas, North Korea will accept generous assistance from Seoul and use it as a springboard to jumpstart its impoverished economy. With the government in Seoul willing to provide support and to fully engage with Pyongyang, the Kim Jong Il regime is eager to extract as many financial gains as possible at the expense of the generosity of Seoul. Pyongyang attempts to compensate for its physical weakness by using tactics to drive a wedge between conservatives and liberals in South Korea and between the United States and South Korea. South Korea's aim is not to hurry national reunification, but to induce the North's reform slowly and incrementally through continuous contact and material exchanges. With Pyongyang not ready to willingly accept liberalization of its system, Seoul needs to be more ingenuous in trying to breed change in the North Korean system.

The following section briefly reviews the evolution of the rivalry between the two Koreas. The third section traces North Korea's changes under Kim Jong Il. The fourth section analyzes North Korea's nuclear issues, and the fifth examines inter-Korean economic cooperation. In the sixth section, Pyongyang's current South Korea policy is discussed. Finally, the seventh section introduces some recommendations for developing a mature inter-Korean relationship and building stable peace in the region.

The Evolution of the South Korean–North Korean Rivalry

Seen from the perspective that war and peace is a dominant feature of world politics, rivalries and rivals demand the keen attention of international relations observers. A major portion of international conflict is waged between rivals.[2] A 55-year-old rivalry is currently unfolding on the Korean peninsula. The two Koreas endured a three-year-long war in the early stage of their rivalry and are still at war in technical terms. The conclusion of peace treaties among the major war participants remains elusive. Throughout its existence, the Seoul-Pyongyang rivalry has had its share of military conflicts, crises, and reconciliations. In the post–Cold War period, South Korea is making every effort to realize the stage of peaceful coexistence between the two Koreas. Currently in the life cycle of a rivalry, it can be assumed that we are in the transitional stage from antagonistic coexistence to peaceful coexistence. This transitional period, not surprisingly, is filled with difficulties and setbacks.

During the Cold War era, the relationship between South Korea and North Korea could have been characterized as hostile. The two rivals experienced tragic confrontation locked in a zero-sum game of conflict. With the end of the Cold War era, South Korea has begun to adopt a different approach toward the North. Instead of seeking peace by deterrence only, successive administrations have been pursuing peace through engagement from as early as the late 1980s. The changes in global political and economic environments as well as the determination and fresh ideas of successive political leaders have made this foreign policy change possible. What is more, Seoul now feels more comfortable dealing with its counterpart in the North than it has in the past. South Korea has been democratized and has a vigorous economy that cannot be matched by North Korea. The fierce competition between the two Koreas seems to be ending with the South emerging victorious. The questions remain as to how it will end and how long the current, outmoded rivalry will endure. The only hope Pyongyang has is to revive its economy with external help by opening itself up to the international community.

President Roh Tae Woo practiced Northern Politics, which resulted in diplomatic normalization with the Soviet Union and China, respectively, in 1990 and 1992. President Roh sought to make inroads into Pyongyang via Moscow and Beijing. Seoul and Pyongyang held several high-level talks between themselves. Under President Kim Young Sam, the first nuclear crisis erupted as North Korea resisted the IAEA's special inspections. North Korea and the United States concluded the Agreed Framework in October 1994, in which Pyongyang promised to freeze its nuclear program in exchange for a U.S. pledge to provide heavy oil and to build two light-water reactors for North Korea. Notwithstanding the resolution of the nuclear issue, the Kim Young Sam regime kept its distance from Pyongyang.

With the rise of the Kim Dae Jung presidency, the mood between the two Koreas began to change again. The South Korean government adopted a Reconciliation and Cooperation Policy, which is commonly known as the Sunshine Policy, toward North Korea. Even during moments of temporary setbacks such as North Korea's missile launching and naval skirmishes in the West Sea in 1999 and again in 2001, Kim Dae Jung's engagement drive made possible a historic summit meeting in Pyongyang between President Kim Dae Jung and Chairman Kim Jong Il in June 2000.[3] Following the 2000 Summit, inter-Korean exchanges proliferated. In 2002, North-South trade recorded US$642 million, and between 1998 and 2002, more than 500,000 South Korean tourists visited Mt. Keumgang in the North. South and North Korea have begun to build railroads and roads connecting the divided country across the DMZ. Hyundai-Asan and North Korea have agreed to build an industrial complex in Kaesung in the North, which is located just seventy kilometers north of Seoul.[4] The amount of official aid that the North received from the South rose to US$135 million in 2002 from US$4.6 million in 1996.[5]

The current administration in Seoul under Roh Moo Hyun vows to tackle the twin tasks of simultaneously mending inter-Korean relations and promoting peace and prosperity in Northeast Asia. Since the June 15 meeting, North and South Korea have held more than one hundred meetings. Roh's Peace and Prosperity Policy seeks to promote peace and prosperity on the Korean peninsula, which will, in turn, build the foundation for peaceful unification of the two Koreas, and further facilitate Northeast Asian economic cooperation and development. There is no doubt that the success of the Peace and Prosperity Policy hinges on the peaceful resolution of the nuclear maze. Nuclear confrontation on the peninsula puts Roh's unification policy in an awkward position. Trapped at the crossroads of rivalry (intranational) dynamics with Pyongyang and alliance (international) dynamics with Washington, Roh's Peace and Prosperity Policy is facing difficulties: Making headway in inter-Korean relations opens the door to a schism in alliance politics in solving the nuclear problem, and vice versa. Roh Moo Hyun is making slow, and yet steady progress in inter-Korean economic cooperation while seeking a breakthrough in multilateral nuclear deals through close coordination with the United States.

For the establishment of peaceful coexistence between the two Koreas, South Korea's engagement efforts alone are not sufficient. North Korea should respond in kind by giving up its nuclear weapons development program and opening up its country via economic reforms.

Ten Years of North Korea Under Kim Jong Il

Following the death of Kim Il Sung, Kim Jong Il inherited the isolated regime already in shambles due to structural inefficiencies and the aftershock of the collapse of the Soviet Union and East European communist countries. What is worse, natural disasters in the mid-1990s compounded by internal and external problems inflicted unbearable sufferings on the North Korean people. Between 1990 and 1998, the North Korean economy recorded negative growth. The Public Distribution System (PDS), which is a state-run system to provide cereal to the people, ceased to function properly. It is estimated that more than one million people starved to death.[6] The collapse of the socialist states worldwide has placed the North Korean regime on the defensive. North Korea has survived "contagion effects," that is, the successive collapse of the neighboring communist states as seen in Eastern Europe, largely because of its relative political autonomy from the Soviet Union. The North Korean regime has been operating like an isolated island, even more so in the post–Cold War context.[7]

Though the North Korean leadership still boasts the unique strength of its socialist regime, created based on juche ideology, North Korea's economic performance has been quite dismal due to inefficiency and low productivity of central planning in industry and collective farming in agriculture. The society is suffering severely from food and energy shortages. More than 40 percent of children under age seven are known to suffer from malnutrition. In spite of a relatively good harvest in the fall of 2003, North Korea is still in need of one million tons of food to feed its population.[8] The North Korean economy, which had been showing signs of decay in the 1980s, took a sharp downturn in the early 1990s as the global network of socialist trading came to a halt. Kim Jong Il once admitted, "the economic conditions in the 1990s were worse than the devastation suffered after the Korean War in the 1950s."[9] Factories throughout the country operate at about 30 percent of their full capacity. For a decade Pyongyang has been unable to initiate any new mid- or long-range economic plans after the ominous failure of its third seven-year economic plan, which ended in 1993. The national budget has dwindled to half the size of that of 1994. The GNP per capita had been reduced from US$1,146 in 1990 to US$573 in 1998. Fortunately, the North has been recording positive growth rates since 1999, and its agricultural output is slowly on the rise.[10] Yet this is not to say that North Korea's difficult days are over.

In the post–Kim Il Sung era, North Korea has been showing signs of change in many aspects. These changes are geared as a means of escape from the paucity of food, living conditions, and isolation from the international community. North Korea's dysfunctional economy dictates its leadership to launch economic restructuring measures in order to sustain the regime and save the people from starvation. Under the new regulation, the cabinet has been assigned the main responsibility for planning and directing the national economy, whereas the intervention of the party in the economic sector has been curtailed.[11] The North Korean regime is not hesitant to use terms such as "market" and "reform," educating its people that working harder to make more money is not against socialist virtues. While upholding socialism, Pyongyang wants its people to become pragmatic in their commercial endeavors. Leadership preaches that the spirits of socialism and pragmatism are not contradictory.

In the post–Kim Il Sung era, one notable change in North Korea is the advance of the military, the Korean People's Army (KPA), as the central organ responsible for preserving the sovereignty of the DPRK. In September 1998, the Supreme People's Assembly (SPA) anointed Kim Jong Il as head of the National Defense Commission (NDC), which was given heightened authority and power according to a revised constitution. Facing economic hardship and regime crisis, Kim Jong Il solidified his power by resorting to ideologies such as *songun-chongchi* (Military-First Politics) and kangsong taeguk (a Strong and Prosperous State).[12] According to Pyongyang's explanation, three pillars—ideology, military, and science and technology—and three principles—self-reliance, self-sustenance, and profit making—are necessary to build a strong and prosperous state. Military-first politics, first appearing in the party organ *Rodong Shinmun* (Worker's Daily) in April 1998, was Kim Jong Il's way of dealing with internal and external threats to the regime's survival: "Kim Jong Il had prescribed 'military-first' politics by giving priority to the military to preserve and protect the sovereignty of the state."[13] Military spirit and military methods have become national slogans that all must blindly recite and follow. For the time being, Kim Jong Il seeks to mobilize his people with the motto of military-first politics.

In July 2002, North Korea introduced yet other measures to revive its economy, which included price reforms and salary hikes. According to the reform measures, the price of rice was fixed at 44 won per kilogram. Local transportation cost 2 won per ride. Average workers receive 2,000 won a month, with miners who have to endure harsh working environments earning from 6,000 to 8,000 won a month. Local enterprises have been allowed to possess higher managerial autonomy than before.[14] There are mixed reports about the interim outcome of this economic restructuring. Some observers lament that the Pyongyang regime's reform efforts are only superficial and insufficient. They assert that only the full-scale adoption of a market economy will revive the autarkic economy. Yet, the Kim Jong Il regime is unlikely to swing open the doors to foreign technology, capital, and influence, so they reason that only regime change can bring life to North Korean society and economy. Many factories are unable to pay their workers; therefore, living conditions of average workers have degenerated. People are suffering more due to steep inflation and scant food rationings.

Yet others see positive changes occurring in many aspects of the Hermit Kingdom. They see changes in people's attitudes and attire. Foreigners have witnessed markets sprouting in big cities, selling various items from vegetables to shoes to consumer electronics. Many have seen street vendors selling drinks and fruits. Those who have observed these changes argue that living conditions have been slowly improving in North Korea. Rick Corsino, who until recently resided in North Korea for three years as the head of the World Food Program observes, "There are more vehicles on the road, and people are dressing more colorfully than in the past. There's more electricity, more shops and restaurants opening."[15] A Japanese businessman was surprised to see notable signs of change when returning to Pyongyang after just ten months: "There were a lot more food stands, people looked more lively, there were more [businesses] catering to foreigners and a drastic increase in the number of bicycles on Pyongyang's streets."[16]

Internationally, Kim Jong Il is actively pursuing foreign policies. The DPRK opened diplomatic relations in succession with Italy, Australia, the Philippines, Great Britain, the Netherlands, Belgium, Canada, Spain, Germany, and others.[17] Since the June summit between the two Koreas, Kim has met several times with Chinese, Japanese, and Russian leaders. In spite of the rise of the new generation of leadership under President Hu Jintao in China, Beijing remains a close guardian of North Korea. While it is true that the once cordial relationship between Pyongyang and Beijing dubbed as "lips and teeth" has all but disappeared, the two still seem to be dependent on each other for geostrategic reasons. China is currently functioning as the mediator between Washington and Pyongyang in an attempt to work out a solution to the recent nuclear negotiations, and by doing so has raised its diplomatic posture in the region to new heights.[18] Recently, in China, there are hints that the Chinese leadership increasingly regards Pyongyang more as a nuisance than as a strategic partner, which would be of grave concern to Kim Jong Il.

Russian leader Vladimir Putin and North Korean leader Kim Jong Il have thrice exchanged visits in July 2000, August 2001, and August 2002. The July 2000 summit meeting marked the first ever visit to Pyongyang by a Russian leader.[19] Putin's Russia aims to become a pragmatic balancer between the two Koreas. Russia's economic interests in the Far East lie in the development of Siberia and the linking of the Trans-Siberian Railroad (TSR) and Trans-Korean Railroad (TKR), for which it feels that North Korean-South Korean-Russian economic coordination is essential.[20] Russia remains an important player in multilateral nuclear negotiations and will play an even bigger role when Northeast Asian economic cooperation talks materialize.

North Korean-Japanese negotiations in September 2002 resulted in a historic visit to Pyongyang by Japanese Prime Minister Junichiro Koizumi. However, talks between the two countries are now in limbo due to revelations regarding North Korea's kidnapping of Japanese nationals, in addition to the nuclear imbroglio. Recently, Pyongyang has been sending signals to Tokyo that it is willing to make concessions on the kidnapping issue in return for progress in bilateral normalization talks.[21] A commentary in the *Rodong Sinmun* notes that Pyongyang is ready to make progress in North Korean-Japanese relations "if Japan respects the DPRK-Japan Pyongyang Declaration and acts in good faith."[22] In spite of Koizumi's additional visit to Pyongyang, the prospects for a smooth process of bilateral normalization talks seem far from rosy in part due to high anti-North Korea sentiment among the Japanese people.

North Korea's recent activities reveal that Pyongyang has set out to reform its defunct economy. Kim Jong Il is ready to accept a "quarantined opening," meaning that Pyongyang "selectively accepts what is needed and the area opened is fenced off from the rest of the economy."[23] Yet North Korea's efforts fall short of accepting full-scale, Chinese-style economic reforms. Given the nature of the regime in Pyongyang, that is, one-man authoritarian rule, hereditary succession, and devotion to the juche ideology, it seems unlikely that it will voluntarily take the liberal path to political and economic reforms.

The North Korean Nuclear Issue and Inter-Korean Relations

The nuclear specter is back on the Korean peninsula. Once again, the peninsula is mired in confrontation over how to solve the North Korean nuclear problem. Three rounds of Six-Party Talks held in Beijing, attended by China, Russia, Japan, the United States, and the two Koreas, have fallen short of resolving North Korea's nuclear problem through peaceful means. With the September 11 terrorist attacks on American soil and the U.S. war on terrorism, a new North Korean nuclear episode is unfolding in ill-fated times. The Bush administration is determined not to reward North Korea's bad behavior, which places Pyongyang's nuclear game in a dangerous position. North Korea and the United States are again at loggerheads and, unfortunately, the South Korean government's desire for inter-Korean reconciliation and eventual integration is once again on hold.

The United States and the Democratic People's Republic of Korea have both stated that they want a diplomatic resolution to the nuclear standoff, but they differ on how to achieve it. North Korea still denies the existence of a highly enriched uranium (HEU) program and continues to argue that it has the right to develop nuclear deterrence as long as the hostile U.S. policy toward Pyongyang persists. Kim Jong Il says that he is willing to negotiate with the United States, with the denuclearization of the peninsula as the final goal. But he also argues that the basic formula for the solution must be "freeze vs. compensation" and involve simultaneous actions on the parts of the United States and North Korea. North Korea wants to be rewarded for each concession it makes toward the incremental disarming of its nuclear capabilities. The Bush administration publicly claims that it is devoted to a peaceful solution of the matter, even though the United States demands that North Korea scrap its nuclear programs completely, verifiably, and irreversibly before receiving any security or economic benefits.[24]

In the early 1990s, North Korea ignited the first nuclear crisis on the peninsula by refusing to accept a special inspection by the IAEA. The Korean peninsula was on the brink of military conflict, but at the final moment North Korea and the United States were able to come to an agreement on freezing Pyongyang's nuclear program in exchange for providing heavy fuel oil and building light-water nuclear reactors in North Korea.[25] It was hoped then that the Geneva Agreed Framework of October 1994 would resolve the nuclear problem and bring stability to Northeast Asia.

Years later, however, another nuclear crisis erupted on the peninsula in October 2002, when North Korea admitted its pursuit of a clandestine nuclear program by enriching uranium. Pyongyang evicted the IAEA nuclear inspectors and withdrew from the NPT successively.[26] On October 2, 2003, Pyongyang announced that it had finished reprocessing 8,000 spent fuel rods and was using the plutonium to make nuclear bombs. A North Korean representative to the United Nations in New York said that North Korea had a nuclear deterrence capability and was continuing to strengthen it. In addition, North Korea declared that it did not plan to export its bombs to other countries.[27]

The first round of Six-Party Talks, held in Beijing in late August 2003, ended in a stalemate, neither a success nor a failure. The six parties laid out their respective positions on the pending nuclear issue. North Korea expressed that it did not intend to build nuclear bombs and was willing to give up its nuclear weapons program in exchange for a nonaggression pact and economic aid. China and Russia concurred that the Korean peninsula should remain nuclear-free and North Korea's security concerns must be addressed. Japan raised the abduction issue in addition to the resolution of the nuclear problem. The United States asserted that North Korea must dismantle its nuclear programs completely, verifiably, and irreversibly. One positive outcome of the Beijing gathering was that the North indicated its final goal was to establish a nuclear-free Korean peninsula. After the talks, Pyongyang claimed that it had no interest in further talks unless the United States changed its hostile attitude. The North also declared that it would pursue concrete steps to enhance its nuclear deterrent capability.[28]

The second round of Six-Party Talks brought a mild thaw over the nuclear issue, but huge differences still remained between Pyongyang and Washington on how to resolve the problem through diplomatic channels. The six parties agreed to set up working groups and to meet again before the end of June. Unable to agree on the exact languages of the official communiqué, the participants had to be content with the chairman's statement, in which they agreed to build a nuclear-weapons-free Korean peninsula. North Korea still adheres to the idea of simultaneous action and wants to be rewarded materially for its nuclear concessions. North Korea has denied the existence of an HEU program while asserting its intention to retain a civilian nuclear power program.[29]

The third round of Six-Party Talks was held in Beijing from June 23–26, 2004. The attitude of the North Korean delegation somewhat mellowed following Kim Jong Il's Beijing visit, and the United States tabled a concrete proposal for the resolution of the nuclear stalemate at the persuasion of its Asian allies. In a closed session, James Kelly remarked that North Korea should expect extraordinary compensation for the complete dismantlement of its nuclear programs. North Korea expressed its willingness to freeze its nuclear facilities in Yongbyon, demanded energy assistance, asked to be removed from the list of terrorist-assisting nations, and asked to be freed of economic sanctions. The United States demanded a complete dismantlement of all the North's nuclear programs following a three-month preparatory stage of freezing. Once North Korea begins to dismantle its nuclear programs, the United States promises to provide a temporary security guarantee and hold talks with the North to discuss the lifting of economic sanctions.[30]

South Korea basically supports the idea of a denuclearized Korean peninsula and of resorting to diplomatic means to achieve that goal. South Korea, using multiple venues, has tried to persuade North Korea to abandon its nuclear programs and accept generous assistance from the international community. South Korea's efforts to persuade North Korea to abandon its nuclear programs continued in Jakarta, Indonesia. During the ASEAN Regional Forum (ARF) meeting, North Korea's Foreign Minister Baek Nam Sun and South Korea's Foreign Minister Ban Ki Mun met to discuss inter-Korean relations and the nuclear problem. The two agreed to continue their cooperation on international issues, but fell short of agreeing on the right formula for resolving the nuclear issue.[31]

Seoul's diplomatic efforts are geared to convince North Korea that it will be better off without nuclear weapons. To date, however, Seoul's sincere advice has largely fallen on deaf ears. To overcome its economic backwardness, Pyongyang needs to forgo its nuclear obsession and instead turn to the international community for economic cooperation. Yet as long as Kim Jong Il believes that the existence of nuclear deterrence will assist his reign of power, he will find it a formidable task to nullify his nuclear programs.

Inter-Korean Economic Cooperation

Economic cooperation between the two Koreas dates back to 1988 when President Roh Tae Woo opened the door to commercial exchanges. After a momentary stall during the first nuclear crisis, inter-Korean talks and cooperation culminated in the June 2000 summit between Kim Dae Jung and Kim Jong Il. The two leaders jointly declared that North and South Korea would seek to raise inter-Korean economic cooperation to a higher level by agreeing to develop the national economy in a balanced way through bilateral efforts. While much of the credit goes to the Kim Dae Jung administration for initiating and maintaining reconciliations in a fierce rivalry that has continued for half a century, North Korea has also responded positively to the South's overtures, albeit with inconsistency.[32]

In spite of the ongoing nuclear standoff, the Roh Moo Hyun administration is seeking ways to improve inter-Korean relations. Pyongyang for its part does not want to disengage fully due to the tempting aid that has been flowing in from Seoul. As the U.S.–North Korean standoff continues, Pyongyang has been tactically leaning toward Seoul and calling for intranational cooperation in the fight against U.S. imperialism.

Seoul-Pyongyang economic exchanges are making headway in multiple areas. In 2003, more than 14,000 South Koreans visited the North and almost 74,000 South Korean tourists visited Mt. Keumgang. The total volume of inter-Korean trade in the same year exceeded US$700 million, placing Seoul as the second most important trading partner of Pyongyang, next to Beijing.[33] The construction of a major industrial park in Kaesong is by far the most important task ever attempted by the two Koreas. The pilot industrial park in Kaesong will open at the end of 2004 with fifteen South Korean firms manufacturing goods using North Korean labor, largely intended for South Korean markets. Among the three planned sections in the Kaesong park, the first will open by 2007. Kaesong is conveniently located near the metropolitan area of Seoul, which will help cut transportation costs. North Korean laborers working for the park will be paid about US$50 a month.[34]

The future of the South's engagement policy toward the North is dependent on the success of the Kaesong project. If it fails, criticism of the idea of engaging Pyongyang will rise to new heights. Many will argue that economic cooperation with North Korea is a mirage. Hitherto, the majority of South Korean businesses investing in the North have failed to make profits. The Kaesong park should create a model that is beneficial to both Koreas. South Korean firms need to start acquiring financial gains from business with the North; economic cooperation should ease the economic difficulties borne by North Korea, and teach the North lessons in conducting business with the outside world.

Railroads and highways on the west and east coasts are being reconnected. The two Koreas agreed to rebuild west coast railroads (*Kyongui* railway) and roads in 2000 and east coast railroads (*Donghae* railway) and roads in 2002. Building railroads and roads crossing the DMZ is not only symbolic as a sign of rapprochement between the two erstwhile enemies, but also is useful in facilitating exchanges of people and goods across the border. The convenience of land transportation is expected to lure more South Korean businessmen to invest in the North and therefore speed integration of the two economies.

In spite of the progress made by the Kumgansan tour, the Kaesong industrial park, and railroad connections, many problems persist in bilateral economic cooperation. Foremost, political instability and security anxiety caused by the North Korean nuclear problem create barriers for the expansion of inter-Korean commercial ventures. Because of the special character of inter-Korean economic cooperation, an early resolution of the nuclear issue and normalization of relations between the United States and North Korea are essential to the rapid progress of North-South ventures. Unless the nuclear issue is resolved, the uncertainty surrounding the Korean peninsula will surely impede the inflow of investment into North Korea. North Korea's unbending attitudes also make business ventures with the North formidable. In the past, numerous adventurous investors, many of them Koreans living abroad, dared to explore investment opportunities in the North, only to fail miserably. The records of Korean businesses following the opening of inter-Korean commercial exchanges are also poor. The shabby condition of North Korea's infrastructure creates barriers to the development of inter-Korean economic cooperation. North Korea badly needs to repair its electricity, transportation, and communication facilities. Due to the lack of infrastructure, many South Korean ventures find it difficult to smoothly manage their operations on Northern soil.

Pyongyang's nuclear ambition constitutes the primary hurdle to the realization of President Roh's Peace and Prosperity Policy. As long as Kim Jong Il holds fast to his nuclear weapons programs, Roh's plan for expanding inter-Korean economic cooperation will have to be put on hold. Currently, the nuclear issue at the international level and economic cooperation between the two Koreas maintain an uneasy coexistence. South Korea wants to resolve the nuclear issue peacefully within the realm of multilateral talks and make progress in the order of cooperation and coexistence between the two Koreas. But the time might come when the two contradict each other.

North Korea's South Korea Policy

Kim Jong Il's primary interest is regime survival. To obtain this goal he seems prepared to make sacrifices in other areas at any cost. In addition, Kim is currently interested in boosting North Korea's economy and enabling his people to meet basic survival needs. In order to reverse the fate of the economy, Kim needs amicable relations with and significant assistance from the surrounding states. Problems arise when Kim's interest in regime survival and economic growth collide. It is more likely that Kim Jong Il will choose to keep his regime afloat at the expense of development. At this juncture, Pyongyang is pursuing both objectives through a controlled opening. The North Korean regime advocates the pursuit of individual benefits and pragmatic attitudes, all the while warning its people to remain vigilant against U.S. aggression.

For the course of a controlled opening to succeed, it is very important for North Korea to keep inter-Korean relations friendly. When the United States seeks to build a united front against North Korea, Seoul's assistance is helpful in breaking out of the trap. At the current juncture, Seoul, along with China, is Pyongyang's most important asset in playing the reverse containment game. Therefore, North Korea is expected to continue to respond positively to South Korea's engagement policy. Pyongyang acknowledges its inferiority vis-à-vis Seoul in terms of economic capacity. Even ordinary North Koreans have learned that their own system is obsolete and backward compared to Seoul's vibrant economy. For the time being, North Korean leadership seems to have decided to bite the bullet and accept Seoul's material assistance. Until the nuclear issue is resolved, the international community is unlikely to make any huge investments in the North. So for Pyongyang, Seoul remains its economic savior for the moment. Given that Pyongyang has allowed Seoul to virtually take over the lands of Kaesong and Kumgangsan, which are strategically important sites for the North's military, the Kim Jong Il regime seems to have accepted the reality that economic cooperation with South Korea is inevitable if it is to rise out of the underdevelopment pit.[35]

But this does not mean that the North has given up its strategic goal of spreading revolution to the South. It seems that Pyongyang is still pursuing this aim, but given the adverse situation, has decided to put it aside for the moment. Pyongyang's urgent task is to improve its economic capabilities. The North is fully aware of the fact that left-wingers are gaining force in political circles, while a liberal, nationalist group holds power in Seoul. South Korea is deeply and evenly divided between old and young generations, and liberal and conservative factions. This weakness and divide in South Korean society is the strength for Pyongyang's unification policy. The Kim Jong Il regime takes advantage of the ideological war in South Korea by playing one against the other. On many occasions, Pyongyang has verbally attacked the conservative faction for blocking progress in the nationalist movement. Within the younger generation, animosity toward North Korea is actually dwindling. Pyongyang seeks to utilize the liberal moment in Seoul to achieve its own ends.

For North Korea, the strong alliance between the United States and South Korea is the primary threat to its regime safety. North Korea will make every effort to widen the gap between the two allies. As North Korea confronts the United States over the nuclear issue, Pyongyang sees the necessity to keep close ties with South Korea. North Korea blames the United States for blocking the advance of inter-Korean relations, facilitated by the June 15 summit. North Korea warns that the Korean nation will not be deterred by the divisive tactics of the United States. Pyongyang is strongly calling for *minjok gongjo* (national coordination) and asks the South Koreans to stop collaborating with the U.S. imperialists. According to the Northern media, *hanmi gongjo* (U.S.–South Korea coordination) is *mangguk gongjo* (coordination of betrayal) and *jeonjaeng gongjo* (war coordination).[36]

North Korea wants the United States to withdraw all of its troops from the peninsula. It has been carefully monitoring the reduction and repositioning of U.S. troops in the South. Pyongyang believes the U.S. hostile policy toward North Korea and U.S. troops in the peninsula are the major barriers to national unification. The North Korean media proposes that Koreans of the North and the South should lead a joint effort to rid themselves of the U.S. army once and for all by 2005. Pyongyang is quite encouraged by the rising tide of anti-American sentiment among the youth in South Korea. The Kim Jong Il regime will continue to stir anti-Americanism in the South Korean populace and use it to advance its own agenda in the South.

For a Mature Relationship

There is no doubt that the trends of the nuclear issue and inter-Korean economic cooperation affect each other. Even though the Seoul government does not explicitly link economic cooperation with Pyongyang with the nuclear issue, it cannot help but control the speed of development of bilateral cooperation in accordance with the phase of the resolution of the North Korean nuclear problem. Strategically speaking, while continuing with the ongoing North-South projects, it is important for Seoul to dispel the illusion that Pyongyang can have both the development of nuclear weapons and the expansion of inter-Korean economic cooperation.

The onus is on North Korea to expeditiously resolve the nuclear issue and start economic revitalization programs, with aid from the international community, to save its starving population. In an unstable environment, even if Seoul wanted to, it would not be able to launch massive investment in the North, given that political instability hinders economic investment. As South Korean Foreign Minister Ban Ki Moon noted on his trip to Washington in early March of this year, "It will be difficult to conduct any major economic exchanges with North Korea until the nuclear problem has been resolved."[37] This means that once Pyongyang forgoes its nuclear programs, Seoul will be ready to embark on grand-scale economic assistance projects for the North.

Even North Korea's close friends such as China and Russia oppose Pyongyang's nuclear maneuvers and strongly favor a nuclear-free Korean peninsula, which renders Kim Jong Il's nuclear armament plan rather difficult. Instead of bickering over the futile issue of who needs to make the first move, the resolution process could consist of three stages following an initial bold step taken by Pyongyang. In the first stage of freezing North Korea's nuclear activities, North Korea could declare its intention to scrap all of its nuclear programs and halt its operation of nuclear facilities in Yongbyon. In exchange, some members of the Six-Party Talks could initiate energy and economic assistance to Pyongyang. Ban Ki Moon and Colin Powell reached an understanding that South Korea along with China and Russia could "provide economic aid to the North if Pyongyang froze its nuclear weapons programs as a step toward scrapping them."[38] In the second stage of reduction, North Korea could make headway for the reduction of its nuclear capability with an aim to eventually eliminate it. The United States could then delist the DPRK as a sponsor of terrorism and lift economic sanctions. In the third and final stage of elimination, the United States and North Korea, and Japan and North Korea would normalize diplomatic relations, and large-scale economic projects involving the Six-Party Talks' members could be launched with an aim to enhance Northeast Asian economic cooperation and link North Korea's economy to the international community.

The fundamental hurdle to overcome for a resolution of the nuclear issue is the deep mistrust between the regimes of North Korea and the United States. Trust needs to be earned. In the North Korean-U.S. negotiations, it is North Korea that has violated the 1994 agreement by its secret HEU nuclear development program. Therefore, Pyongyang should take the first step by declaring its willingness to give up all of its nuclear weapons programs and freeze its nuclear activities. It is not correct to assume that the North can elicit a new deal reminiscent of the 1994 deal. The Bush administration is determined to avoid the same kind of agreement that gave North Korea the leeway to receive economic benefits and to revive its nuclear ventures whenever it felt necessary. Given the international environment in which the United States sees terrorism and WMD proliferation as the utmost threat to its security, Pyongyang's tactics to elicit as many concessions as possible in exchange for the freezing of its nuclear facilities simply will not work.

The United States needs to formulate a definite plan and time schedule to solve the nuclear impasse as soon as possible. The Bush administration is divided over how to solve the North Korean problem, and this split of opinions does not benefit the situation in any way. One group favors a diplomatic deal whereas the other prefers a policy of isolation. Early negotiations with North Korea are preferable to its isolation because postponement of the issue only gives North Korea more time to enhance its nuclear capabilities. Because of Bush's stalling tactics, "a troublesome situation has slipped into being an appalling one."[39] At a Senate panel, James Kelly, the Assistant Secretary of State for East Asian and Pacific Affairs, has testified that it is "quite possible" that North Korea has finished reprocessing all of its 8,000 nuclear spent fuel rods.[40] Furthermore, a strangulation of North Korea at the current juncture would incite dissension among the regional players, and they would be less than willing to lend support to encircling Pyongyang before attempting sincere negotiations first. As Joel Wit, a former U.S. negotiator with North Korea, notes, "Beijing and other regional powers will not support sanctions unless all diplomatic options have been exhausted."[41]

Pyongyang's zeal for regime security and the establishment of a peace regime on the peninsula should be dealt with hand in hand. The United States, along with other members of the Six-Party Talks, can provide security guarantees to North Korea in multilateral and written forms in exchange for Pyongyang's commitment to dismantle its nuclear programs. Pyongyang prefers a bilateral commitment between North Korea and the United States, but Six-Party Talks' members should convince North Korea that a multilateral format would guarantee better protection of North Korean security than a bilateral one. The clause may include a statement requiring North Korea to respect the status quo in the region and to abide by international laws and norms promoting peace and cooperation among states. Furthermore, participants can make a joint effort to induce South Korea, North Korea, and the United States to conclude two separate peace treaties in order to formally terminate the state of war on the Korean peninsula and launch a new era of stable peace.

North Korea needs to metamorphose as quickly as possible. Kim Il Sung and Kim Jong Il have been able to build and sustain a totalitarian regime that has kept its people under tight control for decades. Now surrounded by the bustling economies of Northeast Asia and the growing trend of globalization, North Korea faces a choice of either sinking or swimming. Only by reforming its economy and opening to the outside world can North Korea's regime security be achieved. Aside from isolation, the inefficiency in the socialist mode of production and distribution, and its excessive military expenditures have taken heavy tolls on North Korea's economy. To remedy this distortion, a new approach by Pyongyang is urgently required. The engagement policy by Seoul is based upon the premise that open dialogue and exchanges with the North will bring about incremental changes. Yet, Pyongyang sticks to its old tactics when dealing with Seoul. Against international norms and standards, it frequently fails to deliver its commitments to its counterpart.

Thus far, South Korea has made unilateral concessions to coax North Korea into inter-Korean exchanges and to build a foundation for peace on the peninsula. In the future, South Korea should devise plans whereby commercial exchanges benefit both Koreas. South Korea should no longer support the kind of economic exchanges that are unfruitful and benefit only the North. In this sense, the Kaesong industrial complex project stands to become the watershed in inter-Korean relations. With mixed records historically of success in inter-Korean economic cooperation, Kaesong planners should seek ways to profit both Koreas. The success of these programs will further pave the way for a deepening and widening of economic cooperation. A failure to do so will doom the process. South Korea's engagement policy should not stop at merely granting humanitarian assistance and economic benefits to the North. Seoul needs to develop effective mechanisms and channels to induce change in the North Korean system through bilateral exchanges.

The Cold War structure on the Korean peninsula has not yet been completely dismantled. While South Korea has diplomatic relations with all concerned parties in the region, North Korea does not have diplomatic missions in Tokyo or Washington. This imbalance between the two Koreas does not bode well if a zone of stable peace in the region is to be built. Pyongyang's isolation spells instability for the region and forces it to find other means of survival, resorting to the development of ultimate weapons. A pacific way to relieve Pyongyang of its security anxiety is to cultivate diplomatic relations with the United States and Japan. The idea of cross-recognition had been floated in the region back in the early 1990s. The Seoul government fulfilled its diplomatic missions by normalizing relations with Moscow in 1990 and Beijing in 1992 successively. With Pyongyang still struggling in pitiful isolation, it is about time to mend the diplomatic asymmetry on the Korean peninsula. North Korean–U.S. and North Korean–Japanese diplomatic normalizations will pave the way for increased contact and understanding between the regional actors. In addition, the six parties to nuclear negotiations should toil to facilitate and assist inter-Korean reconciliation efforts. In particular, heightened South Korean–North Korean economic cooperation could become the new method for achieving a stable and prosperous Korean peninsula.

The North Korean problem should be seen from the perspective of stability and progress in the Northeast Asian region. To accelerate the realization of a peaceful and prosperous Northeast Asia, one needs to tackle the North Korean issue directly. In addition to being a security concern for neighboring countries, Pyongyang's economic backwardness sits uneasily with the dynamic economies of East Asia. As long as North Korea remains an isolated island in the middle of the Northeast Asian region, intraregional cooperation will be hampered, if not thwarted entirely. Once North Korea becomes a legitimate player in the region, South Korea, conveniently located at the crossroads between the maritime forces and the continental forces, will be better placed to become the economic hub of the region. Concerned parties can promote large-scale projects that are conducive to regional development, using the local state's capital, technology, and labor force.

It is time for regional organizations to promote peace and prosperity. China and the United States, who have both been shy about establishing a multilateral regime, are now actively pursuing multilateralism in Northeast Asia as a vehicle for solving the North Korean nuclear problem. Concerned parties in the region should devote their time and energy to turning the Six-Party Talks' format into a standing regional forum for peace and prosperity.

Conclusion

Peace comes in many forms. Sometimes it is stable and at other times it is not. The lessons learned from the Cold War days are that peace by deterrence is useful in maintaining the status quo, but it alone does not create the stable and permanent peace that the peoples of the region have long wanted to achieve. Neither was this strategy able to pull the two Koreas together. The Northeast Asian peoples are worthy of a secure and enduring safety net, such as the European Union and North America now enjoy. It remains the ultimate diplomatic task for statesmen of the region to build stable peace, what Karl Deutsch calls a "security community," in the region.[42] The first step toward erecting a pluralistic security community can be taken as we build a non-nuclear security regime on the Korean peninsula.

Ultimately, the security issues of the Korean peninsula boil down to the question of what to do with North Korea. There are two options: One is regime change and the other is regime transformation. The regime change school calls for heightened sanctions and pressure on the North Korean regime to hasten its collapse. It is dangerous in that this strategy could easily invite military confrontation. The regime transformation school takes a longer perspective and seeks to manage the North Korean problem with patience and subtlety. It advocates dialogue and diplomacy as a way to induce internal changes within North Korean society. The more contacts there are, either popular or commercial, the more access and leverage there will be to change North Korea. As webs of knowledge expand among the people, we can influence their way of thinking; as they develop new ideas, changes from below becomes possible. The active engagement strategy envisions a stage in which South Korea and North Korea exchange popular visits and cooperate in mutually profitable ways. Thus, the inter-Korean rivalry will face an eventual dissolution by way of a peaceful transition.

Notes

1. Woo, "North Korea's Food Crisis," 63–65.

2. Thompson, "Why Rivalries Matter," 1–21.

3. Oberdorfer, *The Two Koreas*, chs. 9, 10, 16.

4. Woo, "South Korea's Search," 511, 514–518.

5. Koh, "Prospects for Opening in North Korea," 94, 100–105.

6. Snyder, "The NGO Experience in North Korea," 1–13.

7. Sun-won Park, "Kim Jong Il Sidae Bukhanui Byunhwa: Jinhwaronjeok Jeopgeun" (North Korean Reform in the Kim Jong-il Era from the Perspective of 'Change Within the System,' 1997–2001), 159.

8. Kwon, "Talgukgasahoejuuiui Yeoreo Gilgwa Bukhan" (Pathways from State Socialism and North Korea), 256.

9. Suh, "Military-First Politics of Kim Jong Il," 160.

10. Yeon Chul Kim, "Bukhan Singyeongjae Jeonryakui Seonggong Jogeon" (The Successful Precondition of North Korea's New Economic Strategy), 8–9.

11. Keun-sik Kim, "Kim Jong Il Sidae Bukhanui Dang-Jeong-Gun Gwangye Byeonhwa" (The Change in North Korea's Party-Government-Military Relationship in the Kim Jung-Il Era: The Implications of the Changes of the 'Great Leader'[Suryong] System), 352–356; Sun-won Park, "Kim Jong Il Sidae Bukhanui Byunhwa," 164–169.

12. Oh, "Kim Jong Il Sidae Bukhanui Gunsahwa Gyeonghyange Daehan Yeongu" (Study on the Militarization of North Korea in the Kim Jung-il Era), 213–232; Keun-sik Kim, "Kim Jong Il Sidae Bukhanui Dang-Jeong-Gun Gwangye Byeonhwa," 356–359.

13. Suh, "Military-First Politics of Kim Jong Il," 146, 158–161.

14. Yeon Chul Kim,"Bukhan Singyeongjae Jeonryakui Seonggong Jogeon," 11–13; Cha and Kang, "Can North Korea be Engaged?" 89–95.

15. Nicholas D. Kristof, "Don't Count on a Rebellion in North Korea," *International Herald Tribune*, January 12, 2004, 8.

16. George Wehrfritz, "Nowhere to Go But Up," *Newsweek*, November 17, 2003, 38.

17. Don Oberdorfer, *The Two Koreas*, 435.

18. Charles L. Pritchard, "The Evolution to a Multilateral Approach in Dealing with North Korea." Paper delivered in the conference on North Korea, "North Korea, Multilateralism, and the Future of the Peninsula," Seoul, South Korea, November 20–21, 2003, pp. 8–10; Chong, "Improving Pyongyang-Beijing Ties," 2–7.

19. Kihl, "Security on the Korean Peninsula," 62.

20. Hong, "Putin Sidae Russiaui Sin Hanbandojeonryak" (Russia's New Strategies Toward the Korean Peninsula Under the Putin Administration), 350–355.

21. Hyunki Kim, "Buk, Ilbonae Ittan Hwahae Sonjit" (North Korea Seeks to Mend Relations with Japan), *Joongang Ilbo*, January 12, 2004, 17.

22. "North Korea Renews Its Call for Talks," 37.

23. Koh, "Prospects for Opening in North Korea," 99–100.

24. Associated Press, "Pyongyang to Receive Chinese Legislator," *International Herald Tribune*, October 30, 2003, 3; Donald G. Gross, "U.S. and North Korea: Bush Sees the Light," *International Herald Tribune*, October 25–26, 2003, 10.

25. "The Koreas: A Ray or Two of Light in the Gloom," *The Economist*, August 2, 2002, 23–24.

26. Samuel Len, "North Korea Offers to Halt Nuclear Testing," *International Herald Tribune*, January 7, 2004, 3.

27. George Wehrfritz and Richard Wolffe, "How North Korea Got the Bomb," *Newsweek*, October 27, 2003, 18–21.

28. Glenn Kessler, "U.S. Has a Shifting Script on North Korea," *Washington Post*, December 7, 2003, 25.

29. Joseph Kahn, "North Korea Talks Bring a Mild Thaw," *International Herald Tribune*, March 1, 2004, 1.

30. Pinkston, "Bargaining Failure and the North Korean Nuclear Program's Impact," 5–21.

31. *Joongang Ilbo*, July 2, 2004, 5.

32. Lawrence, Hiebert, Solomon, and Kim, "North Korea Nuclear Crisis," 12–16.

33. "Overview of Inter-Korean Exchange and Cooperation for 2003," *Monthly Report: Intra-Korean Interchange & Cooperation and Humanitarian Projects* (Seoul: Ministry of Unification, December 2003), 163–165.

34. Norimitsu Onishi, "U.S. Allies Help Break Isolation of Pyongyang," *International Herald Tribune*, August 21–22, 2004, 1.

35. Park, "First Year of the Roh Moo-Hyun Administration," 9–22.

36. Ian Bremmer, "Iran and North Korea: The Proliferation Lesson," *International Herald Tribune*, August 21–22, 2004, 6.

37. "North and South Korea Set Factory-Project Start," *International Herald Tribune*, March 6–7, 2004, 4.

38. Ibid.; "The Pleasure of Dealing with North Korea," *The Economist*, December 7, 2002, 13.

39. Nicholas D. Kristof, "Don't Count on a Rebellion in North Korea," *International Herald Tribune*, January 12, 2004, 8.

40. David E. Sanger, "U.S. Voices New Worry on Nuclear Bomb Fuel," *International Herald Tribune*, March 4, 2004, 1.

41. Morton I. Abramowitz and James T. Laney, "Meeting the North Korean Nuclear Challenge," *Report of an Independent Task Force Sponsored by the Council on Foreign Relations*, 2003, 32–42.

42. Adler and Barnett, eds., *Security Communities*.

Part III

Future Prospects

——— 12 ———

Bi-Multilateral Approaches to Defusing Nuclear Crisis

Beyond the Six-Party Talks as Peace Strategy

Young Whan Kihl

The "bi-multilateral" approach to diplomacy toward North Korea, which the Six-Party Talks on North Korea's nuclear standoff epitomize, is neither right nor wrong as a peace strategy. During the first act of the North Korean nuclear standoff in 1992–1994, the United States and the DPRK chose to defuse the nuclear crisis via the direct, face-to-face, talks in Geneva through the bilateral channel of diplomacy.[1] During the second act of the current nuclear standoff, which began in October 2002, the United States chose to confront the DPRK within a multilateral forum of Six-Party Talks involving other regional powers: South Korea, Japan, China, and Russia.

All of these bilateral or multilateral frameworks of diplomatic negotiation and bargaining are basically nothing more or less than diplomatic tools, a means to an end, to gain political settlement. So long as "there is a will, there will be a way" to be found in the quid pro quo settlement of the nuclear standoff. The 2 + 4 formula, which the Six-Party Talks symbolize, is regarded by the Bush administration as more conducive to making the multilateral negotiation process with the DPRK possible, with greater flexibility and credibility, although the venue of bilateral diplomacy cannot be completely ruled out as such, whether within or outside the multilateral diplomatic forum in Beijing.

This chapter on bi-multilateral approaches to defusing North Korea's nuclear crisis in 2002–2005 will proceed in several steps. The prelude to diplomatic opening and China's role in hosting the Six-Party Talks on North Korea will be examined first, to be followed by an analysis of each of the three rounds of Beijing talks held and the reasons why the fourth round of talks was stillborn. In order to address the last issue, the broader context and setting for domestic politics and foreign policy issues linkage in some key member countries of the Six-Party Talks will be explored. For example, the 2004 U.S. presidential election politics and the effects of the Six-Party Talks on the U.S.-ROK alliance played a role. The chapter will conclude by addressing the rationale for going beyond the Six-Party Talks and the challenges of turning it into a regional security forum through institution building in Northeast Asia.

Diplomacy of U.S.-DPRK Nuclear Standoff

Clearly, the United States and the DPRK are locked in high-stakes diplomacy in a game of nuclear brinkmanship and standoff. While the United States was preoccupied with preparation for a possible war against Saddam Hussein's Iraq early in 2003, so as to disarm its WMD program in violation of UN sanctions, the Kim Jong Il regime of North Korea chose to confront the Bush administration in a nuclear showdown. The primary objective of the United States was to checkmate the North Korean strategy of nuclear brinkmanship and risk taking, while continuing the war in Iraq and the postwar reconstruction process.[2]

The Prelude to Diplomatic Opening

When the IAEA governing board voted on February 12, 2003 to cite Pyongyang for defying UN nuclear safeguards and sent the issue to the UN Security Council, Pyongyang accused the IAEA of being "America's lapdog" and urged it to investigate instead "the illegal U.S. behavior that brought a nuclear crisis to the Korean peninsula." Since North Korea had already withdrawn from the NPT in January, the DPRK had no legal obligations to comply with IAEA safeguards, the official KCNA news agency insisted. It also noted that "discussing the nuclear issue through the IAEA was an act of interference in internal affairs."[3] Defense Secretary Donald H. Rumsfeld said North Korea might pose a bigger threat as "a supplier of nuclear weapons" and as "the world's greatest proliferator of missile technology."

The U.S. options under these circumstances were rather severely restricted; the possible measures vis-à-vis the defiant DPRK action might include:

1. Do nothing
2. Try to destroy North Korea's WMD program through surgical air strikes on its nuclear installation at Yongbyon
3. Impose economic sanctions and international pressure through the UN and with support from its allies
4. Seek negotiated settlements directly with the North along the lines of the Geneva Agreed Framework of October 1994

Because none of these policy alternatives as such was judged to be acceptable, the George W. Bush administration decided to seek its own new option based on a combination of stick and carrot, exerting pressure on North Korea while engaging in dialogue through bi-multilateral diplomatic arrangements. Because the timing was ill suited for the United States and favorable to North Korea, the choice of seeking a quid pro quo settlement of the disputes between the two sides (the choice of Pyongyang and that of the Clinton administration) was ruled out as unacceptable, in favor of the stick and carrot alternative.

China Agrees to Host the Six-Party Beijing Talks on North Korea

The result of the Bush administration's deliberation on policy options and was the launching of the multilateral forum on North Korea's nuclear standoff, with the assistance of China as host to the Six-Party Talks on North Korea. On February 13, 2003, Secretary of State Colin Powell told Congress that the United States had forwarded a proposal to hold multilateral talks on North Korea's nuclear weapons program that would include China, Russia, and South Korea but that Pyongyang turned this proposal down.[4] This stalemate was broken, however, when China agreed to host trilateral Beijing talks involving the United States and the DPRK in April 2003. This first effort with North Korea under China's auspices, unfortunately, did not produce any tangible agreement between the contending parties to the nuclear dispute.[5]

The U.S. effort to entice North Korea to a face-to-face meeting within the framework of multilateral talks bore the initial, intended fruit when China announced that it would host such a multilateral meeting in Beijing to address the North Korean nuclear issue. Although China's offer of good offices to the United States and the DPRK, as a preliminary step toward the Six-Party Talks, did not produce any meaningful agreement, as a move toward a multilateral gathering of interested parties it was still useful for providing a face-saving device to both antagonists and resulted in an agreement to launch a multilateral forum, to be participated in by the three neighboring countries of South Korea, Japan, and Russia.

China's hosting of the six-nation talks was expected to enhance the tasks of international agenda setting as well as to seek the formula for obtaining a nuclear-free Korean Peninsula. It was thought that this effort, if successful, might also eventually lead to an international conference on overcoming the legacy of an inconclusive Korean War a half century ago.

In preparation for the Six-Party Talks on North Korea's nuclear issue, a flurry of diplomatic maneuvers and consultations took place among the interested parties in the region. Chinese Vice Foreign Minister Wang Yi met with North Korean officials in Pyongyang to finalize the setting and timing of the Six-Party Talks in Beijing. Chinese Foreign Minister Li Zhaoxing, during his visit to Tokyo, told reporters that the talks would be held in Beijing on August 26, 2003. Whereas the Russian diplomat was in Beijing, South Korea's vice foreign minister visited Moscow to meet with Russian Deputy Foreign Minister Alexander Losyukov who, in turn, met with a North Korean foreign ministry envoy a few days later. U.S., South Korean, and Japanese officials met in Washington for further consultation and policy coordination.

The Bush administration hoisted a trial balloon ahead of the Six-Party Talks first session in Beijing. On August 7, Secretary of State Colin Powell sent a "subtle signal" to Pyongyang that the United States might be prepared to compromise on a top North Korean demand: a written security guarantee that the United States would not attack it. Powell said that there could be a way to "capture assurances to the North Koreans . . . that there is no hostile intent" and added that "there are ways that Congress can take note of it without being a treaty or some kind of pact." A senior State Department official said that this is "not an entirely new formulation."[6]

By virtue of agreeing to host the Six-Party Talks in Beijing, China has become more than an equal partner. It has assumed a greater role as intermediary or third party attempting to fulfill a diplomatic settlement between the DPRK and other participants of the United States, South Korea, Japan, and Russia.

The First Round of Talks

The six-party Beijing talks are a classic example of a two-level diplomacy game played out in a global political arena involving both formal and informal channels. All delegates presented their government's official policy positions at the meeting, while they were also open for and susceptible to informal channels of communication face to face. It was no surprise, therefore, to see that on the first day of the Six-Party Talks on August 27, Assistant Secretary of State James Kelly as chief delegate emphasized in his formal presentation that President Bush had said the United States has no intention of attacking or invading North Korea, while stressing that it would not accept Pyongyang's demand for a nonaggression treaty. He did say, however, that Washington was open to exploring other options.

During an informal bilateral session with the North Korean delegation later on the same day, the North Koreans repeated that they did possess nuclear weapons, and raised the new possibility of conducting a nuclear test to prove they did indeed have such weapons and to show they had the means to deliver a bomb. The North Koreans said they had been forced to go nuclear because of the "hostile policy" of the United States. In response, Kelly said that this was a very serious matter and that the United States would share this information with the other participants. On the second day, August 28, the North Koreans made a long presentation to the entire gathering, by repeating the same points they had made privately to Kelly, to the distress of the other participants.[7]

Despite these unfriendly exchanges between the U.S. and North Korean delegates, Washington was reportedly "pleased" with the outcome of the six-party Beijing talks. "We have a long, long way to go. But the U.S. delegation is recommending that the U.S. stay the course" in continuing the six-nation negotiation process. "We know that the North Koreans are the most difficult interlocutors, but we are committed to the process" and policy direction set by the president. In fact, U.S. officials said they were "pleased by the chemistry of the talks, not between Washington and Pyongyang, but among the other participants: the United States, China, Russia, South Korea, and Japan."[8] The three-day meeting, from the U.S. point of view, had led to a situation where the other nations, except for North Korea, no longer saw the nuclear issue as just a problem between Washington and Pyongyang.

The Beijing talks had become a nuclear poker game with six players at the table, where the negotiators would play hands that ranged from strong to weak. While the first round of the six-party Beijing talks in August was largely unproductive, China was confident that it had impressed the global community, particularly the United States, with its clout with Pyongyang. Despite its vocal rhetoric, claiming that nuclear deterrence was a legitimate tool of self-defense, there were also signs that Pyongyang might be ready for some form of a stand down, as one observer noted. Pyongyang did not carry out its threat of testing potent weapons, such as a nuclear bomb or a medium range missile, on the fifty-fifth anniversary of the founding of the DPRK on September 5.[9]

It was reported that China had also told North Korea to halt its "constant war preparation" and to concentrate instead on building up its feeble economy. Chinese President Hu Jintao allegedly offered three suggestions to the North Korean leader Kim Jong Il, while making it clear that Pyongyang must dismantle its nuclear weapons program: (a) work toward attaining economic self-sufficiency; (b) try out a Chinese-style open-door policy; and (c) improve relations with neighboring countries after halting its WMD program.[10] If true, this is a clear case of the strong-arm diplomatic tactics China exerted toward North Korea in exchange for continuing China's close ties with Pyongyang and also China's desire to improve its future relations with the United States.[11]

The Second Round of Talks

A second round of the Six-Party Talks, tentatively scheduled for mid-December, did not materialize until February 25, 2004. Unlike the first session six months earlier, which nearly broke down after two days of negotiations when North Korea told the United States that it could develop, test, deploy, and even export nuclear weapons, there was a greater expectation that flexibility and civility would prevail this time around. In fact, during the second round of talks, Pyongyang finally said that it would freeze its nuclear program in return for Washington providing energy aid and removing North Korea from a list of nations that allegedly sponsor terrorism.

On the eve of organizing the second round of talks, however, North Korea wanted the United States to know that it now possessed nuclear weapons and had also completed reprocessing nuclear-weapons-grade plutonium. If true, North Korea could acquire the capability to produce five to six atomic bombs within six months to one year's time. North Korea's "nuclear breakout" strategy was clearly aimed at exerting pressure on the U.S. side to negotiate a new nuclear agreement. The U.S. Bush administration strategy, however, was to secure the dismantling (not freeze) of Pyongyang's plutonium- and uranium-based nuclear programs.[12]

Earlier in December 2003 President Bush was firm and clear about what the United States expected North Korea to do. Speaking at a brief news conference with China's visiting Premier Wen Jiabao in December, Bush responded to a question raised by the press by saying that Pyongyang must dismantle its WMD program. "The goal of the United States is not a freeze of the nuclear program. The goal is to dismantle the nuclear weapons program in a verifiable and irreversible way." "That," he said, "is the clear message we are sending to the North Koreans."[13]

It was no surprise, therefore, that the situation was still tense when the negotiators from six countries witnessed no change in the conflicting positions of the United States and North Korea at the opening session of the second round of talks. The U.S. chief delegate James Kelly, during his opening remarks, demanded that the North must first dismantle the nuclear weapons program, both plutonium- and uranium-based, in a complete, verifiable, and irreversible manner, whereas the North's chief negotiator Kim Gye-kwan asked for a package of compensation for the refreeze of its nuclear activities it had resumed in December 2002 while denying the alleged uranium enrichment program of the North.

Despite the difference in basic positions of the United States and North Korea, the other four participants in the talks, notably South Korea and China, exerted their best efforts for leading the negotiations toward success with tangible results. South Korea's chief delegate Lee Soo-hyuck proposed a three-stage solution to the issue, while offering energy to the North in compensation for its freeze and eventual dismantlement of its nuclear weapons program, with support from Russia and China. The Chinese efforts were reflected in the remarks of Wang Yi as its delegate: "We expect the second round of talks to solve some substantial issues . . . to enlarge the common understanding, not 'differences.'"[14]

The Third Round of Talks

Unlike the preceding two rounds of the Beijing talks, the third round of the Six-Party Talks held June 22–26, 2004, worked to narrow the gap between the U.S. and North Korean positions on the conditions for a nuclear settlement. In the opening third session of the Six-Party Talks on June 23, the North Korean chief delegate Kim Gye-kwan stated that the DPRK was willing to give up efforts to develop nuclear weapons "in a transparent way" if the United States ended its "hostile policy" toward the DPRK. If the United States would withdraw its demand for a complete and irreversible dismantling of the program "and accept our compensation demands, we are prepared to submit specific proposals concerning freezing the nuclear program at these talks in order to break the current stalemate and to reinvigorate the Six-Party Talks," Kim said.[15]

The U.S. chief delegate James Kelly said in his opening statement that "We are prepared for serious discussion and we have a proposal to offer" adding, without giving any details, that "a focus on the common objective, and practical and effective means to attain it, will lead in a very positive direction with new political, economic, and diplomatic possibilities." According to David Sanger of the New York Times, U.S. negotiators would offer the DPRK new but "highly conditional" incentives to give up its nuclear weapons at the talks, including a provisional guarantee not to invade. The article quoted U.S. officials as saying President Bush had authorized negotiators to offer the incentives in what would be the first significant, detailed overture to the DPRK since he took office in January 2001. Under the proposal, aid would begin flowing to North Korea once its leader, Kim Jong Il, had made a commitment to dismantle his plutonium and uranium weapons.[16]

The Bush administration was deeply divided on what stance to take toward North Korea, with the state department reportedly urging dialogue and the Pentagon and the vice-president's office urging caution (if not outright hostility) toward Pyongyang. Washington seized upon the six-party formula, however, as a way of maintaining dialogue without having to hold direct bilateral talks with the North Koreans.

The third round of Six-Party Talks, however, was noteworthy for a significant "repackaging" of the Bush administration's proposals. The new plan involved "immediate rewards" for North Korea in the form of heavy fuel oil imported from South Korea, if it agreed to dismantle its nuclear weapons program. This plan could be interpreted as a way to test North Korea's true and serious intentions on denuclearization of the Korean peninsula. It also reflected the pressure that Washington was experiencing from allies of Japan and South Korea to show greater flexibility toward Pyongyang.[17]

Pyongyang's threat of a possible nuclear test, repeated during face-to-face talks with the U.S. delegation, overshadowed the third round of Six-Party Talks. North Korea took a more upbeat and self-assured assessment of its stance, however, when its Foreign Ministry spokesman stated, on June 28, that its delegation had held exhaustive negotiations with the U.S. side, for nearly two-and-a-half hours on the sidelines of the Six-Party Talks. During that time, North Korea claimed to have clarified details concerning the nuclear freeze, on the premise that the United States withdraws its demand for CVID (complete, verifiable, irreversible dismantlement).[18] It also claimed that an agreement was reached on such issues as "taking simultaneous actions" on the principle of "words for words" and "action for action" by insisting that the issue of "reward for freeze" was "positive progress" made at the talks.

If the DPRK's proposal for "reward for freeze" was accepted, Pyongyang reiterated that it would "freeze all the facilities related to nuclear weapons and products" churned out by their operation. This freeze would then lead to the ultimate dismantlement of the nuclear weapons program, because they would not only refrain from producing more nuclear weapons but also from transferring and testing them. "Reward for freeze" should include, Pyongyang insisted, not only U.S. commitment to the lifting of sanctions and blockade against the DPRK but also the energy assistance of 2,000,000 kilowatts through the supply of heavy oil and electricity.[19] This was exactly the same amount of energy supply that would have been provided by the KEDO project, if completed. Following the breakdown of U.S.-DPRK negotiations in October 2002, the KEDO had suspended its operation of heavy fuel oil delivery to the North and the on-site construction of two light water reactors, as provided for by the 1994 Geneva Agreed Framework.

As the third round of multilateral talks ended inconclusively, the PRC Vice Foreign Minister Wang Yi issued the eight-point Chairman's Statement and told reporters that progress was being made even if a "serious lack of mutual trust" still existed among participants. The Associated Press reported that the Bush administration was giving the DPRK at least a passing grade in negotiations to stop its nuclear weapons program and suggested that the slow-moving talks to denuclearize the Korean peninsula might be making headway.[20]

During this session of the Six-Party Talks, the United States reiterated its policy stance on CVID but also outlined "five corresponding measures" in return for a nuclear freeze by the DPRK, which amounted to a package deal of proposals by both sides of Washington and Pyongyang. The U.S. offer included, according to Seoul's Foreign Ministry Web site, (1) heavy oil, (2) a provisional security guarantee, (3) longer-term energy aid, (4) direct talks about the lifting of economic sanctions and removal of the DPRK from its list of terrorist states, and (5) retraining of nuclear scientists during a three-month "preparatory period" of dismantlement.[21]

According to Wang Yi, China's chief negotiator and chairman of the talks, the third round of the Six-Party Talks "forged new steps for reaching the goal of denuclearization and progress has been made in five aspects."[22] Nonetheless, as of the end of 2004, the multilateral negotiation has failed to produce any breakthrough in the preceding three sessions in bridging the gap between the U.S. position on CVID and the DPRK demand for a package deal of concessions in exchange for its agreeing to freeze the ongoing nuclear program.

The five notable new steps mentioned by Wang Yi included:

1. All the relevant parties have offered proposals and plans for the solution to the nuclear issue.
2. The six parties reached a consensus on the first phase of the denuclearization on the Korean Peninsula, that is, the freeze.
3. All parties agreed to take a step-by-step process of "words for words" and "action for action" in search for a peaceful solution to the nuclear issues.
4. The parties approved a concept paper on the working group, that "will help . . . start more effective, regular and practical work" and authorize convening "at the earliest possible date to define the scope, duration and verification, as well as corresponding measures for the first steps for denuclearization."
5. "As appropriate, [all parties will] make recommendations to the fourth round of the talks scheduled to be held by the end of September."[23]

Neither the working group nor the fourth round of the talks were called into session by the end of September 2004, for reasons to be examined subsequently.

Domestic Politics and Foreign Policy Issues Linkage

Before getting into a discussion of how and why the fourth round of the Six-Party Talks was stillborn in 2004, it is necessary to examine the larger context in which these talks were taking place, including the domestic-foreign policy linkages and the effects of the Six-Party Talks on the U.S.-ROK alliance.

Political and Strategic Context

All politics are based on considerations of power, perception, and preference, whether they pertain to domestic politics or foreign policy issues, including policy options on the North Korean nuclear issue. In this sense, "all politics are local" and the politician's desire and need to stay in power and to hold an office will influence foreign policy options and policymaking. The U.S. and ROK alliance and their common strategy toward North Korea's nuclear brinkmanship is no exception to the rule.

In 2004 the respective leadership and foreign policy stances of the ROK President Roh Moo Hyun and U.S. President George W. Bush were motivated by considerations of power in domestic politics. Whereas Roh was focused on winning the April 2004 general election and establishing his ruling party as a majority in the National Assembly, Bush was focused on winning the November 2004 presidential and congressional elections. He was determined to assure that Republican Party dominance in U.S. domestic politics would continue until 2008.[24]

In this battle for an electoral victory, the perception of how each administration (in Seoul and in Washington, D.C.) was doing in domestic politics and public perception by the electoral constituency were critical for building winnable partisan strategy. Policy preferences including those associated with resolving North Korea's nuclear issue would be determined in the final analysis by the strategic calculation that would maximize the chances for electoral victory in national elections in 2004. (The leadership of DPRK's Kim Jong Il in nuclear brinkmanship, although he was not running for election, would likewise be influenced by his regime survival and related political strategy and calculus.)

Given the fact that U.S. domestic politics was heating up as it got closer to the 2004 presidential and congressional elections, the Bush administration was less inclined to take any bold and risky policy initiatives related to the nuclear issue on the Korean peninsula. It sought low war-risk policy options rather than any radical changes in the approach toward the Korean security dilemma. This meant that in the short run, "a formula for a peaceful and diplomatic settlement of the nuclear issue" would characterize American policy rather than a forceful and confrontational approach to nuclear problem solving on the Korean peninsula.

The leadership in both Seoul and Washington were also cognizant of the fact, however, that Pyongyang's Kim Jong Il had his own strategic design. Pyongyang would seek to influence and undermine the domestic political situation in the South, so as to foster public perception favorable to the North. In a way, the latest move of the North in agreeing to accept Six-Party Talks in Beijing on the nuclear issue seemed to reflect this strategic calculus on the part of North Korea's Kim Jong Il.

At that point, the Bush administration was reluctant to characterize the North Korean provocation as a "crisis" that would pose a serious security threat in the

Korean peninsula, and resisted partisan pressure from the Democratic Party leadership to make the North Korean nuclear issue more pressing and dangerous than the U.S. war in Iraq.

In its diplomacy, the Bush administration was trying to downplay the "high stakes and high risk" nature of the North Korean situation. But the time for decision was rapidly dwindling and the element of surprise was increasingly undermined by the North Korean strategy of openness in its acts of escalation and provocation. Unlike the Saddam Hussein's regime practices of "deceit and concealment" of its WMD program, Kim Jong Il's North Korea was more open and public in its posture and approach to using hyperbole and vocal pronouncement of its intentions.

Finally, Kim's strategy of nuclear brinkmanship and risk taking seemed to bear the initial, intended fruit of enticing the United States to a face-to-face meeting within the framework of six-party multilateral talks held in Beijing. This gathering of interested parties of the United States and the DPRK under the auspices of China as the host nation, participated in by the three neighboring countries of South Korea, Japan, and Russia, would give a face-saving device for launching a multilateral forum for international agenda setting and for possible problem solving on Korean peninsula security. That effort might eventually lead to a six-power conference on overcoming the unsolved legacy of an inconclusive Korean War (1950–1953) a half-century ago.

Effects of the Six-Party Talks on the U.S.-ROK Alliance

The stakes were high and getting higher for the success of the Six-Party Talks because their outcome would impact ongoing present U.S.-ROK relations as well as new directions for the alliance in the years to come. As part of the plan for a sweeping reorganization of U.S. troops across Asia, visiting U.S. Secretary of Defense Donald Rumsfeld said in Seoul that the process of policy review would begin "as soon as possible" for relocating U.S. forces back from the highly fortified demilitarized zone. The troop movements "will reflect our new technologies and abilities to deter and defeat any aggressions against allies such as South Korea."[25] Rumsfeld's Seoul visit, to attend the annual U.S. Korea Security meeting, was the third leg of Rumsfeld's six-day Asian trip after Japan and Guam.

South Korea and the United States are in the process of redefining their alliance. Under the fifty-year-old alliance, American soldiers have acted as a "tripwire" along the demilitarized zone to deter an attack from North Korea, which would guarantee American retaliation and involvement in the war. In Seoul, the National Security Council's deputy director, Lee Jong Suk (age 45), who is said to embody many of the so-called 386 generation's views, is reported to have the greatest influence on President Roh Moo Hyun on foreign policy matters. The term "386 generation," borrows from a computer chip code and refers to those young voters who were in their thirties when the term was coined, went to college, and fought in the prodemocracy movement in the 1980s, and were born in the 1960s. A new generation of South Korean leaders, backed by these young voters, is known to be more independent-minded and less beholden to the United States. This generation helped the candidate Roh Moo Hyun to win his December 2002 presidential election in Seoul and tends to regard the United States less as the country that fought in the Korean War and more as the country that backed military dictators in the years before the 1988 democratization.[26]

North Korea's secretly developing a nuclear weapons program was a key justification for the Bush administration's policy of imposing economic sanctions and directing efforts toward further political isolation and a regime change in the North. It also led the U.S. administration to seek a new theater missile defense system, increased military spending, and continued U.S. troop presence in Asia and in South Korea. The September 11, 2001, attacks on America and the Bush administration's resolve to address the transnational terrorism threat to U.S. security has added complexity to an otherwise familiar and conventional episode of the latest nuclear controversy over North Korea.

These and related policies of the U.S. administrations were likely to be undermined by the Six-Party Talks' settlement of the North Korean nuclear issue. Under the regionalization strategy pursued by the Bush administration, the North Korean nuclear issue would become a multilateral agenda of regional diplomacy in Northeast Asia. Seoul would be forced to seek a new strategy to accommodate the changing security dynamics under review.

As stated, in the end, "all politics are local," including the politics of U.S.-Korea alliance relations and Korean security. Clearly, the Roh Moo Hyun administration policy on inter-Korean relations has been impacted by the outcome of the April 2004 parliamentary elections and the results of the November 2004 U.S. presidential election, as will be noted next. "All politics are local," but external pressures (such as China's rise and fall, as well as other factors of geopolitics) will also matter in the Korean context, as proven so many times in the annals of Korea's diplomatic history. Valuable lessons are often drawn by historians who study Sino-Korean relations in terms of establishing causal linkages between Korea and the dynastic cycles of the rise and fall inside China in the historical past.[27]

Sidetracking the Fourth Round of Talks

The fourth round of the Six-Party Talks on the North Korean nuclear issue, scheduled to convene in late September 2004 as agreed upon during the third round of talks, did not materialize. The primary reason was the North Korean refusal to participate because of its perceived lack of progress thus far in the Six-Party Talks. Included in the list of other factors for the failed meeting, however, were domestic political situations in some of the participating countries, like the upcoming U.S. presidential and congressional election. The 2004 electoral politics in the United States had led to political uncertainties and limited the possibilities for achieving a breakthrough in the settlement of stalemated negotiations surrounding the nuclear standoff between Washington and Pyongyang.

During one of the presidential campaign debates on foreign policy issues, President Bush and Senator John Kerry had agreed that the United States must talk to North Korea to resolve concerns over their nuclear activity, but they differed sharply over how to do so. Bush defended his administration's policy, the Six-Party Talks on North Korea's suspected nuclear weapons development, while Kerry said a bilateral track would bring more progress, adding that North Korea had acquired more weapons during Bush's term in office. Bush responded by saying that "It's a big mistake to do that" (hold bilateral talks) "because not only would it undercut the on-going six-party negotiations but also would remove China as a powerful influence on its communist neighbor."[28]

Under these circumstances, North Korea seems to have thought it better to wait for the results of the U.S. election, as it would not benefit from negotiating with "a hostile" party, the U.S. Bush administration, which it chose to characterize as "a crueler tyrant than 'Hitler.'" North Korea also accused the United States of applying double standards to North and South Korea, tolerating nuclear experiments by the South, and it stated it would not attend additional Six-Party Talks until questions were answered about South Korea and its nuclear testing program.[29] South Korea had just disclosed that its scientists had earlier conducted a plutonium-based nuclear experiment in 1982, and a uranium test in 2002, thereby sparking suspicions about the country's development of nuclear weapons.

The Seoul government notified the IAEA that they had conducted laboratory-scale experiments involving plutonium separation and uranium enrichment. This admission led to an IAEA on-site inspection, including a visit by IAEA Director General Mohamed ElBaradei to South Korea in October 2004 as part of the investigation of the unauthorized nuclear research. The subsequent IAEA report to the United Nations Security Council on November 10, 2004, concluded that secret experiments conducted in South Korea had produced small amounts of weapons-grade nuclear material, but quantities were not significant.[30]

The report also said that there was "no indication that the undeclared experiments have continued" but that "although the quantities of nuclear material involved have not been significant, the nature of the activities . . . and the failures of the ROK to report these activities in a timely manner . . . is a matter of serious concern." The report praised South Korea's active cooperation with the IAEA, but it called on the Seoul government to provide more detailed information on the nuclear experiments so that a full investigation could be completed.[31]

In 2004 Japan reportedly deployed Aegis destroyers and reconnaissance aircraft in the Sea of Japan to provide around-the-clock surveillance after detecting signs that North Korea was preparing to launch a Rodong intermediate-range ballistic missile, with a range of 1,300 kilometers.[32] Developed from Soviet Scud missiles, these missiles were successfully test-fired in 1993 and about one hundred of them are believed to have been deployed by the end of 2004. North Korea's *Rodong Shinmun,* in an article, criticized Tokyo by threatening that "If the United States ignites a nuclear war in this part of the world, then U.S. bases in Japan would serve as a detonating fuse that would plunge Japan into a nuclear sea of fire," adding that "if it wants to maintain peace and live safely, Japan should not become an appendage of the war strategy of American imperialism."[33]

North Korea's program to secretly develop nuclear weapons was a key justification for the U.S. Bush administration policy imposing economic sanctions and directing efforts toward further political isolation and regime change in the North. The Bush administration's resolve to address the transnational terrorism threat to U.S. security added new complexity to an otherwise familiar and conventional approach to the latest nuclear controversy over North Korea. America's security strategy in the post–September 11 era has undergone the most sweeping redesign since the days of Franklin D. Roosevelt. The basic direction of this strategy, based on the doctrines of preemption and prevention arising during Bush's first term, is likely to remain the same during his second term in office, according to some analysts.[34]

A new rule set on global security, appropriate for the post–September 11 era, is more likely to be put into effect in the second-term Bush administration.[35] The new PSI (Proliferation Security Initiative) to halt the North Korean export and sale of WMD fuels and technology, for instance, may be a manifestation of such a new strategic design for checkmating Pyongyang's ambitious and intransigent negotiating behavior.

These changes and the related strategy of preemption by the Bush administration in the post–September 11 era have underscored the ways in which the diplomatic settlement of the ongoing Six-Party Talks on North Korea's nuclear issue could be worked out. Under the regionalization strategy pursued by the Bush administration, the North Korean nuclear issue has become part of a multilateral agenda of regional diplomacy in Northeast Asia.

South Korea has been forced to seek a new strategy of its own to accommodate the changing security dynamics and alliance relations with the United States. Clearly, the Roh Moo Hyun administration policy on inter-Korean relations has been impacted by the outcome of their April 2004 parliamentary elections as well as the 2004 U.S. presidential elections. An uncertain security future awaits the Roh Moo Hyun administration in the days ahead, in charting its navigation of its foreign policy between Washington and Pyongyang. Roh's foreign minister Ban Ki-moon, following the U.S. presidential election on November 2, reiterated the need for Seoul and Washington to stand side-by-side in a "horizontal relationship" that would stem from a mutually beneficial U.S.-South Korea alliance.[36]

During his second inaugural address, on January 20, 2005, U.S. President George W. Bush gave his "freedom speech," saying that "the survival of liberty in our land increasingly depends on the success of liberty in other lands" and that "the best hope for peace in our world is the expansion of freedom in all the world." In his address there was no reference to the Korean peninsula security challenges or North Korea as a problem country. However, a few days later, U.S. Secretary of State designate Condoleezza Rice stated, during the Senate Foreign Relations Committee hearing on her nomination, that North Korea was "an outpost of tyranny" with which the United States was not getting along well with diplomatically, together with the five other countries of Cuba, Iran, Belarus, Myanmar, and Sudan.

In his State of the Union address, on February 2, 2005, U.S. President George W. Bush used a remarkably restraining tone by saying that "We're working closely with the governments in Asia to convince North Korea to abandon its nuclear ambitions." This language was in sharp contrast with his designation of the DPRK as a member of the "axis of evil" countries three years ago. This restraint by Bush was also remarkable considering the U.S. newspaper's report one day earlier on U.S. scientists "declaring 90 percent certainty" that North Korea had sold nuclear materials to Libya.[37] If true, this will mean that North Korea was close to crossing an imaginary "red line" of exporting nuclear technology, material, or weapons to states or groups that pose a terrorist threat. In the same State of the Union address, President Bush also noted, "We're cooperating with sixty governments in the Proliferation Security Initiative, to detect and stop the transit of dangerous materials . . . There are still regimes seeking weapons of mass destruction . . . but no longer without attention and without consequence."

The restraint by Bush could also be interpreted as an attempt by Washington to be sensitive to the positions taken by South Korea and China. Neither South Korea nor China, the two states whose cooperation is indispensable for a solution to North Korea's nuclear issue, want to provoke North Korea. Bush's restraint could also be a tacit invitation to Pyongyang to quickly come back to the Six-Party Talks. North Korea must learn to exploit Bush's declared intention to seek solutions through diplomacy and dialogue. Seoul's Foreign Ministry took a positive stance, welcoming the Bush address as an expression of the desire to resolve the North Korean nuclear issue "in a peaceful and diplomatic way." Whether Washington's fundamental views of the North Korean issue have changed, however, will remain to be seen as the call for convening the next round of Six-Party Talks continues.

The dynamics of the Korean peninsula nuclear standoff continues to gyrate with the public statement by Pyongyang on February 10, 2005, that it now possesses nuclear weapons and that it would withdraw from Six-Party Talks.[38] This prompted U.S. Secretary of State Condoleezza Rice to call on North Korea to reconsider its decision to withdraw from the talks, or risk further isolation. Pyongyang's announcement was also met by critical reactions from each of the six-party member countries in Seoul, Tokyo, and Moscow, as well as by "an unusual level of criticism" by China.[39]

In the following weeks, diplomatic consultations would continue between representatives of each of the interested parties. This included scheduled telephone conversations between the Chinese Foreign Minister Li Zhaoxing and U.S. Secretary of State Condoleezza Rice regarding the next moves and common strategy toward resuming the now-stalled Six-Party Talks. A multilateral diplomacy to defuse the Korean security crisis will continue so as to keep the peninsula nuclear free.

Turning the Six-Party Talks into a Regional Security Forum?

A culture of democracy is fundamentally a culture of peace. So long as a nuclear North Korea remains a distinct possibility in terms of Pyongyang's access to bomb materials (this time with highly enriched uranium as well as plutonium), the United

States together with its allies of Japan and South Korea and coalition partners of China and Russia must confront the security challenges posed by the reclusive rogue state. The United States must also entice the nuclear North Korea into a regional security organization that is yet to be established in Northeast Asia.[40] In the following discussion, we will address the question of why North Korea has become a tough bargainer to be followed by the question of what institutional measures are open to go beyond the six-party talks so as to keep the Korean Peninsula nuclear free.

North Korea as a Tough Bargainer

The security dynamics of the Korean peninsula are a classic case of a dilemma arising from the "anarchic" structure of international politics. Under anarchy, independent action taken by one state (in this case the DPRK) to increase its security is taken by the United States and its allies of South Korea and Japan as diminishing their own.

The nuclear standoff as a security dilemma is a type of Prisoner's Dilemma game, where cooperation between North Korea and the United States with its allies is difficult because absence of mutual trust leads to the possibility of defection and cheating. Does this mean that there is no hope or possibility of achieving cooperation in the current anarchic international politics?

According to Robert M. Axelrod's 1984 study, there are three ways of overcoming a security dilemma: the first is by promoting "the mutuality of interests," that is, the extent to which each actor (in a Prisoner's Dilemma situation) can achieve its own interest by acting cooperatively rather than competitively. The second is by lengthening "the shadow of the future," that is, the extent to which actors value future payoffs from further interactions. The third is by limiting "the number of players," because cooperation becomes more difficult as the number of players increases.[41] That the United States chose to involve other actors in the nuclear talks, under the umbrella of the six-party Beijing talks, may make the situation more complex and complicated than if it had confronted North Korea face to face.

Does this mean that future war is unavoidable and inevitable on the Korean peninsula? The answer is "not quite," because it all depends on what the United States and its allies are prepared to do next. The only way to avoid war and conflict in a nuclear standoff, again as Axelrod argues, seems to be by "lengthening the shadow of the future." United States–North Korean dialogue and negotiations over the nuclear issue, or lack of it, reflect what may be called a "tit-for-tat" game, which is usually played by states that are perceived as distrustful: "If you cheat, I will do likewise" and "I will do to you what you did to me." This strategy works, however, only if there is a long shadow of the future.[42] Unfortunately, with the continued stalemate and brinkmanship, this shadow is rapidly dwindling, and, with it, the number of choices is narrowing concurrently with the lessening of the degree of freedom in foreign policy decisionmaking.[43]

On July 2, 2004, U.S. Secretary of State Colin Powell held talks with the North Korean Foreign Minister Paek Nam-sun in Indonesia for about twenty minutes on the sidelines of an ARF (ASEAN Regional Forum) meeting, which the U.S. State Department spokesman called a "conversation." Powell told the press that the two sides had used the opportunity to reaffirm their positions. "These are difficult negotiations, it just doesn't happen overnight. There's a great deal of mistrust between the United States and North Korea," he said.[44] Powell was also quoted as reconfirming that "the U.S. has no intention to attack North Korea" and delivering President Bush's word: "It is possible to cooperate with each other in important areas even if ideologies and political systems are different."

A statement released shortly afterwards by North Korea seemed equally cautious, and quoted Mr. Paek as saying, "If the United States is of the position to improve the bilateral relations, the DPRK also will not regard the U.S. as a permanent enemy."[45] Despite this upbeat claim by Pyongyang, it is clear that the North Koreans were waiting for the outcome of November's U.S. elections, with an expectation that a new president might lead to a situation advantageous to them. It is also clear that this expectation by Pyongyang's leadership failed to materialize when George W. Bush was reelected to serve a second term in office.

On February 10, 2005, North Korea stated that it now possessed nuclear weapons and that it would withdraw from the six-party talks.[46] The DPRK Ministry of Foreign Affairs released a statement to clarify its stand to cope with what it called "the grave situation created by the U.S. hostile policy toward the DPRK." Two specific measures are said to be necessary, the statement noted: First, "We have wanted the six-party talks but we are compelled to suspend our participation in the talks for an indefinite period" because, according to this statement, "there is no justification for us to participate in the six-party talks again given that the Bush administration terms the DPRK, a dialogue partner, an 'outpost of tyranny'..." Second, in the light of U.S. hostile policy, "(T)his compels us to take a measure to bolster its nuclear weapons arsenal in order to protect *the ideology, system, freedom and democracy chosen by its people*" which, according to the statement, reflects "the true spirit of the Korean people true to the Songun (the military-first) politics to respond to good faith and the use of force in kind."[47]

This statement by Pyongyang has prompted U.S. Secretary of State Condoleezza Rice to call on North Korea to reconsider its decision, to withdraw from the talks, or risk further isolation.[48] Pyongyang's announcement was also met by critical reactions by each of the six-party member countries in Seoul, Tokyo, and Moscow as well as by "an unusual level of criticism" by an ally of China toward North Korea.[49] In the pursuing weeks diplomatic consultations continued between representatives of each of the interested parties. This included scheduled telephone conversations between the Chinese Foreign Minister Li Zhaoxing and U.S. Secretary of State Condoleezza Rice regarding the next moves and common strategy toward resuming the now-stalled six-party talks.

During the six-day diplomatic tour to Asia in the third week of March, involving stopovers in Tokyo, Seoul, and Beijing, U.S. Secretary of State Condoleezza Rice used firm language to reiterate Washington's demand that North Korea immediately resume six-party talks to resolve the international standoff over its nuclear weapons programs.[50] But, as North Korea bitterly refused any dealings with U.S. Secretary of State Rice, the Rice diplomatic mission to Asia, so as to entice North Korean participation in the fourth round of the Beijing talks, was judged to be a failure.[51] Nonethless, a multilateral diplomacy to defuse the Korean security crisis, whether within or outside the six-party talks framework, was to continue so as to keep the peninsula nuclear free.

Institution Building Beyond the Six-Party Talks

What are the implications and lessons of the unfolding drama and conflict issues related to the North Korean nuclear standoff for the future of the U.S.-Korea-Japan alliance? To conclude the present discourse on the Six-Party Talks as peace strategy, we will turn next to the broader question of "war and peace" issues on the Korea Peninsula.

Depending on how the current nuclear controversy is addressed and managed, there exists a distinct possibility of the worst-case scenario—a nuclear-armed North Korea and a second Korean War.[52] The danger exists for North Korea's overblown rhetoric of threat and retaliation to come true as a self-fulfilling prophesy. Likewise, the new national security strategy of the Bush administration, proclaimed in order to defeat global terrorism in the post–September 11, 2001, security environment, may be invoked, although this Bush strategy may be ill suited to the Korean security situation. After Iraq, North Korea may be the next target; at least that is what Pyongyang believes.

The literal application of the Bush strategy to North Korea, especially invoking the doctrine of preemptive war, may end up with a greater tragedy, leading to another Korean War. The price of the regime change that results from the war may be too high and costly when directed to the belligerent and bellicose North Korean regime of Kim Jong Il. An outbreak of a second Korean War will need to be avoided by all means; it will not only undermine the economic foundation, but also destroy the fragile peace sustaining the burgeoning political and civil societies of South Korea's new democracy.

"Avoiding apocalypse" on the Korean peninsula will require the United States and its allies to confront the security challenges of the Korean peninsula head on with renewed seriousness.[53] This will require moving the policy debate over "nuclear" North Korea to a higher level of scholarship and fashioning practical strategies that confront issues of "war and peace" head on.[54]

Furthermore, the United States must go beyond the practice of treating Korea policy as a dependent variable in a global calculus or strategy, as an appendage to a larger cause elsewhere in Asia such as the rising China or rearming Japan. The U.S. policy toward Korea, instead, must reflect a partnership with a thriving democratic, prosperous and peaceful South Korea. This partnership will help lay "the proverbial stones in the stream that [can] ensure a geo-strategic current" surrounding the Korean peninsula, that is favorable to both the United States and South Korea, and other Asian allies.[55]

Such a possibility has been suggested by others. Francis Fukuyama in a recent *Foreign Affairs* essay suggested turning the Six-Party Talks into a five-power regional security forum and framework for Northeast Asia during the second Bush Administration.[56] The questions of scope, task, and membership of the proposed regional security organization, however, would need to be spelled out. Whether the security organization will continue to have six charter members or only five, excluding North Korea, would depend on the success or the failure of the ongoing Beijing Six-Party Talks and the responsiveness of North Korea.

The Bush administration may, in fact, have already worked out the details of such a policy plan by proposing to make the Six-Party Talks permanent. U.S. National Security Adviser Condoleezza Rice reportedly had delivered this plan to Chinese leaders during her visit to Beijing in July 2004, proposing the six nation talks be upgraded into a permanent organization. This agenda of raising the Six-Party Talks to a full-fledged security consultation organization, to discuss conventional weapons and missile issues after the North Korean nuclear issue is settled or not was also discussed with South Korea and Japan in an unofficial exchange of opinion.[57]

Concluding Remarks: Korea's Uncertain Security Future

The Bush administration policy toward North Korea, and its strategy of keeping the Korean Peninsula nuclear free, has not worked out as well as expected at the time of this writing. While boycotting its participation in the Six-Party Talks, North Korea has begun to remove the fuel rods from the Yongbyon nuclear reactors in April 2005. If it reprocesses those fuel rods, North Korea could double the number of nuclear warheads in its possession. This will mark the second time in two years, since 2003, that North Korea has been allowed to remove spent fuel rods.[58] With the U.S. CIA estimate that North Korea already possesses from two to eight nuclear weapons, it will be a matter of time before the North Korean claim of being a nuclear weapon state, with an anticipated underground testing of its nuclear device, may come true.

To underscore the significance of this new development, a historical perspective and lesson of the nuclear controversy may be in order. The Bush administration policies toward North Korea have backfired and led the North to churn out nuclear weapons, and they have also antagonized allies of Japan and South Korea, thereby diminishing America's stature in East Asia. If the Bush administration had adopted the policies that Colin Powell had initially pushed for, as one columnist recently noted, the current mess could probably have been averted.[59]

In 1989, during the George H. Bush administration, North Korea extracted enough spent fuel to manufacture one or two nuclear bombs, but agreed to freeze its plutonium program under the 1994 "Agreed Framework" with the Clinton administration. Although adhering to the freeze on plutonium production, North Korea secretly started around 1999 on a second nuclear track involving uranium. Instead of resolving both challenges through negotiation, the Bush administration was victimized by their "A.B.C (Anything But Clinton) approach" and "they blew it" to borrow a characterization by ambassador Charles Prtichard, special envoy and point man for North Korea in the first Bush administration.[60]

In the absence of a breakthrough settlement of the nuclear controversy, with an anticipated resumption and consummation of the fourth round of the Six-Party Talks sometime in 2005, the Six-Party Talks as a mechanism for keeping the Korean peninsula nuclear free is bound to fail. Not surprisingly, in the face of deadlocked Six-Party Talks, an alternative plan of imposing quarantine has been floated that is aimed primarily for the nuclear North Korea. The Bush administration now considers submitting a UN resolution "empowering all nations to intercept shipments in or out of the country that may contain nuclear materials or components."[61]

This plan, as a modified version of the PSI strategy, would allow the United States and other nations to intercept nuclear shipments in the waters off the Korean Peninsula and force down aircraft for inspection. It is unclear, however, whether China or South Korea would support this plan. All efforts would fail if China was "not a full partner" given the fact that its border with North Korea is a primary route for shipments of weapons, drugs, and counterfeit money, which were Pyongyang's main sources of foreign exchange.

On April 13, 2005, North Korea's *Rodong Sinmun* carried commentary headlined "The United States and Japan should be excluded from regional security issues," carried by the North Korean news agency KCNA. "The security of Northeast Asia can only be achieved when all forces of aggression are removed from this region," noted the commentary after severely criticizing the PSI policy adopted by the United States and Japan. It concluded that "countries interested in this security issue of Northeast Asian region and whose lands border on each other's should sit face to face to discuss the security issue and make positive efforts to exclude the United States and Japan from the debate on security issue."[62] To address these and related issues, U.S. Assistant Secretary of State Christopher Hill subsequently left for consultation with Japan, South Korea, and China.[63]

Finally, the Korean Peninsula security situation has made an unfortunate turn and with it the possibility of North Korea softening its hardened stance toward the Six-Party Talks. U.S. President Bush ventured the name of Kim Jong Il twelve times, never using Kim's official title, during his news conference on April 28 by calling Kim a "tyrant" and a "dangerous person" with a "huge concentration camp" who starves his people" and "threatens and brags."[64] Pyongyang's Foreign Ministry spokesman responded by calling Bush "a hooligan" and "a philistine whom we can never deal with. . . . " North Korea "does not expect any solution to the nuclear issue or any progress in (North Korea)-U.S. relations during his term," according North Korea's official Korean Central News Agency.[65]

Bush answered three questions about the nuclear standoff during his news conference and noted concerns about the capacity of North Korean missiles to carry nuclear warheads. He said, "One of the reasons why I thought it was important to have a missile defense system is for precisely the reason that you brought up: Perhaps Kim Jong Il has got the capacity to launch a weapon: wouldn't it be nice to be able to shoot it down?" He stressed, after noting the possibility of referring the nuclear issue to the UN Security Council, that the best "way to deal with this issue diplomatically is to have four other nations beside ourselves dealing with" Kim Jong Il.[66]

A U.S. defense intelligence official also noted during his appearance at a U.S. Senate committee hearing that North Korea had mastered the technology for arming its missile with nuclear warheads, that would threaten Japan and possibly Western U.S.[67] North Korea test-fired a missile into the Sea of Japan, on May 1, as if to substantiate the U.S. intelligence assessment. Although this missile launch was about sixty-five miles off the North Korean coast, it was not the first, because such attempts had already been made. The U.S. White House Chief of Staff Andrew H. Card, Jr., denounced the North Korean move as "bullies" and called their leader, Kim Jong Il, "not a good man."[68]

White House and Pentagon officials have reportedly been closely monitoring a recent stream of satellite photographs of North Korea that appear to show rapid extensive preparations in a nuclear weapons test, including the construction of a reviewing stand.[69] Despite the inconclusive nature of intelligence on signs of North Korea's nuclear test plans, and China's reported undercutting of U.S. strategy on sanctions on North Korea, the fact remains that North Korea has never tested a nuclear weapon and its so doing will clearly violate the redline set by U.S. strategy with anticipated retaliation and sanctions.[70]

North Korea said, in a statement, that it had removed 8,000 spent fuel rods from a reactor at its main nuclear complex at Yongbyon as one of several "necessary measures" to bolster its nuclear arsenal.[71] In the meantime, the Bush administration official, national security adviser Stephen J. Hadley, has warned North Korea for the first time in public that if it conducted a nuclear test the United States together with its allies in the Pacific would take punitive action, stopping short of saying what kind of sanctions that would entail.[72]

While North Korea remains intransigent diplomatically, by boycotting the fourth round of the Six-Party Talks in Beijing, it continues to play nuclear hardball by strengthening its WMD capability at home. The signs of diplomatic opening arose, however, from the U.S.-ROK summit meetings on June 10, when the visiting South Korean president Roh Moo Hyun met with the U.S. president in the White House, to reaffirm their determination "to pursue peaceful settlement of the North Korean nuclear problem and denuclearization of the Korean peninsula." A week later the North Korean leader Kim Jong Il met with the visiting South Korean official delegation in Pyongyang, led by the ROK Unification Minister. Kim was quoted as saying during this meeting that his country was ready "to resume the Six-Party Talks as early as July, provided that the United States treated it with respect" and, if the nuclear crisis were resolved, "to rejoin the Nuclear Non-Proliferation Treaty and allow international inspectors inside his country."[73]

In closing, it is hoped that next time around not only will the Korean peninsula successfully denuclearize but the unfinished legacy of the Korean War a half-century later will also finally come to be settled. This can be done as a package deal, together with the conventional arms control and the WMD nonproliferation measures, by a newly envisioned security forum that reaches beyond the six-party talks in the Northeast Asia region.

Notes

1. For the first act of the U.S.-DPRK nuclear standoff in 1993–1994, and its diplomatic settlement in the form of the Geneva Agreed Framework of October 24, 1994, see Kihl and Hayes, *Peace and Security in Northeast Asia*. Also, see Wit, Poneman, and Gallucci, *Going Critical*.

2. Some information in this section is derived from the author's book, *Transforming Korean Politics*, 333–337.

3. "North Korea Accuses Nuke Agency of Meddling," Associated Press (Seoul), February 14, 2003.

4. "Powell Says North Korea Rejects U.S. Proposal for Regional Talk," Associated Press (Washington), February 14, 2003.

5. As for a chronology of events leading to the Six-Party Talks, and the statements on the issues surrounding North Korea's nuclear weapons program, see Manyin, Chanlett-Avery, and Marchart, *North Korea: A Chronology of Events*.

6. Andrea Koppel, "U.S. Lays Ground for North Korea Meet," CNN.com, August 9, 2003.

7. John King, "North Korea 'Ready to Show' Nuke Capability," CNN.com, August 29, 2003.

8. Mike Chinoy, "Washington 'Pleased' with Talks," CNN.com, August 29, 2003.

9. Willy Wo-Lap Lam, "China Seeks Payback for North Korea Efforts," CNN.com, September 16, 2003.

10. Willy Wo-Lap Lam, "Time to Act, China Tells North Korea," CNN.com, August 25, 2003.

11. Ibid.

12. U.S. Vice President Dick Cheney made a trip to China on April 13, 2004. His main purpose was to present new information to Chinese leaders on North Korea's nuclear program based on highly enriched uranium obtained through the A.Q. Khan connection. "Cheney Pushes China on North Korea," CNN.com, April 14, 2004.

13. "North Korea Nuclear Deal Rejected," CNN.com, December 9, 2003.

14. Chong, "Tough Multilateral Negotiations," 2–5. For the list of additional details of events building up to the second and the third Six-Party Talks in 2004, see Manyin et al., *North Korea: A Chronology of Events*, 30–43.

15. "Envoy: Pyongyang Willing to Give Up Nukes," Associated Press, June 23, 2004.

16. David Sanger, "U.S. to Offer Incentives to Sway North Korea in Nuclear Talks," *New York Times*, June 23, 2004, A-3.

17. Jonathan Marcus, "High Stakes at North Korea Talks," BBC News, June 25, 2004.

18. Korean Central News Agency, "DPRK Foreign Ministry Spokesman on Six Party Talks," June 28, 2004, as posted in *NAPSNET Daily Report*, June 29, 2004, 2, available at www.bbc.co.uk/worldservice/index.shtml.

19. Ibid.

20. "State Dept. Credits North Korea with Constructive Negotiations," Associated Press, June 28, 2004.

21. "U.S. Offers 5-Point Proposal to North Korea," *Korea Times*, July 13, 2004.

22. Chong, "Six-Way Talks in New Stage," 2–7.

23. Ibid., 4–5.

24. Kihl, *Transforming Korean Politics*, especially the launching of the Roh Moo-Hyun

administration in chapter 8 and the epilogue. Also, see a collection of essays in *International Journal of Korean Studies* 8, no. 1 (Fall/Winter 2004), a publication of the International Council on Korean Studies in Washington, DC.

25. "U.S. Talks Korea Strategy Shift," CNN.com, November 17, 2003.

26. Norimitsu Onish, "U.S. and South Korea Try to Redefine Their Alliance," *New York Times,* December 26, 2003, A-8.

27. Han Kyo Kim, "Korean Unification in Historical Perspective," 17–28.

28. This particular exchange took place during the first of the three scheduled presidential candidates debates, held in Tallahassee, Florida. See "Bush and Kerry Agree on Talks with North Korea, But Differ on the Method," Associated Press, September 30, 2004.

29. "North Korea to Boycott Nuke Talks over S. Korea," United Press International, September 16, 2004.

30. "IAEA Slaps Seoul over Nuke Tests," CNN.com, November 11, 2004.

31. Ibid.

32. The *Yomiuri Shimbun* report, as cited in "Japan on Alert following Signs of North Korean Missile Launch," *Digital Chosunilbo,* September 23, 2004, available at http://english.chosun.com/

33. "North Korea Threatens to Turn Japan into 'Nuclear Sea of Fire,'" *Digital Chosunilbo,* September 23, 2004, available at http://english.chosun.com/

34. On the likely direction of mid-course adjustment to Bush's post-9/11 strategy of preemption, see Gaddis, "Grand Strategy in the Second Term," 2–15.

35. Barnett, *The Pentagon's New Map.*

36. "Relationship with U.S. Is Changing: Ban," *Korea Herald,* November 11, 2004.

37. David Sanger, "North Korea Sold Uranium to Libya," *New York Times,* February 2, 2005, A-1.

38. "North Korea Says It Has Nuclear Weapons," CNN.com, February 10, 2005.

39. Keith Bradsher and James Brooke, "In China, an Unusual Level of Criticism Toward an Ally," *New York Times,* February 13, 2005, A-12.

40. See Cho, "Vision of Northeast Asian Peace," 42–52.

41. Axelrod, "Conflict of Interest," 87–99.

42. Ibid.

43. Nye, *Understanding International Conflict,* 78–79.

44. "Powell Confers with North Korean Minister," CNN.com, July 2, 2004.

45. "Powell Meets N. Korean Minister," BBC News, July 2, 2004.

46. "North Korea Suspends Nuclear Talks," BBC News, February 10, 2005; "North Korea Says It Has Nuclear Weapons," CNN.com, February 10, 2005.

47. Emphasis added. "Pyongyang, February 10 (KCNA), The DPRK Ministry of Foreign Affairs released a statement Thursday to clarify its stand to cope with the grave situation created by the hostile U.S. policy toward the DPRK." BBC News/Asia-Pacific/North Korea's Statement in Full. February 10, 2005, available at www.bbc.co.uk/worldservice/index.shtml

48. "Rice Urges North Korea to Return to Nuclear Talks," CNN.com, February 10, 2005.

49. Bradsher and Brooke, "In China, an Unusual Level of Criticism Toward an Ally," *New York Times*, February 13, 2005, A-12.

50. "Rice Talks Tough Over North Korea," CNN.com, March 19, 2005; "North Korea: We've Built More Nukes," CNN.com, March 25, 2005.

51. "Angry North Korea Refuses Rice Talks," CNN.com, March 16, 2005; "Rice Presses China on North Korea," CNN.com, March 20, 2005.

52. Cha and Kang, *Nuclear North Korea.*

53. Noland, *Avoiding the Apocalypse.*

54. Cha and Kang, *Nuclear North Korea.*

55. Ibid., 10, 185.

56. Fukuyama, "Re-Envisioning Asia," 75–87.

57. "U.S. Proposed to Make Six-Party Talks Permanent: Nikkei," *Digital Chosunilbo*, November 19, 2004, available at www.bbc.co.uk/worldservice/index.shtml.

58. David E. Sanger, "Steps at Reactor in North Korea Worry the U.S.," *New York Times*, April 18, 2005.

59. Nicholas D. Kristof, "North Korea, 6, and Bush, 0," *New York Times*, Op-Ed, April 26, 2005.

60. Ibid.

61. David E. Sanger, "White House May Go to U.N. Over North Korean Shipments," *New York Times*, April 25, 2005.

62. "North Korea Paper Wants USA, Japan, Excluded from Regional Security Talks," BBC Monitoring Asia-Pacific–Political Supplied by *BBC Worldwide Monitoring*, April 14, 2005.

63. "U.S. Envoy Downbeat Over NK Talks," CNN.com, April 26, 2005; James Brooke, "U.S. Weapons Envoy Pessimistic About Talks with North Korea," *New York Times*, April 30, 2005.

64. Excerpts from Bush's news conference, *New York Times*, April 29, 2005; "U.S. Will Pursue 'Common Approach' to North Korea, Bush Says," States News Service, Washington, April 28, 2005.

65. "North Korea: Bush a 'Hooligan,'" CNN.com, May 2, 2005.

66. Excerpts from Bush's news conference, *New York Times*, April 29, 2005; "U.S. Will Pursue 'Common Approach' to North Korea, Bush Says."

67. David S. Cloud and David E. Sanger, "U.S. Aide Sees Arms Advance by North Korea: Cites Skill to Fit Nuclear Weapons on Missile," *New York Times*, April 30, 2005.

68. Interview with Andrew Card; Interview with Mowaffak Al-Rubaie, CNN Late Edition with Wolf Blitzer, 12:00 PM EST, May 1, 2005. Wolf Blitzer and Brian Knowlton, "U.S. Denounces North Korea After Reports of Missile Test," *New York Times*, May 2, 2005.

69. David E. Sanger and William J. Broad, "U.S. Cites Signs of Korean Steps to Nuclear Test," *New York Times*, May 6, 2005.

70. Joseph Kahn and David E. Sanger, "China Rules Out Using Sanctions on North Korea, Undercuts U.S. Strategy," *New York Times*, May 11, 2005; Joseph Kahn, "China Says U.S. Impeded North Korea Talks," *New York Times*, May 13, 2005.

71. James Brooke, "North Koreans Claim to Extract Fuel for Bombs from a Nuclear Reactor," *New York Times*, May 12, 2005; David E. Sanger, "What Are Koreans Up To? U.S. Agencies Can't Agree," *New York Times*, May 12, 2005.

72. David E. Sanger, "U.S. Is Warning North Koreans on Nuclear Test," *New York Times*, May 16, 2005.

73. Norimitsu Onishi, "North Korea's Leader Says He's Ready to Resume Talks to End Nuclear Standoff," *New York Times*, June 18, 2005, A5; Sohn Jie-ae, "Kim Meets South Korean Official," CNN.com, June 17, 2003; "Hopes Raised Over Korean Détente," CNN.com, June 15, 2005.

13

Why Hasn't North Korea Collapsed?

Understanding the Recent Past,
Thinking About the Future

Nicholas Eberstadt

Can the Democratic People's Republic of Korea survive—as a distinct regime, an autonomous state, a specific political-economic system, and a sovereign country? Can it continue to function in the manner in which it has been performing since the end of 1991—that is to say, since the final collapse of the Soviet empire? Or is it doomed to join the Warsaw Pact's failed Communist experiments in the dustbin of history? Or might it, instead, adapt and evolve—"surviving" in the sense of maintaining its political authority and power to rule, but transforming its defining functional characteristics and systemic identity?

Back in 1994, I would not have expected to be writing on this particular theme a decade later. My own work on the North Korean economy has generally been associated with what others have termed the "collapsist"[1] school of thought, and not unfairly. As far back as June 1990, I published an op-ed essay titled "The Coming Collapse of North Korea"[2]; since then, my analyses have recurrently questioned the viability of the DPRK economy and system.[3]

It is perhaps especially fitting, then, that, having imagined the odds of the DPRK's post-Soviet survival to be very low, I should be charged with explaining just how the North Korean system *has* managed to survive these past fourteen or so years—and with speculating about the possibility of sustainable pathways that might permit regime, state, and system to endure that far, or further, into the future.

The following pages proceed through four sections. The first discusses the epistemology of state collapse, focusing on a particular historical example of potential relevance. The second focuses on some of the factors that may have abetted state survival in the DPRK case in recent years. The third will discuss the sustainability of North Korea's current economic modus operandi. The fourth will examine some of the questions pertaining to a DPRK transition to a more pragmatic variant of a planned socialist economy.

The Epistemology of State Collapse: A Cautionary Ottoman Tale

Although major efforts have been undertaken to systematize the study of state failure,[4] the simple fact is that the modern world lacks anything like a corpus of science by which to offer robust predictions about impending episodes of social revolution, systemic breakdown, or state collapse. At the very best, the anticipation of such dramatic political events might aspire to *art* rather than *science*[5]—just as the technique of successful stock picking (or short-selling) has always been, and still remains, an art and not a science.[6] A common set of factors, furthermore, consigns both of these endeavors to the realm of art: the extraordinary complexity of the phenomena under consideration; the independent and unpredictable nature of the human agency at their center; and the ultimately irresolvable problem of asymmetries of information.

All of this is to say there is no reason to expect that students and analysts should be able to predict in advance the breakdown for political systems with any degree of accuracy on the basis of any regular and methodical model. Indeed, predicting breakdown for Communist systems is arguably even more difficult than for open societies, insofar as the problem of asymmetries of information is—by systemic regime design—that much more extreme.[7]

If anticipating state collapse is—at best—a matter of art, it is an art whose most obvious failures might be classified into two categories of error. First, there are the failures to predict events that did actually take place: the 1989–1991 collapse of all the Warsaw Pact states—an upheaval that caught almost all informed Western observers unawares[8]—is certainly the most memorable recent example of this type of error. Second, there is the error of predicting upheaval and abrupt demise for states or systems that do *not* end up suffering from such paroxysms: this category of error would encompass, *inter alia*, the past century of Marxist-Leninist prognoses for Western Europe; the apocalyptic assessments from the 1970s and 1980s on the future of South Africa,[9] the premature predictions of the fall of Soviet Communism[10]—and, of course, at least to date, the presentiments of the collapse of the DPRK.

These particular types of mistakes can be likened to "Type I" and "Type II" errors in statistical inference—but for our purposes here we should emphasize that the family of analytical errors that can attend assessments of state failure or collapse is *not* dichotomous. Other types of errors can also occur. Among these, the one I wish to draw attention to for the moment is *failure to recognize imminent, but averted, collapse.*

This is not a fanciful hypothetical category. To the contrary, history is replete with examples of this phenomenon. One particular example worth recalling involves the collapse of the Ottoman Empire, and the battle of Gallipoli.

As early as 1853,[11] the Ottoman Empire had been dubbed "the sick man of Europe" by those other Great Powers engaged in the struggle for mastery of the continent. With a sclerotic and corrupt Byzantine administrative system and an over-taxed, underinnovating economy,[12] Constantinople was set on a course of steady relative decline.[13]

In the event, the Ottoman invalid survived for almost seventy years after that dip-lomatic diagnosis of its poor political health: the Empire was finally laid to rest in 1922/23, with Mustapha Kemal Ataturk's revolution and the founding of the modern Turkish state. What is less well known, however, is that the Ottoman Empire very nearly came to an end in 1915—in the World War I campaign that came to be known as Gallipoli.

The Gallipoli campaign of 1915–1916 is remembered as a military debacle for the forces of France and, more particularly, the British Empire. In a bold and risky bid to capture Constantinople by naval attack and amphibious invasion, the Allied troops were instead trapped on their own beachheads on the Gallipoli peninsula, unable to displace the Ottoman forces from their fortified positions on the high grounds above. For months the soldiers of the British Commonwealth—quite a few of them Austra-lian and New Zealand regulars—were slaughtered in futile attempts to break the Ot-toman line. (The plight of these unfortunates is vividly portrayed in Peter Weir's 1982 movie, *Gallipoli.*) At the end of 1915, with more than 100,000 Commonwealth casu-alties having been sustained in the campaign, the British began a total evacuation of the surviving combatants. In the course of the Gallipoli campaign, Ottoman General Mustapha Kemal secured his reputation as a brilliant and heroic military leader, while Winston Churchill, the then-young Lord Admiral of the British Navy, was obliged to resign his post in humiliation.

Gallipoli is considered a classic military blunder today—literally a textbook case. (The campaign was included in an influential contemporary treatise on great military mistakes,[14] and for decades beforehand it was studied in military academies around the world.) What is not commonly appreciated, however, is that the Franco-British naval assault that was to become Gallipoli very nearly *did* succeed—and indeed came within an ace of toppling the Ottoman Empire.

In early March 1915, a Franco-British flotilla that included sixteen capital ships (battleships, cruisers, and destroyers) commenced Churchill's plan to "force" the Dardanelles Strait. Artillery fire from the Turkish gun emplacements proved ineffec-tual against these mighty warships. On March 18, 1915, the flotilla prepared to ad-vance through the Dardanelles Strait and into the Sea of Marmora—from whence they would steam on to Constantinople. Over the course of a daylong battle between big guns, the Allied fleet slowly moved forward against the Ottoman emplacements. Then, in the late afternoon, three British ships—one of them a battleship—unexpect-edly struck mines and suddenly sank. The British commander of the operation, Rear Admiral John de Roebeck, was severely shaken by this setback (apparently he felt certain he would be sacked for the loss of those ships).[15] At the end of the day the Allied fleet regrouped—but did not pursue its assault the next day, or indeed in the weeks that immediately followed. As David Fromkin notes, "only a few hundred casualties had been suffered, but the Admiralty's Dardanelles campaign was over."[16]

De Roebeck could not have known at the time about the circumstances on the other side of the barricades. With the benefit of Ottoman and German records and memoirs, however, historians have described these for us now: the Ottoman administration and its German military advisers were grimly convinced the Allied assault would spell doom for Constantinople—for they had no hope of putting up a successful resistance.

As chronicler Alan Moorehead recounts, Ottoman Minister of the Interior Talaat himself was utterly despondent. As early as January he had called a conference (with the top German military allies and advisers). All agreed that when the Allied Fleet attacked it would get through.[17]

In the days before the attempt to "force" the Dardanelles, indeed, Constantinople had begun to take on the smell of a defeated capital. Thus David Fromkin stated:

Morale in Constantinople disintegrated. Amidst rumors and panic, the evacuation of the city commenced. The state archives and the gold reserves of the banks were sent to safety. Special trains were prepared for the Sultan and for the foreign diplomatic colony. Talaat, the Minister of the Interior, requisitioned a powerful Mercedes for his personal use, and equipped it with extra petrol tanks for the long drive to a distant place of refuge. Placards denouncing the government began to appear in the streets of the city. . . . The [German ship] *Goeben* made ready to escape to the Black Sea. . . . [Ottoman War Minister] Enver bravely planned to remain and defend the city, but his military dispositions were so incompetent that—as [German military adviser General Otto] Liman von Sanders later recalled—any Turkish attempt at opposing an Allied landing at Constantinople would have been rendered impossible.[18]

Among the disadvantages weighing on the beleaguered Turks was the fact—unappreciated by de Roebeck—that the defenders were virtually out of artillery shells. As Moorehead commented,

[nothing] could alter the fact that they had so much ammunition and no more. . . . [I]f the battle went on and no unforeseen reinforcements arrived it was obvious to the commanders that the moment would come when they would be bound to order their men to fire the last round and then to retire. After that they could do no more.[19]

As an historian who fought in Gallipoli would later note, the official records of Minister Enver's German advisers jotted the following entry on the fateful day of March 18, 1915:

Most of the Turkish ammunition has been expended; the medium howitzers and mine fields have fired more than half their supply. Particularly serious is the fact that the long-range high explosive shells, which alone are effective against British Ship's armor are all used up. We stress the point that Fort Hamidieh has only seventeen shells and Kalid Bahr Fort only ten: there is also no reserve of mines; what will happen when the battle is resumed.[20]

The Ottoman government and its German advisers could not believe their good fortune when the Allied naval assault inexplicably (from their perspective) halted. Looking back later, Enver is reported to have commented:

> If the English had only had the courage to rush more ships through the Dardanelles, they could have got to Constantinople; but their delay enabled us thoroughly to fortify the Peninsula, and in six weeks' time we had taken down there over 200 Austrian Skoda guns.[21]

General Liman von Sanders, for his part, later commented tersely that the evacuation procedures underway in Constantinople in March 1915:

> were justified. . . . Had the [Allied landing] orders been carried out . . . the course of the world war would have been given such a turn in the spring of 1915 that Germany and Austria would have had to continue without Turkey.[22]

Fromkin stated the matter more plainly: "The Ottoman Empire, which had been sentenced to death, received an unexpected last-minute reprieve."[23]

The notion that a state might be on the verge of collapse without interested outsiders' fully understanding that this was in fact the case is not merely an abstract theoretical possibility. The example of Gallipoli offers us an "existence proof" that such things do indeed happen in real life—sometimes with great historical consequence. (Here again, we note the role of asymmetries of information in the outsider's analytical failure—circumstances that tend to be most acute in times of hostility, with little regular communication between the actors in question, and with strategic deception being actively practiced in the quest for state survival.)

From this Turkish parable, let us return to North Korea. The DPRK continues to function as a sovereign and independent state to this very writing. But is the North Korean state's recent survival a modern-day variant of the Gallipoli phenomenon—a case, in other words, of imminent but averted collapse?

Financing the Survival of the North Korean State

The speculative questions I have just posed are unfortunately unanswerable—and for now, quite untestable. We will probably have to await the eventual opening of the Pyongyang state archives to delve into those issues with any satisfaction—assuming that the DPRK's official files and data offer a sufficiently coherent and faithful record of events to aid such historical inquiries.

Available data do, however, cast light on one aspect of the DPRK's struggle to avoid collapse in the wake of the Soviet Bloc's demise. These are the international data on North Korean trade patterns as reported by the DPRK's trade partners—"mirror statistics," as they are known by their users. Mirror statistics cannot tell us how close North Korea may have come to collapse in recent years: but they can help us explain how North Korea has managed to *finance* state survival.

Although the analysis of the modern North Korean economy has always been hampered by the extraordinary paucity of reliable data that might facilitate independent assessments, it is not exactly a state secret that the DPRK national economy was in the grip of stagnation—or incipient decline—in the 1980s, and began to spiral downward once the aid and subsidized trade from the erstwhile Soviet Bloc suddenly ceased at the start of the 1990s.

The steep and apparently unbroken decline in North Korean economic performance in the first half of the 1990s led to the outbreak of famine in the DPRK by the mid-1990s—the first and only instance of such mass hunger in an industrialized and literate society during peacetime. North Korea's patent economic dysfunction, and its leadership's seeming unwillingness or incapacity to confront and correct it, seemed to me to raise the possibility of one very particular kind of systemic collapse: namely, *economic collapse.* I addressed this prospect in some detail in my 1999 book, *The End of North Korea.*[24]

In discussing economic collapse, of course, I was not venturing guesses about the possibility of some dramatic *political* event that might bring the North Korean regime to an end—a coup at the top, say, or a revolt from below. (Then, as now, the sorts of information that might permit such a judgment were unavailable to outside observers—especially those with no access to confidential sources of intelligence.)

Economic collapse, for its part, may have seemed an exceedingly elastic term—but I attempted to use it with some conceptual precision. In my analysis, economic collapse was *not* defined as an economic shock, or an economic dislocation, or a severe depression, or even a famine. Instead it was offered as a term to describe *the breakdown of the division of labor in the national economy*—the process through which ordinary people in complex productive societies trade their labor for food. (This conception of economic collapse was, to my knowledge, first developed and defined by Jack Hirshleifer of UCLA and RAND.[25])

North Korea in the mid- and late-1990s, I argued, was set on a trajectory for economic collapse—for its domestic economy was incapable of producing the requisite goods necessary for the maintenance of a division of labor, and the regime seemed utterly unable to finance their purchase from abroad. Although it was impossible to determine from outside the precise breaking point at which the division of labor would unravel, events were incontestably bringing the DPRK system progressively closer to that point.

The situation in early 2004 looks somewhat different. The ordinary North Korean today, of course, does not exactly live in the lap of luxury. On the other hand, by most accounts he no longer suffers from the desperate privation that character-

Figure 13.1   **North Korean Merchandise Imports, 1989–2003**

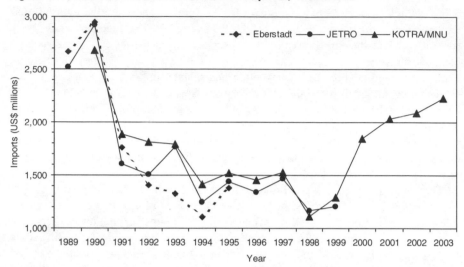

Sources: Eberstadt, Nicholas, "Economic Recovery in the DPRK: Status and Prospect," *International Journal of Korean Studies,* IV:1 (Fall/Winter 2000); JETRO; KOTRA; ROK Ministry of Unification (MNU).

ized the mid-to-late 1990s. As best can be told, the worst of the North Korean famine—which almost certainly claimed hundreds of thousands of victims, and may well have killed a million people between 1995 and 1998[26]—ceased raging over five years ago.

Officially, the North Korean leadership evinced a new confidence in the DPRK's staying power back in September 1998, at the same Supreme People's Assembly that formally elevated Kim Jong Il to "the highest position of state." That convocation publicly declared the "Arduous March" of the previous several years over, and announced that the DPRK was now on the road to becoming a "powerful and prosperous state" (kangsong taeguk).[27]

Whether or not the North Korean economy has enjoyed actual growth since 1998—a question that remains a matter of some contention—it is clear that the economic situation has in some meaningful sense stabilized and improved since the grim days of the Arduous March. But how was this accomplished? Mirror statistics provide some clues.

We can begin by looking at reconstructions of North Korea's overall trends for merchandise imports[28] (see Figure 13.1). In 1990, the reported value of imports was nearly $3 billion (in current U.S. dollars). Eight years later, the reported level had dropped below $1.2 billion—a catastrophic fall of over 60 percent. After 1998, however, North Korea's imports rebounded markedly. By 2001, the reported level exceeded $2 billion—and appears to have risen further since then. To go by these numbers,

Figure 13.2   **North Korean Merchandise Exports, 1989–2003**

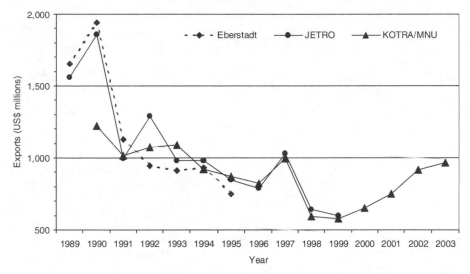

Year

Sources: Eberstadt, Nicholas, "Economic Recovery in the DPRK: Status and Prospect," *International Journal of Korean Studies,* IV:1 (Fall/Winter 2000); JETRO; KOTRA; ROK Ministry of Unification (MNU).

North Korea was obtaining fully twice as much in the way of goods from abroad in 2003 as it had in 1998. In the year 2003, in fact, the current dollar volume of North Korean merchandise imports was at the highest level registered since the collapse of the Soviet Union.

And how did North Korea pay for this upsurge in imports? To judge by the mirror statistics, it did so *not* through any corresponding jump in reported export revenues (see Figure 13.2). Between 1990 and 1998, North Korea's reported merchandise exports collapsed, plummeting from about $2 billion to under $600 million. By 2003, these had recovered somewhat, to a reported level of just under $1 billion. Nevertheless, by any absolute measure, the DPRK's reported export level remained remarkably low in 2003—only half as high as it had been in 1990, and actually slightly lower than it had been in the bitter Arduous March year of 1997.

In a purely arithmetic sense, North Korea succeeded in effecting a substantial increase of merchandise imports by managing to increase its reported balance of trade deficit appreciably (see Figure 13.3). In the Arduous March period—the famine years of 1995–1998—North Korea's reported surfeit of imports over exports averaged under $600 million a year. By contrast, in the years 2000–2003 (the kangsong taeguk era) the DPRK's reported trade deficit averaged about $1.2 billion annually.

But how was this reported trade deficit financed? After all, North Korea is a state with a commercial creditworthiness rating of approximately zero, having maintained

Figure 13.3 **North Korean Merchandise Trade Deficit, 1989–2003**

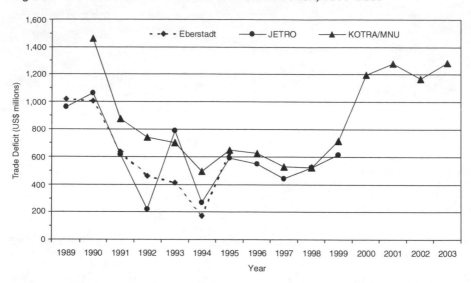

Sources: Eberstadt, Nicholas, "Economic Recovery in the DPRK: Status and Prospect," *International Journal of Korean Studies,* IV:1 (Fall/Winter 2000); JETRO; KOTRA; ROK Ministry of Unification (MNU).

for a generation its posture of defiant de facto default on the Western loans it contracted in the 1970s.

Historically, the DPRK relied upon aid from its Communist allies—principally, the Soviet Union and China—to augment its imports. After the collapse of the USSR, China perforce emerged as North Korea's principal foreign patron, and Beijing's largesse extended beyond its officially announced subventions for Pyongyang. The DPRK's seemingly permanent merchandise trade deficit with China constitutes a broader and perhaps more accurate measure of Beijing's true aid levels for Pyongyang (insofar as neither party seems to think the sums accumulated in that imbalance will ever be corrected or repaid).

Implicit Chinese aid, however, cannot account for North Korea's import upsurge of 1998–2003. To the contrary, China's implicit aid to North Korea—i.e., its reported balance of trade deficit—was essentially the same in 1998 and 2003 ($339 million vs. $341 million, in current U.S. dollars). North Korea's non-Chinese balance of trade deficit, by contrast, apparently soared upward (see Figure 13.4). Whereas in 1997 the DPRK reportedly only managed to obtain a net of $50 million more merchandise from abroad than its commercial exports would have paid for—after factoring out China—by 2003 the corresponding total was well over $900 million.

Indeed, if we remove China from the picture, the line describing North Korea's net imports of supplies from abroad rises steadily upward between 1997 and 2003. It is

Figure 13.4 **North Korea's Merchandise Trade Deficit,1990–2003, Excluding Trade with China**

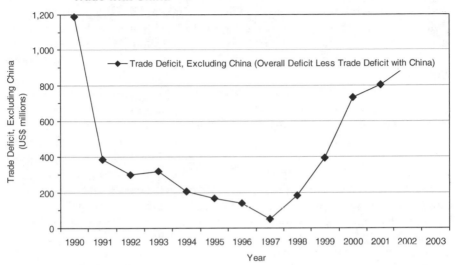

Sources: Eberstadt, Nicholas, "Economic Recovery in the DPRK: Status and Prospect," *International Journal of Korean Studies,* IV:1 (Fall/Winter 2000); JETRO; KOTRA; ROK Ministry of Unification (MNU); PRC General Administration of Customs, China's Customs Statistics, various volumes.

this graphic that captures the economic essence of North Korea's shift from its Arduous March period to its kangsong taeguk epoch.

And how was this jump in non-Chinese net imports financed? Unfortunately, we cannot be precise about this, since many of the sources of funds involve illicit transactions. North Korea's international counterfeiting, drug trafficking, weapons, and weapon technology sales all figure here, although the sums raised from those activities are a matter of some dispute.

Nor do we yet know exactly how much of the South Korean taxpayers' money was furtively channeled from Seoul to Pyongyang during this period. One set of prosecutorial investigations has convicted former President Kim Dae Jung's national security adviser and several other aides of illegally transferring up to $500 million to Kim Jong Il's "Bureau 39" on the eve of the historic June 2000 Pyongyang summit.[29] The possibility of other unreported official Seoul-to-Pyongyang payoffs during the 1998–2002 period cannot be ruled out—nor of course can the potential volume of any such attendant funds be determined.

Broadly speaking, however, we can explain the timing and the magnitude of the 1998–2002 upswing in North Korea's non-Chinese net imports by looking at policies that were embraced during those years by the United States and its Northeast Asian allies. The year 1998 heralded the inauguration of ROK President Kim Dae Jung and the advent of South Korea's "Sunshine Policy" for détente and reconciliation with the

North. In 1999, the United States followed suit, unveiling the "Perry Process" (the "grand bargain" approach to settling outstanding disputes with the DPRK that was hailed by the ROK Foreign Minister in the year 2000 as "based on our engagement policy toward North Korea"[30]). Japan and the EU both joined in the pursuit of engagement with North Korea during these years as well, although in differing degrees.

In their strict performance specifications—their defining actions, as opposed to their official rationales or stated intentions—"Sunshine Policy" and "engagement policy" effectively meant organized activity by Western governments to mobilize transfers of public resources to the North Korean state. If this formulation sounds provocative, reflection on the particulars of those multilateral polices—e.g., the Hyundai/ ROK National Tourism Office payments for vacations to Mt. Kumgang; the U.S. "inspection fee"[31] of 500,000 tons of food aid granted in 1999 in exchange for permission to visit a suspect underground North Korean facility at Kumchang-ri; the continuing food and fertilizer shipment from Seoul and the occasional food transfers from Japan; the secret payments for the historic June 2000 Pyongyang summit; and the new, albeit modest, flows of aid from EU countries in the wake of the flurry of diplomatic normalizations between Pyongyang and EU states in 2000/2001—will indicate it is also functionally accurate. Thus, it is perhaps not surprising that North Korea's financial fortunes should have improved so markedly in 1998 and the years immediately following.

It may be perplexing and counterintuitive to see the United States—the DPRK's longtime principal opponent and antagonist in the international arena—described as a major backer of the North Korean state. Yet this is now in fact the case. Figures compiled by Dr. Mark Manyin of the Congressional Research Service provide the details (see Table 13.1). In the 1996–2002 period, Washington awarded Pyongyang just over $1 billion in food aid, concessional fuel oil, and medical supplies. (Interestingly enough, nearly $350 million of these resources were transferred in the years 2001 and 2002— under the purportedly hostile aegis of the George W. Bush administration.)

By the second half of the 1990s, it may be noted, North Korea's reliance on U.S. aid for financing its international purchases and supplies of good was, in some quantifiable respect, more pronounced than for almost any other state for which Washington funded military, economic, and/or humanitarian assistance programs. This may be seen in Table 13.2 (p. 280). Total American aid allocations to key recipients Israel and Egypt for the five years 1996–2000, for example, amounted to 34 percent and 67 percent of those states' respective export earnings for the year 2000. U.S. 1996–2000 assistance to North Korea, by contrast, actually exceeded the DPRK's reported year 2000 commercial export revenues. (Incidentally, since most of the American aid resources in Table 13.1 were not tallied in the international commercial ledgers upon which "mirror statistics" rely,[32] the DPRK's actual level of reliance upon non-Chinese net supplies from abroad was consistently higher for the years 1998–2003 than the graphic in Figure 13.4 suggests.) Ironic though it may seem, when considered in relation to the economy's evident capability to finance its international needs from its own regular commercial exports, Washington's aid lifeline for the DPRK in recent

Table 13.1

U.S. Aid and National Exports, Selected Comparisons

Current Comparison to Selected Countries

	Total military and economic aid, 1996–2000 (US$)	Exports of goods and services, 2000 (US$)	Total aid as percentage of exports
Pakistan	253,300,000	9,575,000,064	2.65
Ukraine	743,400,000	19,522,000,896	3.81
El Salvador	234,700,000	3,645,691,392	6.44
Nicaragua	206,600,000	962,200,000	21.47
Jordan	1,221,000,000	3,534,132,736	34.55
Israel	14,880,000,000	44,146,860,032	33.71
Egypt	10,595,200,000	15,931,033,600	66.51
Haiti	485,000,000	506,236,864	95.80
DPRK	661,500,000	653,100,000	101.29

Sources: Manyin (DPRK Total Aid, 1995–2002); KOTRA/Korean Ministry of Unification (DPRK Exports, 2002); USAID (Total Military and Economic Aid); International Bank for Reconstruction and Development, *World Development Indicators 2002* (Washington, DC: World Bank, 2002), CD-ROM (Export Revenues).

Historical Comparison to Taiwan and the ROK

	Total military and economic aid (US$)[1]	Total exports ($US)[2]	Total aid as percentage of exports
DPRK	1,021,800,000	751,100,000	136.04
Taiwan	2,512,100,000	220,750,000	1137.98
ROK	4,346,200,000	56,000,000	7761.07

Sources: Manyin (DPRK Total Aid, 1995–2002); KOTRA/Korean Ministry of Unification (DPRK Exports, 2002); USAID (Total Military and Economic Aid); and IMF International Financial Statistics (ROK and Taiwan Exports, 1962).

[1] For DPRK, figures represent total aid for 1995–2002; for Taiwan and ROK, total aid for 1955–1962.

[2] For DPRK, total exports for 2001; for Taiwan and ROK, total exports for 1962.

years looks more consequential than any of the bilateral assistance relationships that Washington has arranged for treaty allies or friendly states in any spot on the globe.

This is not the first time, of course, that American aid has helped a state on the Korean peninsula to survive. After the 1953 Korean Armistice, Washington devoted tremendous resources to propping up and strengthening the Syngman Rhee government in Seoul—a regime fascinated with "aid-maximizing stratagems"[33] and manifestly disinterested in improving its then-miserable export performance. To be sure, judged by the metric of U.S. aid to recipient-country exports, the American

Table 13.2

U.S. Assistance to North Korea, 1995–2004

Calendar or fiscal year	Food aid (per FY)		KEDO assistance (per calendar year; US$ million)	Medical supplies (per FY; US$ million)	Total (US$ million)
	Metric Tons	Commodity value (US$ million)			
1995	0	0.00	9.50	0.20	9.70
1996	19,500	8.30	22.00	0.00	30.30
1997	177,000	52.40	25.00	5.00	82.40
1998	200,000	72.90	50.00	0.00	122.90
1999	695,194	222.10	65.10	0.00	287.20
2000	265,000	74.30	64.40	0.00	138.70
2001	350,000	102.80	74.90	0.00	177.60
2002	207,000	82.40	90.50	0.00	172.90
2003	40,170	33.60	2.30	0.00	35.90
2004	60,000	n.a.	0.00	0.00	n.a.
Total	1,953,864	$648.80	$403.70	$5.20	$1,057.60

Sources: Figures for food aid and medical supplies from USAID and U.S. Department of Agriculture; KEDO (Korean Peninsula Energy Development Organization) figures from KEDO. Courtesy of Mark Manyin, Congressional Research Service.

Cold War project for preserving the ROK was *vastly* more intensive than Washington's post–Cold War programs sustaining the North Korean state (see Figure 13.2). In the late 1950s, on the other hand, U.S. bilateral aid was just about the only game in town for states seeking Western largesse—in marked contrast to today. And if we were able to consider all the aid packages—overt, covert, or semi-formal—that were extended to the DPRK by Western governments in the kangsong taeguk period, we might well discover that the ratio of such outside assistance to local commercial earnings began to approach the scale of disproportion earlier witnessed in, say, the late-1950s U.S. project to preserve the independence of the Republic of China (Taiwan). To be clear here, earlier Taiwan effort would have undoubtedly been the more aid-intensive by our selected metric; while lower, however, the aid-intensity of the recent DPRK arrangements would perhaps fall within the same approximate order of magnitude.

At the end of the day, we can never know what would have happened if the United States and its allies in Asia and Europe had refrained from underwriting the survival of the North Korean state in the late 1990s and the early years of the present decade. (Such exercises in counterfactual speculation—"imaginary history," as they are known to their modern-day devotees[34]—can make for fascinating reading, but are ultimately inconclusive.) We do not know, furthermore, just how close North Korea came to the critical breaking point of an economic collapse during the Arduous March period between Kim Il Sung's death and Kim

Jong Il's formal anointment. What we know—or think we know—is that the DPRK was failing economically in the mid-1990s, coming steadily closer to the notional point of an economic collapse—but that the prospect of economic collapse was subsequently diminished materially by an upsurge in provisions of goods from abroad. What seems beyond dispute is that the increase of Western aid for the DPRK under the Sunshine and engagement policies played a role—possibly an instrumental role—in reducing the risk of economic collapse, and increasing the odds of survival for the North Korean state.

Current Parameters in Financing State Survival for the DPRK: Ideological and Cultural Infiltration, and Military-First Politics

Although North Korea's flirtation with economic collapse did not commence until after the disintegration of the Soviet Bloc, the DPRK's relative (and perhaps also its absolute) economic decline has been a long-term process, and by some indicators was already well underway in the Cold War era. The country's trade performance vividly describes this record of long-term economic decline, and since international trade bears more than incidentally upon the state's risk of economic collapse, on systemic survival prospects as well. From our twenty-first century vantage point, we may not recall how steep and steady this long decline has been.

There was a time—within living memory—when the DPRK was *not* known for being an international trade basket case. In 1970, the level of per capita exports in North and South Korea was roughly comparable ($21 vs. $27—in then-much-more-valuable dollars).[35] As late as 1980, in fact, North Korea's export profile, though hardly robust, was not manifestly disfigured. That year, for example, the DPRK's level of reported per capita exports was just slightly higher than Turkey's, and over five times higher than India's (see Table 13.3). At the same time, North Korea's reported imports exceeded reported export revenues, but by a margin that was in keeping with the performance of other developing economies, including quite successful ones. The DPRK's 1980 ratio of imports-to-exports, for example, was just slightly higher than Chile's—but it was a bit lower than either Thailand's or South Korea's (see Table 13.4).

By 1990 the picture had worsened considerably (see Tables 13.5 and 13.6). Despite a politically determined surge in exports to the USSR under the terms of the 1985–1990 Soviet-DPRK Economic Cooperation accord, per capita exports now ranked in the lowest quartile of the world's economies—in a league with Equatorial Guinea and Kenya—and the ratio of exports to imports had risen, so that North Korea was among the quartile of states where this imbalance was greatest. (By 1990, the disproportion between North Korea's import and export revenues already placed in the ranking next to such heavily aid-dependent economies as Jordan and Ghana.)

By 2000 the DPRK was an outlier within the world system (see Tables 13.7 and 13.8). That year, the DPRK's reported per capita export level would have ranked 158 among the 168 countries so tracked by the World Bank's *World Development*

Table 13.3

Per Capita Exports: DPRK Rank in World, 1980 (out of 134 countries)

Rank	Country	Exports (US$)	Population	Per capita exports (US$)
108	DPRK	1,414,100,000	17,113,626	82.63
109	Turkey	3,660,084,493	44,484,000	82.28
114	Haiti	316,099,994	5,353,000	59.05
119	Chad	175,041,754	4,477,000	39.10
121	Pakistan	2,958,199,994	82,730,330	35.76
127	Burkina Faso	172,600,568	6,962,000	24.79
128	Burundi	81,022,222	4,130,000	19.62
129	Uganda	242,000,000	12,806,900	18.90
130	Guinea-Bissau	14,039,310	763,000	18.40
131	India	11,249,000,000	687,332,000	16.37
133	China	14,327,813,120	981,235,000	14.60
134	Bangladesh	995,270,012	85,438,000	11.65

Sources: International Bank for Reconstruction and Development, *World Development Indicators 2003* (Washington, DC: World Bank, 2003), CD-ROM; U.S. Bureau of the Census; KOTRA; ROK Ministry of Unification (MNU).

Table 13.4

Exports as a Percent of Imports: DPRK Rank in World, 1980 (out of 132 countries)

Rank	Country	Imports (US$)	Exports (US$)	Exports as a percent of imports
60	Spain	37,942,881,948	32,740,267,959	115.89
62	Greece	13,560,731,209	11,526,621,528	117.65
64	Chile	7,438,435,984	6,291,974,407	118.22
65	Philippines	9,253,067,162	7,661,066,650	120.78
66	Mexico	25,215,695,652	20,806,478,261	121.19
67	DPRK	1,714,400,000	1,414,100,000	121.24
73	Korea, Rep.	25,245,953,457	20,369,193,589	123.94
74	Brazil	26,571,483,281	21,276,141,968	124.89
75	Botswana	704,709,213	562,918,168	125.19
76	Thailand	9,825,161,457	7,801,035,704	125.95
77	Vanuatu	47,384,760	37,603,233	126.01
78	Argentina	4,989,979,960	3,895,791,461	128.09

Sources: International Bank for Reconstruction and Development, *World Development Indicators 2003* (Washington, DC: World Bank, 2003), CD-ROM; KOTRA; ROK Ministry of Unification (MNU).

Table 13.5

Per Capita Exports: DPRK Rank in World, 1990 (out of 162 countries)

Rank	Country	Exports (US$)	Population	Per capita exports (US$)
120	Lebanon	511,008,107	3,635,000	140.58
121	Bhutan	80,434,166	600,110	134.03
122	Nigeria	12,365,872,842	96,203,000	128.54
123	Cape Verde	43,051,774	341,400	126.10
124	Equatorial Guinea	42,485,125	352,000	120.70
125	DPRK	1,939,000,000	20,018,546	96.86
126	Albania	312,500,000	3,277,000	95.36
127	Kenya	2,205,890,747	23,354,000	94.45
129	Haiti	502,200,000	6,473,000	77.58
130	Central African Republic	219,621,201	2,945,000	74.57
131	Congo, Democratic Republic	2,757,935,431	36,999,000	74.54

Sources: International Bank for Reconstruction and Development, *World Development Indicators 2003* (Washington, DC: World Bank, 2003), CD-ROM; U.S. Bureau of the Census; KOTRA; ROK Ministry of Unification (MNU).

Table 13.6

Exports as a Percent of Imports: DPRK Rank in World, 1990 (out of 152 countries)

Rank	Country	Imports (US$)	Exports (US$)	Exports as a percent of imports
108	India	31,485,000,000	23,028,000,000	136.72
109	Yemen, Rep.	969,083,969	689,312,977	140.59
110	Niger	544,691,917	372,432,639	146.25
111	Dominica	133,948,146	90,718,517	147.65
112	Grenada	138,799,998	93,796,295	147.98
113	Jordan	3,727,972,374	2,489,182,055	149.77
114	Pakistan	9,350,911,782	6,216,942,715	150.41
115	DPRK	2,945,405,700	1,938,861,818	151.91
116	Ghana	1,521,547,091	993,434,057	153.16
117	Greece	23,434,020,455	15,180,855,017	154.37
118	Solomon Islands	153,748,814	98,821,575	155.58
119	Albania	487,500,000	312,500,000	156.00
120	Romania	10,026,785,816	6,406,250,166	156.52
121	Ethiopia	850,961,538	534,884,615	159.09
122	St. Kitts and Nevis	132,366,664	82,385,184	160.67
123	Egypt, Arab Republic	14,109,376,402	8,646,612,831	163.18
124	Vanuatu	117,153,596	70,912,344	165.21

Sources: International Bank for Reconstruction and Development, *World Development Indicators 2003* (Washington, DC: World Bank, 2003), CD-ROM; KOTRA; ROK Ministry of Unification (MNU).

Table 13.7

Per Capita Exports: DPRK Rank in World, 2000 (out of 168 countries)

Rank	Country	Exports	Population	Per capita exports
157	Chad	233,152,617	7,694,000	30.30
158	DPRK	653,100,000	21,647,682	30.17
159	Niger	320,655,075	10,832,000	29.60
160	Uganda	656,000,000	22,210,000	29.54
161	Mozambique	469,194,516	17,691,000	26.52
162	Eritrea	97,489,583	4,097,000	23.80
163	Sierra Leone	110,005,233	5,031,000	21.87
164	Burkina Faso	236,804,405	11,274,000	21.00
165	Rwanda	149,602,258	7,709,000	19.41
166	Congo, Dem. Rep.	963,872,464	50,948,000	18.92
167	Ethiopia	984,250,978	64,298,000	15.31
168	Burundi	62,164,375	6,807,000	9.13

Sources: International Bank for Reconstruction and Development, *World Development Indicators 2003* (Washington, DC: World Bank, 2003), CD-ROM; U.S. Bureau of the Census; KOTRA; ROK Ministry of Unification (MNU).

Indicators: below Chad, and at less than half of India's level. (Reported per capita exports for Turkey were now nearly twenty-five times as high as those for the DPRK.) Although the nominal level of per capita exports for the world was nearly 2.5 times higher in 2000 than in 1980,[36] North Korea's nominal reported per capita export level fell by almost two-thirds over those years. At the same time, North Korea's imbalance between reported import and export earnings (with the former 2.8 times as great as the latter) looked to be among the ten most extreme recorded that year. While a glaring discrepancy between imports and exports did not automatically betoken aid-dependence—in the case of several outliers in Table 13.8, Lesotho and West Bank/Gaza among them, it speaks to the importance of remittances in the local balance of payments—North Korea's ratio of reported commercial export revenues to reported imports was even lower in 2000 than in such all-but-permanent wards of the ODA community as Haiti and Burkina Faso.

When it comes to trade performance and patterns of international finance, North Korea's downward trajectory and its current straits—its structural descent, so to speak, from Turkey to Haiti in just one generation—represents in part the misfortune of circumstance. The sudden and unexpected downfall of the Soviet Bloc was a disaster for the North Korean economic system: a disaster, indeed, from which the DPRK economy has not yet recovered.

But it would be a mistake for us to ignore the degree to which North Korea's aberrant and seemingly dysfunctional trade regimen today is actually a result of conscious purpose, deliberate design, and considered official effort. There is a deeply embedded *regime logic,* in other words, in the DPRK's tangential and precarious

Table 13.8

Exports as a Percent of Imports: DPRK Rank in World, 2000 (out of 158 countries)

Rank	Country	Imports (US$)	Exports (US$)	Imports as a percent of exports
146	Burundi	162,210,166	62,164,375	260.94
147	Haiti	1,321,141,442	501,946,403	263.20
148	Cape Verde	344,211,362	130,517,532	263.73
149	Burkina Faso	657,602,742	236,804,405	277.70
150	DPRK	1,847,800,000	653,100,000	282.93
151	Rwanda	441,108,545	149,602,258	294.85
152	Mozambique	1,526,308,504	469,194,516	325.30
153	Lesotho	762,704,061	226,049,911	337.41
154	French Polynesia	952,020,780	192,401,162	494.81
155	West Bank and Gaza	3,085,316,244	603,791,679	510.99
156	Eritrea	498,593,750	97,489,583	511.43
157	Timor-Leste	160,000,000	25,000,000	640.00
158	Palau	127,100,000	11,500,000	1105.22

Sources: International Bank for Reconstruction and Development, *World Development Indicators 2003* (Washington, DC: World Bank, 2003), CD-ROM; KOTRA; ROK Ministry of Unification (MNU).

relationship with the world economy—and far from being irrational, it is based on careful and cool-headed calculations about regime survival.

Consider the DPRK's trade performance over the past generation with the twenty-nine countries the IMF terms the "advanced economies"[37] (or what North Korean terminology would designate as the "capitalist" or "imperialist" countries). Between 1980 and 2000 the total size of the import market for this collectivity grew from about $1.8 trillion to about $6.1 trillion.

The DPRK, we recall, is precluded from exporting any appreciable volume of goods to the United States—the world's single largest import market—by Washington's thicket of sanctions and restrictions. But if we exclude the United States from the picture, the remaining advanced economy market for foreign imports is nevertheless vast and (at least in nominal terms) rapidly expanding—growing from about $1.5 billion in 1980 to $4.6 billion in 2000. DPRK exports to this group, however, remained negligible and stagnant over these decades—even after the loss of Soviet Bloc markets would seem to have added some urgency to cultivating new sources of commercial export revenue. In 1980 and 1990, North Korea's reported sales to this grouping totaled roughly $430 million and roughly $470 million, respectively. In 2000, the reported aggregate was about $560 million—but that total may have been inflated somewhat by an unusual and perhaps questionable $60 million in North Korean imports recorded that year by Spain. Yet even accepting that year's exceptional

Spanish data, the real level of North Korean exports to these "capitalist" countries would have been substantially lower in 2000 than it had been two decades earlier.[38]

Pyongyang's remarkably poor long-term performance in the advanced economies' huge markets is no accident. Rather it is a direct consequence of official DPRK policy and doctrine—including the special DPRK conception of "ideological and cultural infiltration." Official North Korean pronouncements relentlessly decry this danger: it is said to be an established technique by which outsiders attempt to undermine the foundations of established Communist states. A recent declamation will give the flavor of the general argument:

> It is the imperialist's old trick to carry out ideological and cultural infiltration prior to their launching of an aggression openly. Their bourgeois ideology and culture are reactionary toxins to paralyze people's ideological consciousness. Through such infiltration, they try to paralyze the independent consciousness of other nations and make them spineless. At the same time, they work to create illusions about capitalism and promote lifestyles among them based on the law of the jungle, in an attempt to induce the collapse of socialist and progressive nations. The ideological and cultural infiltration is their silent, crafty and villainous method of aggression, intervention and domination. . . .
>
> Through "economic exchange" and personnel interchange programs too, the imperialists are pushing their infiltration. . . . Exchange and cooperation activities in the economic and cultural fields have been on the rise since the beginning of the new century. The imperialists are making use of these activities as an important lever to push the infiltration of bourgeois ideology and culture. . . .
>
> The imperialists' ideological and cultural infiltration, if tolerated, will lead to the collapse and degeneration of society, to disorder and chaos, and even to the loss of the gains of the revolution. The collapse of socialism in the twentieth Century— and the revival of capitalism in its place—in some countries gave us the serious lesson that social deterioration begins with ideological degeneration and confusion on the ideological front throws every other front of society into chaos and, consequently, all the gains of the revolution go down the drain eventually.[39]

DPRK party lecture notes published in South Korea late in 2002 put the point more succinctly:

> The capitalist's ideological and cultural infiltration will never cease, and the struggle against it will continue, as long as the imperialists continue to exist in the world. . . .
>
> The great leader, Kim Jong Il, pointed out the following: "Today, the imperialists and reactionaries are tenaciously scheming to blow the wind of bourgeois liberalism into us." . . .
>
> Under these circumstances, if we turn away from reality and we regard it as someone else's problem, what will happen?

People will ideologically degenerate and weaken; cracks will develop in our socialist ideological position; and, in the end, our socialism will helplessly collapse. A case in point is the bitter lesson drawn from the miserable situations of the former Soviet Union and Eastern European countries.[40]

"Economic exchange" with the "capitalist" world, in other words, is explicitly and officially regarded by Pyongyang as a process that unleashes powerful, unpredictable and subversive forces—forces that ultimately erode the authority of socialist states. Viewed from this perspective, North Korea's record of trade performance vis-à-vis the advanced market economies though a record of failure—i.e., failure to integrate into the world economy—is at the same time a mark of *success*—i.e., effective containment of a potentially lethal security threat.

Moreover, it is worth recalling that the DPRK's public misgivings about ideological and cultural infiltration are longstanding, almost precisely paralleling the state's record of minimal export outreach to advanced market economies over the past generation. Although Pyongyang's pronouncements about ideological and cultural infiltration have attracted some attention abroad since the downfall of Soviet Bloc socialism, the slogan itself was *not* a response to that defining historical event. To the contrary, North Korean leadership had been highlighting the dangers of that tendency for at least a decade *before* the final collapse of the Soviet Union. At the Sixth Congress of the Korean Workers' Party in 1980, for example, Kim Il Sung inveighed against the dangers of cultural infiltration. And by 1981, he was urging North Korea's "workers and trade union members" to "combat the ideological and cultural infiltration of the imperialists and their subversive moves and sabotage."[41]

It is true that official directives from Pyongyang have from time to time discussed the desirability of significantly increasing the DPRK's volume of international trade. Against such comments, North Korea's extraordinary and continuing weakness in export performance may seem especially curious (insofar as it would be at least in theory so very easy to redress). But Pyongyang's conspicuous neglect of the revenue potential from trade with advanced market economies is not to be explained away as a prolonged fit of absent-mindedness. Instead it speaks to fundamental and abiding calculations in the DPRK's strategy for state survival.

If staying out of the poisonous embrace of the world economy is viewed as an imperative for survival by DPRK leadership, a corollary question inevitably arises: how to generate sufficient international resources to forestall economic collapse? To date, Pyongyang's answer has been: through nonmarket transactions. The DPRK has always pursued an aid-seeking international economic strategy—but in the post–Soviet Bloc era, the particulars of that approach have perforce mutated. In the kangsong taeguk era, North Korea's main tactics for generating international resources are viewed through the prism of the current state campaign for "Military-First Politics" (songun-chongchi).

Like the concept of ideological and cultural infiltration, the theory of Military-First Politics has received a tremendous amount of airtime in the North Korean media over the past five years. As a long official analysis in March 2003 instructed, it was a renewed emphasis on military development that enabled North Korea to conclude its Arduous March and to step onto the pathway to power and prosperity:

> Today, the peoples' struggle for their nations' independent development and prosperity is waged in an environment different from that of the last century. . . . In building a state in our era, it is essential to beef up the main force of the nation and fortify the revolutionary base, and, in this regard, it is most important to build up powerful military might. In today's world, without powerful military might, no country can . . . achieve development and prosperity.
>
> During . . . "the Arduous March" in our history, great Comrade Kim Jong Il firmly believed that the destiny of the people and the future of the revolution hinged on the barrel of a gun, and that we could break through the difficulties and lead the revolution to victory only by depending on the Army. . . . Through the arduous practice in which the Army was put to the fore and the unheard-of trials were overcome, the revolutionary philosophy that the barrel of a gun was precisely the revolution and the barrel of a gun was precisely the victory of socialism was originated.
>
> Our theory on the construction of a powerful state . . . is the embodiment of the profound truth that the base of national strength is military might, and the dignity and might of a country hinges on the barrel of a gun. . . . In a powerful state, the defense industry takes a leading and key position in the economy. . . .
>
> Today, by firmly adhering to the principle of putting prime effort into the defense industry and, based on this, by developing the overall economy ceaselessly, our party is brilliantly resolving the issue of consolidating the national strength of a powerful state.[42]

And how exactly does military power conduce to prosperity? The answer was strongly hinted at in a statement the following month:

> A country's development and the placement of importance on the military are linked as one. . . .
>
> Once we lay the foundations for a powerful *self-sustaining national defense industry*, we will be able to rejuvenate all economic fields, to include light industry and agriculture and enhance the quality of the people's lives.[43] [emphasis added]

This is a fascinating, and revealing, formulation. In most of the world today, a country's defense outlays are regarded as a weight that must be shouldered by the value-adding sectors of the national economy (hence the phrase "military burden"). North Korea's leadership, however, evidently entertains the concept of a "self-sustaining" defense sector—implying that Pyongyang views its military activities as *generating* resources rather than absorbing them. In the enunciated view of Pyongyang's leadership, the DPRK's military sector is the key to financing the recovery of the national economy.

It does not require a great deal of imagination to spell out the operational details of this approach. While forswearing any appreciable export revenues from legitimate commerce with advanced market economies, North Korean policy today seems to be banking on the possibility of financing state survival by exporting *strategic insecurity* to the rest of the world. In part, such dividends are derived from exports of merchandise (e.g., missile sales, international transfer of WMD technology). But these revenues also depend heavily on what might be described as an export of services: in this case, military extortion services (might we better call them "revenue-sensitive threat reduction services"?) based upon Pyongyang's nuclear development and ballistic missile programs.

The export of strategic insecurity can arguably account for much of the upsurge in North Korea's unexplained surfeit of imports over commercial export revenues since 1998—especially to the extent that Western aid policies in recent years can be described as appeasement motivated.[44] In an important tactical sense, that approach has enjoyed success—it has facilitated state survival under imposing constraints. But the territory demarcated by ideological and cultural infiltration on one side and Military-First Politics on the other is also, quite clearly, a sort of no-man's land—an inherently unstable niche in which survival is utterly contingent, and sustained development is utterly unlikely. North Korea's current strategic policy, in short, may be deferring the question of economic collapse—but it has not yet answered it.

Avoiding Economic Collapse Through Economic Reform Policies?

If the DPRK is sustaining its system through aid-seeking stratagems grounded in military menace, it would seem to have settled upon a particularly meager and highly uncertain mode of state finance. Even today, when this approach is "working," it is not clear that it generates sufficient funding to maintain (much less improve) the nation's aging and badly decayed industrial and transport infrastructure. Moreover, it may fail at any time for any number of reasons (donor "aid fatigue," DPRK miscalculation, or an external push for "regime change" in Pyongyang being but three of these).

Under these circumstances, a pragmatic reorientation of Pyongyang policy toward promoting sustained growth might serve as a more secure path to avoiding economic collapse and preserving the sovereignty of the North Korean state. It is widely argued that China and Vietnam have already demonstrated that it is feasible for a Marxist-Leninist government in an Asian setting simultaneously to execute a shift to an outward-oriented economic regimen, to achieve rapid economic growth, and to maintain leadership authority and political stability.

Whether "reform" and "outward orientation" could be consonant with the preservation of unquestioned power for North Korea's leadership is a question that will not detain us here.[45] Nor will we be diverted by a discussion of the potential problems and preconditions of any "reform" worthy of the name under contemporary North

Korean conditions. Instead we will briefly address two practical and subsidiary questions. First, how far have North Korea's much discussed "reforms" progressed to date? Second, if the DPRK were truly moving in the direction of "reform" and self-sustaining growth, how would we tell and what would we see?

North Korea's Economic Reforms to Date

Predictions that the DPRK would soon be embracing economic reform come from a family tree that is, if anything, even more prolific and even older than the lineage of predictions about imminent or eventual DPRK collapse. Scholars and analysts have been detecting quiet signs of reform and opening in the North Korean system since at least the 1980s.[46] The intensity of these premonitions typically waxed and waned according to the current temperatures in Pyongyang's relations with Washington and/or Seoul.[47] In July 2002, however, Pyongyang enacted a package of macroeconomic policy changes that marked a notable departure from DPRK practices over the previous generation. Moreover, North Korean leadership now sometimes openly describes these measures as economic reform[48]—a term the DPRK had vigorously rejected heretofore, on the grounds that no reforms were needed for the existing DPRK system.

The specifics of the July 2002 measures have been described in detail elsewhere.[49] Scholars and analysts have in addition offered some initial assessments of their significance and portent.[50] It may be cheering, of course, to see *anything* self-described as "reform" emanating from the organs of power in the DPRK. And by comparison to North Korea's economic policy adjustments since, say, the late 1960s, these measures may indeed be described as bold and experimental steps. Yet in a sense this only attests to how impoverished our expectations for DPRK policy have become over the decades. Viewed for what they are—rather than for what we might hope they will prefigure—the July 2002 package of economic changes can best be described as rather modest: both by comparison to economic reforms undertaken in other troubled economies and by comparison to the job that needs doing in the DPRK.

In practical terms, the July 2002 reform package—consumer price increases, wage hikes, currency devaluation, and ration system devolution—accomplished one important function: it re-monetized a limited portion of the DPRK domestic economy. By the late 1980s, the DPRK was already a shockingly demonetized operation: back of the envelope calculations for the year 1987 suggest that the wage bill in that year would have amounted to only about a third of North Korea's official net material product. Over the following decade and a half, the role of the national currency in domestic economic activity was progressively diminished. By the turn of the century, North Korea was perhaps the modern world's most completely demonetized economy—excepting only Khmer Rouge Cambodia, where for a time money was abolished altogether.

The re-emergence of money in North Korean economic life—and with it, the reemergence of a limited measure of open market activity—mark a critical improvement for the DPRK's tiny consumer sector. But it is important also to recognize just what this July 2002 package does *not* signify. It does *not,* to begin, represent an unambiguous move toward market principles. To the contrary, re-monetization of the domestic economy would be a sine qua non for the resurrection of the DPRK's badly broken central planning mechanism ("a planned economy without planning," in Mitsuhiko Kimura's apt phrase[51])—which has not managed to launch another multiyear national plan since the last one was concluded in 1993.

Limited re-monetization of the domestic economy, furthermore, does not signify transformation of the DPRK's badly distorted production structure. To the contrary, the manifestly limited supply-response of the DPRK economy to the July 2002 measures is indicated on the one hand by the subsequent steep drop in the black market exchange rate for the DPRK won,[52] and on the other by Pyongyang's hurried introduction, barely ten months after the July 2002 package, of new "people's life bonds"— worthless, utterly illiquid, and involuntarily assigned—in lieu of wages for workers or payments for enterprises.[53]

To be sure, the limited reintroduction of money in the DPRK domestic economy may elicit *some* supply response: a Leibenstein-style increase in "x-efficiency," for example.[54] But without the possibility of a reallocation of state resources in accordance with new demand conditions—and that possibility presently does not exist in the DPRK—the supply response must perforce be tepid and superficial. Thus, it should come as no surprise that, a year and a half into the new North Korean reform program, the World Food Program (WFP) should warn prospective donors that North Korea faced an imminent return to mass hunger barring an influx of new food aid into the relief pipeline[55]—heartening signs of newly sprouted "people's markets" and all the rest notwithstanding. The contrast is not a contradiction, but rather a faithful reflection of the scope and limits of the July 2002 reforms.

The July 2002 reforms, in brief, do not in themselves stave off the specter of DPRK economic collapse. Nor do they have any obvious or direct bearing on the prospects for a shift to China-style or Vietnam-style export-led growth. One need only contrast North Korea's patterns of trade performance over the past generation with those of China and Vietnam to appreciate this (see Figures 13.5 and 13.6). Vietnam began its push for export-orientation when its Soviet subsidies abruptly ended—whereas North Korea's export performance markedly worsened, and its aid dependence increased, after 1991. Though still predominantly agrarian societies, Vietnam and China both manage to export far more merchandise on a per capita basis today than does the ostensibly industrialized DPRK (precisely because of the linkages and supply-response mechanisms that the DPRK has assiduously prevented from taking root). At the risk of belaboring the obvious, the DPRK has not even begun to tinker with the macropolicies, or to promote the micro-institutions, that would permit a China- or Vietnam-style export response.[56] Thus, for the time being, economic survival through export-orientation is simply not in the cards for North Korea.

Figure 13.5   **Per Capita Exports, 1977–2003: China, Vietnam, and DPRK**

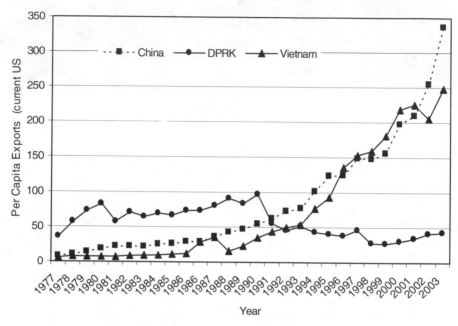

Figure 13.6   **Imports as a Percent of Exports, 1977–2003: China, Vietnam, and DPRK**

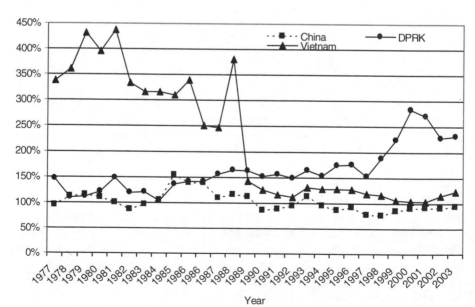

What Would a Genuine Reform and Opening Look Like for North Korea?

Let us here address three essential and inextricably linked features: the outward opening itself, military demobilization, and normalization of relations with the ROK.[57]

1. Economic Opening. If Pyongyang were to embark upon a genuine move toward an economic opening, what initial signs would outsiders be able to see? Some of these might include: (a) a meaningful departure from old economic themes, and a new a dialogue about economic issues, in DPRK propaganda and guidance organs; (b) doctrinal reorientation regarding profit-generating transactions in official DPRK pronouncements—especially those transactions involving foreign concerns; (c) an attempt on the part of the DPRK to settle its longstanding international "debt default" problems;[58] (d) a move toward greater economic transparency, that is, the publication of economic and social statistics describing the North Korean domestic situation; and (e) serious attempts to promulgate a legal framework for potential investors that might attract profit-seeking overseas entrepreneurs to North Korean soil. Although some observers may see glimmers of conditions (a) and (b), none of these "blinker lights" is flashing brightly and consistently in North Korea today.

2. Military Demobilization. Military demobilization would represent a critical aspect of North Korean "reform" and "opening" insofar as (a) a dismantling of Pyongyang's WMD programs would indicate that North Korean leadership was committed to earning its living from activities other than international military extortion, and (b) a reallocation of resources from the hypertrophied military to the civilian sectors would permit much more potentially productive economic activity in the DPRK.

To date, there is little evidence that North Korea has ever, at any point in its more than five decades of existence, voluntarily abjured any new instrument of military force that might possibly lie within its grasp. Today, indeed, such a renunciation would seem fundamentally inconsistent with the state's established policies of kangsong taeguk and military-first politics. Moreover, North Korea's commitment to developing weapons of mass destruction was implicitly reaffirmed in the exhortation that "We should hold fast to the military-first politics *and build up our military strength in every possible way*"[59] [emphasis added].

If North Korea *were* to head in a different direction with respect to proliferation, the first clear sign would be a new stance toward outside verification of North Korean WMD activities. For the time being, however, Pyongyang maintains that the U.S. calls for verification conceal "a dark ulterior motive to thoroughly investigate our national defense and military bases . . . [a plot to] completely dig out our interior organs [*sic*] . . ."[60] and that "the issue [of verification] can never be on the agenda for DPRK-U.S. talks."[61]

3. Normalization of DPRK-ROK Relations. The DPRK cannot execute a successful economic opening unless it demobilizes, and it cannot demobilize unless it comes to terms with the right of the Republic of Korea to co-exist with it on the Korean

peninsula. Consequently, one indispensable marker of movement would be a change in North Korea's official posture on the legitimacy of the ROK.

If North Korea were to undertake this change, the indications would be direct and unmistakable: its highest political figures and its official media would disclose that they were prepared to accept the existence of the South Korean state, that they recognized the ROK's right to conduct its own foreign policy, and that they respected (while respectfully disagreeing with) Seoul's decision to maintain a military alliance with the United States. Suffice it so say that no such disclosures have been offered to date.

In sum, there is little evidence that North Korea has yet embarked upon a path to reform and opening, with all the transformations in polity this path would foreshadow. That oft-discussed strategy for economic survival appears, as yet, to be an option unchosen by the DPRK's own leadership.

How long the DPRK can survive on its current trajectory is anyone's guess—and my personal guesses on this score have admittedly been somewhat off the mark, for the reasons indicated above. Nevertheless, the specter of economic collapse haunts the DPRK to this very day—and will not be exorcized until North Korea's leadership agrees to undertake what, in a very different context, they have called "a bold switchover." Whether Pyongyang accepts such a challenge remains to be seen.

Notes

This is an extended version of a paper originally prepared for an AEI-Korean Economic Institute (KEI)–Korea Institute for International Economic Policy (KIEP) conference in February 2004, and subsequently published in *Policy Review*, no. 127 (2004). The author wishes to thank Ms. Heather Dresser of AEI and Mr. Jay Philip Nash of Georgetown University for their research assistance.

1. See, for example, Noland, "Korea After Kim Jong-il," 12–19.

2. Nicholas Eberstadt, "The Coming Collapse of North Korea," *Wall Street Journal*, June 26, 1990. Students of miscellany and minutiae may be interested in the story of how that essay came to bear that particular title. I myself did not suggest it. In fact, when I picked up the morning paper and read it (this was before the email revolution), I was quite surprised—although as I reflected upon it, I realized it did fairly capture the thrust of my argument. The *Wall Street Journal* editorialist who wrote the title for my piece was a young man named David Frum—who, among many other accomplishments in a later life, would be widely credited with crafting the "Axis of Evil" language in President George W. Bush's 2002 State of the Union Address.

3. Perhaps most memorably, including this quote from my 1995 study *Korea Approaches Reunification:* "There is no reason at present to expect a reign by Kim Jong Il to be either stable or long."

4. Cf. the large interdisciplinary State Failure Task Force, the U.S. government-funded undertaking that spent six years attempting to devise econometric formulae by which to predict political upheaval and/or breakdown. (A report from this project can be accessed electronically from the University of Maryland's Center for International Development and Conflict Management, at www.cidcm.umd.edu/inscr/stfail.)

5. The distinction between art and science is elucidated in many places, but perhaps nowhere better and more clearly than in the writings of Michael Oakeshott. See Michael Oakeshott, *Rationalism in Politics*.

6. This is not to gainsay the utility of new mathematical or quantitative techniques used by particular contemporary stock-pickers and investors (e.g., Black-Sholes option pricing models, etc.). Some principals have enjoyed fantastic success with these tools and have amassed enormous personal wealth as a result. The point is that these successes are not *generalizable*, as scientific knowledge in principle always is. George Soros and Warren Buffett are practitioners of art, not science (as they themselves have often said).

7. One scholar who has explored aspects of this asymmetry is Timur Kuran. See, in particular, Timur Kuran, "Sparks and Prairie Fires," 41–78; Kuran, "The East European Revolution of 1989," 121–125; Kuran, "Now or Never," 7–48; and Kuran, "The Inevitability of Future Revolutionary Surprises," 1528–1551.

8. For an inventory and analysis, see Lipset and Bence, "Anticipations of the Failure of Communism," 169–210.

9. For example, Johnson, *Can South Africa Survive?* Seventeen years before the RSA peace transition to pan-racial democracy, Johnson explained why this occurrence was an impossibility.

10. Cf. Amalrik, *Will the Soviet Union Survive to 1984*. In a bitter historical irony, the USSR *did* last to 1984—but Amalrik did not.

11. Christopher de Bellaigue, "Turkey's Hidden Past," *New York Review of Books*, March 8, 2001.

12. For some background on the long relative decline of the Ottoman economy, see Faroqhi, McGowan, Quataert, and Pamuk, *An Economic and Social History of the Ottoman Empire*.

13. An indication of that decline may be gleaned from estimates by the economic historian Angus Maddison. In 1870, by his reckoning, per capita GDP for modern-day Turkey would have been $825 (in 1990 international dollars)—or about 39 percent of the contemporary level for Western Europe. By 1913—on the eve of World War I—Turkey's per capita GDP had risen to an estimated $1,213: but its relative standing had dropped to just 34 percent of the Western Europe level. (Derived from Angus Maddison, *The World Economy: Historical Statistics*, Paris: OECD Development Research Centre, 2003, 61, 156.)

14. Cohen and Gooch, *Military Misfortunes*.

15. Stephens has surmised that de Roebeck's "naval timidity" can be explained in part by "the high regard for battleships at that time. The loss of even one battleship was considered a national tragedy, more so than the loss of several thousand troops." Lt. Col. Cortez D. Stephens, "Gallipoli—What Went Right?" *Marine Corps Gazette*, vol. 77, no. 10 (October 1993), 73–77, citation at 74.

16. Fromkin, *A Peace To End All Peace*, 154.

17. Moorehead, *Gallipoli*, 72.

18. Fromkin, *A Peace To End All Peace*, 152.

19. Moorehead, *Gallipoli*, 77. In recent years a revisionist literature has challenged the notion that the Turkish and German defenders were critically short of ammunition. See, for example, Erickson, "One More Push," 158–176. The literature does not account for, or explain, Ottoman and German military officers' own contemporary reports—and subsequent reminiscences—to the contrary.

20. Watson, "The Gallipoli Blunder," 179.

21. Cited in Nevinson, *The Dardanelles Campaign*, 62.

22. Moorehead, *Gallipoli*, 74.

23. Fromkin, *A Peace To End All Peace*, 154.

24. Eberstadt, *The End of North Korea*.

25. Cf. Hirshleifer, *Economic Behavior in Adversity*.

26. See Goodkind and West, "The North Korean Famine," 219–238. Goodkind and West's modeling conjectures center on a range of 600,000 to 1,000,000 deaths for the late 1990s.

27. Not too long thereafter, the ROK Bank of Korea (BOK) declared that North Korea's economy had resumed economic growth; BOK reports, in fact, have suggested positive growth in the DPRK for 1999, and every subsequent year. Whether the BOK analysis can withstand

scrutiny is another question. For a skeptical look, see Eberstadt, "Prospects for Economic Recovery," 1–25.

28. The methods used here in reconstructing North Korea's patterns of merchandise trade are outlined in Eberstadt, "Prospects for Economic Recovery."

29. For some of the details, see Andrew Ward, "Six Convicted for Korea Payments," *Financial Times*, September 27, 2003, 9; Samuel Lem, "Seoul Court Convicts 6 over Summit Funds," *International Herald Tribune*, September 27, 2003, 2.

30. "Seoul Firmly Backs 'Perry Process,'" *Korea Times*, February 7, 2000.

31. Pyongyang's description of the transaction.

32. In theory, none of these American assistance resources should be included in "mirror statistics," but real-world practice is more haphazard. U.S. heavy fuel oil shipped to the DPRK in South Korean vessels, for example, has often been registered as "North-South trade" in the ROK Ministry of National Unification's inter-Korean trade statistics.

33. In the felicitous phrase of Cole and Lyman, *Korean Development*.

34. Interestingly, enough, a growing number of eminent historians and respected social scientists seem to be engaging in this pastime. See, for example, Polsby, *What If?*; Ferguson, *Virtual History*; and Cowley, *What Ifs? Of American History*.

35. Eberstadt, *Korea Approaches Reunification*, chapter 1.

36. Global calculations derived from IMF World Economic Outlook Database (September 2003), available at www.imf.org/external/pubs/ft/2003/02/data/index.htm and UN Population Division World Population Prospects Database, available at http://esa.un.org/unpp.

37. This grouping includes twenty-four of the current thirty OECD members (omitting the Czech Republic, Hungary, Mexico, Poland, the Slovak Republic, and Turkey) and five others: Cyprus, Hong Kong, Israel, Singapore, and Taiwan.

38. Between 1980 and 2000, the U.S. producer price index—the more appropriate deflator for international tradables—rose by 51 percent. Using that deflator, North Korea's inflation-adjusted export volume to this grouping of countries would have declined by about 16 percent between 1980 and 2000. Note that the grouping includes South Korea, and figures in inter-Korean trade.

39. *Nodong Sinmun*, April 20, 2003, translated as "DPRK Organ Scores 'Imperialists' for Ideological, Cultural Infiltration Schemes," U.S. Foreign Broadcast Information Service (FBIS), AFS Document Number KPP20030429000057.

40. *Chosun Ilbo*, December 20, 2002, translated as "'Full Text' of DPRK Lecture Program in Capitalists' 'Ideological and Cultural Infiltration,'" FBIS, AFS Document Number KPP20021222000016.

41. KCNA, November 30, 1981, reprinted as "Kim Il-sung's Speech to Trade Union Congress," *BBC Summary of World Broadcasts*, FE/6896/B/1, December 3, 1981.

42. *Nodong Sinmun*, March 21, 2003; translated text available on Nautilus Institute's Web site at www.nautilus.org/pub/ftp/napsnet/special_reports/MilitaryFirstDPRK.txt.

43. *Nodong Sinmun*, April 3, 2003; translated text available on Nautilus Web site at www.nautilus.org/pub/ftp/napsnet/special_reports/MilitaryFirstDPRK.txt.

44. Even ostensibly humanitarian food aid transfers to North Korea are informed by the reality of military extortion: think in particular of Kumchang-ri, and more generally whether the opaque rules under which food relief is administered in the DPRK would be tolerated by the international donor community in any other setting.

45. We may note in passing, however, that both Robert Scalapino and Ezra Vogel have suggested that North Korea might plausibly evolve from today's hermetic juche totalitarian system to a more familiar, Park Chung-Hee type authoritarian state—and the judgment of these two leading American authorities on modern Asia should be respectfully weighed in this consideration. (Scalapino, *The Last Leninists*, and Ezra Vogel, personal communications with the author, 1994–2004.)

46. See, for example, Lee, "North Korea's Closed Economy," 1264–1279; Oh, "North Korea's

Response to the World"; and Merrill, "North Korea's Halting Efforts at Economic Reform," 139–153. Each of these papers was written and initially presented in the 1980s.

47. The announcement of the Pyongyang North-South Summit occasioned an especially vigorous pulsation of such premonitions. Thus, for example, Marcus Noland in June 2000: "The secret visit to Beijing last month by Kim Jong Il supports the argument that this is the real deal and that the North Koreans are serious about opening to the outside world." (Marcus Noland, "The Meaning in the Meeting of the Two Koreas: Out of Isolation," *Washington Post*, June 12, 2000, A21.) This, of course, was before the "outside world" had learned the true details of the "real deal" underpinning that historic summit.

48. Thus SPA President Kim Yong Nam in August 2002 in a conversation with UN officials: "We are reactivating the whole field of the national economy. . . . We are reforming the economic system on the principle of profitability." (Cited in United Nations, *Consolidated Inter-Agency Appeal 2003: Democratic People's Republic of Korea* (November 2002), 127, available at www.reliefweb.int/appeals/2003/files/dprk03.pdf.

Note, however, that the term "reform" has not yet been accepted by the DPRK media, which still treats the concept as anathema. This March 2003 formulation from *Minju Choson* remains representative: "Even though the imperialists are trying to stifle our economy by inducing it to 'reform' and 'opening,' our economic management is being improved without deviating even an inch from socialist principles." (*Minju Choson*, March 6, 2003, translated as "DPRK Cabinet Organ Discusses Improving Economic Management," FBIS, AFS Document Number KPP 20030313000122.)

49. See, for example, United Nations, *Consolidated Inter-Agency Appeal 2003: Democratic People's Republic of Korea* (November 2002), 127–132, available at www.reliefweb.int/appeals/2003/files/dprk03.pdf.

50. For cautiously optimistic analyses, see Marcus Noland, "West-Bound Train Leaving the Station: Pyongyang on the Reform Track," October 2002, available at www.iie.com/publications/papers/noland1002.htm; Ruediger Frank, "A Socialist Market Economy in North Korea? Systemic Restrictions and a Quantitative Analysis" (unpublished paper, Columbia University, 2003); and Ruediger Frank, "North Korea: 'Gigantic Chance' and a Systemic Change," *NAPSNET Policy Forum Online PFO 3–31*, May 9, 2003, available at www.nautilus.org/for a/security /0331_Frank.html. For a more cautiously skeptical assessment, see William J. Newcomb, "Economic Development in North Korea: Reflections on North Korea's Economic Reform," in *2003 Korea's Economy* (Washington, DC: Korea Economic Institute, May 2003), 57–60.

51. Mitsuhiko Kimura, "A Planned Economy Without Planning: *Su-ryong's* North Korea," *Discussion Paper F-081*, March 1994, Faculty of Economics, Tezukayama University.

52. The initial July 2002 exchange rate was set at 153 won to the U.S. dollar. By October 2003, DPRK government foreign exchange booths in Pyongyang were paying 900 won per dollar. *Yonhap* (Seoul), "N. Korea Depreciate (*sic*) Its Currency. Adopts Floating Rates: Asahi," October 4, 2003. By July 2004—two years into the July 2002 measures—the unofficial rate for the DPRK won was reportedly about 1,600 to the U.S. dollar. (*Chosun Ilbo*, July 27, 2004; translated as "South Korea Reports Defections Rising Despite North Efforts to Tighten Border," *BBC Worldwide Monitoring*, July 29, 2004.) By those numbers, the pace of depreciation against the dollar (a serviceable proxy for the implied pace of domestic price inflation) averaged 10 percent per month since the advent of the new economic measures. And the decline continues, in August, 2004, the director of the World Food Programme office in Pyongyang stated that prices in local North Korean markets had risen 10–15 percent during the previous two months. (Cindy Sui, "No Turning Back for North Korea's Reforms: UN Official," Agence France Presse, August 18, 2004.) If that estimate is roughly correct, the rate of inflation in these markets is running at an annualized rate of 75 percent to 130 percent per annum—fairly compelling testimony that too much currency is still chasing too few goods in the DPRK domestic market. ROK government reports, for their part, put the unofficial exchange rate in North Korea at 2,000 DPRK won to the dollar as of September 2004. (Personal communica-

tion with S. H. Chung, ROK Embassy, Washington D.C., September 2004.) To go by those numbers, the value of the won has been falling by about 10 percent a month, or 228 percent a year, since the advent of the July 2002 "reforms."

53. KCNA, May 8, 2003, reprinted as "North Korea Reports 'Brisk' Sale of Public Bonds," *BBC Worldwide Monitoring*, May 8, 2003.

54. Leibenstein, "Allocative Efficiency Versus 'X-Efficiency," 392–415.

55. Kim So-young, "WFP Warns of N.K. Food Crisis," *Korea Herald*, February 11, 2004; Joe McDonald, "WFP Makes Emergency Food Appeal for North Korea, Saying Supplies Nearly Exhausted," Associated Press, February 9, 2004. The WFP's own institutional interests, to be sure, comport with an alarmist reading of the North Korean food situation—but that does not mean the WFP's warnings were unfounded.

56. To date, the only appreciable movement in these general areas would seem to be the events that found their denouement in the September–October 2002 Yang Bin fiasco.

57. The following paragraphs draw on Eberstadt, "If North Korea were Really Reforming," 20–46.

58. For the past quarter century, the DPRK has been in effective default on roughly $1 billion in European, Japanese, and Australian loans contracted in the early 1970s. For more detail, see Eberstadt, *Korea Approaches Reunification*, chapter 1.

59. *Nodong Sinmun*, June 1, 2001, translated as "DPRK Daily Full Front-Page Article Discusses 'National Pride,'" FBIS-EAS-2001–0629, July 3, 2001.

60. *Pyongyang Central Broadcasting Station*, July 8, 2001, translated as "North Korea Demands Compensation from USA for Delay to Reactor Project," *BBC Monitoring Asia Pacific–Political Supplied by BBC Worldwide Monitoring*, July 8, 2001.

61. *Yonhap* News Service, August 1, 2001, reprinted as "ROK's Yonhap: N.K. Says U.S. Demands for Verification Ruse to Disarm It," *FBIS*-EAS-2001–0801, August 2, 2001.

Bibliography

Abramowitz, Morton I., and James T. Laney. 2003. "Meeting the North Korean Nuclear Challenge." Report of an independent task force sponsored by the Council on Foreign Relations.

Adler, Emanuel, and Michael Barnett, eds. 1998. *Security Communities.* Cambridge: Cambridge University Press.

Albright, Madeleine. 2003. *Madam Secretary—A Memoir.* New York: Easton Press.

Amalrik, Andrei. 1970. *Will the Soviet Union Survive to 1984?* New York: Harper & Row.

An, Tai Sung. 1983. *North Korea in Transition: From Dictatorship to Dynasty.* Westport, CT: Greenwood Press.

Armstrong, Charles K. 2003. *The North Korean Revolution: 1945–1950.* Ithaca, NY, and London: Cornell University Press.

Axelrod, Robert M. 1967. "Conflict of Interest: An Axiomatic Approach." *Journal of Conflict Resolution* 11: 87–99.

Barnett, Thomas P.M. 2004. *The Pentagon's New Map: War and Peace in the Twenty-First Century.* New York: G.P. Putnam & Sons.

Becker, Jasper. 2005. *Rogue State: The Continuing Threat of North Korea.* New York: Oxford University Press.

Bermudez, Joseph S. 2001. *Shield of the Great Leader: The Armed Forces of North Korea.* Canberra, Australia: Allen and Unwin.

Bermudez, Joseph S. Jr. 1998. *North Korean Special Forces,* 2nd ed. Annapolis: Naval Institute Press.

Breen, Michael. 2004. *Kim Jong Il: North Korean Leader.* New York: John Wiley & Sons.

Buzo, Adrian. 1999. *The Guerilla Dynasty: Politics and Leadership in North Korea.* Boulder, CO: Westview Press.

Campbell, Kurt M. 2001. "Bush's First 100 Days in Asia." *Far Eastern Economic Review* (May 10): 32.

Carpenter, Ted Galen, and Doug Bandow. 2005. *The Korean Conundrum: America's Troubled Relations with North and South Korea.* New York: Palgrave Macmillan.

Cha, Victor D. 2002. "Korea's Place in the Axis." *Foreign Affairs* 81, no. 3 (May/June): 79–92.

Cha, Victor D., and David C. Kang. 2003. *Nuclear North Korea: A Debate on Engagement Strategies.* New York: Columbia University Press.

———. 2004. "Can North Korea Be Engaged? An Exchange Between Victor D. Cha and David C. Kang." *Survival* 46, no. 2 (Summer): 89–95.

Chanda, Nayan. 2001. "Kim Flirts with Chinese Reform." *Far Eastern Economic Review* (February 8): 26.

Chanlett-Avery, Emma. 2003. "North Korean Supporters in Japan: Issues for U.S. Policy." *CRS Report for Congress* (RL32137) (November 7). Washington, DC: Congressional Research Service, The Library of Congress.

Chin, Yong-san. 2002. "China-DPRK Economic Ties—Impact on Life in DPRK Society." *Proceedings of the 1st World Congress of Korean Studies,* Vol. 2. Seoul: Academy of Korean Studies.

"China to Provide US$50 Million to Finance Glass Plant in North Korea." 2003. *Vantage Point* (July): 56.

"Chinese Fuel, Grain Exports to North Korea Dwindle in 2002." 2003. *Vantage Point* (July): 56.

Chinhung Trading Company. 2001. "North Korea's Overseas Trade." Seoul.

Cho, Seung-ryoul. 2004. "Vision of Northeast Asian Peace and Cooperation Regime in Relation to Six-Party Talks." *Vantage Point* 27, no. 3 (March): 42–52.

Chong, Bong-uk. 1999. "Military Rule in Full Swing." *Vantage Point* (April): 2–9.

———. 2003. "A Year After Radical Economic Reforms." *Vantage Point* (July): 2–8.

———. 2003. "Improving Pyongyang-Beijing Ties." *Vantage Point* (August): 2–7.

———. 2003. "The Project of Issuing Public Bonds." *Vantage Point* (May): 14–18.

———. 2004. "Economic Programs and State Budget," *Vantage Point* (April): 2–8.

———. 2004. "Economic Reforms Under Way." *Vantage Point* 27, no. 10 (October 4): 2–7.

———. 2004. "Kim Jong-Il's Military-First Politics." *Vantage Point* 27, no. 9 (September): 2–8.

———. 2004. "North Korean Leadership After Kim Il-Sung." *Vantage Point* 27, no. 6 (June): 2–9.

———. 2004. "Six-Way Talks in New Stage." *Vantage Point* 27, no. 7 (July): 2–7.

———. 2004. "Tough Multilateral Negotiations." *Vantage Point* 27, no. 3 (March): 2–5.

Choong, Yong Ahn, ed. 2003. *North Korea—Development Report 2002/03*. Seoul: Korea Institute for International Economic Policy.

Chung, Yun-ho. 2003. "The Prospects for Economic Reform in North Korea and the Direction of its Economic Development." *Vantage Point* (May): 43–53.

"Civic Efforts on to Keep Inter-Korean Tour." 2004. *Vantage Point* (March): 25–27.

Clinton, William J. 2004. *My Life.* New York: Random House.

Cohen, Elliot, and John Gooch. 1990. *Military Misfortunes: The Anatomy of Failure in War.* New York: Vintage Press.

Cole, David C., and Princeton Lyman. 1971. *Korean Development: The Interplay of Politics and Economics.* Cambridge, MA: Harvard University Press.

"Construction of Kaesong Industrial Park." 2004. *Vantage Point* (July): 23–24.

Cornell, Erik. 2002. *North Korea Under Communism: Report of an Envoy to Paradise.* London: Curzon Press.

Council on Foreign Relations. 1995. *Success or Sellout? The U.S–North Korean Nuclear Accord.* Report. New York: CFR and the Seoul Forum for International Affairs.

Cowley, Robert. 2003. *What Ifs? Of American History: Eminent Historians Imagine What Might Have Been.* New York: G.P. Putnam.

Cumings, Bruce. 1993. "The Corporate State in North Korea." In *State and Society in Contemporary Korea,* edited by Hagen Koo, 197–230. New York: Cornell University Press.

———. 1997. *Korea's Place in the Sun: A Modern History.* New York: Norton.

———. 2004. *North Korea: Another Country.* New York: The New Press.

Dictionary of Political Terminology (North Korean). 1970. Pyongyang: The Social Science Publishing House.

Eberstadt, Nicholas. 1995. *Korea Approaches Reunification.* Armonk, NY: M.E. Sharpe.

———. 1997. "Hastening Korean Reunification." *Foreign Affairs* 76, no. 2 (March/April): 77–92.

———. 1997. "Why North Korea Will Muddle Through?" *Foreign Affairs* 76, no. 4: 105–18.

———. 1999. *The End of North Korea.* Washington, DC: The AEI Press.

———. 2001. "Prospects for Economic Recovery: Perceptions and Evidence." In *Joint US-Korean Academic Studies,* 1–25. Washington, DC: Korea Economic Institute.

———. 2002. "If North Korea Were Really Reforming, How Could We Tell—and What Would We Be Able to See?" *Korea and World Affairs* 26, no. 2 (Spring): 20–46.

Eberstadt, Nicholas, and Richard J. Ellings, eds. 2001. *Korea's Future and the Great Powers.* Seattle: University of Washington Press.

Eliot Jung, Young-soo Kim, and Takayuki Kobayashi. 2003. *Confrontation and Innovation on the Korean Peninsula.* Washington, DC: Korea Economic Institute.

Erickson, Edward J. 2001. "One More Push: Forcing the Dardanelles in March 1915." *Journal of Strategic Studies* 24, no. 3 (September): 158–76.

Faroqhi, Suraiya, Bruce McGowan, Donald Quataert, and Sevket Pamuk. *An Economic and Social History of the Ottoman Empire: Volume Two, 1600–1914.* New York: Cambridge University Press.

Feffer, John. 2003. *North Korea/South Korea: U.S. Policies and the Korean Peninsula.* New York: Seven Stories Books.

Feickert, Andrew. 2003. *North Korean Ballistic Missile Threat to the United States.* Washington, DC: Congressional Research Service (October 1).

Ferguson, Joseph. 2003. "A Chilly Fall for U.S.–Russia Relations." *Comparative Connections* 5, no. 4: 59–66.

Ferguson, Niall, ed. 1997. *Virtual History: Alternatives and Counterfactuals.* London: Picador.

"Five Foreign Firms Prospecting for Oil in North Korea." *Vantage Point* (October): 57.

Fromkin, David. 1989. *A Peace to End All Peace: Creating the Modern Middle East 1914– 1922.* New York: Henry Holt.

Fukuyama, Francis. 2005. "Re-Envisioning Asia." *Foreign Affairs* 84, no. 1 (January/February): 75–87.

Furukawa, Katsu. 2003. "Japan's View of the Korea Crisis." North Korea Special Collection (March 31). Monterey, CA: Monterey Institute of International Studies.

Gaddis, John Lewis. 2005. "Grand Strategy in the Second Term." *Foreign Affairs* 84, no. 1 (January/February): 2–15.

Gills, B.K. 1996. *Korea Versus Korea: A Case of Contested Legitimacy.* London: Routledge.

Goodkind, Daniel, and Loraine West. 2001. "The North Korean Famine and Its Demographic Impact." *Population and Development Review* 27, no. 2 (June): 219–38.

Grinker, Roy Richard. 1998. *Korea and Its Future: Unification and the Unfinished War.* New York: St. Martin's Press.

Gurtov, Mel. 2002. "Common Security in North Korea: Quest for a New Paradigm in Inter-Korean Relations." *Asian Survey* 42, no. 3 (May–June): 397–418.

Handbook on North Korea. 1998. 1st revision. Seoul: Naewoe Press.

Harnisch, Sebastian. 2002. "U.S.–North Korean Relations Under the Bush Administration— From 'Slow Go' to 'No Go.'" *Asian Survey* (November/December): 856–82.

Harrison, Selig. 2002. *Korean Endgame: A Strategy for Reunification and U.S. Disengagement.* Princeton: Princeton University Press.

———. 2005. "Did North Korea Cheat?" *Foreign Affairs* 84, no. 1 (January/February): 99–110.

Hirshleifer, Jack. 1987. *Economic Behavior in Adversity.* Chicago: University of Chicago Press.

Hong, Ihk-pyo. 2002. "A Shift Toward Capitalism? Recent Economic Reforms in North Korea." *East Asia Review* 14 (Winter): 93–106.

Hong, Kwanhee. 1996. "North Korea's Foreign Policy for National Security: A Regime Survival Strategy." *The Korean Journal of Unification Studies* 5, no. 2: 55–82.

Hong, Soon-Jick. 2003. "North Korean Nuclear Crisis: Prospects and Policy Directions." *East Asian Review* (Autumn): 23–38.

Hong, Wan-Suk. 2001. "Putin Sidae Russiaui Sin Hanbandojeonryak: Bunseokkwa Daeeung" (Russia's New Strategies Toward the Korean Peninsula Under the Putin Administration: Analysis and Response). *Hanguk Jeongchihak Hoebo* (Korean Political Science Review) 35, no. 3 (Autumn): 350–55.

Hunter, Helen-Louise. 1999. *Kim Il-song's North Korea.* Westport, CT: Praeger.

Hwang, Eui-gak. 1993. *The Korean Economies.* Oxford: Clarendon Press.

Hwang, Jang-yop. 1999. *Memoir: Naneun Yoksa'e Jinrireul Boatta* (Memoir: I Saw the Truth of History). Seoul: Hanul.

———. 2000. *Nation's Life Is More Important than Individual Life* (in Korean). Seoul: Shidae Jungshin.

International Institute for Strategic Studies (IISS). 2004. *North Korea's Weapons Programmes: A Net Assessment.* London: IISS.

Johnson, R.W. 1977. *Can South Africa Survive?* New York: Oxford University Press.

Joo, Seung-Ho, and Tae-Hwan Kwak. 2001. "Military Relations Between Russia and North Korea." *The Journal of East Asian Affairs* 15, no. 2 (Fall/Winter): 305–6.

Jung, Eliot S., Yongsoo Kim, and Takayuki Kobayashi. 2003. "North Korea's Special Economic Zones: Obstacles and Opportunities." In *Confrontation and Innovation on the Korean Peninsula.* Washington, DC: Korea Economic Institute.

Kang, Chol-Hwan, and Pierre Rigoulot. 2001. *The Aquariums of Pyongyang: Ten Years in the North Korean Gulag.* Translated by Yair Reiner. New York: Basic Books.

KIEP. 2004. *North Korea Development Report: 2003/04.* Seoul: Korea Institute for International Economic Policy.

Kihl, Young Whan. 1984. *Politics and Policies in Divided Korea: Regimes in Contest.* Boulder, CO: Westview.

———, ed. 1994. *Korea and the World: Beyond the Cold War.* Boulder, CO: Westview.

———. 1997. "North Korea's Political Problem: The Regime Survival Strategy." *The Economics of Korean Reunification* 2, no. 2 (Summer): 82–97.

———. 2000. "The DPRK and Its Relations with the ROK." In *Korea Briefing 1997–1999: Challenges and Change at the Turn of the Century,* edited by Kongdan Oh, 123–44. New York: The Asia Society and M.E. Sharpe.

———. 2001. Overcoming the Cold War Legacy in Korea? The Inter-Korean Summit One Year Later. *International Journal of Korean Studies* 5, no. 2 (Fall/Winter): 1–24.

———. 2002. "Security on the Korean Peninsula: Continuity and Change." *Security Dialogue* 33, no. 1 (March): 59–72.

———. 2005. *Transforming Korean Politics: Democracy, Reform and Culture.* Armonk, NY: M.E. Sharpe.

Kihl, Young Whan, and Peter Hayes, eds. 1997. *Peace and Security in Northeast Asia: The Nuclear Issue and the Korean Peninsula.* Armonk, NY: M.E. Sharpe.

Kim, Gye-dong. 1999. "North Korea's Military-First Politics and Anti-South Strategy." *Vantage Point* (January): 9.

Kim, Hakjoon. 2003. "North Korea Since Kim Jong Il Became General Secretary of the Korean Workers' Party in 1997." *Korea and World Affairs* 27, no. 4 (Winter): 511–43.

Kim, Han Kyo. 1994. "Korean Unification in Historical Perspective." In *Korea and the World,* edited by Young Whan Kihl, 17–28. Boulder, CO: Westview Press.

Kim, Hong Nack. 1994. "Japan and North Korea: Normalization Talks Between Pyongyang and Tokyo." In *Korea and the World: Beyond the Cold War,* edited by Young Whan Kihl, 111–29. Boulder, CO: Westview Press.

———. 1998. "Japan in North Korean Foreign Policy." In *North Korean Foreign Relations in the Post–Cold War Era,* edited by Samuel S. Kim, 117. New York: Oxford University Press.

———. 2003. "U.S.–North Korean Relations Under the Bush Administration: Problems and Prospects." *Korea and World Affairs* (Spring): 34–66.

———. 2004. "Japanese-North Korea Relations After the 2002 Pyongyang Summit: Problems and Prospects." *Korea and World Affairs* 28, no. 2 (Summer): 163–97.

Kim, Hong Nack, and Jack L. Hammersmith. 2000. "Japanese–North Korean Relations in the Post Kim Il-Sung Era." *Korea and World Affairs* (Winter): 611–16.

Kim, Ilpyong J. 1973. *The Politics of Chinese Communism: Kiangsi Under the Soviets.* Berkeley: University of California Press.

Kim, Ilpyong J. 2003. *Historical Dictionary of North Korea.* Lanham, MD, and Oxford: Scarecrow Press.

"Kim Jong Il Era Dawns with Military Status Enhanced." 1988. *Vantage Point* (September).

Kim, Keun-sik. 2002. "Kim Jong Il Sidae Bukhanui Dang-Jeong-Gun Gwangye Byeonhwa" (The Change in North Korea's Party-Government-Military Relationship in the Kim

Jong-Il Era: The Implications of the Changes of the 'Great Leader' [Suryong] System). *Hanguk Jeongchihak Hoebo (Korean Political Science Review)* 36, no. 2 (Summer): 352–56.

Kim, Kyoung-soo. 2002. "North Korea's CB Weapons Threat and Capability." *Korean Journal of Defense Analysis* 14, no. 1 (Spring): 69–95.

Kim, Samuel S., ed. 1998. *North Korean Foreign Relations in the Post–Cold War Era.* Hong Kong and New York: Oxford University Press.

———. 2001. "North Korea in 2000—Surviving Through High Hopes of Summit Diplomacy." *Asian Survey* 41, no. 1 (January/February): 12–29.

———. 2001. "The Making of China's Korea Policy in the Era of Reform." In *The Making of Chinese Foreign and Security Policy in the Era of Reform,* edited by David M. Lampton, 371–408. Stanford, CA: Stanford University Press.

———, ed. 2001. *The North Korean System in the Post–Cold War Era.* New York: Palgrave.

———. 2003. "China's Path to Great Power Status in the Globalization Era." *Asian Perspective* 27, no. 1: 35–75.

———, ed. 2004. *Inter-Korean Relations: Problems and Prospects.* New York: Palgrave Macmillan.

Kim, Samuel S., and Tai Hwan Lee, eds. 2002. *North Korea and Northeast Asia.* Lanham, MD: Rowman & Littlefield.

Kim, Taeho. 1999. "Strategic Relations Between Beijing and Pyongyang: Growing Strains and Lingering Ties." In *China's Military Faces the Future,* edited by James R. Lilley and David Shambaugh, 306–8. Armonk, NY: M.E. Sharpe.

Kim, Yeon Chul. 2002. "Bukhan Singyeongjae Jeonryakui Seonggong Jogeon: Sijangjaedo Hyeongseonggwa Talnaengjeon Gukjaehwangyeong" (The Successful Precondition of North Korea's New Economic Strategy: The Formation of Market Institutions and Post–Cold War International Environment). *Gukga Jeonryak (National Strategy)* 8, no. 4 (Winter): 8–9.

Kleiman, Aaron. 1997. North Korean Decision-Making and Rational Choice Theory, available at www. personal.umich.edu/~rtanter/F97PS472Papers/Kleiman.Aaron.

Koh, Byung Chul, ed. 2004. *North Korea and the World: Explaining Pyongyang's Foreign Policy.* Seoul: Kyungnam University Press.

Koh, Dae-Won. 2004. "Dynamics of Inter-Korean Conflict and North Korea's Recent Policy Changes." *Asian Survey* 44, no. 3 (May/June): 422–41.

Koh, Hyunwook. 2002. "Prospects for Opening in North Korea and Inter-Korean Economic Cooperation." *Asian Perspective* 26, no. 3: 94, 100–5.

"Korean Banks to Support Firms in North Korean Industrial Complex." 2004. *Vantage Point* (July): 57.

Kuran, Timur. 1991. "The East European Revolution of 1989: Is It Surprising That We Were Surprised?" *American Economic Review* 81, no. 1: 121–25.

———. 1989. "Sparks and Prairie Fires: A Theory of Unanticipated Political Revolution." *Public Choice* 61, nos. 1–2 (April): 41–78.

———. 1991. "Now or Never: The Element of Surprise in the East European Revolutions of 1989." *World Politics* 44, no. 1 (October): 7–48.

———. 1995. "The Inevitability of Future Revolutionary Surprises." *American Journal of Sociology* 100, no. 4 (May): 1528–51.

Kwak, Seung-ji. 2002. "Sinuiju Special Administrative Region." *Vantage Point* (October): 2–10.

———. 2003. "Solution to the North's Nuclear Weapons Problem." *Vantage Point* (November): 2–8.

Kwak, Tae-Hwan, ed. 1997. *The Four Powers and Korean Unification Strategies.* Seoul: Kyungnam University Press.

Kwon, Manhak. 2001. "Talgukgasahoejuuiui Yeoreo Gilgwa Bukhan: Bunggoewa Gaehyuk" (Pathways from State Socialism and North Korea: The Political Economy of Collapse and Reform). *Hanguk Jeongchihak Hoebo (Korean Political Science Review)* 35, no. 4 (Winter): 256.

Kwon, Soyoung. 2003. "State Building in North Korea: From a 'Self-Reliant' to a Military-First State." *Asian Affairs* 34, no. 3 (November): 286–95.

Lampton, David M., and Richard Daniel Ewing. 2004. *The U.S.–China Relationship Facing International Security Crises: Three Case Studies in Post-9/11 Bilateral Relations.* Washington, DC: The Nixon Center.

Laney, James T., and Jason T. Shaplen. 2003. "How to Deal with North Korea." *Foreign Affairs* (March/April): 16–30.

Lankov, Andrei N. 2002. *From Stalin to Kim Il Sung: The Formation of North Korea, 1945–1960.* London: Hurst.

———. 2004. *Crisis in North Korea: The Failure of De-Stalinization, 1956.* Honolulu: University of Hawaii Press.

Lawrence, Susan V., Murray Hiebert, Jay Solomon, and Jung Min Kim. 2002. "North Korea Nuclear Crisis: Time to Talk." *Far Eastern Economic Review* (January 23): 12–16.

Lee, Chong-Sik. 1978. *Korean Workers' Party: A Short History.* Stanford, CA: Hoover Institution Press.

Lee, Hy-Sang. 1988. "North Korea's Closed Economy: The Hidden Opening." *Asian Survey* 28, no. 12 (December): 1264–79.

———. 2001. *North Korea: A Strange Socialist Fortress.* Westport, CT: Praeger.

Leibenstein, Harvey. 1996. "Allocative Efficiency Versus 'x-Efficiency.'" *American Economic Review* 56, no. 3 (June): 392–415.

Li Gun. 2004. "Various Requisites for Resolving the Nuclear Question." *The People's Korea* (February 28): 3–4.

Li, Jong Seok. 2001. *PukHan-Chungkuk Kwankyae 1945–2000* (DPRK-PRC Relations, 1945–2000). Seoul: Jungsim.

Lim, Hyun-Chin, and Chung Young Chul. 2004. "Is North Korea Moving Toward a Market Economy?" *Korea Focus* 12, no. 4 (July–August): 49–79.

Lintner, Bertil. 2004. "North Korea, Shop Till You Drop." *Far Eastern Economic Review* (May 13): 14–19.

Lipset, Seymour Martin, and Georgy Bence. 1994. "Anticipations of the Failure of Communism." *Theory and Society* 23, no. 2 (April): 169–210.

Liu Jinzhi and Yang Huaisheng, eds. 1994. *Zhongguo dui Chaoxian he Hanguo zhengci wenjian huibian (1958–1962)* (A Collection of Documents on China's Policy Toward the Democratic People's Republic of Korea and the Republic of Korea [1958–1962]), Vol. 3. Beijing: Zhongguo shehui kexue chubanshe.

Liu Ming. 2003. "China and the North Korean Crisis: Facing Test and Transition." *Pacific Affairs* 76, no. 3: 370–72.

Luse, Keith, and Frank Jannuzi. 2004. *North Korea: Status Report on Nuclear Program, Humanitarian Issues and Economic Reforms.* Washington, DC: U.S. Government Printing Office.

"Manufactures Selling Consumer Goods on Markets." 2004. *Vantage Point* (January): 28.

Manyin, Mark E., Emma Chanlett-Avery, and Helene Marchart. 2005. *North Korea: A Chronology of Events, October 2002–December 2004.* CRS Report for Congress, The Library of Congress (January 24).

Mazarr, Michael J. 1995. *North Korea and the Bomb.* New York: St. Martin's Press.

McCormack, Gavan. 2004. *Target North Korea: Pushing North Korea to the Brink of Nuclear Catastrophe.* New York: Nation Books.

McVadon, Eric A. 2001. "China's Goals and Strategies for the Korean Peninsula." In *Planning for a Peaceful Korea,* edited by Henry D. Sokolski, 170. Carlisle, PA: Strategic Studies Institute.

Merrill, John. 1991. "North Korea's Halting Efforts at Economic Reform." In *North Korea in Transition,* edited by Chong-Sik Lee and Se-Hee Yoo, 139–53. Berkeley, CA: Institute of East Asian Studies.

Ministry of Unification. 2003. "Overview of Inter-Korean Exchange and Cooperation for 2003." *Monthly Report: Intra-Korean Interchange & Cooperation and Humanitarian Projects*. Seoul.

Moltz, James. 2000. "Russian Nuclear Regionalism: Emerging Local Influences over Far Eastern Facilities." *NBR Analysis* 11, no. 4 (December): 35–57.

Moltz, James Clay, and Alexandre Y. Mansourov, eds. 2000. *The North Korean Nuclear Program: Security, Strategy, and New Perspectives from Russia.* London: Routledge.

Moon, Chung In, ed. 1998. *Understanding Regime Dynamics in North Korea.* Seoul: Yonsei University Press.

———. 2004. "North Korean Foreign Policy in Comparative and Theoretical Perspective." In *North Korea and the World: Explaining Pyongyang's Foreign Policy,* edited by B.C. Koh, 327–68. Seoul: Kyongnam University Press.

Moon, Chung-in, and David I. Steinberg, eds. 1999. *Kim Dae-jung Government and Sunshine Policy—Promises and Challenges.* Seoul: Yonsei University Press.

Moorehead, Alan. 1956. *Gallipoli.* London: Hamish Hamilton.

"Mt. Kumgang Inn to Reopen after Renovations." 2004. *Vantage Point* (June): 56.

"Mt. Kumgang Attracts Over 530,000 Tourists." 2003. *Vantage Point* (November): 57.

Nam, Kwang-sik. 2004. "North Korea Heading Toward Market Economy." *Vantage Point* (February): 8–11.

———. 2004. "North Korea, European Union Caught in Nuke Issue." *Vantage Point* (June): 10–12.

Nam, Sung-wook. 2002. "Prospects for Pyongyang's Economic Reforms." *Vantage Point* (October): 11–15.

Natsios, Andrew. 1999. *The Politics of Famine in North Korea.* U.S. Institute of Peace Special Report, Washington, D.C.

Nevinson, Henry W. 1929. *The Dardanelles Campaign.* London: Nisbet & Co.

Noland, Marcus. 1997. "Why North Korea Will Muddle Through." *Foreign Affairs* 76, no. 4: 105–18.

———. 2000. *Avoiding the Apocalypse: The Future of the Two Koreas.* Washington, DC: Institute for International Economics.

———. 2002. "Human Rights in North Korea: Testimony to the Congressional Human Rights Caucus" (April 17). Washington, DC.

———. 2002. "The Future of North Korea's Economic Reform." *Korea Journal of Defense Analysis* 14, no. 2: 73–90.

———. 2003. "Famine and Reform in North Korea." Working Paper 03–5. Washington, DC: Institute for International Economics.

———. 2004. "Korea After Kim Jong-il." *IIE Policy Analyses in International Economics* #71 (January): 12–19. Washington, DC: IIE.

North, Douglass C. 1990. *Institutions, Institutional Change and Economic Performance.* New York: Cambridge University Press.

"North Korea Aims to Secure US$150 Billion Foreign Investment in Sinuiju." 2002. *Vantage Point* (November): 57.

"North Korea Expands Foreign Investors' Share of Joint Venture." 2002. *Vantage Point* (October): 57.

"North Korea Renews Its Call for Talks to Normalize Ties with Japan." 2004. *Vantage Point* 27, no. 2 (February): 37.

"Number of Pyongyang's Markets Increasing Rapidly." 2004. *Vantage Point* (January): 29.

Nye, Joseph S. Jr. 2003. *Understanding International Conflict: An Introduction to Theory and History,* 4th ed. New York: Longman.

O'Hanlon, Michael, and Michael Mizoguchi. 2003. *Crisis on the Korean Peninsula: How to Deal with a Nuclear North Korea.* New York: McGraw-Hill.

Oakeshott, Michael. 1991. *Rationalism in Politics and Other Essays.* Indianapolis, IN: Liberty Press.

Oberdorfer, Don. 1997. *The Two Koreas: A Contemporary History.* Reading, MA: Addison Wesley.

———. 2001. *The Two Koreas: A Contemporary History.* Revised and updated. New York: Basic Books.

Oh, Il-Whan. 2001. "Kim Jong Il Sidae Bukhanui Gunsahwa Gyeonghyange Daehan Yeongu" (Study on the Militarization of North Korea in the Kim Jung-il Era). *Gukjae Jeongchi Nonchong (Korean Journal of International Relations)* 41, no. 3: 213–32.

Oh, Kongdan. 1990. "North Korea's Response to the World: Is the Door Ajar?" RAND Paper Series P-7616.

Oh, Kongdan, and Ralph C. Hassig. 2000. *North Korea Through the Looking Glass.* Washington, DC: Brookings Institution Press.

Oh, Seung-yul. 2003. "Changes in the North Korean Economy: New Policies and Limitations." In *Korea's Economy 2003,* vol. 19, 72–78. Washington, DC: Korea Economic Institute.

"One Thousand Hectares of Fish Farms Built in 2001." 2002. *Vantage Point* (February): 13.

Pan, Zhenquang. 2004. "Solution for the Nuclear Issue of North Korea, Hopeful But Still Uncertain: On the Conclusion of the Second Round of the Six-Party Talks." *The Journal of East Asian Affairs* (Spring/Summer): 19–46.

Park, Han S. 1995. "The Nature and Evolution of Juche Ideology." In *North Korea: Ideology, Politics, Economy,* edited by Han. S. Park, 9–18. Englewood Cliffs, NJ: Prentice Hall.

———. 2002. *North Korea: The Politics of Unconventional Wisdom.* Boulder, CO: Lynne Rienner.

Park, Hyeong Jung. 2004. "First Year of the Roh Moo-Hyun Administration." *Korea and World Affairs* (Spring): 9–22.

Park, Jae Kyu, ed. 1999. *North Korea in Transition and Policy Choices: Domestic Structure and External Relations.* Seoul: Kyungnam University Press.

Park, Kyung-Ae. 2004. "North Korea in 2003—Pendulum Swing Between Crisis and Diplomacy." *Asian Survey* 44, no. 1 (January/February): 139–46.

Park, Suhk-sam. 2004. "An Analysis of Economic Effects of the Kaesong Industrial Park." *Vantage Point* 27, no. 8 (August): 40–50.

Park, Sun-won. 2002. "Kim Jong Il Sidae Bukhanui Byunhwa: Jinhwaronjeok Jeopgeun" (North Korean Reform in the Kim Jong-il Era from the Perspective of 'Change Within the System,' 1997–2001). *Hanguk Jeongchihak Hoebo* (Korean Political Science Review) 36, no. 3 (Autumn): 159.

Perl, Raphael F. 2003. "Drug Trafficking and North Korea: Issues for U.S. Policy." *CRS Report for Congress* (RL32167) (December 5). Washington, DC: Congressional Research Service, The Library of Congress.

Perry, William J. 1999. *Review of U.S. Policy Toward North Korea: Findings and Recommendations* (October 12). Washington, DC: Department of State.

Pinkston, Daniel A. 2003. "Bargaining Failure and the North Korean Nuclear Program's Impact on International Nonproliferation Regimes." *KNDU Review* 8, no. 2 (December): 5–21.

Pinkston, Daniel A., and Stephanie Lieggi. 2003. *North Korea's Nuclear Program: Key Concerns.* Monterey Institute of International Studies Center for Nonproliferation Studies (January 17).

Pollack, Jonathan, and Chung-min Lee. 1999. *Preparing for Korean Unification.* Santa Monica, CA: RAND.

Polsby, Nelson W., ed. 1982. *What If? Explorations in Social-Science Fiction.* Lexington, MA: Lewis.

Pritchard, Charles L. 2003. "The Evolution to a Multilateral Approach in Dealing with North Korea." Paper delivered at the conference on North Korea "North Korea, Multilateralism, and the Future of the Peninsula" (November 20–21). Seoul.

Quinones, C. Kenneth. 1998. "North Korea: From Containment to Engagement." In *North Korea After Kim Il Sung,* ed. Dae-sook Suh and Chae-jin Lee, 101–119. London Lynn Rienner.

———. 2003. "Dualism in the Bush Administration's North Korea Policy." *Asian Perspective* 27, no. 1.

————. 2004. "North Korea Nuclear Talks: The View from Pyongyang." *Arms Control Today* 34, no. 47 (September).

Quinones, C. Kenneth, and Joseph Tragert. 2004. *Understanding North Korea.* New York: Penguin Alpha Books.

Reese, David. 1998. *The Prospects for North Korea's Survival.* Adelphi Paper 323. International Institute for Strategic Studies. Oxford: Oxford University Press.

Roh, Tae Woo. 1992. "Declaration of Non-nuclear Korean Peninsula Peace Initiatives, Seoul, November 1991." In *Intra-Korean Agreements.* Seoul: National Unification Board.

ROK Ministry of Unification. 2003. *Promoting Peace and Cooperation: Five Years of the Kim Dae-jung Administration.* Seoul.

Rozman, Gilbert. 2003. "Japan's North Korea Initiative and U.S.–Japanese Relations." *Orbis* (Summer): 527–30.

Scalapino, Robert A. 1992. *The Last Leninists: The Uncertain Future of Asia's Communist States.* Washington, DC: Center for Strategic and International Studies.

————. 1997. *North Korea at a Crossroads.* Stanford: Stanford University Hoover Institution.

Scalapino, Robert A., and Chong-Sik Lee. 1972. *Communism in Korea.* 2 vols. Berkeley: University of California Press.

Scobell, Andrew. 2002. "Crouching Korea, Hidden China—Bush Administration Policy Towards Pyongyang and Beijing." *Asian Survey* 42, no. 2 (March/April): 343–68.

————. 2004. *China and North Korea: From Comrades-in-Arms to Allies at Arm's Length.* Carlisle, PA: Strategic Studies Institute.

Seliger, Bernhard. 2004. "Economic Reform in North Korea." In *Korea's Economy 2004,* 77–86. Washington, DC: Korea Economic Institute.

Shambaugh, David. 2003. "China and the Korean Peninsula: Playing for the Long-Term." *Washington Quarterly* 26, no. 2 (Spring): 43–56.

Shigemura, Toshimitsu. 2003. *Saishin Kita Chosen Deta Bukku.* Tokyo: Kodansha.

Shim Jae Hoon. 1999. "A Crack in the Wall." *Far Eastern Economic Review* (April 29): 11.

Sigal, Leon V. 1997. *Disarming Strangers: Nuclear Diplomacy with North Korea.* Princeton: Princeton University Press.

"60,000 Tons of Fertilizer from EU Arrive in North Korea." 2003. *Vantage Point* (May): 18.

Snyder, Scott. 1999. *Negotiating on the Edge: North Korean Negotiating Behavior.* Washington, DC: United States Institute of Peace Press.

————. 2003. "The NGO Experience in North Korea." In *Paved with Good Intentions: The NGO Experience in North Korea,* edited by L. Gordon Flake and Scott Snyder, 1–13. Westport, CT: Praeger.

————. 2004. "Can China Unstick the Korean Nuclear Standoff?" *Comparative Connections* 6.1 (April): 98. Available at www.csis.org/pacfor/cc/0401Q.pdf.

Snyder, Seiler A. 1994. *Kim Il-Song 1941–1948.* Lanham, MD: University Press of America.

Song, Dexing. 1998. "Lengzhan hou DongbeiYa anquan xingshe de bianhua" (Changes in the Post–Cold War Northeast Asian Security Situation). *Xiandai guoji guanxi* (Contemporary International Relations) 9: 37.

"South Korea Sends US$135.39 Million in Aid to North Korea Last Year." 2002. *Vantage Point* (February): 57.

Spurr, Russell. 1988. *Enter the Dragon: China's Undeclared War Against the U.S. in Korea, 1950–1951.* New York: Newmarket Press.

"State Bank to Cover Losses from Trade with North Korea." 2004. *Vantage Point* (June): 57.

Stueck, William. 2002. *Rethinking the Korean War: A New Diplomatic and Strategic History.* Princeton: Princeton University Press.

Suh, Dae-Sook. 1988. *Kim Il Sung: The North Korean Leader.* New York: Columbia University Press.

————. 2002. "Military-First Politics of Kim Jong Il." *Asian Perspective* 26, no. 3: 145–67.

Suh, Dae-Sook, and Chae-Jin Lee, eds. 1998. *North Korea After Kim Il Sung.* Boulder, CO: Lynne Rienner.

Swaine, Michael D., and Alastair Iain Johnston. 1999. "China and Arms Control Institutions." In *China Joins the World: Progress and Prospects,* edited by Elizabeth Economy and Michel Oksenberg, 101. New York: Council on Foreign Relations Press.

Thompson, William R. 1999. "Why Rivalries Matter and What Great Power Rivalries Can Tell Us About World Politics." In *Great Power Rivalries,* edited by William R. Thompson, 1–21. Columbia: University of South Carolina Press.

Toloraya, George. 2003. "President Putin's Korean Policy." *The Journal of East Asian Affairs* 17, no. 1 (Spring–Summer): 33–51.

Triplet II, William C. 2004. *Rogue State: How a Nuclear North Korea Threatens America.* Washington DC: Regnery Publishing.

"Two-Thirds of Tenth Term SPA Members Are Newcomers." 1998. *Vantage Point* (August): 11.

United Nations Conference on Trade and Development. 2003. *World Investment Report, 2003.* New York: United Nations.

United Nations Environment Programme. 2003. *DPR Korea: State of the Environment 2003.* UNEP.

"U.S. Sees Korean Nuclear Threat." 2001. *Far Eastern Economic Review* (December 6): 10.

"U.S. Spies Convinced on Korean Bomb." 2002. *Far Eastern Economic Review* (May 2): 9.

Vollertsen, Norbert. 2004. *Inside North Korea.* San Francisco: Encounter Books.

Wada, Haruki. 1998. *Kita Chosen: Yugekitai Kokkano Gensai* (North Korea: Guerrilla State). Tokyo: Iwanami Shoten.

Wang, Yizhou. 1999. "Mianxiang ershi shiji de Zhongguo waijiao: sanzhong xuqiu de xunqiu jiqi pingheng" (China's Diplomacy for the Twenty-First Century: Seeking and Balancing Three Demands). *Zhanlue yu guanli* (Strategy and Management), no. 6: 18–27.

Watson, Lieutenant Colonel S.H. 1982. "The Gallipoli Blunder." *The Army Quarterly and Defence Journal* 112, no. 2 (April): 178–83.

Wit, Joel S., Daniel B. Poneman, and Robert C. Gallucci. 2004. *Going Critical: The First North Korean Nuclear Crisis.* Washington, DC: The Brookings Institution Press.

Woo, Seongji. 2003. "South Korea's Search for a Unification Strategy." *Orbis* (Summer): 511, 514–18.

———. 2004. "North Korea's Food Crisis." *Korea Focus* (May–June): 63–65.

World Bank. 1991. *World Development Report 1991: The Challenge of Development.* New York: Oxford University Press.

Yang, Ho-min. 1998. "North Korea Placed Officially Under Military Rule in 1998." *Vantage Point* (December): 16–19.

Yang, Sung Chul, 1999. *The North and South Korean Political System: A Comparative Analysis.* Seoul: Hollym.

You Ji. 2001. "China and North Korea: A Fragile Relationship of Strategic Convenience." *Journal of Contemporary China* 10, no. 28 (August): 389–90.

Yun, Duk-min. 2004. "Long-Range Missiles." In *North Korea's Weapons of Mass Destruction: Problems and Prospects*, edited by Kim Kyoung-soo, 121–48. Seoul: Hollym.

Zong, Hairen (pseudonym). 2003. "Hu Jintao Writes to Kim Jong-il to Open Door to Six-Party Talks." *Hong Kong Hsin Pao* (Hong Kong Economic Journal) (August 28), trans. in FBIS-CHI-2003–0828, August 29, 2003.

List of Contributors

The Editors

Young Whan Kihl (Ph.D., New York University) is Professor of Political Science at Iowa State University. He has written sixteen books on comparative foreign policy, Asian security, and Korean politics. His most recent books include *Transforming Korean Politics* (2005); *Peace and Security in Northeast Asia* (coeditor, with Peter Hayes, 1997); and *Korea and the World* (editor, 1994, selected by CHOICE as an outstanding academic book). Kihl is editor-in-chief of *International Journal of Korean Studies* and contributing editor to *Korea Journal*. He is a recipient of the 2005 Regents Faculty Excellence Award from the State of Iowa.

Hong Nack Kim (Ph.D., Georgetown University) is Professor of Political Science at West Virginia University. He was a visiting Fulbright Fellow at Keio University (1979, 1982) and Fulbright Professor of Political Science at Seoul National University (1990–1991). Formerly editor-in-chief of the *International Journal of Korean Studies*, he has contributed over 120 articles to major journals, including *Asian Survey*, *Pacific Affairs*, *Current History*, *World Politics*, and *Problems of Communism*. He has also authored or edited seven books on East Asian affairs. He will be a visiting POSCO Fellow at East-West Center, Honolulu, Hawaii, in the fall of 2005.

The Contributors

Nicholas Eberstadt (Ph.D., Harvard University) holds the Henry Wendt Chair in Political Economy at the American Enterprise Institute in Washington DC, and is Senior Adviser to the National Bureau for Asian Research in Seattle, WA. He is the author of many studies on demography, development, and international security. He earned his AB, MPA and Ph.D at Harvard and his M.Sc. at the London School of Economics.

Ilpyong J. Kim (Ph.D., Columbia University) is Professor Emeritus of Political Science at the University of Connecticut. He has lectured at Brown, Indiana, Harvard and Yale universities and was Fulbright Professor at Tokyo University in 1976–1977 and Seoul National University in 1991–1992. He has authored or edited fifteen books and contributed more than three dozen articles to academic journals. One of his most recent publications is *Historical Dictionary of North Korea* (2003).

Samuel S.Kim (M.I.A., Ph.D., Columbia University) is Adjunct Professor of Political Science and Senior Research Scholar at the Weatherhead East Asian Institute, Columbia University. He is the author or editor of twenty-one books including *North Korea and Northeast Asia* (2002), *The International Relations of Northeast Asia* (2004), and *The Two Koreas in the Global Community* (forthcoming). In addition, he has contributed numerous articles to leading international relations journals.

Alexandre Y. Mansourov (Ph.D., Columbia University) is Associate Professor at the Asia-Pacific Center for Security Studies, Honolulu, and a specialist in Northeast Asian security, politics, and economics. He has widely published on Korean and Northeast Asian affairs including *The North Korean Nuclear Program: Security, Strategy, and New Perspectives from Russia* (coeditor), *Bytes and Bullets: Information Technology Revolution and National Security on the Korean peninsula* (editor) and *A Turning Point: Democratic Consolidation in the ROK and Strategic Readjustment in the U.S.-ROK Alliance* (editor, forthcoming).

Peggy Falkenheim Meyer (Ph.D., Columbia University) is Professor of Political Science at Simon Fraser University in Burnaby, B.C., Canada. She has published widely on Russia's relations with Japan, China and the two Koreas, the Russian Far East's foreign economic relations, and Sino-Japanese and Sino-U.S. relations. Her publications have appeared in *Pacific Affairs*, *Asian Survey*, *Dmocratizatsiya*, *The Journal of East Asian Affairs*, *International Journal of Korean Studies*, *World Policy Journal*, and others.

Dick K. Nanto (M.A., Ph.D., Harvard University) is Head of the Asian Section at the Congressional Research Service. Formerly, he was an Assistant Professor of Economics at Brigham Young University. A specialist on U.S. trade and financial relations with China, Japan, and Korea, he has published numerous articles, chapters in books, and government reports on U.S. economic relations with the countries of Northeast Asia.

Larry Allen Niksch (MSFS, Ph.D., Georgetown University) is a Specialist in Asian Affairs with the Congressional Research Service. He specializes in U.S. security policy in East Asia, political conditions of the countries of the region and regional foreign policy developments. In addition to publishing numerous articles, he is a Senior Adviser on East Asia to the Political Risk Services Group and is a consultant to Lloyd, Thomas and Ball international business consulting service.

C. Kenneth Quinones (Ph.D., Harvard University) has been involved with Korea since 1962 as a soldier, scholar and diplomat. His Ph.D. is in History and East Asian Languages. Since retiring from the U.S. Foreign Service in 1997, he has been director of Korean Peninsula Program in Washington, D.C. His publications include three books about U.S.-Korea relations, and numerous articles in academic journals and newspapers in the United States, Japan, South Korea and Canada.

Robert A. Scalapino (Ph.D., Harvard University) is Robson Research Professor of Government Emeritus in the Department of Political Science, University of California, Berkeley. He was Director of the Institute of East Asian Studies between 1978 and 1990. He is currently a Fellow of the American Academy of Arts and Science, and a member of the boards of the Asia Foundation, the Atlantic Council, the National Bureau of Asian Research, and others. Included among his numerous scholarly publications is the prize-winning book (with Chong-Sik Lee) *Communism in Korea* (2 vols.) (1972).

Seongji Woo (Ph.D., Indiana University) is Assistant Professor of Kyung Hee University School of International Studies. Previously, he was Assistant Professor at the Institute of Foreign Affairs and National Security of the ROK Ministry of Foreign Affairs and Trade. His articles have appeared in *Orbis* and *Issues & Studies*. His current research is on the dynamics of inter-Korean reconciliation process, especially in the early 1970s.

Index